The Obama Victory

The Obama Victory

How Media, Money, and Message
Shaped the 2008 Election

KATE KENSKI

BRUCE W. HARDY

KATHLEEN HALL JAMIESON

OXFORD
UNIVERSITY PRESS

2010

OXFORD
UNIVERSITY PRESS

Oxford University Press, Inc., publishes works that further
Oxford University's objective of excellence
in research, scholarship, and education.

Oxford New York
Auckland Cape Town Dar es Salaam Hong Kong Karachi
Kuala Lumpur Madrid Melbourne Mexico City Nairobi
New Delhi Shanghai Taipei Toronto

With offices in
Argentina Austria Brazil Chile Czech Republic France Greece
Guatemala Hungary Italy Japan Poland Portugal Singapore
South Korea Switzerland Thailand Turkey Ukraine Vietnam

Copyright © 2010 by Oxford University Press, Inc.

Published by Oxford University Press, Inc.
198 Madison Avenue, New York, New York 10016

www.oup.com

Oxford is a registered trademark of Oxford University Press

Library of Congress Cataloging-in-Publication Data
Kenski, Kate.
The Obama victory : how media, money, and message shaped
the 2008 election / Kate Kenski, Bruce W. Hardy, Kathleen Hall Jamieson.
p. cm.
Includes bibliographical references and index.
ISBN 978-0-19-539955-4; ISBN 978-0-19-539956-1 (pbk.)
1. Obama, Barack. 2. Presidents—United States—Election—History—Statistics.
3. Mass media—Political aspects—United States. 4. Public television—United States.
I. Hardy, Bruce W. II. Jamieson, Kathleen Hall. III. Title.
JK524.K36 2010
324.973'0931—dc22   2009047182

1 3 5 7 9 8 6 4 2

Printed in the United States of America
on acid-free paper

Contents

Introduction, 1

PART I. THE FORCES AND MESSAGES THAT PERVADED
THE CAMPAIGN

ONE: The Economy and the Unpopular Incumbent, 13

TWO: McSame versus the Tax-and-Spend Liberal, 27

THREE: McCain: Out of Touch/Too Old, 53

FOUR: Obama: Not Ready to Lead, 71

PART II. SHIFTS IN MOMENTUM: FIVE PERIODS

FIVE: Period One: McCain Gains Energy (June 7–August 22), 109

SIX: Period Two: Impact of the Vice Presidential Selections and
Conventions (August 23–September 9), 123

SEVEN: The Impact of Sarah Palin and Joseph Biden, 149

EIGHT: Period Three: The Campaigns Confront the Economic Collapse
(September 10–October 14), 175

NINE: Period Four: The McCain Surge (October 15–28), 203

TEN: Period Five: Be Very, Very Afraid/Be Reassured
(October 29–November 4), 233

PART III. THE NEW CAMPAIGN LANDSCAPE

ELEVEN: Absentee and Early Voting in the 2008 Campaign, 251

TWELVE: Spending Differences and the Role of Microtargeting, 265

THIRTEEN: The Effect of Messages, 287

Afterword, 303
Appendix, 315
Notes, 319
Index, 369

Acknowledgments

THE DIVISIONS OF LABOR IN ANY BOOK ARE COMPLEX. *THE OBAMA Victory* reflects Kate Kenski's interests in gender and politics and in early voting, Bruce Hardy's knowledge of the ways in which candidate traits and character function and matter, and Kathleen Hall Jamieson's belief that understanding campaign rhetoric should be a starting point in any project involving the creation of surveys of the electorate and analysis of results.

Our debts are many. Consultants from both sides of the aisle shared their perspectives on campaign strategy and substance. We are grateful to Democrats David Axelrod, David Plouffe, Anita Dunn, Jim Margolis, Joel Benenson, Jon Carson, and Danny Jester, and to Republicans Steve Schmidt, Nicolle Wallace, Bill McInturff, Chris Mottola, Mark Wallace, Fred Davis, Kyle Roberts, and Rebecca Kimbro. Helping us unpack of the role of the parties and independent expenditures were Rich Beeson, Ricky Feller, Karen Finney, Ed Patru, Cecile Richards, Lawrence R. Scanlon Jr., Rodger Schlickeisen, and Scott Wheeler. Peter Hart's Annenberg Public Policy Center focus groups informed the book in ways both obvious and not. The staff of the Annenberg Public Policy Center's FactCheck.org helped us assess the accuracy of advertised claims. Our thanks to Brooks Jackson, Viveca Novak, and Lori Robertson.

To analyze the impact of ads, we relied on data from CMAG, Nielsen, Media Monitors, the cable and broadcast networks, local stations, and the campaigns. Thank you to Jeff Gottfried for gathering the local market data that enabled us to cross-check the accuracy of our other sources. Were it not for Kyle Roberts' patient tutorials, Dan Sinagoga's explications of hard and soft buys, and Tim Kay's technical consultations, we never would have made sense of syscodes and interconnects. Special thanks to David Cohen, who made time when we most needed his help.

We have drawn extensively on the good will and talent of Chris Adasiewicz, who like Kate and Bruce is an Annenberg graduate and who is the guru who matched disparate time-buy data sets to the NAES surveys and charted spending. Without Chris, we would not have been able to write the chapter he coauthored on the impact of the differences between Obama and McCain on spending in broadcast, cable, and radio. Also indispensable to our work was our colleague Ken Winneg, managing director at NAES, whose real-world experience as a pollster saved us many headaches. Without Annenberg researcher Jackie Dunn there would not have been an Annenberg election debriefing from which to draw insight or a footnote-creation and checking process better than any we have ever before experienced. Annenberg undergrads Jae Bang, Ina Cox, Maggie Devitt, Emily Fox, Ruben Henriquez, Andrew Karter, Christine Nieves, Andrew Reich, Erica Stone, and Rachel Weisel spent endless hours downloading and coding radio. Gary Gehman and Aous Abbas created our database structure. Michael Hennessey and Amy Bleakley continue to serve as our APPC gurus in residence. Seven scholars went beyond the call of friendship to provide us with wise counsel. Thank you to Larry Bartels, Henry Brady, Michael Delli Carpini, Larry Jacobs, Ben Page, Bob Shapiro, and John Zaller. We are thankful as well to Richard Johnston for midwifing our rolling cross-sectional survey.

From start to finish, Oxford's David McBride has been the critic we needed and the champion we aspire to deserve. This is Jamieson's ninth book with Oxford and the second edited by Dave McBride. She is grateful to both. Were it not for the diligence of Alexandra Dauler and Keith Faivre, the book never would have made its way into press, and David Klein's copyediting saved us from the sorts of errors that give scholars nightmares. The National Annenberg Election Survey would not exist were it not for the generosity and vision of two individuals no longer with us. We remember Walter and Lee Annenberg with gratitude and affection.

We dedicate this book to Kate and Bruce's children and Kathleen's grandchildren in the hope that Henry (Kenski) Anicker, Eva and Stella Hardy, and Finnian, Sylvia, Ava, and Gabrielle Jamieson grow up to participate in elections that make them and the country proud.

Kate Kenski
University of Arizona

Bruce Hardy
University of Pennsylvania

Kathleen Hall Jamieson
University of Pennsylvania

The Obama Victory

Introduction

F ROM AMONG THE HUNDREDS OF THOUSANDS OF WORDS HE SPOKE
in public in the fall of 2008, we think we know which ones Republican
Party nominee John McCain would take back if given the chance. We also
have a pretty good guess about the sentence his Democratic counterpart, Barack
Obama, would rewind if opportunity permitted. Our choice on the Republican
side occurred on September 15 as the country was plummeting into the worst
recession in recent memory. On that date, the Arizona senator said, "The fundamentals of the economy are strong." For the Democrat, the moment occurred days
before the final presidential debate, when, in a chance encounter in the crucial
battleground state of Ohio, the Illinois senator told a plumber, "I think when you
spread the wealth around, it's good for everybody." Each ill-phrased opinion elicited hours of commentary on cable, in broadcast news, and on the pages of the
nation's newspapers and found an afterlife in debates, ads, e-mails, late-night comedy, and on YouTube. Each altered its creator's prospects, if, in one case, only for a
short time.

From the Reverend Jeremiah Wright's "God damn America" to Tina Fey's
"I can see Russia from my house," the 2008 election brimmed with attention-
grabbing communication. "For 20 years, Barack Obama followed a preacher of
hate," alleged an independent expenditure ad. "Obama takes great care to conceal
the fact that he is a Muslim," asserted a viral e-mail. "How many houses does he
own?" asked a message sponsored by the campaign of Democratic Party nominee
Barack Obama. "John McCain says he can't even remember anymore." "Erratic,"
said an Obama spokesperson of the Arizonan. "A celebrity but not ready to lead,"
responded the Republicans. "Likely to die in office, leaving the country in the

hands of Sarah Palin," whispered partisans on the Left. "Unpatriotic, angry, risky," suggested those on the Right. Barack Obama had been "palling around with terrorists," contended Republican vice presidential nominee Sarah Palin. Within his first six months in office, Obama "would be tested," forecast the Delaware senator holding the second spot on the Democratic ticket.

In the chapters that follow, we ask whether support for one major-party nominee or the other shifted when money was married to such messages, or media highlighted them. To answer that question, *The Obama Victory* concentrates on the processes at play in presidential elections, the factors that affect their outcomes, and the mechanisms by which these effects occur. In the chapters that follow, we draw on a survey of over 57,000 voters, an analysis of campaign messages, and a comprehensive data set of media buys to explain the extraordinary election that occurred in the middle of the worst economic meltdown since the Great Depression and pitted a 72-year-old Vietnam War hero against a 47-year-old African-American whose prime credential was prescient opposition to the war in Iraq.

Throughout the book, we assess the effects of factors the candidates did not control, such as the economy and the record of unpopular incumbent President George W. Bush, as well as choices about media, messages, and money that the campaigns themselves made. To capture the former, we separately use "objective" economic indicators as well as citizens' retrospective evaluations of the performance of the economy. To make sense of the latter, we track the ways in which the skilled professionals running the campaigns masterminded messages about the character and dispositions of their candidates, chose the issues and traits to feature, and capitalized on or neutralized the effects of events over which they exerted no direct control. McCain's campaign, for example, reframed Obama's pre-convention speech in Berlin as evidence that the Democratic nominee was a lightweight celebrity who, unlike the maverick war hero, put himself first. We then assess the impact, if any, of those messages on those we surveyed.

Our overarching goal is addressing the question found in our subtitle: What part, if any, did media, money, and message play in shaping the 2008 election? Our answer focuses on the communication disseminated by the campaigns, the media's treatment of it, and voters' responses. Those messages include ones making incumbent George W. Bush central to one's vote.

Drawing on our analysis of message, media treatment, and meaning for voters, we explore the push and pull exerted by McCain's age and Obama's race. We also study the Democratic moves to tie McCain to the unpopular incumbent and the Republican efforts to disassociate the two. We probe the impact of challenges to Obama's readiness and McCain's judgment. The ups and downs of the vice presidential candidates are a focus as well. In our account of the postprimary period, we examine the contest in summer over which offered the better energy policy, and in fall over their alternative tax policies and plans for the economy. In the end, we hope to have produced a compelling account of the complex factors at play in the 2008 outcome, including the roles of a wide disparity in the two campaigns' ad spending and the impact of their sophisticated microtargeting on cable and radio.

To organize our analysis, we divide *The Obama Victory* into three parts: "The Forces and Messages That Pervaded the Campaign," "Shifts in Momentum," and "The New Campaign Landscape." Four chapters fall into part I. In the first, we capture the variables of special concern to our colleagues in political science. Then in chapters 2 through 4, we explore the candidates' central messages about themselves and their opponent. In part II, which encompasses chapters 5 through 10, we make sense of the postprimary season by dividing the June-through-November calendar into five periods coinciding with shifts in momentum. Finally, in part III, we explore the effects of a campaign environment that included massive early voting and unprecedented Obama spending and microtargeting. We also compare the relative impact messages have on vote preference to other factors, such as party identification. We close by thinking aloud about the implications of new media, microtargeting, early voting, and candidate rejection of federal financing.

In addition to acknowledging the fact that distinguished political scientists accurately forecast both Obama's win and the final vote spread between the tickets, in the first chapter of part I we create our own estimates of the predictive power of the perceived health of the economy, the popularity of the incumbent, and party identification. We then parcel the dominant messages offered by the Obama and McCain campaigns into discussions titled "McSame versus the Tax-and-Spend Liberal," "McCain: Out of Touch/Too Old," and "Obama: Not Ready to Lead." In each chapter, we account for the forces that influenced voters' acceptance of one set of these disparate characterizations over the other. Put simply, part I is set up to detail the factors the candidates had to address, specifically their kinship or antipathy to George W. Bush and their take on the economy, as well as the messages they chose to convey about themselves and each other.

In the process, we recount the thrust and parry involving the themes of the campaign that pervaded the periods into which we divide the events of the election. So, for example, in chapter 2, "McSame versus the Tax-and-Spend Liberal," we concentrate on the tactics Obama's campaign employed to both blunt the claim that he was an old-style liberal and assume the mantle of change while denying John McCain the maverick label and linking him to unpopular incumbent George W. Bush. At the same time, we chronicle the ways in which the Republicans and McCain worked to tag Obama as not the new-style reformer he cast himself to be but rather a traditional tax-and-spend liberal. In chapter 3, "McCain: Out of Touch/Too Old," we show how Democratic messages amplified the content of news and the popular culture to characterize the 72-year-old Republican nominee as out of touch while also asserting that he was erratic and implying that he was too old to serve as president in troubled economic times. Turning to the other side, in chapter 4 we probe the Republican argument that Obama was unready to lead, a claim tied to fears—including some that were race based—that Obama was unpatriotic, angry, and a poseur. The central themes identified in part I's four chapters are then threaded throughout the five periods on which we focus in the second part of the book, a part that accounts for shifts in momentum (see figure 1).

As figure 1 illustrates, these periods coincide, albeit roughly, with shifts in advantage. Surprisingly, in an election all but ordained to be a Democratic win, our data suggest that the Arizona senator was actually either ahead or tied, in period one just before the Democratic convention, and in period two just after his own. Also running counter to the expectations of political scientists is McCain's momentum after the third debate in mid-October. However, once Obama took the lead in mid-September, at the national level at least, he never lost it.

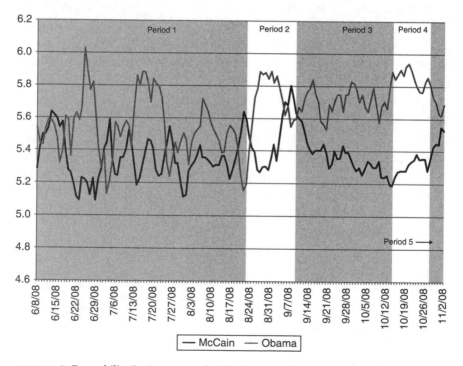

FIGURE 1 Favorability Ratings across the Five Periods of the General Election (5-day PMA). Note: Between June 1 and July 31, the average N was 68 respondents per day. After August 1, it increased to 244 respondents per day. PMA = Prior Moving Average. *Source*: NAES08 telephone survey.

Although we will argue that something important changed within the days surrounding the break points among these periods, we cannot calibrate precise turning points. Making sense of the campaign requires some license to roam in and out of these bracketed periods. Accordingly, we ask readers to think of them not as precise periods but rather as a rough-hewn but functional template.

One of the reasons we consider these periods helpful is that they tell a story with evolving themes. So, for example, in period 1 (June 7–August 22) with news reports casting energy policy as the central issue troubling the economy, Senator McCain gained traction with his support of offshore oil drilling. By contrast, in period 2 (August 23–September 9) the news media wrapped a competence/incompetence, knowledgeable/ignorant frame around Sarah Palin but not Joseph Biden. However, her selection energized the Republican base and drew support from white women. After his convention, McCain was marginally ahead in the polls.

We demarcate period 3 as the time between September 10, a point by which the Republican convention bounce had dissipated, and October 14, the eve of the third and final debate. In this time frame, the intense media focus on the economy made it difficult if not impossible for the McCain campaign to secure news coverage of its controversial attacks on Obama's association with former Weather Underground member William Ayers and convicted felon and former Obama fundraiser Tony Rezco. Meanwhile, McCain's response to the crisis was cast negatively by both the Obama campaign and the press. During these weeks, the candidates' relative command of the economic crisis became the test of whether they deserved to win and how they would govern.

In period 4, tax policy became the lens through which McCain urged voters to assess the candidates as leaders. In the back-and-forth leading up to these weeks, the Obama campaign displayed its skill by convincing voters that McCain was more likely than the Democratic Party nominee to raise taxes. However, in the time between the last debate on October 15 and October 28, McCain gained momentum with the argument that he, not Obama, had the better economic plan for those like Joe the Plumber. That gambit played on a long-standing public belief that liberals expand big government and redistribute wealth. Rather than resolving the economic crisis, argued McCain, Obama's tax proposals would worsen it.

To blunt McCain's surge, in the final week (October 29–November 4) Obama used his substantial financial advantage to vivify the "McSame" image and to argue from his own biography, endorsements and proposals that he shared voters' values. In the end, a center right electorate was persuaded that a candidate perceived to be a liberal shared its values more so than a person thought to be closer to its ideological bent.

Where in part I we set in place the central messages of the campaign and in part II explain the shifts in momentum across the postprimary season, in part III we step back to examine the factors that distinguished the 2008 campaign from those that had come before. The first seismic change occurred because of unprecedented levels of early voting; put simply, for about a third of the electorate, Election Day occurred before November 4. In an effort to understand the implications of this phenomenon, in chapter 11 we ask: How much of a buffer or cushion against last-minute McCain movement in polls did Obama secure because of early voting? And were these votes he would have gotten later anyway and hence inconsequential, or ballots by individuals whose votes might have been changed in the presence of information available only after their vote had been cast? Among other changes, Obama's rejection of federal financing opened the way for him to create a contest very different from the ones that scholars have studied since campaign finance reform more or less leveled the playing field between the parties. In 2008, Obama had the capacity to both outspend his opponent and to do so on a grand scale. Scholars of communication have long believed that the effects of messages usually cancel themselves out when two sides spend comparable amounts airing them. In chapter 12, we confirm that the difference between Obama's media spending and McCain's moved voters' dispositions.

Of course, voters are not equally susceptible to persuasion. Partisans and those with high levels of knowledge are more resistant[1] than not. But even their minds can be changed if they are subjected to cross-pressuring on issues that they care about.[2] Campaigns of course have always been preoccupied with reaching persuadable voters with messages capable of moving them. Microtargeting does just that. In chapter 13, we show the implications of the breakthroughs in microtargeting of cable and radio in 2008. We also argue that the advent of widespread use of the Internet, microtargeting through cable and radio, and the demise of federal financing have fundamentally and perhaps irrevocably altered the communication dynamics of presidential campaigns.

As students of communication, we start from the assumption that media, messages, and money matter. Our case for the importance of communication in the 2008 campaign begins with the notion that messages were vehicles that tied McCain to the environmental factors that predicted an Obama vote. We recognize that before McCain or Obama's messages mentioned either the incumbent or the economy, both had a powerful hold on voters' dispositions. Still, we argue that their effect was enlarged by skillfully deployed messages. As evidence, we note fluctuations in the perception that electing McCain meant a third Bush term. The difference between Bush and McCain widens in period one, closes during the Democratic convention, and opens back up again as the rhetoric of the Republican convention sinks in. Although McCain painted himself as a maverick, the

Democratic forces succeeded in casting him as either Bush's kin or clone. As a result, our survey data from the beginning of period one to election eve show an upward trend in the belief that McCain equals Bush. We take this to mean that communication strengthened the relationship between McCain and Bush. At the campaign's end, McCain is seen as McSame in part because the Democrats scraped the maverick label from him and melded his identity to that of the star-crossed incumbent.

On the economy, the process of persuasion worked by reassuring the electorate that Obama was ready to handle the issue and, for a variety of reasons, McCain was not. In other words, in a season dominated by the plummeting market, the contest was not focused on the state of the economy but rather on which candidate could break its free fall and fashion a recovery. In the gospel according to McCain, the Democratic nominee's disposition to tax and transfer wealth might turn a recession into a depression. In Obama's scripture, the Republican could not create needed change because he was out of touch with the concerns of Middle America and a proponent of the Bush policies that had birthed the crisis. In the end, Obama won by convincing a majority that he shared its values and was the candidate better suited to fix what ailed the economy. Where at the height of McCain's convention bounce, the two candidates were both attracting about 45 percent saying he could better handle the economy, on election eve the gap separating them was over 10 percent. At that point, Obama was securely above 50 percent and McCain below 40.

In other words, on these fundamentals we tell a familiar story. Communication did its job in linking the candidates to the conditions that political science considers important in voting decisions. But even after rhetoric's role in tying voters to fundamentals has been estimated, there is unexplained variance. Here the predictive power of communication comes in. When deciding for whom to vote, it matters whether an individual thinks that Obama rather than McCain is the one who would raise taxes; the perception that one more than the other shares voters' values has an effect as well; and thinking that Palin isn't ready to assume the presidency makes a difference, too.

What all of this means is that campaigns are not simply black boxes that telegraph that one candidate is tied to the incumbent and deserving of credit or blame for the state of the economy. Campaign messages also change the standards of judgment that voters use in evaluating the candidates and frame the way that the contenders, their stands on issues and their character and temperament are understood. And those factors can affect how some say they will vote.

Our case for communication effects is built on the notion that people don't make decisions on the basis of all available evidence. Nor as they cast their ballots do they consider all the issues or attributes potentially at play. Instead, through a cognitive process known as priming, some factors become more important or salient than others. The priming hypothesis assumes that individuals embrace criteria for assessment on the basis of accessibility—how quickly and automatically such criteria come to mind. If a criterion has been the subject of a lot of attention, it will be accessible. For example, if discussions of the economy dominate news commentary and other issues receive less attention, then the economy will become more salient to news consumers than issues that are featured less. By focusing on some issues and ignoring others, the media and campaigns prime the criteria by which we evaluate leaders and policies.[3]

Both issues and traits can be made more salient through priming. Since some issues or attributes benefit one candidate more so than the other, the content that is primed matters. Make terrorism or the war in Iraq more salient and McCain gains; prime the economy or health care and Obama is advantaged. Stress old age and McCain is hurt; activate the notion of "angry black male with criminal ties" and Obama is disadvantaged.

The campaigns and the media primed issues and attributes throughout the months that we study. In what we call period one, the pre-convention months of summer, McCain gained ground in part because the media had primed energy prices as the central problem endangering the economy and "offshore drilling for more oil" had more support than the usual Democratic alternatives. By contrast, the Wall Street meltdown of major financial institutions in period three vilified natural Republican allies, big business, and Wall Street while also increasing the salience of the economy, an issue on which Democrats enjoyed an advantage. The momentum McCain unexpectedly gained after the third debate was driven by his move to persuade voters that Obama would provide the undeserving with welfare in the form of taxpayers' hard-earned money.

Attributes were primed as well. Where "strong leader" was a trait the 2000 campaign stressed, its equivalent in 2008 was "shares my values." Obama's rhetoric of reassurance persuaded voters that the change he proposed was rooted in valued principles. From June 7 to November 3, perception that he shared voters' values increased by .002 points a day for an overall increase of .3 on a 10-point scale.

Also central to our analysis is the cognitive process that works through priming, known as framing. Scholars define a framing effect as "one in which salient attributes of a message (its organization, selection of content, or thematic structure) render particular thoughts applicable, resulting in their activation and use in evaluations."[4] Media frames are organizing structures that tell audiences "what the issue is through the use of selection, emphasis, exclusion and elaboration."[5] Frames "affect the likelihood that a particular option will be selected" by audiences.[6] In the process, frames increase the importance of some arguments over others, some evidence over others.[7] Put simply, frames are a way of seeing the world.

In elections, voters are asked to select among competing constructions of reality. Is McCain a war hero and maverick who opposed George W. Bush on a wide menu of issues, from climate change legislation to a ban on torture, and opposed the first two Bush tax cuts, or is he out of touch and infirm McSame, a Bush booster who, like the incumbent, championed the war in Iraq and wants to retain the Bush tax cuts on high-income individuals? Is Obama a presumptuous, lightweight tax-and-spend liberal with a thin legislative résumé who catapulted to power on the strength of his ability to deliver the scripted words of others or a Lincolnesque prophet whose prescient opposition to the war in Iraq and bipartisan legislative achievements forecast the change for which the country hungered?

The 2008 contest between vice presidential nominees Senator Joe Biden and Governor Sarah Palin illustrates the fact that a frame can be selectively applied. Where Palin's preparedness, competence, and knowledge were questioned, Biden's were presumed. The media framed Biden as a candidate disposed to speak without thinking and Palin as an inarticulate candidate without coherent thoughts. With that standard in place, her interviews with Charlie Gibson of ABC and CBS's Katie Couric and her performance in the vice presidential debate were scrutinized through a frame in which the burden of proof was on her to establish readiness for high office, where for Biden competence was a given. Accordingly, her misstatement of the first name of a general in their vice presidential debate was treated as evidence of lack of knowledge, whereas Biden's placement of executive power in the wrong article of the Constitution was not. And her inability to identify something Gibson called the Bush Doctrine, a construction the incumbent had never himself used, was seen not as an indictment of the questioner but as evidence of Palin's ignorance. Where her jumbled sentences were parodied by Tina Fey on *Saturday Night Live*, the odd locutions Biden laced into his convention address were ignored.

Because both framing and priming work by making concepts salient, the camp with the financial wherewithal to purchase greater exposure for its messages has a natural advantage at each. Since some topics are more salient to some audiences than are other topics, use of targeted media can magnify priming and framing effects.

When we argue that some act of communication moved voters, we risk being foiled by what psychologists call selective exposure. Specifically, individuals are drawn to speakers they admire and messages with which they already agree. Compounding the problem, strategists seek out persuadable audiences. As a result, our analysis of message effects could mistakenly credit the campaign's exhortations with bringing agnostics to religion when instead the congregants had rushed to the sanctuary, hymnals in hand.

To protect ourselves from that trap, in many of our statistical models that show communication effects, we include stringent controls, ranging from party identification and respondents' self-placement on the ideological spectrum to their view of the candidate. For example, in our analyses showing the impact of convention speeches on vote preference, we control for respondents' favorability ratings of the candidates. This, in effect, takes out the influence of Obama supporters eagerly watching him accept the nomination and vice versa for McCain supporters, and allows us to detect the direct impact of convention viewing.

In grappling with the questions asked in this book, one of our comparative advantages resides in the ability of the rolling cross-sectional design to detect message and event effects. Another lies in the range of our data and in our multi-methodological approach to the "why," "how," and "with what effect" of the campaigns' media, money, and messages. In the following pages, we combine rhetorical analysis of messages with survey data capturing the effects of key maneuvers and moments.

The polling data on which we rely include 57,000 National Annenberg Election Survey (NAES) telephone interviews conducted with prospective voters from December 2007 through the election, a postelection panel of 3,700, and a postelection survey focused on what respondents did and did not believe of the claims and counterclaims offered up in debates, ads, and viral e-mail. To study the effects of paid media, we marry these surveys to a comprehensive compilation of candidate radio, cable, and TV ad purchases. For a sense of topics at play in the broad communication environment, we rely on the results of Nexis searches (which we label the TV News Frequency Index) and a sophisticated Web-spidering program (which we call a Cultural Communication Index) developed by a research team at the State University of New York at Stony Brook. Our reports about the goings-on inside the McCain and Obama campaigns come from interviews with key players and from the Annenberg election debriefing conducted in Philadelphia and Washington, D.C., in December 2008. More information on all of these bodies of information can be found on the Web site (www.annenbergpublicpolicycenter. org/obamavictory) we have posted and on which we house the sorts of technical detail off-putting to general audiences but indispensable to our scholarly colleagues. To alert readers that we have lodged support material on the Internet site, we add an asterisk to the relevant argument.

PART I

The Forces and Messages That Pervaded the Campaign

ONE

The Economy and the Unpopular Incumbent

D URING ELECTIONS, DISCUSSIONS IN THE PRESS AND AMONG pundits focus on the role of the candidates, their strategies, and messages in securing the votes needed to assume the White House. Polls chronicle the incumbent president's standing and report which issues voters consider paramount. There is ample talk about national conditions, as well as progress or lack thereof in wars. News accounts feature indicators of the health of the economy, such as the unemployment rate, housing starts, the GDP, the Dow, and, in 2008, gas prices and foreclosure rates. Political conventions remind voters of a candidate's ties to a political party, a notion capable of activating a complex amalgam of information, inferences, and inclinations among those who consider themselves political kin of FDR, JFK, and Clinton or Reagan, and perhaps George W. Bush.

Before asking how messages, media, and money shaped the 2008 general election campaign, we focus here on the supposition that a combination of fundamental factors ensured that in 2008 the stars were aligned for the Democrats. Among them, the incumbent Republican president was unpopular, the premises of the war that he had launched in Iraq discredited, and the economy faltering. In party identification, the Democrats held the advantage. On handling the economy—the issue mattering most to voters—they had the edge as well.

We begin by documenting George W. Bush's subterranean polling numbers, move to note that leading indicators suggested an economy on the wrong track, proceed to note that on handling the economy the Democrats had the advantage, and conclude by showing that the electorate was populated with higher numbers of Democratic than Republican identifiers. After exploring the blessings this bundle of factors bestowed on the eventual Democratic nominee, we set the stage for our argument that message, media, and money nonetheless contributed to Obama's ballot total by isolating the percentage of the 2008 presidential vote intention that can be predicted by party preference, ideological placement, economic conditions, and disapproval of the presidency of George W. Bush alone.*

An Unpopular President

President George W. Bush was the albatross circling the candidacy of Republican nominee John McCain. Not since Hubert Humphrey in 1968 had a presidential candidate so desperately needed to decouple his fortunes from those of his party's incumbent. Bush's "job approval is almost as poor as that of King George III among the colonists 240 years ago,"[1] posited Peter Brown, assistant director of the Quinnipiac University Polling Institute in late March 2008. "The failure of the Bush presidency is the dominant fact of American politics today," observed Jeffrey Bell in the *Weekly Standard* that same month. "It has driven every facet of Democratic political strategy since early 2006, when Democrats settled on the campaign themes that brought them their takeover of the House and Senate in November 2006. Nothing—not even the success of the American troop surge in Iraq—has altered or will alter the centrality of George W. Bush and his failed presidency to Democratic planning in the remainder of 2008."[2]

At no point in 2008 did a major public opinion poll find more than 43 percent of the public approving of the incumbent's presidency.[3] As 2008 was drawing to a close, a survey conducted by the Pew Research Center found that "just 11% said Bush will be remembered as an outstanding or above average president—by far the lowest positive end-of-term rating for any of the past four presidents."[4] The 25 percent at which the 43rd president's approval ratings landed on October 5, noted an article in the *National Journal*, was "only 1-percentage point higher than President Nixon's low of 24 percent, reached shortly before he resigned, and 3 points above President Truman's low of 22 percent."[5]

On average from mid-December 2007 through Election Day 2008, Bush scored 3.8 on a 10-point NAES favorability scale.[6] Were the presidency a college course, one would be hard-pressed to read this as a pass. Related measures told the same story. During the general election, 77 percent believed the country was "seriously off on the wrong track."[7]

When asked about the incumbent, voters served up a wide range of both conventional and unexpected language expressing dismay and disdain. On May 12, 2008, for example, an Annenberg-sponsored focus group[8] of undecided independents in Charlottesville, Virginia, responded to moderator Peter Hart's request for "a word or phrase to describe your opinion of George Bush as president" by saying:

DANNY: Disappointing.

DORITA: That was my word, too. Exact word. I'm thinking, okay, yes. I was expecting more.

SUSAN: Well, I don't like to be disrespectful of the president, but I think he's worthless.

NOLA: Not surprising.

BOB: Misleading.

MONIQUE: Awful.

DOLORES: Can a toilet brush go with a toilet... I don't want to be disrespectful either. I'm going to say scary.

DENNIS: I just say he's in a difficult position.

WILLIAM: I think he's very gullible.

JOSH: Solitary.

PATRICK: War monger.

MELINDA: I don't know. I don't know what to say. I don't have one word. All I know is I wouldn't want to be in his shoes.

Four months later, a focus group of citizens in Bedford, New Hampshire, offered answers no more likely to gladden the 43rd president's heart:

TOM: Incompetent.

SHANNON: Illiterate.

DAVID: Blew it.

JOAN: Scary.

KATHY: ...disappointed.

BILL: Unqualified and incompetent.

ELIZABETH: Embarrassing.

EMILY: That's what I was going to say, embarrassing.

JANE: I was going to say sympathy.[9]

The implications were not lost on the Republican ticket. "We're up against a lot," noted McCain's running mate, Governor Sarah Palin of Alaska, in an interview with NBC's Brian Williams on October 24. "We're up against a very unpopular president, Bush's administration right now, and those who want to link us to that administration."[10]

A Faltering Economy

As the presidential candidates assembled for their preprimary debates in fall 2007, the Dow was setting records, peaking in early October at 14,164.[11] Still, the country was anxious. In a *Wall Street Journal*/NBC News poll taken at the time, three-quarters of respondents reported that the nation was on the wrong track. By the eve of the second general election presidential debate a year later, the Dow had lost more than 4,000 points to close on October 7, 2008, at 9,447. And the bottom wasn't in sight.

Where in the third quarter, the GDP growth was minus one-half of 1 percent,[12] in the fourth, the contraction rate was negative 6.2 percent.[13] Put simply, the economic quarter that included the last five weeks of the election was dismal.[14] Harking back to the early 1980s, an account in the *Wall Street Journal* characterized the U.S. economy's performance in the closing months of 2008 as "its worst…in a quarter-century…"[15] In that period, business sales plunged and consumer spending dropped at a rate "marking the worst back-to-back declines since quarterly records began in 1947."[16]

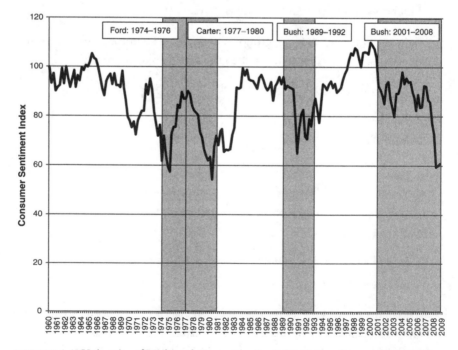

FIGURE 1.1 University of Michigan's Consumer Sentiment Index. *Sources*: Survey of Consumers, Reuters, and University of Michigan, http://www.sca.isr.umich.edu/

Nor were other economic indicators reassuring. In the fourth quarter of 2008, "[h]omebuilding tumbled at a 23.6% pace, and commercial real estate started to crumble. As federal spending rose, state and local governments [were] pulling back. Exports growth fell at a nearly 20% rate."[17]

The other news for individuals was troubling as well. "Personal income decreased 1.2 percent for the quarter."[18] Because scholars peg electoral outcome from inferences based largely on gains or losses in personal income and the popularity of the president, the drop in income was especially noteworthy. If past is prologue, the University of Michigan Consumer Sentiment Index also forecast a script that ended with Barack Obama in the White House. Driven by a collapse in housing prices and a dramatic fall in the stock market, consumer confidence in fall 2008 was plummeting.

"When the party in power wins, the Michigan consumer sentiment index is at least 96," recalled McCain pollster Bill McInturff. "The three times it's been in the '70s, the party in power has lost: Jimmy Carter, Gerry Ford and George H.W. Bush in '92. In October [2008] the number was 58. In other words, there's not a number like this. When you look at those numbers, you conclude that we're going to lose the election"[19] (figure 1.1).

A Democratic Advantage on Handling the Economy

At the very beginning of the election season, Iraq surpassed the economy as the issue most saw as the central concern facing the country. But its position at the top of the list was short-lived. Thereafter, the focal issue was the economy writ large (figure 1.2). NAES data tell us that the economy was the most important issue for respondents regardless of their race, gender, age, education, political identification, and so on.*

Even before the first Iowa voter braved the ice and snow to caucus, the issue landscape looked sunny and cloud-free for the Democrats. "The Republican Party was in a much stronger position on issues in January 2004, 10 months before President George W. Bush won re-election and the Republicans retained their majority position in Congress," noted a November/December 2007 Gallup Poll report.[20] When asked which party could better handle the situation in Iraq, the public had shifted from preferring the Republicans by 16 percent in 2004 to favoring the Democrats by 10 in late 2007. On the economy, the Democratic advantage had risen from 4 percent to 12 in the same period, and on health care from 21 to 30 percent. Even on taxes, an issue the Republicans had owned in the1980s, the Democrats and Republicans were basically at parity both in 2004 (when the Democrats were up 4) and in late 2007 (when they were ahead by 2).

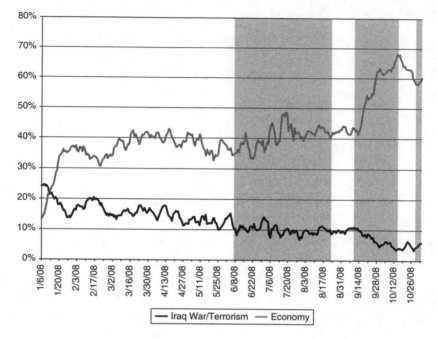

FIGURE 1.2 Percent of Respondents Who Cited "Iraq War/Terrorism" and
the "Economy" as the Most Important Problem (5-day PMA). *Source*: NAES08
telephone survey.

The Economy

After looking back at its measures since 1982, Gallup concluded in late 2007 that
its "long-term trend for which party can better handle the economy finds the
Democrats doing well on a historical basis."[21] The country's oldest polling firm
then offered an ominous forecast for the Republicans. "[W]hile it is not unusual
for the Republicans to be at parity with or behind the Democrats on this measure,
their current 12-point deficit is on the high side. If a disadvantage this large persists in 2008, it could spell trouble for the party if the economy figures as a major
issue for voters."[22] In February 2008, Pew confirmed that "a majority (53%)...says
the Democrats are better able to handle the economy, which has become the leading issue in the presidential campaign."[23] In every head-to-head comparison in
the *Washington Post*/ABC survey between March and Election Day 2008, Obama
topped McCain on this issue.[24] Not since the Dukakis-Bush race of 1988 had the
Post-ABC poll showed a Republican outpacing the Democrat on this question
as Election Day neared.[25] Throughout the general election season, data from the
NAES show an Obama advantage on the perceptions of which candidate would
best handle the economy as well (figure 1.3).

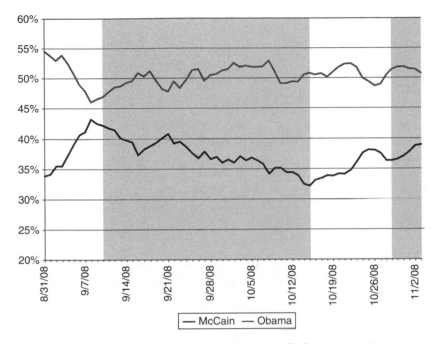

FIGURE 1.3   Perceptions of Which Candidate Would Handle the Economy Better
(5-day PMA). *Source*: NAES08 telephone survey.

A Democratic Advantage in Party Identification

The disposition of individuals to tell a pollster that they were Republicans began
dissipating after the 2004 election (figure 1.4).

The effects of a frustrating war, faltering economy, and failing president are
reflected in the outcome of the 2006 election, which flipped control of both the U.S.
House and Senate to the Democrats and spiked the number of voters calling themselves
Democrats. That shift continued into the 2008 election. In 2004, a Pew survey found
33 percent identified as Republicans and 35 percent as Democrats. In 2008, 27 percent
were self-described Republicans and 36 percent self-identified as Democrats. The 2008
NAES produced similar results (26.7 percent Republicans, 36.1 Democrats).[26]

In the contest to sign up adherents, the Democrats handily bested those on
the other side as well. Almost 74 percent (73.5) of those eligible were registered by
Election Day—an increase of 10.1 million. While from 2004 to the end of 2008
Democratic registration increased 1.4 percent, or 2,916,000 million, during the
same period, the Republicans tallied only half that amount (1,458,000).[27]

Of course, identification doesn't necessarily translate into election of the
advantaged party's presidential nominee. "[T]he Republican Party apparently

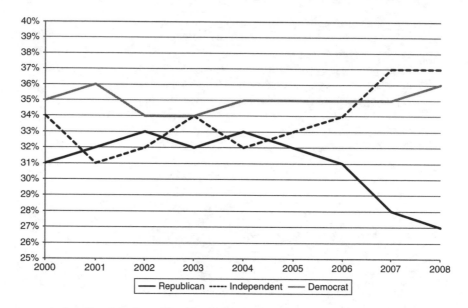

FIGURE 1.4 Trends in Party Identification, 2000 to 2008. *Source*: Pew Research Center for the People & the Press, "Fewer Voters Identify as Republicans. Democrats Now Have the Advantage in 'Swing' States," March 20, 2008 (http://pewresearch.org/pubs/773/fewer-voters-identify-as-republicans).

enjoyed a party-identification advantage among actual voters (that is, nonvoters are omitted) in all contests from 1904 through 1932, and the Democrats an advantage in all contests from 1936 through 2000," notes political scientist David Mayhew. "Yet in only fourteen of these twenty-five instances did the party that actually won the presidency enjoy a party-identification edge among voters at the time. Coin flips would have brought twelve and a half such victories, barely a worse showing."[28]

One explanation may be that voters sometimes consider the other party's nominee an ideological kin. If so, Obama's party identification and voter registration surplus might be trumped by McCain's ideological advantage. In 2008, 38.4 percent of those surveyed by the NAES (by telephone) said they were very or somewhat conservative, while only 26 percent said they were very or somewhat liberal.[29] This trend has proven durable; the share of Americans calling itself liberal, moderate, or conservative has remained stable for decades. This was true even as the Democratic Party identification advantage was widening.[30]

According to the NAES data, Democrats and independents are less ideologically predictable than their Republican counterparts.* Sixty-eight percent of self-identified Republicans consider themselves conservative, compared to the

42 percent of Democrats who see themselves as liberal. However in our data, party identification is a slightly stronger predictor of how a person will vote than ideology, adding weight to the Obama party advantage.[31]

Still all of this raises the question: how did a person widely perceived to be liberal (figure 1.5) win the votes of conservatives?

The cross-ideological draw of the senator from Illinois was stronger than that of the Republican Party nominee.* Not only did the Democrat do better with self-identified liberals than McCain did with self-identified conservatives, but he decisively carried moderates. Similar to our data, exit polls showed that 20 percent of conservatives voted for Obama. The Illinois senator also carried a majority of those who considered themselves to be neither Republicans nor Democrats but independents. Still, both candidates carried over 85 percent of those who identified with their own party.[32]

Using the 2008 NAES phone postelection panel data to compare the 17.4 percent of conservatives voting for Obama against other conservatives, we find that those for the Democratic ticket were significantly more likely to be black, Hispanic, lower income, and inclined to believe that their personal economic situation had worsened in the past year.* The largest and most robust predictor in our statistical model is race. Among conservatives, blacks are 40.79 times more likely

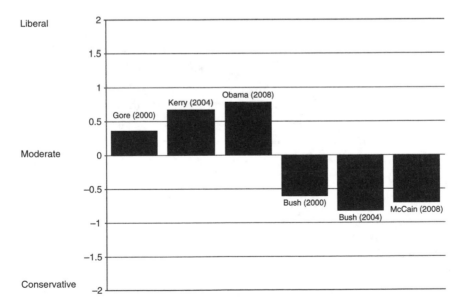

FIGURE 1.5 Perceptions of Candidate Ideology. *Sources*: NAES00 telephone survey, 6/01/00 to Election Day, N = 38,764; NAES04 telephone survey, 6/01/04 to Election Day, N = 40,898; NAES08 telephone survey, 6/01/08 to Election Day; N = 25,654.

to vote for Obama than nonblacks. In our postelection survey over 85 percent of black conservatives reported voting for Obama.

In electoral college terms, these shifts meant that liberal Obama took back states that had been won by centrist Clinton in 1992 and/or 1996 but had been taken by Bush in 2000 and/or 2004: Colorado, Florida, Iowa, Nevada, New Mexico, and Ohio. Obama did not win some states won by Clinton, including Arkansas (home to Clinton), Tennessee (home to Gore) and West Virginia, but picked up states Clinton did not carry: Virginia, North Carolina, and Indiana. The fact that McCain contested Pennsylvania to the end indicates how difficult his task was. Pennsylvania has been won by the Democratic presidential nominee since 1992. Of the states that Bush won in 2004, Obama recaptured nine: Colorado, Florida, Indiana, Iowa, New Mexico, Nevada, North Carolina, Ohio, and Virginia.

Unsurprisingly, voters did not necessarily pull the same party's lever in the voting booth in 2008 as they had in 2004. In the 2008 NAES postelection panel, 17 percent of respondents who said that they voted for incumbent president George W. Bush in 2004 reported balloting for Obama, while 7.6 percent who said that they voted for Democratic Senator John Kerry in 2004 did the same for Senator McCain, a net advantage of almost 10 percent for the Democrats. Moreover in 2008, Democratic turnout was up and Republican down. This proved particularly important in North Carolina and Virginia, which both moved to Obama's column.

Party, Ideology, Incumbency, and the Economy in Predicting the 2008 Vote

Scholars of politics have found that economic growth and the incumbent's popularity account for most of the variance in presidential vote.[33] The predictions are less reliable when the so-called fundamentals do not dramatically tilt in one direction or the other;[34] when the country is at war, as was the case in 1952 and 1968;[35] or, as Gore's failure in 2000 suggests, when one campaign neglects to do something the models presuppose, such as claiming credit for prosperity that occurred when the candidate's party controlled the White House.[36]

In most years, forecasts modeled by political scientists have been accurate within a percent or two[37] and as we noted earlier the forecasters anticipated a clear Democratic victory in 2008. In retrospect, it is unsurprising that the McCain advisors could not conjure up a plan that might have taken them to victory because their assessment was on the same page as the forecasters. In lay terms, a faltering economy and an unpopular incumbent predict a win for the party peering at the White House from outside the wrought iron gates on Pennsylvania Avenue.

Here we replicate these assumptions as best as our survey questions permit, using the 2008 telephone NAES postelection panel to see how well party identification, ideological placement, incumbent approval rating and economic perceptions predict vote in 2008. Table 1.1 outlines a probit regression model predicting an Obama two-party vote. The predictor variables in the model[38] are party identification, ideology, voting for Bush in 2004, Bush approval ratings, the belief that the national economy is worse than a year ago, and the belief that personal economy is worse than a year ago. These last two variables are often thought of as sociotropic voting and pocketbook voting.[39] The dependent variable in the model is from the postelection wave of the panel while the predictor variables come from the pre-election wave.

We apologize for the use of terms such as "explained variance," which is the percentage of variability in a dependent variable, that is, an Obama vote that can be statistically attributed to independent variables. For a simple example, knowing a person's birthday can explain his or her age by 100 percent. Knowing a person's eating habits may only partially explain his or her body mass index (BMI), since other variables, such as genetics, physical activity, and so on, can explain other variance in BMI.

Examining explained variance allows us to see how much of an impact these fundamental variables have on vote decisions. Therefore, the first statistic of note is the McKelvey and Zavoina R^2, which estimates the variance in our dependent variable explained collectively by our independent variables.[40] It suggests that 77 percent of the variance in the Obama two-party vote variable is explained by these few variables. When one adds to this finding the fact that Obama outspent McCain and ran a better campaign, the likelihood that he would win was high. In the chapters that follow, we will factor the power of campaign messages into our explanation. Then, in chapter 12, we will add the money advantage to the equation.

TABLE 1.1. Predicting Obama Two-Party Vote

	Probit Coefficient		Standard Error	Z
Intercept	−0.722		0.194	−3.72
Party Identification	0.283	***	0.022	12.66
Ideology (Conservative high)	0.378	***	0.040	9.28
Vote for Bush in 2004	−0.626	***	0.088	−7.09
Approve Bush	−0.621	***	0.045	−13.76
National Economic Conditions Worse	0.030		0.081	0.37
Personal Economic Conditions Worse	0.032		0.075	0.43
McKelvey & Zavoina's R^2:			0.766	

*** $p < .001$
Data: NAES08 postelection panel telephone survey; $N = 3{,}004$

Finally, in chapter 13, we will ask what difference, if any, campaign messages made, over and above the effects of party identification, ideology, incumbent popularity, and perception of the economy. We will also ask what effect, if any, campaign communication had on perceptions of the economy and the candidates' ability to handle it.

A few points of note: First, in this model, party identification and ideology are strong predictors of how individuals say they voted.[41] Approval of Bush's handling his job as president and voting for Bush in 2004 produced equally strong effects in the model. This suggests, as we will discuss in chapter 2, that President Bush played a large role in this election. The respondent's assessment of his or her personal economic condition or national economic conditions did not predict an Obama vote in this model. There are a few reasons for this. First, 83.9 percent of respondents reported that their economic situation was either the same as or worse than it was a year ago. With such a high ceiling effect and a lack of variance within this predictor variable, meaningful relationships are difficult to tease out statistically.

Second, we are looking at individual-level data and perceptions of the economy, not an aggregate economic indicator. Political scientist Gerald H. Kramer noted many discrepancies between macro- and micro-level studies linking the economy to vote choice and argued that aggregate-level time-series analyses produce better results. In other words, the individual-level data reported here may not detect the economy's role in the outcome. We did find a moderate correlation at the aggregate level. However, our economic indicator did not produce a lagged effect on voting behavior, suggesting that although these two variables may move together, shifts in economic conditions do not appear to precede and influence votes for Obama.[42]*

As we will show in chapter 8, the economy was at play in this election, even though we do not show statistical evidence for that here. In a later chapter, we will suggest that perceptions of the candidates' abilities to handle the economy were directly linked to vote choice in the presence of controls.

One explanation for the minimal net effect of campaign communication may of course be that two equally skilled and comparably financed teams cancel out the effects of each other's messages and media.[43] Messages may have specific, short-lived influences on certain groups of people, but when taken together the net effect of all campaign communication from both parties on an election outcome may be limited.

If campaigns do matter, some surmise that it may be by activating such "fundamentals" as perception of the strength of the economy and of party identification and political ideology. In other words, campaigns may serve simply to vivify existing voter preferences or, in the phrasing of political scientists Andrew Gelman and Gary King,[44] foster "enlightened preferences." Echoing Gelman and King, political scientist Thomas Holbrook found that campaigns basically provide voters with information that helps them align with the candidate to whom they were predisposed all along.[45]

The communication effects that have been located have in general been minor and, as such, not likely to undermine the standard models' predictions. So, for example, Bartels found small changes in percent of vote due to priming in the 1980 and 1996 elections[46] and also identified small instances of persuasion effects on candidates' image in 1980, 1984, and 1988. He concludes, "While persuasion effects of this magnitude are clearly large enough to be electorally significant under the right circumstances, they are also clearly small enough to be roughly consistent with aggregated-level evidence that 'the outcome of recent elections can be predicted within a few percentage points in the popular vote, based on events that have occurred before Election Day.' "[47]

Before we move to chapters on the overarching themes of the 2008 general election, it is important that we note that messages and money aren't factors in the forecasting models that correctly predicted more than two months before Election Day that Obama would win handily.[48] Much of the past research on the impact of campaigns assumes that during the general election the two major-party candidates are running campaigns with equal resources and skill. Under those circumstances we would expect the communication of each side to simply cancel out the effects of the other.[49] Nor did the 2008 models anticipate the collapse of the U.S. economy in mid-September, a change that should have widened the gap separating the Democratic ticket's final vote total from that of its Republican counterpart.

With an estimated $5.3 billion spent by candidates, political parties, and interest groups, the 2008 campaign was the costliest in U.S. history.[50] If equally distributed between the two major presidential campaigns, past research suggests that the simple fact of heavy spending wouldn't affect outcome. However, hamstrung by McCain's decision to accept federal financing, in the 2008 general election, the Republicans were swamped by a message tsunami from a campaign able to outspend them nationally and in virtually every battleground state. In other words, the financial advantage resided on the same side as the structural one. To compound Obama's advantage, he also ran what even his opponents characterized as an almost flawless general election campaign, while, as we will show in later chapters, McCain and his running mate stumbled at key points in the general election. We wonder why the Obama spending and tactical advantage didn't widen the margin between the two candidates beyond the forecasters' predictions. By the end of the book, we hope to have provided a preliminary answer to the question of whether the Obama campaign's saturation of the paid media affected the disposition to vote for Obama in the general election. And did the messages purchased with that money matter?

TWO

McSame versus the
Tax-and-Spend Liberal

❧

I N THE WORLD CONSTRUCTED BY THE OBAMA CAMPAIGN, GEORGE W. Bush aspired to a third term. "The most influential politician in 2008 won't be on the ballot," forecast Democratic consultant David Axelrod in a memo to the Illinois lawyer he helped elect to the Senate in 2004.[1] "His name is George W. Bush. With few exceptions, the history of presidential politics shows that public opinion and attitudes about who should next occupy the Oval Office are largely shaped by the perceptions of the retiring incumbent."[2] In 2008, the task of Republican nominee Arizona Senator John McCain was to become one of those exceptions. The responsibility for ensuring that he didn't do so resided with the Illinois senator turned Democratic Party nominee.

In this chapter, we examine the most frequently aired attacks by and against each of the two major-party candidates: McCain as "McSame" versus Obama as a "tax-and-spend liberal." Specifically, where Obama defined himself as the agent of needed change and equated McCain both with Bush and the failed politics and policies of Washington, McCain cast himself as a maverick and contended that the liberal changes Obama proposed would worsen the economy and harm the middle class. Obama parried the tax-and-spend charge by arguing his Republican counterpart would push up taxes and perpetuate policies that had mangled the economy and mired the country in Iraq. Meanwhile, the Democrat blunted charges of out-of-touch liberalism with autobiographical vignettes steeped in American middle-class values. By contrast, McCain drew sustenance for his claims that he had and would place country first from his heroic defiance of his North Vietnamese captors in a war beyond the memory of most of the electorate.

Lost in the crossfire were two key facts. First, although the prime beneficiaries of the proposals differed, the plans of both presidential contenders contained new taxes and increased spending. Second, the Obama-McCain-Bush record of alliance and attack was more complex than either candidate admitted. So for example, in a number of instances, Obama had sided with Bush when McCain had not. In others, both had come down on the same side as or taken a view opposed to the president's. Specifically, Obama voted for and McCain against Bush's energy bill, while both agreed with the incumbent on the basic contours of immigration reform. There were also instances in which the two nominees embraced a policy anathema to Bush, such as the use of cap and trade to address climate change.

The Backdrop: An Unpopular President

Although both Bush's approval ratings and the growth in the economy were sub-par, the biography of the Republican Party's nominee challenged an assumption embedded in past elections and hence the theorists' models of them. Not since Governor Adlai Stevenson and General Dwight D. Eisenhower ran to succeed President Harry Truman in 1952 had the presidential contest failed to include either a vice president seeking election or an incumbent bent on retaining the key to the Oval Office. In other words, unlike most of the elections modeled in the television age, in 2008 the outgoing president did not have a lineal heir in the race.

Instead, the Republican nominee had fiercely fought George W. Bush for his party's nomination in 2000 and during the Texan's eight-year term had amassed a list of significant defections from the president's policies. McCain, for example, had opposed the first two Bush tax cuts, voted against the prescription drug benefit, supported reimportation of pharmaceutical drugs from Canada, championed the Patients' Bill of Rights Act, cast some of the administration's "enhanced interrogation techniques" of suspected terrorists as "torture," argued for closing the detention center at Guantanamo Bay, opposed a Constitutional amendment banning gay marriage, challenged administration-imposed restrictions on embryonic stem cell research, taken on Secretary of Defense Rumsfeld, pushed for an increase in troop levels in Iraq that came to be known as the surge, and sponsored legislation to deal with global warming. Further muddling some of the models, halfway into Bush's second term, the 2006 elections swept the Democrats into control of the House and Senate, which meant that the economic woes of 2008 happened with a Republican in the White House and Democrats on the other end of Pennsylvania Avenue, a configuration that opened the question, "Which party, if either and not both, would be blamed for the mess?"

One dilemma for the senior senator from Arizona was that the success of the surge strategy that he championed moved the Iraq war out of the headlines and subordinated the question, "Who would be the better Commander-in-Chief?," on which McCain consistently topped Obama, to one which McCain never held a lead—"Who was better at handling the economy?" Another problem for the Republican standard-bearer was that in his pursuit of his party's prize he had either downplayed or fled from the credentials that bolstered his prospects with independents in the general election. The price of nourishing his chances with party regulars in the winter primaries was undercutting them with moderates in the fall election.[3]

Additionally, throughout the contest for the Republican nomination, the Arizonan was hammered from the Right, a phenomenon that increased the likelihood that, without intense courting, portions of the Republican conservative base might sit the election out. Conservatives' discomfort with McCain was stoked by his co-sponsorship of immigration reform legislation and "campaign finance rules that many on the right consider a violation of free speech. And he made a deal with Democrats to break a deadlock on judicial nominations that many on the right considered near treasonous."[4] In a harbinger of problems to come, at the 2007 meeting of the Conservative Political Action Conference, McCain was booed.[5] Moreover, in the early primaries, conservative icon Rush Limbaugh routinely railed against his bid.[6] Our NAES data suggest that the political talk-show host's attacks increased his listeners' perceptions that the Arizonan was a Machiavellian moderate in conservative's clothing.[7]

Complicating matters for the GOP contender was the fact that throughout their face-off in the primaries, well-financed former Massachusetts governor Mitt Romney tried to outflank him from the right by stressing McCain's heretical views. "Senator McCain was one of two Republicans who voted against the Bush tax cuts," noted Romney in the Fox News debate in early January.[8] In Romney's view, McCain was for all intents and purposes a Democrat who was "pushing the Democrat position on immigration, taxes, energy."[9]

However if other facets of his life story are highlighted, the Vietnam War hero seemed surprisingly liberal. In its editorial endorsement of his bid for the Republican Party nomination, the New York Times, for example, applauded the very positions that had earned Limbaugh's opprobrium: McCain-Kennedy (immigration reform), McCain-Feingold (campaign finance reform), and McCain-Lieberman (climate change legislation). "Senator John McCain of Arizona is the only Republican who promises to end the George Bush style of governing from and on behalf of a small, angry fringe," noted that Times encomium. "With a record of working across the aisle to develop sound bipartisan legislation, he would offer a choice to a broader range of Americans than the rest of the Republican field."[10]

By emphasizing McCain's impulse to safeguard taxpayers' dollars and police government spending, others made the case that he was a true fiscal conservative. "While other conservatives failed to see how corporations were insinuating themselves into their movement," noted right-of-center *New York Times* columnist David Brooks in November 2007, "McCain went after Boeing contracts. While others failed to see the rising tide of corruption around them, McCain led the charge against Jack Abramoff. While others ignored the spending binge, McCain was among the fiscal hawks."[11]

By adopting the label "maverick," McCain harmonized these disparate perceptions and drew a contrast with the incumbent. The strategy was simple. If McCain was a maverick then he could not be McSame. Still, the association between Bush and McCain was plumped up every time a pollster or pundit asked, "In an election in which the economy is in peril and the president a pariah, can a self-described maverick from the president's party unhitch himself from the record of a president whose approval ratings are setting record lows?" Also hampering McCain's ability to slip the knot on the central issue of the economy was the fact that after objecting to Bush's spending and taxing plans in the Republican primaries of 2000, and after voting against the first two of the Bush tax cuts, McCain had campaigned at Bush's side in 2004 and, in the 2008 Republican primaries, supported retaining those tax reductions beyond their 2010 expiration date. Additionally, although he was a deficit hawk who opposed earmarks, McCain had been part of the Senate when, with a Republican in the White House, the country had, over his futile objections, but in four instances[12] with his vote, nearly doubled its national debt.[13] At the same time, the Arizonan's history of support for deregulation, insistence on retaining the tax cuts for upper-income earners, and support for four of the Bush proposed budgets made it possible for the Obama campaign to concede McCain's maverick credentials in some areas, while indicting his embrace of the administration's economic policies and philosophy.

Principled War Hero

As a third-generation son of military officers whose father and grandfather were both four-star admirals, John McCain was a prized captive when his plane was downed during a 1967 bombing run over Hanoi during the Vietnam War. Imprisoned from 1967 to 1973 and tortured in what was known as the Hanoi Hilton, the Arizonan refused release unless those captured before he had been were repatriated as well. In the primaries and general election, the starting premise of the McCain campaign was that his behavior in Hanoi demonstrated that he was a strong, principled individual. In the postprimary season, the message that he had and would put "country first" was evident from his biography as well. When the central issue in voters' minds was the Iraq War, the slogan "Country First" whispered McCain's military credentials and prescience in advocating the surge. But when the economy displaced concerns about distant wars and both candidates endorsed the Wall Street rescue package or bailout of September, the theme lost much of its power to distinguish one candidate from the other.

The Alternative Narrative: "Keating Five" Tied to the Crash of 2008

McCain's credibility as a reformer depended in part on how much culpability one ascribed to his role in the so-called Keating Five scandal of the late 1980s and early '90s and whether one approvingly credited that part of his past to his resulting crusade to diminish the role of money in politics. Whatever its political implications, the rhetoric of that scandal hurt McCain by creating the telegraphic label "Keating Five" on which to hang memories of the staggering government bailout of the savings and loan industry after the collapse of over 700 poorly regulated savings and loans. Labeling him one of the "Keating Five" fused McCain and Keating and the S & L crisis in memory and invited the assumption that each of the five implicated Senators was as guilty as the other, an assumption that in McCain's case was belied by the facts.

Substantively what the label meant was that McCain was one of five U.S. senators accused of intervening in a 1987 federal investigation of Charles Keating, a major campaign contributor and family friend who headed a failed savings and loan association. Four were Democrats; McCain was the only Republican. Since the Democrats controlled the Senate, the possibility existed that the Arizonan had been swept into the investigation to ensure that it did not exclusively implicate Democrats, a conclusion bolstered in 2008 when Robert Bennett, the Democratic lawyer who served as special counsel to the committee, told the *Washington Post* that the committee chair, former Sen. Howell Heflin (D-Ala.), did not want "a month of public hearings 'with no Republicans in the dock.' "[14]

When his Lincoln Savings and Loan Association went under in 1989, Keating, who ultimately was convicted of federal conspiracy charges, became a symbol of the corruptive influence of money in politics. In 1991, the Senate Ethics Committee reprimanded two of the five senators for interfering with the earlier investigation of his activities but cleared McCain and former astronaut John Glenn (D-Ohio) of wrongdoing. "I'm sure that my political obituary will always have something about the Keating Five in it," McCain nonetheless said in March 1991. "I don't see how that could be avoided."[15]

By meeting with regulators, albeit as part of a group, on a case involving a major benefactor, McCain recognized that he had created the appearance of impropriety without actually engaging in outlawed conduct. The Senate committee agreed, finding his actions neither improper nor unlawful but instead an instance of poor judgment. Responding to the lesson he learned in his Keating Five experience, McCain championed campaign finance reform, leading a national effort that in 2002 led to passage of the Bipartisan Campaign Reform Act, known as McCain-Feingold.

In early October, the Obama team tried to transform that part of McCain's past into a coherent narrative about a person whose bad judgment and dangerous ideological dispositions contributed to the savings and loan debacle, as well as the 2008 Wall Street meltdown. Obama campaign manager David Plouffe[16] explained the storyline in a carefully worded e-mail to supporters:

> During the savings and loan crisis of the late '80s and early '90s, McCain's political favors and aggressive support for deregulation put him at the center of the fall of Lincoln Savings and Loan, one of the largest in the country. More than 23,000 investors lost their savings. Overall, the savings and loan crisis required the federal government to bail out the savings of hundreds of thousands of families and ultimately cost American taxpayers $124 billion.
>
> In that crisis, John McCain and his political patron, Charles Keating, played central roles that ultimately landed Keating in jail for fraud and McCain in front of the Senate Ethics Committee. The McCain campaign has tried to avoid talking about the scandal, but with so many parallels to the current crisis, McCain's Keating history is relevant and voters deserve to know the facts—and see for themselves the pattern of poor judgment by John McCain....[17]

The e-mail invited the inference that McCain was found guilty by the Senate Ethics Committee, while at the same time suggesting that he had played a "central" role in costing taxpayers billions. The indictment of his judgment is more telling because that is, in fact, the language used by the Senate Ethics Committee and the words on which Obama was resting his case for his readiness to be president.

Still, the Obama high command recognized that if any Republican contender had the opportunity to detach himself from the Bush presidency, that individual was John McCain. "John McCain remains the odds on favorite to win the Republican nomination," noted David Axelrod in that 2006 memo. "[He] is the best chance the Republicans have to break from Bush and offer their own version of change. His speech after the 2006 election to a conservative audience, rebuking the party for 'drifting from its principles and reformist commitments' was excellent."[18]

Obama's top strategist also observed: "McCain has a well-established reputation—as a feisty independent reformer.... [t]hrough his battles on such issues
as campaign financing, remarks on environment, and his willingness to buck the
President and his party on a wide range of issues.... But his nomination won't
come without a fight or a cost. He remains anathema to many activists within the
party from the religious right, which is deeply suspicious of his secular politics, to
the tax cut purest, to K-street. He knows he will have a fight, and this has caused
him to make a series of Faustian bargains with the right. From the dalliance with
Jerry Falwell to his embrace of the anti-immigration panderers and gay marriage
militants in his last campaign, McCain's straight talk express has taken many awkward detours."[19]

The Contest over Change: Obama's Efforts to Own the Issue

In a change election, Barack Obama embodied that central message in ways that
his 72-year-old opponent could not. In August 2008, the Democratic Party asked a
country in which the majority of voters are white and whose past includes slavery,
lynching, and Jim Crow to elect a 47-year-old, Harvard-educated former community
organizer who characterized his racial identity by saying that his father came from
Kenya and mother from Kansas. The Democratic standard-bearer signaled the sym-
bolic significance of his biracial heritage when he noted that, "When I raise my hand
and take that oath of office, I think that the world will look at us differently.... And
millions of kids across this country will look at themselves differently."[20] Throughout the election season, pundits wondered whether the change that Obama capsulized with that remark would net out in his favor or cost him the election, a question
we address in the next chapter. As a candidate twenty-five years younger than his
Republican rival, a person of color, highly educated, and a liberal, Obama presented
an identity that coincided with that of his most ardent supporters.

At the same time, incumbent George W. Bush's disapproval ratings meant
that the election was also a contest over which nominee would bring a fundamentally new direction. Each wrapped himself in the mantle of change. "[T]the core
message didn't change much," recalled David Plouffe. "You need to change Washington. We need an economy that works for the middle class."[21] "[W]e're going to
have to change the culture in Washington so that lobbyists and special interests
aren't driving the process and your voices aren't being drowned out," noted the
Democratic nominee in the second debate.[22] In the same face-off, McCain tried to
link the Democrats to the status quo. "[T]he Democrats in the Senate and some—
and some members of Congress defended what Fannie and Freddie were doing,"
argued McCain. "They resisted any change."

On issue after issue, Obama promised dramatic change from the Bush-Mc-Cain status quo. "That is a fundamental difference that I have with Sen. McCain," noted the Democratic nominee in the October 7 debate. "He believes in deregulation in every circumstance. That's what we've been going through for the last eight years. It hasn't worked, and we need fundamental change." Indicting McCain's health care plan, Obama argued, "That, I don't think, is the kind of change that we need." Of foreign policy, the Illinois senator contended, "[T]he strains that have been placed on our alliances around the world and the respect that's been diminished over the last eight years has constrained us being able to act on something like the genocide in Darfur, because we don't have the resources or the allies to do everything that we should be doing. That's going to change when I'm president, but we can't change it unless we fundamentally change Sen. McCain's and George Bush's foreign policy. It has not worked for America."[23]

Where the McCain campaign all but abandoned self-promotional ads in the final weeks of the campaign, Obama's team maintained a track of advertising that promoted his credentials as an agent of fundamental change throughout the primaries and general election. "We are one nation and our time for change has come," Obama argued in an ad aired in February.[24] "We Can Change the World. Change Begins with You," read the print on the screen in the closing moments of another.[25] In the primaries, the Illinois senator's ads promised "a fundamentally new direction." Specifically, he forecast bringing the country together to "fix healthcare and make college affordable, become energy independent and end this war."[26] He promised as well to end "the tax breaks for companies that ship our jobs overseas. And put a middle class tax cut into the pockets of working Americans."[27] When editorial endorsements echoed Obama's theme, his ads quoted the testimonials. "There's a reason every major newspaper's endorsed Barack Obama," noted an ad aired in Pennsylvania in the run-up to that state's primary. "'Obama can change the way business is done in Washington,' says the *Daily News*.... 'Obama offers real change in the White House,' says the *Patriot-News*. 'He isn't tied to lobbyists and special interests.'"[28]

Throughout the campaign, the incantation "yes we can" and "yes you can" invited Obama supporters to participate in the process of altering the country's course. In Oregon in May, Obama said in an ad, "Some people say we can't change Washington. I'm Barack Obama and I approve this message to say this time you can."[29] As the campaign shifted its focus to the general election, the theme "Change You [We] Can Believe In" gave way to "For the Change We Need."

Central to the Obama message was the contention that "the ways of Washington must change."[30] To tie McCain to the failures of the past, the Democrats cast his platform as "same old politics, same failed policies,"[31] themes we will explore in a moment. Where the Democrats portrayed McCain as "Washington's biggest celebrity,"[32] Obama cast himself as the embodiment of the American dream. Where Democratic rhetoric situated McCain and Bush "in the pocket of big oil,"[33] Obama was the candidate who stood for building "the next generation of fuel efficient vehicles."[34] When McCain and Washington weren't synonyms in Obama ads, they were partners. "Corning shuts down its plant in Pennsylvania," reported a September 16 Obama ad. "Hundreds lose their jobs. Then, the workers are rehired to disassemble the plant and ship the equipment to China. Washington sold them out with the help of people like John McCain."[35]

If voters entered the voting booth asking, "Who will deliver needed change in Washington?" Obama had a decisive edge. In their May 2008 national poll, which showed McCain and Obama neck and neck in the horse race, the Democrats found that McCain "was not perceived as a change agent." Examining "essential change attributes," Obama's pollster Joel Benenson[36] reports that Obama was leading decisively on "putting the middle class first ahead of special interests, putting partisan politics aside, the basic attribute on bringing fundamental change to Washington and our surrogate for straight talk, 'tell people what they need to know, not what they want to hear.'" "Not only did we have commanding leads on those change attributes, except for straight talk where we were at parity," recalls Benenson, "but we had double digit leads on all of them."[37]

To undercut the Democratic advantage on the argument for change, the Republicans raised two incompatible concerns about Obama: First, he was unready to lead and as a result could not actually bring about change. Second, the change Obama would bring was retreaded big-government, tax-and-spend liberalism that would turn a crisis into an irreparable catastrophe. If the Illinois Democrat were indeed unable to lead, then voters need not fear his plans, because they would never be translated from rhetoric to reality.

Obama's Change Will Make Things Worse

In mid-September, McCain/Palin ads tailored to individual battleground states bore the tag "Change is Coming"; in mid-October, the McCain-RNC hybrid attack ads did the same.[38] For McCain, the new direction Obama forecast was not new at all but hoary liberalism in disguise. In this world, Obama's proposals would worsen the financial crisis. "His [Obama's] response to our economic crisis," said a Republican spot at the end of October, "is to spend and tax our economy deeper into recession."[39] In the closing days of the election, Florida Governor Jeb Bush suggested that an Obama administration would "raise your taxes" and "spend us deeper into debt."[40] The final McCain broadcast ad of the fall election offered this choice: "For higher taxes (Obama's picture on screen). For working Joes (McCain's picture on screen)." Then, as pictures of Obama and McCain alternated, the contrasts continued. "Spread your income. Keep what's yours. A trillion in new spending. Freeze spending, Eliminate waste. Pain for small business. Economic growth." The final contrast identified the changes Obama would bring as "Risky." And McCain's as "Proven."[41]

John McCain as Maverick

As we noted earlier, McCain fought the charge that he was "McBush" or "McSame" with the counterclaim that he was a reformer and its synonym, a "maverick." In the preconvention period, the Republican's ads took the "McCain equals Bush" claim head-on. Some of the evidence of McCain's independence was issue-specific. "John McCain stood up to the president and sounded the alarm on global warming five years ago," said one aired in mid-June.[42]

Others linked biography to philosophy. In its most expensive television buy in mid-summer, the McCain campaign concentrated just under $10 million in July on a sixty-second spot that opened with scenes from 1967's "summer of love." "It was a time of uncertainty, hope and change: the summer of love," said the announcer. "Half a world away, another kind of love...of country. John McCain. Shot down, bayoneted, tortured. Offered early release, he said no. He'd sworn an oath."[43] The ad then tracked McCain's life from military service to elected office. "Home, he turned to public service. His philosophy: before party, polls and self: America." Then the key identifying concept: "A maverick, John McCain tackled campaign reform, military reform, spending reform. He took on presidents, partisans, and popular opinion." A shift to present tense followed: "He believes our world is dangerous, our economy in shambles." "Economy in shambles" tacitly indicted the status quo and with it the incumbent president. The message then pivoted to an implicit indictment of Obama. "John McCain doesn't always tell us what we 'hope' to hear. Beautiful words cannot make our lives better." The final lines praise McCain's dedication to country and imply that, by contrast, Obama is self-absorbed, a notion that forecast the "celebrity" attacks of August. "But a man who has always put his country and her people before self, before politics, can," said the McCain ad in closing. "Don't 'hope' for a better life. Vote for one."[44]

In a similar vein, an August McCain ad bluntly said, "Washington's broken. John McCain knows it. We're worse off than we were four years ago. Only McCain has taken on Big Tobacco, drug companies, fought corruption in both parties." Then in a contention on which the fall campaign would be fought, the ad promised, "He'll reform Wall Street, battle Big Oil, make America prosper again. He's the original maverick. One is ready to lead—McCain."[45]

To sunder McCain from the unpopular incumbent during period three (September 10-October 14), the Republican campaign concentrated its TV dollars in September and October on an ad titled "Original Mavericks." At a cost of over $6.5 million in air time, that spot opened with photos of McCain and Palin superimposed on a flag as the announcer said, "The original mavericks" and continued, "He fights pork barrel spending. She stopped the Bridge to Nowhere." As the screen shows an *Associated Press* headline saying, "McCain Calls for Permitting the Importation of Prescription Drugs from Canada" overlaid on a close up of McCain, the voice-over adds, "He took on the drug industry. She took on Big Oil. He battled Republicans and reformed Washington. She battled Republicans and reformed Alaska." The ad closes: "They'll make history. They'll change Washington." The final screen proclaims, "The Original Mavericks," as the announcer says, "McCain/Palin: Real Change."[46]

After months of trying to gain ground with a pro-McCain message, the Republican consultants retired that tactic. "We tested months of positive McCain stuff and it didn't move a single number," recalls McCain pollster Bill McInturff.[47] "To the extent that we had a chance, this race had to be about Senator Obama."[48] As a result, the Republicans moved to high-dollar attack ads whose titles suggest their focus:

Expensive Plans (just under $8 million in TV spending)
Dangerous (Just under $6 million)
Unethical (Just under $6 million)
Ambition (Just under $5 million)[49]

As the Obama campaign tightened the tie between McCain and Bush, the Republicans made a decisive move to sever it in the third and final presidential debate. The Democratic premise of the "Maverick v. McSame" exchange was set in place when Senator Obama noted, "So one of the things that I think we have to recognize is pursuing the same kinds of policies that we pursued over the last eight years is not going to bring down the deficit. And, frankly, Senator McCain voted for four out of five of President Bush's budgets. We've got to take this in a new direction, that's what I propose as president."[50]

McCain's widely reported response was, "Senator Obama, I am not President Bush. If you wanted to run against President Bush, you should have run four years ago. I'm going to give a new direction to this economy in this country...."[51] Without wasting time, the Obama campaign turned the McCain rejoinder into an ad acknowledging that the Arizonan wasn't in fact Bush but adding McCain's admission that he had voted with him over 90 percent of the time.[52]

In the debate itself Obama countered by challenging the notion that McCain differed from Bush on the central issue facing the country: the economy.

So the fact of the matter is that if I occasionally have mistaken your policies for George Bush's policies, it's because on the core economic issues
that matter to the American people, on tax policy, on energy policy, on
spending priorities, you have been a vigorous supporter of President
Bush.... We need to move in a new direction.[53]

In a serious strategic lapse, McCain responded with a series of noneconomic
differences.[54]

During this same period, the McCain ads disparaged the past two Bush terms.
"The last eight years haven't worked very well, have they?" McCain asks in a direct-
to-camera ad that began airing October 17. "I'll make the next four years better.
I have a plan for a new direction for our economy."[55]

The Republican's efforts to disentangle himself from Democratic portraits of
him in Bush's embrace escalated in a *Washington Times* interview published October 23. There, McCain indicted Bush policies, including "Spending, the conduct of
the war in Iraq for years, growth in the size of government, larger than any time
since the Great Society, laying a $10 trillion debt on future generations of America,
owing $500 billion to China, obviously, failure to both enforce and modernize the
[financial] regulatory agencies that were designed for the 1930s and certainly not for
the twenty-first century, failure to address the issue of climate change seriously."[56]

Three days later (October 26) on *Meet the Press,* the Republican nominee
reprised the argument he had made in the final debate. "But the fact is I am not
George Bush. The fact is that I was not popular within my own party. The fact is
that when I said that we were failing in Iraq and we were going to lose, I was criticized by Republicans. The fact is when I did campaign finance reform with Russ
Feingold, I was opposed by my own party and my own president. So do we share
a common philosophy of the Republican Party? Of course. But I've, I've stood
up against my party, not just President Bush, but others; and I've got the scars to
prove it, including taking up, with Ted Kennedy, immigration reform, knowing
full well that that was going to hurt my chances in the primaries. So I could go
down a long list of issues with you."[57]

He then expanded his case to encompass economic grounds as well:

Do I respect President Bush? Of course I respect him. But I pointed out
we were on the wrong track in a whole lot of ways, including a $10 trillion
deficit, including saying we got to rein in Fannie Mae and Freddie Mac
and, and propose legislation to try to fix it before that triggered the housing collapse, including today, when I'm saying they should be going out
and buying up these mortgages and giving people mortgages that they
can afford, rather than bailing out the banks.

When pundits speculated about the general election advantages of McCain's maverick past, they assumed, incorrectly as it turned out, that most voters were aware of his party-bucking credentials. "We discovered in May that we were much better defined with the electorate than John McCain was," recalled Democratic pollster Joel Benenson.[58] "[T]he one thing that was clear when the election campaign started," noted David Axelrod, "was that as much as people in Washington and elites had a clear sense of who John McCain was, there wasn't a real clear sense among voters of who he was."[59]

That knowledge gap eased the Democrat's task of reducing McCain's relationship with Bush to bites of sight and sound digested in telegraphic visuals of the two, side by side, arm-in-arm, embracing on the 2004 campaign trail or conversing in the Oval Office. When the McCain campaign launched its attack on Obama's celebrity status in August, these visuals provided a ready rebuttal. "For decades, he's been Washington's biggest celebrity," the announcer said of McCain in one Democratic ad. The spot then cut to a photo of McCain awkwardly embracing Bush at a rally as the voiceover intoned, "And as Washington embraced him, John McCain hugged right back."[60] Unspoken in the Democratic ads was a fact that we will explore in the next chapter. Specifically, the Oval Office footage on which a number of the ads relied was captured when Bush conceded that McCain had a veto-proof majority for a ban on torture that Bush and Cheney had aggressively opposed.

Complicating McCain's efforts to sever his attachment to the incumbent was the fact, as Obama adviser David Axelrod observed, that, "Throughout the primary campaign, he [McCain] was forced at times to defend his fealty to George Bush." "As you know," Axelrod recalled, "there was a lot of tape of him talking about how he voted with Bush 90 percent of the time and [saying] he couldn't think of a major issue on which he had a disagreement with Bush, and so on. We made good use of that tape throughout the campaign."[61] McCain had uttered the sound bites on which the Obama attacks relied while courting conservative voters and fending off the Romney challenge.

Over the course of the campaign, the Obama team spent more than $14 million on broadcast ads to familiarize the public with McCain's avowals of fealty to the incumbent's plans. This menu of statements included, "I voted with the president over 90% of the time. Higher than, uh, a lot of my, uh, even Republican colleagues."[62] That contention was the centerpiece of the most aired Obama ad in the preconvention period, a message underwritten with just over $6 million in airtime between August 31 and the end of September. The spot featured pictures of Bush and McCain in frame after frame as the words THE SAME were overlaid on the screen. To explain the pictures, the announcer intoned, "They share the same out-of-touch attitude. The same failure to understand the economy. The same tax cuts for huge corporations and the wealthiest one percent. The same questionable ties to lobbyists. The same plan to spend ten billion a month in Iraq when we should be rebuilding America." McCain is then shown declaring, "I voted with the president over 90% of the time. Higher than, uh, a lot of my, uh, even Republican colleagues." The announcer closed, "We just can't afford more of the same" as the tag on the screen set the Obama-Biden ticket as the remedy to the Bush-McCain years by noting, "Obama Biden: For the Change We Need."[63]

In a similar move, the Democrats spent almost $8 million on national cable from mid-October to early November on an ad titled "90 percent" whose opening footage was drawn from the final debate:

SENATOR MCCAIN: Senator Obama, I am not President Bush.

TEXT: Voted with Bush 90%

ANNOUNCER: True but you did vote with Bush 90% of the time.

FOOTAGE: Senator McCain at debate

TEXT: Tax breaks for big corporations and the wealthy

Center for American Progress Action Fund, 6/18/08

GRAPHIC: Still of McCain and Bush

TEXT: Nothing for the middle class

ANNOUNCER: Tax breaks for big corporations and the wealthy. But almost nothing for the middle class: same as Bush

FOOTAGE: Senator McCain at debate

GRAPHIC: Still of McCain and Bush

ON SCREEN: Spend $10 billion a month in Iraq (CRS Report, 7/14/08)

ANNOUNCER: Keep spending ten billion a month in Iraq while our own economy struggles: same as Bush

GRAPHIC: Still of McCain and Bush

ANNOUNCER: You may not be George Bush, but..."

FOOTAGE: McCain TV clip

TEXT: I voted with the President over 90% of the time

MCCAIN: I voted with the President over 90% of the time. Higher than uh, a lot of my, uh, even Republican colleagues.

ANNOUNCER: We just can't afford more of the same.

So pervasive was the 90 percent claim in Democratic rhetoric that it became the premise of a *Saturday Night Live* skit in which Darrell Hammond, playing John McCain, squirmed out of camera range as Will Ferrell, portraying George W. Bush, told the *SNL* audience, "John was there for me 90 percent of the time over the last eight years. When you think of John McCain, think of me, George W. Bush. Think of this face.... A vote for John McCain is a vote for George W. Bush."[64]

An overtime examination of the public's belief in the "McSame" charge reveals that there was a slight but statistically significant upward trend in the percentage believing that electing McCain would in essence create a Bush third term.[65] Between June 9 and November 11, each day was associated with a 0.035 percent increase in the public buying the McSame argument.

As shown in figure 2.1, respondents' belief in the "McSame" charge is related to party identification. In the final weeks of the campaign, nearly two-thirds of Democrats embraced the McCain-Bush link; approximately 40 percent of independents did the same and that view was shared by between 10 to 20 percent of Republicans.

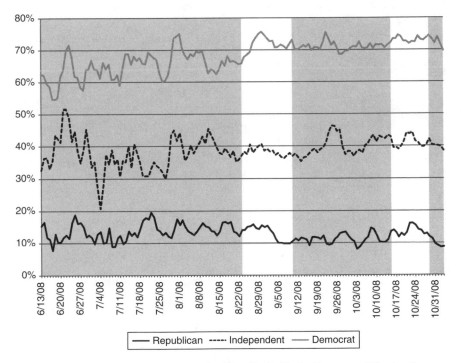

FIGURE 2.1 Percent of Respondents Who Identified with the Statement "Electing Senator John McCain for President Would Be Like Electing George W. Bush for a Third Term" by Party Identification (5-day PMA). *Source*: NAES08 telephone survey.

The NAES also shows that both news and ad viewing affected the belief that installing John McCain in the White House would be extending the Bush presidency. The more one watched television news, read the newspaper, or went online for campaign information, the more likely one was to embrace the notion of McCain as "McSame." Talk radio, a fortress of the conservative media establishment, significantly blunted this effect. As we show in chapter 13, the difference between Obama and McCain's ad spending is statistically related to believing that electing Senator John McCain is like electing George W. Bush for a third term. If Obama's ads increased the odds that a viewer would ally McCain with Bush, we would also expect that heavy viewers of evening TV would, even in the presence of controls, be more likely to report that conviction.

The audiovisual record of McCain's embrace of Bush complicated the Republican's task in the general election. Recalled McCain advisor Steve Schmidt,[66] "Our ballot was tied to the perception 'you're four more years [of] President Bush' or not. When that number went down, our ballot went up. When that number went up, our ballot went down."[67] Those fluctuations are a tribute to the success of the

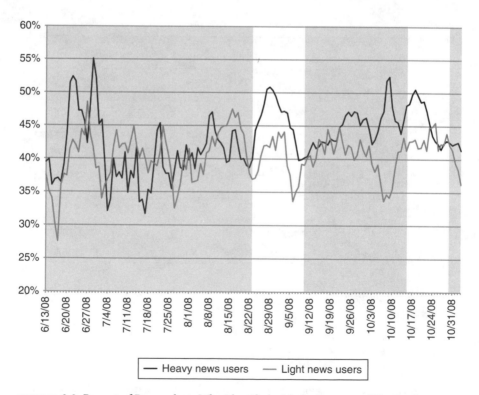

FIGURE 2.2 Percent of Respondents Who Identified with the Statement "Electing Senator John McCain for President Would Be Like Electing George W. Bush for a Third Term" by News Use (5-day PMA). *Source*: NAES08 telephone survey.

messages first of one campaign, as McCain disentangled perceptions of himself from those of the incumbent, and then, the other, as the Obama campaign wrapped the two back together again, a process we will unpack in the chapters that follow.

The following chart shows the extent to which "heavy" news users and "light" news users (figure 2.2) tied McCain to Bush.[68] Our data also suggest that news viewing, in the presence of controls, increased viewers' association between the incumbent and his party's nominee.

Using Radio Ads to Undercut McCain's Argument That He Was a Maverick

The arguments that we have tracked to this point occurred in nationally televised debates and widely accessible broadcast and cable ads. Under the press's radar screen, the Obama campaign opened a second assault on McCain's reputation as a maverick not in a new medium but in radio, an understudied venue that has been part of presidential campaigns for more than a century. The Democrats attacked McCain's reputation as a social moderate by stretching the truth to imply that he opposed abortion even in pregnancies resulting from rape and incest, arguing that he was responsible for derailing immigration reform, and suggesting that he opposed embryonic stem cell research. We will explore the effects of one facet of this narrowcasting strategy in chapter 12. Since our concern here is on the broader themes into which the more targeted ones were set, we turn next to the most aired attack made on the Democratic nominee by the Republicans.

Obama Is a Tax-and-Spend Liberal

With the amount of foreign-owned public debt at worrisome levels and the country's largest creditor an at-best-ambivalent Asian power, the debate over taxing and spending assumed added urgency. Neither party has consistently commanded the taxation issue across the past decade and a half. Instead, as Gallup noted in a 2007 survey, "The lead in perceived handling of taxes has shifted back and forth between the Democrats and Republicans over the years," with the parties "roughly at parity" in late 2007.[69]

Implicit in every attack is a point of contrast. By asserting that electing Obama meant higher taxes and more spending, the Republicans invited the inference that McCain was less disposed to do either. Complicating the attack, as the Arizona senator conceded, was the fact that Republicans had squandered their once cherished identity as the champions of fiscal constraint.[70] At $5.73 trillion when George W. Bush assumed the presidency in 2001, by the end of his second term, the national debt had reached $10.63 trillion.[71] During most of that time, Congress was securely in Republican hands.

The debate about each candidate's disposition to spend occurred in a world in which the economic collapse evoked widespread expert agreement that massive new governmental spending was desirable. Nonetheless, bespeaking their lack of confidence in the intelligence of the huddled masses, each major-party candidate promised a net cut in spending, while also prophesying that government outlays would explode were his opponent elected. As the country devolved into a deep recession, and economists cringed or dismissed the candidates' rhetoric as meaningless posturing, Obama and McCain clung to that script. "[W]e've got to cut spending," announced the Republican in the first debate of the fall. "... [W]e've let government get completely out of control."[72] "I'm cutting more than I'm spending," said the Democrat in the second debate, "so that it will be a net spending cut."[73] But even as he promised a real spending cut, Obama's rhetoric betrayed his own reservations. "[Y]es, we may have to cut some spending," he said leaning on the subjunctive in that same forum.

When asked for specific cuts he would make, Obama punted; by contrast in the first debate of the general election (September 26), McCain proposed an across-the-board spending freeze that exempted defense, veterans affairs, and entitlement programs. Obama opposed that freeze on the grounds that he wanted to take a scalpel, not a hatchet to the federal budget and reserve the option to increase funding for some underfunded programs.

The case McCain made for his disposition to cut spending pivoted on his fabled opposition to earmarks and his objections to a product central to the well-being of a key electoral state. "I oppose subsidies for ethanol," McCain noted in the third debate "because I thought it distorted the market and created inflation."[74] Facing a probable trouncing, McCain had ducked the Iowa primary contest in 2008. By contrast, after Obama bested John Edwards and Hillary Clinton there, Iowa propelled him to front-runner status. Unsurprisingly, given his home state's ties to the ethanol industry and his desire to win in the Hawkeye State, Obama supported ethanol subsidies. He embraced this position with nary a cry from liberal environmental groups that, were they not desperate to change the party in control of the White House, would vocally have protested that not only do the environmental costs of producing ethanol exceed the benefits but also that by turning food into fuel, subsidizing its production ups grocery bills.

If the contest were over which candidate was the more likely to pare down federal expenditures, McCain would have been the easy winner. Obama worked aggressively to blunt that advantage. When McCain argued that he had a history of working to harness earmarks and pork, Obama countered by noting that McCain had supported "almost all" of George W. Bush's budgets.[75] When McCain claimed credit for saving the taxpayers money by killing wasteful or unnecessary projects, Obama responded that, while commendable, the amounts were minuscule. "Earmarks account for .5% of the total federal budget," he observed in the third debate.

Still, where the most aired Democratic claim against the Republican nominee was "McCain equals Bush," the most often broadcast McCain attack against the Democratic standard-bearer was the durable one that has characterized Republican rhetoric throughout the history of televised campaigns. "The real Obama promises higher taxes, more government spending,"[76] is the way the Republicans put it in an ad aired at an almost $5 million level from August through October. In short, Obama is a big-government, tax-and-spend liberal.

This line of attack was clear in a spot the Republicans launched during their convention. "Barack Obama and out-of–touch congressional leaders have expensive plans. Billions in new government spending, years of deficits, no balanced budgets, and painful tax increases on working American families. They're ready to tax, ready to spend, but not ready to lead."[77] "Obama and his liberal congressional allies want a massive government," said the ad titled "Dome." "Billions in spending increases, wasteful pork. And we would pay painful income taxes, skyrocketing taxes on life savings, electricity, and home heating oil. Can your family afford that?" asked that ad.[78] "The *National Journal* says he's the Senate's most liberal" reported another McCain ad.[79] Obama says he's a tax cutter, noted another. "But he voted 94 times for higher taxes."[80] In July, the "celebrity" attack against Obama that we will discuss in chapter 4 came wrapped in a claim about taxation as well. "He'll raise taxes on electricity. High taxes."[81]

As we argue in chapter 10, in the weeks after the final presidential debate, McCain managed to gain some ground by translating an Obama misstep in a conversation with "Joe the Plumber" into a more compelling version of the liberal tax-and-spend claim. And overall, as we will show in that same chapter 10, the Republicans succeeded in marginally increasing the perception that Obama was a liberal at the end of the election.

Obama Counters the Tax-and-Spend Charge with Kansas Values

Both McCain and Obama anchored their core messages in biography. As we noted a moment ago, McCain's maverick credential was built on his defiance of his captors in the Hanoi Hilton. To counter Republican attacks that he was a dangerous liberal and at the same time protect their candidate from insinuations that he was somehow un-American, in an insulating tactic we will explore in more detail in chapter 4, the Democrats used Obama's mother and maternal grandparents' roots in Kansas to establish that he shared voters' values.

Kansas values have been evoked before in the history of presidential campaigning. The advertising with which he launched his 1952 bid identified Dwight Eisenhower as "The Man from Abilene," who came from the nation's "heartland."[82] Popular culture enhanced the currency of Kansas values by capturing Dorothy's yearning for a return to her Kansas home in *The Wizard of Oz*. However, identification with a mother and grandparents from Kansas opened another possible storyline premised not on Auntie Em and Uncle Henry but instead on "Bloody Kansas's" 1850s battle between pro- and anti-slavery forces, a contest in which Obama's maternal slave-owning ancestors were on the wrong side of history.[83] Obama benefitted whether audiences heard Kansas as heartland or as a state torn apart by the controversy over slavery. Where Kansas-as-middle-America certified that Obama was in touch with the values of voters, recalling Bloody Kansas reminded audiences that his was a reconciling candidacy borne of parentage that symbolized a nation ready to end racial division, an argument he made explicitly in his speech at the anniversary of the Selma March.[84]

Had they been more extensively covered or artfully exploited by his opponents, three biographical embellishments had the potential to derail Obama's claim to basic Kansas values by suggesting a disposition to construct rather than recount his life story. Where in the Selma speech Obama claimed that his parents got together and he was born "because of what happened in Selma," the *Chicago Sun-Times* reported, "Marking the anniversary of the March 1965 'Bloody Sunday' in Selma, Ala., Obama, speaking at a church, said his parents got together 'because of what happened in Selma.' Obama was born in 1961."[85] The discrepancy attracted some press notice but little additional attention.

Obama's biographical rhetoric also diverged from reality when he suggested both in the Selma speech and in his address on the occasion of Edward Kennedy's endorsement that his father's trip to the U.S. had been sponsored by JFK. Indeed Obama credited his "very existence" to the generosity of the Kennedy family, but as the *Washington Post* reported:

> It is a touching story—but the key details are either untrue or grossly oversimplified. Contrary to Obama's claims in speeches in January at American University and in Selma last year, the Kennedy family did not provide the funding for a September 1959 airlift of 81 Kenyan students to the United States that included Obama's father.[86]

And Obama sinned by omission when he reported that his job as a community organizer "made $12,000 a year plus car expenses."[87] As *The Boston Globe* noted, "The initial salary of $10,000 came with a $2,000 travel allowance, which Obama spent on a used Honda, but it was soon bumped up to $20,000 and by the time he left he was making the worldly sum of $35,000."[88] The hazard for Obama, of course, was that these embellishments and omissions would be framed by his opponents and the press in the same way that Gore's statements both about his role in the creation of the Internet and about the cost of his mother-in-law's medications were in 2000, as evidence of a deep-seated character flaw.

By locating his values in Kansas and not Chicago, the Obama narrative also sidestepped his connections, however tenuous, to "Chicago Machine politics," a phrase as resonant in the political culture as "Keating Five." In chapter 4, we will show the ways in which the Republicans questioned both Obama's claim to disavow special interests and his judgment by suggesting that he was entangled in and indebted to old-style corrupt Chicago politicians, such as Governor Rod Blagojevich and wheeler-dealers such as Tony Rezko. So, for example, a McCain ad called "Chicago Machine," which began airing September 22, opened with the line, "Barack Obama: born of the corrupt Chicago political machine."[89]

In a campaign that grounded the rhetoric of his candidacy in biography, these sins of omission or commission could have called the veracity of the rest of the narrative, and with it the truthfulness of the candidate, into question. One might surmise that the reason the biographical misstatements did not elicit attacks from his opponents was the basic element of truth in each of them. Obama's parents were an interracial couple; JFK had sponsored an African exchange program, although not the one that brought Obama's father to America; even after it escalated, Obama's salary as a Chicago organizer was hardly princely. Still it is surprising that neither his opponents nor the press translated Obama's embellishments and omissions into questions about his character.

After all, finding an empirical foundation for exaggerations has not deterred past attacks on them. The case of Al Gore in 2000 is illustrative.[90] To undercut Gore's trustworthiness, the Bush 2000 campaign released a general election ad that said:

ANNOUNCER: Remember when Al Gore said his mother-in-law's prescriptions cost more than his dog's? His own aide said the story was made up. Now Al Gore is bending the truth again. The press calls Gore's Social Security attacks "nonsense." Governor Bush sets aside $2.4 trillion to strengthen Social Security and pay all benefits.

AL GORE: There has never been a time in this campaign when I have said something that I know to be untrue. There's never been a time when I have said something untrue.

ANNOUNCER: Really?[91]

Although his mother-in-law wasn't taking one of them, some medications are prescribed for animals at a lower cost than that available for treatment of humans. In a related situation, the Republicans attacked Gore for saying he had invented the

Internet, when instead he had said he had played a role in its inception. For practical purposes, the difference between 2000 and 2008 was not in the level of underlying truth in the lapses. In 2000, the Republicans relentlessly attacked Gore's truthfulness in ads and the press uncritically underscored those attacks; by contrast in 2008, both Obama's opponents and the press were largely silent, perhaps because, unlike 2000, when the economy was thriving and the country at peace, in 2008 the economy was collapsing and the post-9/11 country mired in two wars. Attacks that seemed consequential in 2000 may have sounded unseemly or trivial in such a context.[92]

Allegations of Ties to the "Chicago Machine"

The reason that the "Chicago Machine" attack failed to gain traction is more complicated. Although his campaign exaggerated the extent to which he fought the entrenched establishment, the so-called Chicago machine hadn't backed Obama's failed run for Congress, his successful bid for a state Senate seat, or his party's nomination for the Senate.[93] Moreover, by the third week in September, the country had had extensive experience with Obama and as a result could draw its own conclusions about his integrity. Additionally, after the mid-September economic collapse, a political give-and-take on any topic other than the economy was unlikely to garner much news attention. Compared to the fears of a global economic meltdown that were dominating the headlines, ads about a candidate's political past seemed petty.

Having set Kansan (not Kenyan or Chicago) values as a touchstone, the senator from Illinois then enumerated virtues central to the American self-image: "Accountability and self-reliance, love of country, working hard without making excuses, treating your neighbor as you'd like to be treated." These values "guided" him as he "worked" his way up, "taking jobs and loans to make it through college." They motivated his rejection of Wall Street jobs to "go to Chicago instead, helping neighborhoods devastated when steel plants closed." They grounded his legislative instincts. "That's why I passed laws moving people from welfare to work, cut taxes for working families, extended health care for wounded troops who'd been neglected."[94]

We can't determine what specific effect, if any, these biographical disclosures had on voters, but we do know that regardless of party identification, NAES respondents placed Obama on the liberal side of the ideological continuum (figure 2.3).

We also know that most forms of news exposure increased the likelihood that our respondents would report that the Democratic nominee belonged on that end of the ideological spectrum.[95*] Reported consumption of presidential information from TV news, the Internet, and talk radio all increased the chances that a respondent would place Obama on the Left. Newspaper reading did not produce this effect.

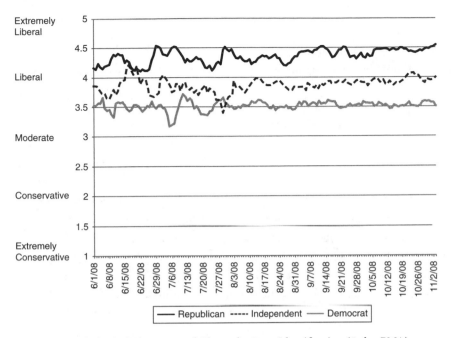

FIGURE 2.3 Ideological Placement of Obama by Party Identification (5-day PMA).
Source: NAES08 telephone survey.

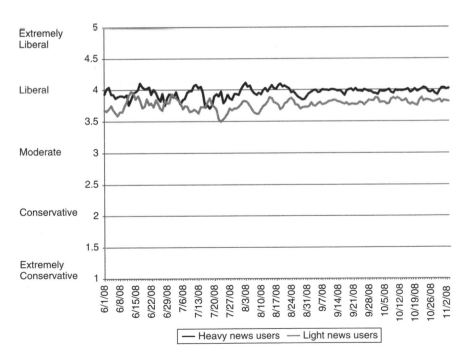

FIGURE 2.4 Ideological Placement of Obama by News Consumption (5-day PMA).
Source: NAES08 telephone survey.

Throughout the campaign, heavy news consumers perceived Obama as marginally more liberal than did those who watched news less often (figure 2.4).

Turning the Tax-and-Spend Argument against McCain

In a clever move, the Democrats turned the central Republican attack on its head by arguing that McCain was the big taxer and Obama the one who would reduce taxes for the middle class. At the same time, the Democrats asserted that the Arizona senator was a big spender ready to commit billions to corporations while short-changing average workers. The tax claim, which we examine at length in chapter 10, was based on a distortion of McCain's health care reform proposal. "McCain's health plan would tax benefits for the first time," said a number of Obama ads, "meaning higher income taxes for millions." By contrast, "Barack Obama: No tax hikes on families earning less than a quarter million dollars and three times as much middle-class tax relief as McCain for the change we need." Consistent with this message, Obama's tax relief targeted those making less than $150,000, and his spending plans focused on those likely to elicit empathy. Analysts who examined the two tax programs did confirm that Obama provided more middle-class tax relief.[96]

In the rhetoric of the Obama campaign, McCain was the big-spending champion of corporations, while Obama would "invest" in the middle class. "John McCain's tax plan," said an ad aired in August, "[F]or big corporations, $200 billion in new tax breaks. Oil companies, 4 billion...100 million Americans get no tax relief at all...For the change we need, Barack Obama. A plan that cuts taxes for middle class families three times as much as John McCain."[97] Another version of that message argued that "McCain pledges hundreds of billions in corporate tax breaks. Billions for oil companies. But for the hundred million households. Nothing."[98] A third continued the rhetoric: "Under McCain, insurance companies prosper," said one general election ad, "Nevadans pay."[99]

The Obama team did not simply argue that McCain favored the corporate class but also that he rewarded corporations that hurt American workers. In particular, McCain was accused of supporting both "tax breaks for corporations that ship jobs overseas, selling out American workers,"[100] and an economic philosophy identified as "George Bush economics." "We can't afford more of the same."[101] Similarly, in an ad that indicted McCain as both wealthy and out of touch with Detroit autoworkers, viewers in Michigan were shown the Arizonan saying, "I've bought American literally all my life." "But John McCain owns thirteen vehicles," added the announcer, "including three foreign cars...McCain even refused to support loan guarantees for the auto industry..."[102]

Because they were central campaign themes, we will revisit the tax-and-spend charge against Obama and the McSame claim against McCain in many of the coming chapters before showing in chapter 13 how they factored into the final vote. In the pages that follow, we will argue that overall, the Obama campaign blunted the "tax-and-spend, big-government liberal" label's ability to translate into two key inferences: that Obama did not share voters' values and was not able to handle the economy. The Democrats' success in doing so helps explain why a right-of-center country elected a person perceived to be liberal. Where the Democrats parried the central McCain allegation levied against their standard-bearer, the Republicans failed to dispatch the Obama assertion that McCain equaled Bush.

Before documenting those outcomes, however, we need to explain how the campaigns linked their attacks on policies to their critiques of the persons who would implement them. In the coming chapters we will show that in the view of the Obama campaign, McCain was not only McBush but out of touch. On the other side, the McCain campaign pictured Obama as a tax-and-spend liberal who was not ready to lead and who failed to share basic American values.

THREE

McCain: Out of Touch/Too Old

I N MOMENTS DEMANDING PRESIDENTIAL LEADERSHIP, SUCH AS THE
Soviet launch of Sputnik in 1957, the 1979 Soviet invasion of Afghanistan,
9/11, or the financial meltdown of fall 2008, the temperament and character
of the president are important predictors of performance. To prophesy that the
competing suitor would prove unreliable in such trying times, each candidate in
2008 argued that the other was unconnected to basic American values. In an effort
to undermine the Arizonan's credibility, the Democrats packaged "McSame" as
out of touch with what was going on in the economy and with resulting middle-
class concerns, while also whispering that he was also too old to be president. For
those who had long admired McCain, this inference raised the possibility that the
Republican nominee had once been but no longer was suited to that high office.
If successful, this move rendered his past leadership on key issues and principled
defiance of his own party admirable but irrelevant.

Meanwhile, in a strategy that we will examine in the next chapter, the Republicans cast Obama as a profligate liberal who was not ready to lead, a notion they
occasionally freighted with the implication that he was an unpatriotic radical
who disdained basic American values. Just as "out of touch" could be heard as *no
longer* ready to be president, a phrase spoken with regret that the Arizonan had
not won the 2000 race, in its benign form, "not ready to lead" could be understood by those sympathetic to Obama as "not *yet* ready," and as such an invitation
to cache their inclination to support the Illinois senator for a future election.

No serious student of politics doubts that the faltering economy and failed
incumbent boosted the Democratic Party's presidential prospects in 2008. There
were other pluses on the Obama-Biden balance sheet as well. For a number of

reasons, it was easier for the Illinois Democrat to establish that he was "ready to lead" than for his counterpart from Arizona to confirm that he was "in touch." Where the culture is rich with tales of a neophyte proving adept, there are fewer accounts of a suspected dodderer revealing that he is instead wily and wise. And where Obama could mobilize black votes to compensate for those lost to race-based reservations among whites, there wasn't an under-energized constituency waiting to champion a septuagenarian standard-bearer.

Moreover, "age" stereotypes offered a grid into which any fumble by the 72-year-old McCain could be fit. If, for example, both candidates tripped over words in a late-afternoon speech, mental decline might well come to the fore as an explanation for his lapse, where for the younger candidate the presumed explanation would be inadvertence or fatigue.[1]

In the following pages, we focus on Democratic contentions that the Republican's presidential nominee was "out of touch" and the whispers that he was also too old. In this chapter's conclusion, we will answer a series of questions including, how, if at all, perceptions that McCain was too old and Obama too young to be president changed across the election. What sorts of voters perceived McCain's age to be a problem? How did media reinforcement affect the perception that the Republican nominee's age was a liability? And how did his age affect voters' perception that McCain shared their values?

One question unresolved by past presidential campaigns was not whether a novice could establish preparedness for the nation's highest office but whether the presidential bid of the son of a black father and white mother who was "black enough to have trouble catching a cab in New York City"[2] would be helped or hurt by his multiracial identity, "rooted," as he put it, "in the African-American community but not limited to it."[3] After devoting this and the next chapter to the give-and-take about age and race that lurked beneath the allegations that one candidate was out of touch and the other unready, we will return to the larger question of how, if at all, Obama's race affected the election's outcome at the end of the next chapter.

Out of Touch

The language in which Senator Obama cast his bid was as serviceable against his primary-season nemeses as against his general-election opponent. "America is ready to turn the page... This is our time. A new generation is prepared to lead,"[4] the Illinois senator said in late 2006. Throughout his showdown with New York Senator Hillary Rodham Clinton, the Illinois Democrat made three arguments easily retooled against McCain: "This election is about the past versus the future"[5] and a referendum on "the same old Washington politics,"[6] not a return to "the same fights that we had in the 1990s."[7] Each of these themes suggested that Obama was the antithesis of both McCain and Bush.

Obama bested Hillary Clinton's argument that, if elected president, she—and implicitly not he—was prepared to field a 3 A.M. phone call. He did so by contrasting her vote to authorize the use of military force against Iraq with his own opposition, a tactic that set his judgment against her experience. The nomination secured, the Democrat from Illinois adopted a move Clinton had pressed against him in the Pennsylvania primary to make the case that McCain was "out of touch." In the Pennsylvania primary, the former first lady had revived her prospects by attaching that label to the front-runner's suggestion at a closed-door San Francisco fund-raiser that in difficult times those in small towns "cling to guns or religion...as a way to explain their frustrations."[8] In one of the New York senator's ads, for example, a young African-American woman responded to Obama's ill-advised statement by saying, "I was very insulted by Barack Obama. It just shows how *out of touch* Barack Obama is (emphasis added)."[9]

Where Clinton portrayed her opponent as a patronizing elitist disposed to derogate the beliefs of religious adherents and gun owners, the Obama send-up of McCain[10] hinted instead that the Republican was cocooned in his own wealth and callous to the suffering of others. Into those meanings, the Democrats also insinuated the implication that the senior senator from Arizona was caught in a time warp, set in his ways, and out of contact with reality. "Things have changed in the last 26 years," said the announcer in one Democratic ad. "But McCain hasn't. He admits he still doesn't know how to use a computer. Can't send an e-mail. Still doesn't understand the economy...[A]fter one president who was out of touch, we can't afford more of the same."[11]

The Democrats also bundled the assumption that Republicans are the party of big business into an indictment of their rival. McCain supported "200 billion in tax cuts for corporations, but almost nothing for the middle class," announced one Obama ad. "After one president who was out of touch, we just can't afford more of the same..."[12] Raising a question Democrats had posed since the days of FDR, another asked, "Who's on your side?" Ads aired both in English and Spanish then chronicled ways in which McCain's policies hurt, and Obama's helped, the middle class.[13] "I don't know who Senator McCain is looking out for," says a woman in one ad, "but it's not us."[14] Another ad pictured Bush at McCain's side as the announcer reported of the Republican nominee, "He's out of ideas. Out of touch and running out of time...with no plan to lift our economy up."[15]

History

At 72 and 47, both McCain and Obama were well above the minimum age the Constitution sets for election to the presidency.[16] However, where a handful of presidents younger than Obama had been elected (e.g., Teddy Roosevelt at 42, Kennedy at 43, Grant and Clinton at 46), some of whom are well regarded by history, McCain would have been the oldest individual ever inaugurated to a first term.[17] As a result, comparisons to TR, JFK, and Bill Clinton helped Obama; by contrast, McCain had little to gain by arguing from the successes of the Reagan administration that age was no barrier to presidential accomplishment. After all, not long after leaving office, the Gipper, who had been inaugurated just before his 70th birthday, revealed his diagnosis of Alzheimer's disease. Still within ready recall of the more senior reporters covering the campaign was a fact refreshed by Anna Quindlen. Reagan's "press contingent saw signs during his second term consistent with the Alzheimer's with which he was later diagnosed."[18]

Nor could McCain draw a road map from the dexterous way in which Reagan dealt with the "age" issue in 1984. After a faltering performance in the first presidential debate of that year, the 73-year-old incumbent dispatched the issue in the second debate with a line that elicited a laugh from the audience and a smile from his 56-year-old challenger, former Vice President and Minnesota Senator Walter Mondale. "I will not make age an issue of this campaign," said the Gipper with an aw-shucks grin. "I am not going to exploit, for political purposes, my opponent's youth and inexperience."[19]

When employed by a candidate seeking re-election, such a comeback draws on evidence unavailable to one aspiring to a first term. Among other things, by 1984, Reagan's conduct in office had allayed the fears fomented by the 1980 Carter campaign. Social Security had not been dismantled, for example, nor had the actor-turned-governor-turned-president rushed the country into war. Moreover, the economy had so clearly improved on Reagan's watch that his re-election campaign relied on the simple theme, "It's Morning Again in America." Reagan also brought a unique piece of history to the age argument in 1984. In his first term, the 40th president had survived an assassination attempt while displaying the same sort of humor represented in that debate riposte.[20] Because his competence was presupposed and his first term successful, 66-year-old President Dwight D. Eisenhower was insulated from Governor Adlai Stevenson's age- and health-related attacks in 1956, as well.[21]

Age and Race as Subtext

Active in any communication equation are the cultural assumptions that prompt voters to hear allusions and draw implications from content others see as straightforward. We will argue in a moment that, even as the campaign gurus high-mindedly contended that they were leaving "race" and "age" alone, both Republicans and Democrats trafficked in them. Moreover, whether prompted or not, age and race were in the wings. "People knew he was 72-years old," reported Obama pollster Joel Benenson of McCain. "That was coming back loud and clear." When a May Democratic poll tested perceptions of whether each candidate had "the energy and the vigor to meet the demands of presidency," the Obama campaign found "a big difference" between perceptions of the two [candidates]. "And what it told us," said Benenson, "was, just leave it alone."[22] "It's the same thing as race," added McCain pollster Bill McInturff. "John's 72."[23]

Priming McCain's Age in News

When it came to his age, news coverage was not McCain's friend. A search of print, broadcast, and cable transcripts from June 1 to November 4, 2008 (McCain, 71; McCain, 72; Obama, 46; Obama 47) reveals that McCain's name was tied to his age 1,390 times and Obama's to his, 898 times.[24] "John McCain, 71, will be the oldest president ever elected if he goes on to win his party's nomination and the White House in November," noted a February article in *Newsweek*.[25] To the notion that McCain would be the "oldest person ever to ascend to the presidency," *Time* added the warrant that it used to justify concern about McCain's age. "He has suffered serious skin cancers over the years, not to mention brutal physical torture as a prisoner of war." From that nexus between age, illness, and biography, the article concluded "His age and health, therefore, are of legitimate concern to voters."[26]

Our two indices of the communication environment, the Cultural Communication Index (CCI)[27] and the Television News Frequency Index (TNFI),[28] show how the strong the tie between McCain and the word "old" was throughout the election. Mentions of McCain and "old" appeared in a wide range of Internet, broadcast, and print news sources, reaching a peak as the financial crisis began to dominate headlines (figure 3.1). Although there are fluctuations in the number of times news media connected McCain to "old" during the economic collapse, we do not see a direct increase in the numbers of respondents in our survey who say McCain is "too old to be president" during this period.

It is important to point out the CCI, a tool developed by researchers at Stony Brook University for our use in 2008, is not a standardized Web searching tool but the output of many internet spider searches. What this means is that we can neither compute a percentage of coverage from it nor make broader statements about the overall nature of campaign coverage. However, we can track the relative changes in the occurrence of two entities within a sentence. The convergence of results from the CCI and the TVFI strengthens our confidence in our interpretations.

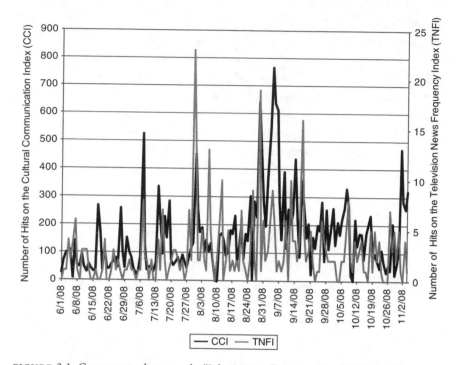

FIGURE 3.1 Concurrence between the "John McCain" and the Word "Old" within a Single Sentence. *Source*: Lydia News/Media Analysis System and Lexis Nexis.

Throughout the campaign, some in the media explicitly fielded the notion that "aging" signaled "mental decline." "How Old is Too Old?" read the headline on Anna Quindlen's February 4, 2008 column in *Newsweek*. The piece went on to argue, "It's significant that while the old mandatory retirement age of 65 has been largely junked, there are still age limits for jobs like airline pilot or police officer, the kinds of jobs that require some of the same skills as the presidency—unwavering mental acuity and physical energy."[29]

Reporters speculated as well on the tactical disadvantage McCain's advanced years carried. After reviewing the Republican and Democratic ads of the primary season of 2008, for example, *The Atlantic*'s Jim Fallows forecast McCain's general election debate performance by saying, "Worse, he will look and sound old and weak next to Obama. Ronald Reagan was about McCain's current age when he ran for re-election against Walter Mondale, but Reagan looked 10 years younger than McCain does now.... [L]acking Reagan's outward haleness, he risks coming across like Dole against Clinton—or, more ominously, his fellow ex-POW [Ross Perot's running mate] James Bond Stockdale, who turned in a notoriously lost-and incoherent-sounding performance against [Bill Clinton's running mate] Al Gore and [George H.W. Bush's vice president] Dan Quayle in the 1992 vice-presidential debates."[30]

The Link between "Out of Touch" and "Old"

Whether the notion that McCain is a septuagenarian signals senility or sagacity depends in part on one's own date of birth and on which of the stereotypes latent in the culture is front and center as we mull the questions, Does age 72 signal experience and wisdom, incipient senility and imminent death, something else altogether, or is age simply irrelevant in this calculus? Does 72 evoke the stereotype "Elder of the tribe," "wise old man," or "temperamental codger?"

Backdrop assumptions are also at play in our perceptions of youth. When considering a presidential aspirant, does 47 signal "Vigorous, energetic, brimming with fresh ideas" or "'wet behind the ears' upstart" and "unready to lead?" Of course, before one is inclined to ask such questions, age must be made salient enough to be part of the discussion. As we noted a moment ago, the media ensured that that conversation happened. As we will document, McCain's opponents did the same. By contrast, the focus by the press, pundits, and the McCain campaign on Obama's readiness or lack thereof was not tied to his age.

In 2007, Gallup hinted at the ways in which race, age, and inexperience might play out in 2008. When asked to assess various characteristics of a presidential candidate, roughly one in two of those surveyed reported that being "70 years of age or older" was undesirable, while just over one in ten said the same about being "a member of a racial or ethnic minority group." At the same time, just over four in ten put having "limited experience in Washington" in the negative column.[31] Age, of course, was a concern for the Republican nominee, and race and limited experience an issue for the Democratic standard-bearer.

Just as inexperience had been deployed against Obama throughout the primary season, age had been raised against McCain. In January 2008, for example, Mike Huckabee–backing actor Chuck Norris suggested that the presidency accelerates the aging process and asked: "[I]f John takes over the presidency at 72 and he ages three to one, how old will he be in four years? He'll be eighty-four."[32]

Complicating the Republican nominee's efforts to slip the so-called age issue was the fact that during a March trip that included a stop in Amman, Jordan, he had confused the Shia with the Sunnis, a mistake he corrected only after Senator Joe Lieberman's promptings.[33] Moreover, even as Obama was shown playing an aggressive game of basketball with his staff or sinking a three-point shot while in the Middle East,[34] injuries McCain sustained as a prisoner of war in Vietnam meant, as reporters occasionally reminded readers, that the Republican nominee walked haltingly and could not raise his arms high enough to comb his own hair. "Mr. McCain's difficulty raising his arms and his sometimes awkward gait are remnants of severe, untreated injuries he suffered in Vietnam," reported the *New York Times* on October 20.[35] However, any invocation of McCain's Vietnam service risked reminding voters under 35 that he was part of a generation in its prime before they were born. The resulting dilemma caused sleepless nights for one of McCain's media advisers, who had confronted the same problem in making the case for Bob Dole in 1996.[36]

If McCain's awkward gait evoked memories of his war heroism, it also fed stereotypes about a person whose age was a media preoccupation. So, for example, humorists responded to McCain's stilted moves across the stage in the town hall debate with age-related parodies. On Comedy Central's *The Daily Show,* Jon Stewart suggested that as he meandered across the stage, McCain was muttering absentmindedly that he was searching for his little dog "Puddles," a not-so-subtle suggestion of incontinence.[37]

Meanwhile, in late-night comedy, the Arizonan's age became a signal of bodily decline and imminent death. *Tonight Show* host Jay Leno, for example, joked, "And do you know John McCain does not use the Secret Service protection? Yes. Yes. He hasn't been using them. He has his own team. It's like, you know, what you call those six guys who surround John McCain all the time? Pallbearers."[38] Leno also reported that "John McCain got some good news today: *The Charleston Daily Mail* endorsed him, saying that since he will only be a one-term president, he can do the right thing to make tough decisions. When they told him the endorsement was for only four years, McCain said, "Four years—that's great. My doctor only gave me two."[39] Jimmy Kimmel played on the same trope with the observation that, "Truth be told: John McCain is doing darn well for a guy who passed away 20 years ago."[40] The prospect of a president dying in office, of course, raises the importance of the credentials of his running mate. As the perception that Sarah Palin was unqualified to be president rose, a phenomenon we explore in chapter 7, jokes about McCain's probable death in office became more problematic for the Republican ticket.

When they were not foreseeing his need for a cemetery plot, late-night humorists were assuming that McCain's age denoted bodily decline. "You don't suspend your campaign," said David Letterman after McCain had done just that in late September. "This doesn't smell right. This isn't the way a tested hero behaves. I think someone's putting something in his Metamucil."[41] "Colin Powell is in the news because he endorsed Barack Obama," reported Craig Ferguson.

"I wonder how John McCain feels about Colin Powell endorsing Obama. He's probably all right with it. Men his age are used to having colon problems.[42]" Between August 23 and November 3, the Center for Media and Public Affairs reports that Jay Leno and David Letterman told 658 jokes about McCain and only 243 about Obama, with the jokes about the Arizona senator most likely to focus on his age.[43]

Because he had been treated for cancer, questions about McCain's age were inevitably tied to those of health. In late September, one independent expenditure group calling itself "Brave New PAC and Democracy for America" conjured the link by showing a close-up of the left side of McCain's face stitched after surgery for melanoma. "John McCain is 72 years old and had cancer four times," says the announcer. A person identified as an MD then appears and reports in part, "Melanoma is the deadliest of skin cancers, and the chances of survival if you have melanoma spread through your body are very, very slim." There was no publicly accessible evidence that McCain's melanoma had spread through his body. However, since his campaign had limited the time that select reporters could spend with his medical records, the ad could play on doubts about what they hadn't had the opportunity to find. "Why won't John McCain release his medical records?"[44] it asked at the end. Brave New Films, a kindred group funded by the same Democratic activist, ran a print ad in the New York Times on October 3 headlined "2,768 doctors call on Senator McCain to issue a full, public release of his medical records."[45]

Reporters did uncover one troubling, although contested, finding in McCain's health records. Where, according to a New York Times report, McCain's Mayo Clinic doctors said that, "All four melanomas that Mr. McCain experienced were primary, or new, and there was no evidence that any of them had spread," a report by two Armed Forces pathologists "suggested that the left-temple melanoma had spread from another melanoma, known as a metastasis or satellite lesion." If the left-temple melanoma "was a metastasis," noted the Times medical reporter, "it would be classified as Stage III. The reclassification would change his statistical odds for survival at 10 years from about 60 percent to 36 percent, according to a published study.... The fact that Mr. McCain has had no recurrence for eight years is in his favor. But cancer experts see the tenth anniversary as an important statistical benchmark, and that would not occur until 2010."[46]

As a wiry, 47-year-old three-point basket-shooter, Obama didn't trigger suspicions about concealed health problems. Even though, until recently, he had been a chronic cigarette smoker, and even though his mother had died at a young age of cancer, there were no ads questioning the fact that Obama's disclosure of his health records made McCain's seem exhaustive by comparison.

How the Obama Campaign Primed Age

Reinforcing an assumption to which the audience is disposed is of course easier than forging a new attitude. And an inference is more readily elicited when other forces in the culture, such as news reports, opinion columns, and comedy, are making the same point. Throughout the postprimary period, the Obama ads built on this cultural reservoir to attach negative notions of "old" to the Republican nominee. The age-related threads in Obama's ads included:

John McCain is blaming Barack Obama for gas prices? The same old politics.[47]

John McCain: He's been in Washington for 26 years.[48]

John McCain: Same old politics, same failed policies.[49]

Lurching to the right, then to the left. The old Washington dance. Whatever it takes. A Washington celebrity playing the same old Washington games.[50]

For 26 years in Washington, John McCain played the same old games.[51]

Other spots implied incipient senility:

[W]hen asked how many houses he owns, McCain lost track. He couldn't remember.[52]

How many houses does he own? John McCain says he can't even remember anymore.[53]

It's one more thing John McCain doesn't get about our economy.[54]

John McCain: He just doesn't get it.[55]

[I]n this economic crisis, its McCain who's careened from stance to stance, been erratic. . . . Yes, McCain's been erratic. What he hasn't been, is on your side.[56]

In the financial crisis, Obama had "the steady hand." McCain was "erratic."[57]

Visuals within the Democratic ads reinforced the message when a replayed video sequence slowed the images and suppressed the conversation from an Oval Office "press opportunity" involving Bush and McCain. Had their words been played, viewers would have heard George W. Bush embracing the ban on torture that McCain had marshaled through Congress with a veto-proof majority in the face of opposition from the White House.[58] To transform that moment, which should have put McCain in good stead with many independents and Democrats, into a confirmation of McCain's age-related infirmity, the Democrats slowed the silenced footage by half. As a result, the Republican nominee's movements are jerky, his blinks halting, his expressions discomfiting.[59] In August, that visual sequence was intercut into narration that said:

ANNOUNCER: Call it country club economics. How many houses does he own? John McCain says he can't even remember anymore. Well, it's seven. No wonder McCain just said the fundamentals of our economy are strong.[60]

The impact of the editing was magnified by the announcer's statement that McCain "says that he can't even remember anymore" how many houses he owns. The Arizonan's actual response to a query about his houses instead went like this:

QUESTION: How many houses do you and Ms. McCain have?

MCCAIN: I think I will have my staff get to you. I will talk to you about that. (crosstalk)

MCCAIN: It's condominiums ownership. It's further. I will have them get to you.[61]

For McCain, any direct answer to the question about his houses was an indictment-in-waiting. Admit to owning more than two, and the sound bite confirms out-of-the-ordinary wealth at a time in which many Americans were struggling to meet the rent or make their mortgage payments on a single home. Alternatively, explaining that some of the homes were in a trust controlled by his wife would have accentuated his wealth even more. Get the number wrong, a possibility since two of the McCain condominiums were being consolidated into one, and the resulting sound bite would suggest age-based confusion.

To complement their visual recasting of the Arizona senator, the Democratic campaign added the word "erratic" as a synonym for age-related disability, an association revealed when Obama spokesperson Robert Gibbs tied it to a recommendation to flee the sidewalk if McCain was behind the wheel of a car in your area. Specifically, when asked how McCain had been erratic, Gibbs said:

Look, just yesterday, John McCain said we shouldn't fix blame, took a breath and then fixed blame. He said the fundamentals of our economy are strong and he flip-flopped. He opposed the bailout of AIG and then he supported it. This guy zigzags. If he's driving a car, get off the sidewalk.[62]

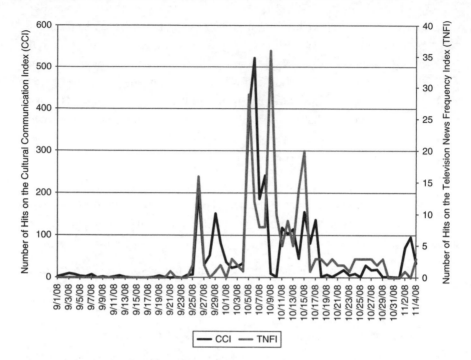

FIGURE 3.2 Concurrence between the "John McCain" and the Word "Erratic" within a Single Sentence. *Source*: Lydia News/Media Analysis System (CCI) and Lexis Nexis (TNFI).

The Democratic campaign's success in insinuating "erratic" into the media's lexicon is evident in the appearance and rapid rise of the word tied to McCain reflected in our searches in the CCI and TNFI (figure 3.2).

The political advantage gained by making erratic a synonym for McCain is evident in our finding that the more survey respondents thought the term applied to the Arizonan, the more likely they were to report that he was too old to be president, a finding that holds in the presence of controls.*

Erratic wasn't the only age-tied weapon in the Obama arsenal. When asked whether attacking McCain over the number of houses he owned wasn't "practicing the kind of slash-and-burn tactical politics that he [Obama] used to condemn," Obama spokesperson Robert Gibbs responded that McCain may have misplaced the keys to the houses, may not even remember how many houses he owns, or may simply be lying. This litany culminates in the conclusion that the Republican nominee is "out of touch."

WALLACE: So he's running for president, to talk about how many houses John McCain has?

GIBBS: Well, somebody's got to talk about how many houses John McCain has, because he either forgot how many he has, misplaced the keys to those houses, or he just wasn't being truthful with those reporters.

That answer illuminates whether or not you're in touch with that family in Youngstown, Ohio, or Scranton that's struggling to make that mortgage payment just this month. And I think you're out of touch if you have seven houses and don't even remember it or can't even admit it.[63]

Among its other meanings, "out of touch" is, of course, a euphemism applied to those of advanced years suffering mental decline, a link between age and incapacity that Anna Quindlen made explicitly in the *Newsweek* piece we cited previously and Gibbs offered by association. Obama did the same thing when he suggested that his opponent was "losing his bearings."[64]

Allegations about McCain's Temper and Temperament

Alleged in some news accounts and implied by the word "erratic" was the suggestion that the Arizona senator had a combustible temper. "My temper has often been both a matter of public speculation and personal concern," conceded McCain in his 2002 book, *Worth Fighting For*. "I have a temper, to state the obvious, which I have tried to control with varying degrees of success because it does not always serve my interest or the public's."[65]

Described by *The Arizona Republic* as "volcanic"[66] in 1999, McCain's temperament was used against him by pro-Bush forces in 2000. During that contest, anonymous sources also spawned a whispering campaign alleging that the Vietnam War veteran had suffered a mental breakdown in Hanoi, from which he had never fully recovered. To undercut that allegation, the McCain campaign released 1,500 pages of medical records, including interviews with military psychiatrists showing that he had a clean bill of mental health.

Concerns about his temper resurfaced in the 2008 campaign. Headlines addressing it included, "The Temperament Factor: Who's Best Suited to the Job,"[67] "McCain's History of Hot Temper Raises Concerns,"[68] "John McCain, Flexible Aggression,"[69] "McCain: A Question of Temperament,"[70] and "McCain's Temper Back on Campaign's Front-Burner."[71]

A related indictment alleged that McCain was dangerously impulsive:

"I like McCain. I respect McCain. But I am a little worried by his knee-jerk response factor," said retired Maj. Gen. Paul Eaton, who was in charge of training the Iraqi military from 2003 to 2004 and is now campaigning for Clinton. "I think it is a little scary. I think this guy's first reactions are not necessarily the best reactions. I believe that he acts on impulse."[72]

Some saw the pick of Sarah Palin as the sort of impulsive move that worried his critics.[73] Alternatively, Obama campaign manager David Plouffe characterized the selection as "a reckless stunt."[74]

Just as exposure can help a candidate establish that he is as ready as his opponent to be president, conduct under the stress of the campaign can rebut suggestions that a candidate is volatile or temperamental. McCain's performance in the primary debates suggested a steadiness that seemed to counter the assertion that he harbored a volcanic temper. Meanwhile, when the issue was raised, the candidate and the campaign dismissed it by suggesting that his anger was directed at wasteful spending and corrupt political behavior and, as such, was a credential for high office, not a disqualifier.

To determine what effect these characterizations had on perceptions of the Republican's presidential candidate, we asked three questions. How, if at all, did perceptions that McCain was too old and Obama too young to be president change across the election? Did media reinforcement affect perception that his age was a liability? And did his age affect voters' perception that McCain shared their values? It is to these questions that we now turn.

Changes in Perception That McCain Was Too Old to Be President and Obama Was Too Young

When NAES asked if respondents thought McCain was too old to be president and, correspondingly, Obama, too young, the question elicited more concerns about the Republican nominee than the Democratic one (see figure 3.3). As the campaign progressed, worries about the Democratic nominee's youth were minimized and concerns about the Republican's age magnified.[75] Curve estimation analyses over 245 days of the campaign confirmed that there was a significant linear increase in the percentage of the public that believed that McCain was "too old to be president." Each day that passed was associated with a 0.04 percent increase in the "too old" belief.

What Sorts of Voters Found McCain's Age Problematic?

Figure 3.4 shows that the increase in this perception is driven by Democrats and independents. Figure 3.5 reveals that the divergence by party in the

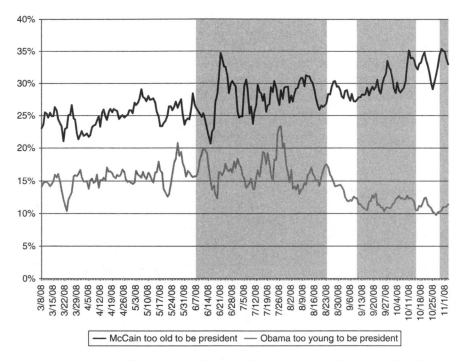

FIGURE 3.3 Percent of Respondents Who Said "McCain is Too Old to Be President"
Compared to the Percent of Respondents Who Said "Obama is Too Young to Be President"
(5-day PMA). *Source*: NAES08 telephone survey.

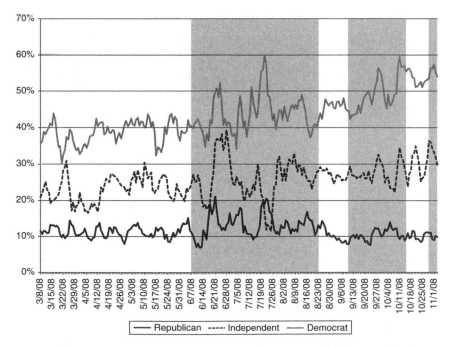

FIGURE 3.4 Percent of Respondents Who Said "McCain is Too Old to Be President"
by Party Identification (5-day PMA). *Source*: NAES08 telephone survey.

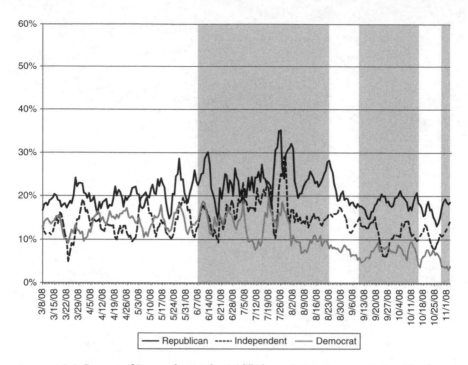

FIGURE 3.5 Percent of Respondents Who Said "Obama is Too Young to Be President" by Party Identification (5-day PMA). *Source*: NAES08 telephone survey.

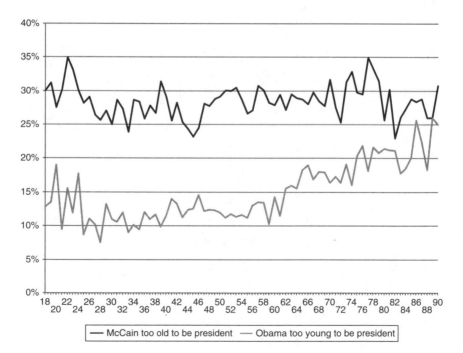

FIGURE 3.6 Percent of Respondents Who Said "McCain is Too Old to Be President" Compared to the Percent of Respondents Who Said "Obama is Too Young to Be President" by Age of Respondent. *Source*: NAES08 telephone survey.

perception about Obama's youth is not as great as the divergence in the perception of McCain's age.

As our data indicate, in the presence of controls older respondents are significantly more likely than younger ones to see McCain as too old to be president.* However, the pattern suggests that respondent age is not the driving factor in the perception that his age disqualifies McCain. Older respondents also are more likely to say Obama is too young (figure 3.6).

The Role of the Media in Priming McCain's Age

An analysis of the NAES data shows that exposure to news media (i.e., television news, newspapers, and Internet news) is significantly related to believing that McCain is too old to be president.* The perception that McCain's age was problematic was higher among those unlikely to vote for him in any event and lower among those who shared his party identification and who considered themselves conservatives. The media findings hold when these variables are controlled.

Effect of Perception that McCain Was Too Old on "Shares My Values"

In chapter 13, we will suggest that concerns about McCain's age translated into doubts that he shared respondents' values which in turn influenced vote intention. Here we set up the first building block of that argument by noting that worries about age appear to have driven down the perception that McCain "shares my values," an inference that makes sense if we assume that someone who is "too old" is "out of touch," and someone who is "out of touch" cannot "share one's values." In the 2008 NAES data, those who believed that McCain was too old to be president were significantly less likely to believe that the Arizonan "shared their values."[76]*

Perceptions that the Arizona senator was too old rose across the election, while those that Obama was too young dropped. Reservations about McCain's age and the resulting erosion of the perception that he shared the voters' values meant that this was an issue that the Republican campaign needed to reframe. By campaigning tirelessly, appearing regularly with his 96-year-old mother (born February 7, 1912) and parlaying comments about age into self-deprecating analogies, such as, "I'm older than dirt, with more scars than Frankenstein,"[77] the Arizona senator worked to disassociate age from dementia. Less apt and more likely to fan concerns that he was "out of touch" was McCain's awkward contention that he retained "the vigor."[78]

Undercutting concerns that age signals inevitable decline is complicated and perhaps even more difficult than dispatching race-based ones. Cognitive scientists tell us that humans "encode" age, but not necessarily race, "in an automatic and mandatory fashion," a conclusion that suggests that race-based stereotypes may be easier to dispatch than those based on age.[79]

Moreover, even in a world of "young old" and "old old" in which the medical literature confirms that people "age" at different rates, age has a chronological reality. After all, one has lived a documentable number of days.[80] And a straightforward appeal to the science regarding "age" carried some cautions for McCain. Although senescence is by no means inevitable, and individuals die at very different ages as well, the person in his 70s is more likely than the one in his 40s to confront certain disabilities.[81]

If age shadowed the McCain campaign, race did the same for the Obama effort. It is to the argument that Obama was not ready to be president and its attendant race-tied appeals that we turn in chapter 4.

FOUR

Obama: Not Ready to Lead

W HERE THE DEMOCRATS HINTED THAT MCCAIN WAS PAST HIS
prime and out of touch with the concerns of Middle America, the
Republicans suggested that Obama was unready to lead, presumptu-
ous, and a profligate liberal. Into that set of indictments they then insinuated the
suspicion that his temperate demeanor masked an unpatriotic radical who disdained basic American values.

The McCain campaign opened its case against Obama with three related
attacks: (1) Obama's inconsistencies signaled that he was untrustworthy,
(2) the length of his elective service meant that he had not banked the wherewithal to create needed change, and (3) he was a self-important celebrity whose
prime talent was speechmaking. To this menu, the Republican National Committee, independent expenditure groups, and viral sources added race-tinged
arguments that Obama was allied with suspect individuals—some criminal,
some extremist—a case capsulized in allegations that Obama was indebted to
a convicted felon and sympathized with the views of both a former member of
the Weather Underground and an America-hating black minister. After exploring these charges, we will outline the strategy of reassurance Obama deployed
in response. Finally we will close by asking whether race helped or hurt Obama's
candidacy.

The truth on which the GOP assaults relied was that by most, but not
all, historical measures, Barack Obama was short on legislative and executive
experience. On the day he won the presidency, the contender from Illinois had
served less than four years in the U.S. Senate, with much of that time running
for higher office. His state legislative pedigree consisted of three two-year terms

as a senator. By contrast, JFK, whose presidency yielded the calamitous Bay of Pigs invasion within its first months, had served six years in the House and one full term in the Senate before becoming president; Bill Clinton brought 12 years' experience as governor to the Oval Office, as well as two as state attorney general, and had chaired the National Governors Association. Within recent memory, the last Democrat and Republican elected with a level of experience close to Obama's had failed; Jimmy Carter brought a double two-year term in the state Senate and one four-year term as governor to Washington. George W. Bush came to the White House after six years as a governor. Obama partisans turned to more distant history to remind voters that Abraham Lincoln's national service consisted of one low-profile term in the House. Behind the GOP attacks was the assumption that the more the public knew of Obama's actual past and record, the less it would like what it found. The Obama campaign made the opposite assumption. Each side, of course, was featuring different facets of the aspirant's résumé.

Undermining Obama's Credibility by Charging Inconsistency

When a charge of flip-flopping sticks, it simultaneously undercuts the trustworthiness, judgment, and decisiveness of the attacked candidate. In one of the ironies of presidential campaigns, the need to persuade one's base in the primaries and then to convince the center in the general election all but ensures that, once the nomination is within sight, prospective standard-bearers of both the Left and Right will open themselves to attack as political changelings by moderating some positions.

With the nomination in hand, Obama did just that by inching back from his pledge to meet with leaders of Iran, Cuba, and North Korea, locating an individual right to bear arms in the Second Amendment,[1] accepting offshore drilling as part of a broader energy package,[2] and voting not to punish the telecoms that had released phone records at the Bush administration's request.[3] The McCain campaign responded, "[A]pparently on several items Senator Obama's word cannot be trusted."[4] "Positions that helped him win the nomination. Now Obama is changing to help himself become president," said a mid-July ad.[5] Similarly, a conservative group calling itself Let Freedom Ring alleged that the Democrat shouldn't be called a flip-flopper because that label only applies to those who hold one position at a time. Instead, the group said, Obama holds "two positions at the same time. Both ways on banning handguns. Both ways on public campaign financing. And now both ways on withdrawing from Iraq. He's Both Ways Barack. Worse than a flip-flopper."[6]

Unprepared to Be President

The Republicans' strongest assault on the Democratic nominee's preparedness drew not on his words but on those of Joe Biden. "What does Barack Obama's running mate say about Barack Obama?" asked the first of three ads making this move. Aired two days after the Delaware senator's nomination was announced, the ad then cut to Biden in a primary debate declaring, "I think he can be ready, but right now, I don't believe he is."[7]

As we will note in greater detail in chapter 9, from mid-October Republican messages hammered home the notion that in uncertain times the country could not afford to entrust its highest office to "one of the least experienced people ever to run for president,"[8] a person whose own vice presidential nominee prophesied would be tested by "the world" in the form of "an international crisis" within six months of his election.[9] We examine the effects of this end-of-the-campaign appeal in that chapter. Here we note simply that throughout the election season the Arizonan trumped the junior senator from Illinois on "experience [needed] to be president" and "ready to be Commander-in-Chief" (see figures 4.1 through 4.6). However, with Democrats and independents Obama passed the midpoint on the Commander-in-Chief scale.

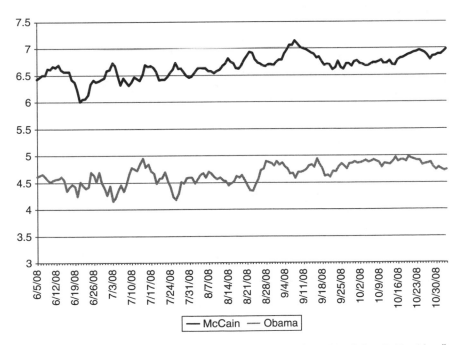

FIGURE 4.1 Perceptions of the Candidates: "Has the Experience Needed to Be President" (10-point scale, 5-day PMA). *Source*: NAES08 telephone survey.

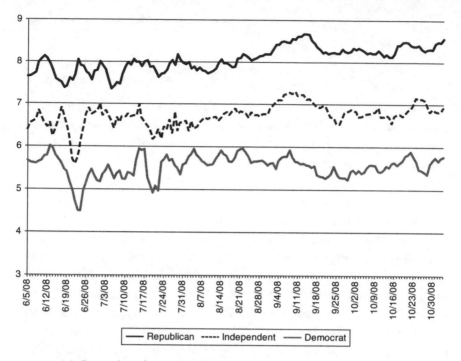

FIGURE 4.2 Perceptions that McCain "Has the Experience Needed to Be President" by Party Identification (10-point scale, 5-day PMA). *Source*: NAES08 telephone survey.

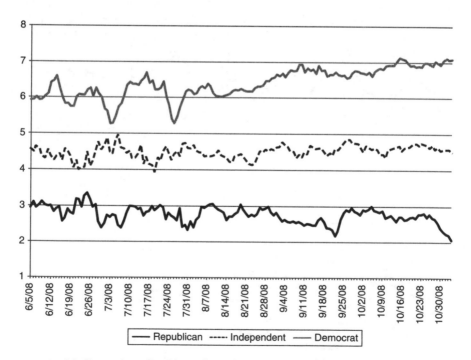

FIGURE 4.3 Perceptions that Obama "Has the Experience Needed to Be President" by Party Identification (10-point scale, 5-day PMA). *Source*: NAES08 telephone survey.

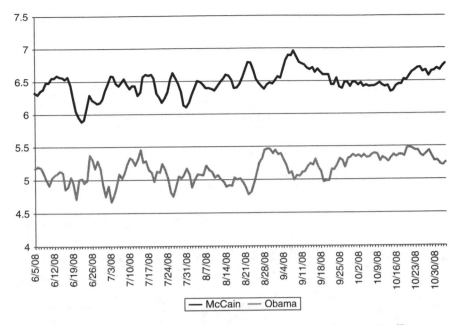

FIGURE 4.4 Perceptions of the Candidates: "Ready to Be Commander-in-Chief"
(10-point scale, 5-day PMA). *Source*: NAES08 telephone survey.

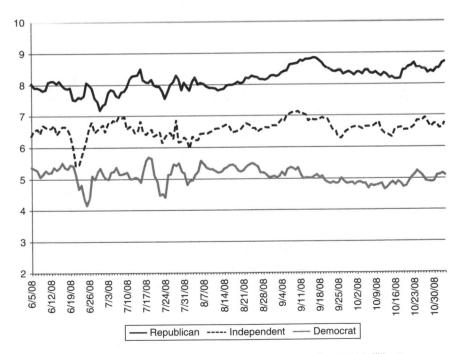

FIGURE 4.5 Perceptions of McCain as "Ready to Be Commander-in-Chief" by Party
Identification (10-point scale, 5-day PMA). *Source*: NAES08 telephone survey.

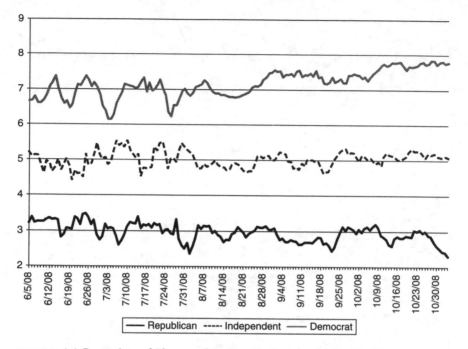

FIGURE 4.6 Perceptions of Obama as "Ready to Be Commander-in-Chief" by Party Identification (10-point scale, 5-day PMA). *Source*: NAES08 telephone survey.

Lightweight, Unprepared Celebrity

Obama's July 17–26 tour of the Middle East and Europe established that he could comfortably deal with heads of state. The sojourn also neutralized the McCain charges that he had neither been to Iraq nor met with General Petraeus outside Washington. For all intents and purposes, the trip's visuals served as unpaid ads asserting that the presidency would be safe in Obama's hands. While engaged in conversation with heads of state on that trip, the Democrat tried on the role of diplomat-in-chief. Meetings with the military invited news viewers to see him as Commander-in-Chief. His ability to draw an audience worthy of a popular U.S. president in Berlin vivified the notion that he would restore world respect for the United States and repudiate Bush's "my way or the highway" foreign policy. So effective was the Obama campaign's news management that *The Daily Show*'s Jon Stewart forecast that Obama's next stop was his birthplace in Bethlehem.[10]

Of even greater importance to the Democratic campaign was a statement by the Iraqi prime minister that silenced controversy generated by Obama's call for withdrawal of U.S. troops within 16 months of taking office. Specifically, two days before their scheduled face-to-face meeting, Iraqi Prime Minister Nuri-al-Maliki told *Der Spiegel* that "U.S. presidential candidate Barack Obama talks about 16 months. That, we think, would be the right timeframe for a withdrawal, with the possibility of slight changes."[11] "Iraqi PM Backs Obama Troop Exit Plan" read the July 19 Reuters headline.[12] The significance of Maliki's embrace of Obama's position was not its effect on the polls but rather its impact on the debate. The prime minister's statement simultaneously accomplished three Democratic objectives: exploding John McCain's assertions that Obama's plans for troop withdrawal would squander success in Iraq, vanquishing debate about the merits of a timetable, and trumpeting the conclusion that Obama was a foreign policy sophisticate. However, unfortunately for this book's authors, the Obama trip and the Maliki moment occurred at a time in which, in an effort to conserve resources, we were surveying only 50 respondents a day, too few to permit us to discern a possible effect.

Recognizing that Obama's tour would dominate the news, the McCain campaign counter-programmed with a series of July and August Web and cable ads that metacommunicated that Obama was a self-absorbed, self-important lightweight. "We used the 'celebrity' ads as a tactic to try to stay in the race and to say something about Senator Obama that would resonate with people and raise a doubt about the excesses of enthusiasm from our perspective [which we humorously conveyed as] 'The One,'" recalled Steve Schmidt. "Humor's an effective weapon in a campaign.... [B]eginning with a series of Web videos, we were able to take some control of the viral space on YouTube, an arena [in which] we'd been just completely manhandled by the Obama campaign."[13]

The McCain campaign's riff on "the one" was forecast by Hillary Clinton's earlier send-up of her charismatic opponent:

> Now, I can stand up here and say, let's just get everybody together. Let's get unified. The sky will open. The light will come down. Celestial choirs will be singing. And everyone will know we can do the right thing and the world will be perfect. Maybe I've just lived a little long, but I have no illusions about how hard this is going to be. You are not going to wave a magic wand and have the special interests disappear.[14]

The Republican rescripting of that idea brimmed with religious overtones as it playfully ascribed messianic illusions to the Illinois democrat:

> ANNOUNCER: It should be known that in 2008 the world will be blessed. They will call him, The One.
>
> SENATOR OBAMA: A nation healed. A world repaired. We are the ones we've been waiting for. (*applause*)

ANNOUNCER: And he has anointed himself ready to carry the burden of the world. To quote Barack, "I have become a symbol of America returning to our best traditions." He can do no wrong.

INTERVIEWER: Do you have any doubts?

OBAMA: Never.

ANNOUNCER: Can you see the light?

OBAMA: A light will shine down from somewhere. It will light upon you. You will experience an epiphany, and you will say to yourself, "I have to vote for Barack."

ANNOUNCER: And the world shall receive his blessings.

OBAMA: This was the moment when the rise of the ocean began to slow and our planet began to heal.

CHARLTON HESTON (as Moses): Behold his mighty hand [raising staff and parting Red Sea. Obama seal emerges from waters].

ANNOUNCER: Barack Obama may be the one. But is he ready to lead?[15]

Depending on one's point of reference, the notion that Barack Obama was "the one" evoked very different associations. Perhaps Obama was akin to the "anointed one," for whom the chosen people waited in the Old Testament, or in the gospel according to Oprah, the one who would lead the nation out of slavery.[16]

By analogizing the Democratic nominee to Moses in the movie *The Ten Commandments,* the Web ad titled "The One" played on the idea that Obama was not, as he thought, Moses leading his people to the Promised Land but, instead, an actor or poseur, played by Charlton Heston. In that role, Obama as Heston raises his staff to the heavens as technicians create the illusion that his divinely directed incantations are actually parting the Red Sea. The Obama-as-Heston-as-Moses message was one in a series suggesting that the Illinois senator was an empty suit. What insulated the McCain campaign from easy counterattack was the fact that the ad replayed Obama's own words to make its points.

The tightrope that the McCain campaign was walking with "The One" was revealed when respected commentator and former Reagan and Clinton advisor David Gergen responded to it by saying, "As a native of the South, I can tell you, when you see this Charlton Heston ad, 'The One,' that's code for 'he's uppity. He ought to stay in his place.' You know, everybody gets that who is from, you know, a Southern background."[17]

A follow-up attack juxtaposed Obama speaking to the stadium-size crowd in Berlin with photos of vacant pop-cultural icons Britney Spears and Paris

Hilton. "He's the biggest celebrity in the world," intoned the announcer. "But is he ready to lead?" On the audio track, the chant of the crowd creates a sense of vague menace. Fred Davis, who masterminded the spot, and fellow Foxhole producer Chris Mottola recall that the audio under the "Celeb" ad (that included Spears and Hilton) was a mix created in postproduction, augmented from elements captured by a McCain film crew with audio from a live news feed.[18]

With almost 2.2 million views, the McCain "Celeb" ad was his most often watched video on YouTube.[19] Interestingly, nearly two years before the ad aired, Obama himself had made the comparison to Hilton when he reported that, "I'm so overexposed, I'm making Paris Hilton look like a recluse."[20]

Underlying the celebrity series was the inference that Obama was a hypocrite, an assumption that only made sense if it could drive or reinforce the notion that he was untrustworthy. Throughout the election, McCain held a slight edge on that trait (figure 4.7). Since both candidates remained above the 5-point level on a 0-to-10 scale, we surmise that a lack of trustworthiness was not a liability for either candidate.

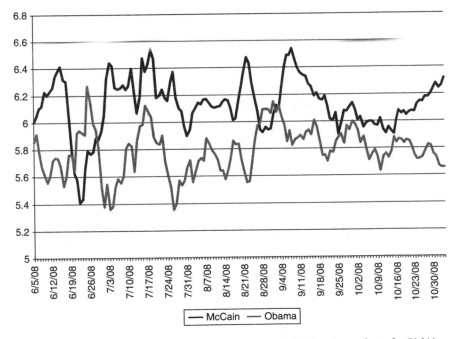

FIGURE 4.7 Perceptions of the Candidates: "Trustworthy" (10-point scale, 5-day PMA). *Source*: NAES08 telephone survey.

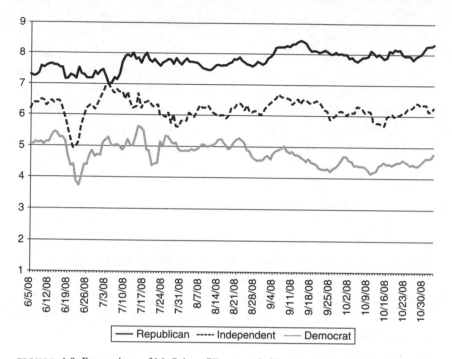

FIGURE 4.8 Perceptions of McCain as "Trustworthy" by Party Identification (10-point scale, 5-day PMA). *Source*: NAES08 telephone survey.

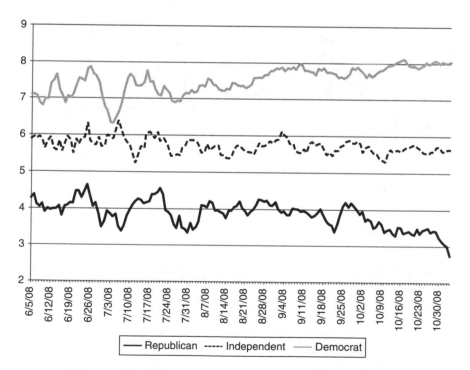

FIGURE 4.9 Perceptions of Obama as "Trustworthy" by Party Identification (10-point scale, 5-day PMA). *Source*: NAES08 telephone survey.

The celebrity theme also was used to turn the tables on Obama, to suggest that he, and implicitly not McCain, was the one who was out of touch. "Celebrities don't have to worry about family budgets," said one spot, "but we sure do. We're paying more for food and gas, making it harder to save for college, retirement."[21] "Life in the spotlight must be grand," said one ad, "but for the rest of us, times are tough."[22] Consistent with the other ads of this type, this one then pivots to the dominant campaign theme of taxes. "Obama voted to raise taxes on people making just $42,000. He promises more taxes on small business, seniors, your life savings, your family. Painful taxes. Hard choices for your budget. Not ready to lead."[23] "Take away the crowds, the chants, all that's left are costly words," said another hybrid RNC/McCain ad.[24]

Rather than legitimizing the "celebrity" attacks by taking them on directly, the Obama campaign responded with humor. At the Al Smith Dinner in New York on October 16, for example, the Democratic nominee revealed that

> Contrary to the rumors that you've heard, I was not born in a manger. I was actually born on Krypton and sent here by my father, Jor-El, to save the planet earth! Many of you know that I got my name "Barack" from my father. What you may not know is "Barack" is actually Swahili for "That One." And I got my middle name from somebody who obviously didn't think I'd ever run for president![25]

The long-term problem McCain would confront with the line "Ready to tax. Not ready to lead"[26] was that Obama had insulated his campaign from it with his pledge to lower taxes for most Americans. Fact checkers concluded that both would reduce taxes for the middle class but Obama more so than McCain. The inconsistency in McCain's argument was that Obama could not both be an empty suit and a menacingly predictable-tax-and-spend liberal. He had to be one or the other.

Who Is Obama?

Since even Obama described himself as "like a Rorschach test,"[27] a "blank screen on which people of vastly different stripes project their own views,"[28] it is unsurprising that the McCain campaign attacked his supposedly meager accomplishments and celebrity status with the question "Who is Obama?" McCain's answer introduced what could be heard as a race-based stereotype by suggesting that Obama was angry:

> You know, it's as if somehow the usual rules don't apply. And where other candidates have to explain themselves in their records, Senator Obama seems to think he's above all that. Whatever the question, whatever the

issue, there's always a back story with Senator Obama. All people want to know is what has this man ever actually accomplished in government.

What does he plan for America? In short, who is the—who is the real Barack Obama? But my friends, you ask such questions and all you get in response is another angry barrage of insults.[29]

The Angry Black Male

If the Republicans succeeded in persuading voters that Obama's calm demeanor masked seething anger, they could not only elicit race-tied fears but also undercut the disposition of nonblacks to get to know and like him. Where negative emotion fuels stereotypic reactions, positive emotion can thwart them.[30] The "anger" attack played on a primal instinct. Neurocientists report that nonblacks respond almost instantaneously with heightened vigilance to blacks with whom they are unfamiliar.[31] Still, "angry" was an unlikely characterization of the candidate dexterously characterized by his campaign as "No Drama Obama," a moniker that carried into news analysis.

Instead of ready anger, Obama's vulnerability seemed to be irritability at being challenged, a posture on display in his tone and nonverbal reactions to reporters' questions in early March. Those queries concerned two controversies potentially implicating the senator from Illinois. The first involved his dealings with his fundraiser and friend Tony Rezko, whose wife sold the Obamas part of a lot next to their home at a time when Rezco was under federal investigation. The second controversy involved allegations that the Democrat's protectionist rhetoric on NAFTA was political positioning and not a policy forecast.[32] "Toward the end of the press conference, the question of [Obama adviser Austan] Goolsbee's meeting [with Canadian officials about the difference between Obama's actual and campaign-inspired position on NAFTA] was raised again. Obama *answered curtly and then walked out* after a staffer called for the last question. The press erupted with shouts, but Obama continued to walk out," reported MSNBC. "He paused only to say, 'Come on, guys; I answered like eight questions. We're running late (emphasis added).'"[33,34]

The same tendency was evident during the primaries in South Carolina, when a *New York Times* reporter insisted that Obama had not answered the question, "Are you letting Bill Clinton get inside your head?" "Don't try cheap stunts like that, Jeff," Dan Balz and Haynes Johnson report Obama responded after he "turned, flashed a grin that seemed to hide his peevishness."[35] A related susceptibility was evident in the detachment glimpsed briefly in a pre-New Hampshire Democratic primary debate when, head down, he responded to Hillary Clinton's acknowledgment of his likeability and assertion of her own, by saying without warmth or conviction, "You're likeable enough, Hillary."[36] If, as social psychologist Susan Fiske suggests, warmth and competence reduce stereotypes, then cues conveying emotional detachment were counterproductive.[37] So too were suggestions after his Iowa caucus victory that the nominee was, in the words of his senior campaign advisor, "doing victory laps."[38] However, by identifying Obama as one who issues an "angry barrage of insults," McCain was painting a picture at odds with the candidate voters were increasingly coming to know.

"Pride in Country"

Two moments in the campaign risked reinforcing the stereotype of the "angry black" being invited by Republican rhetoric. The first occurred in Milwaukee, Wisconsin, on Monday, February 18, when Michelle Obama suggested that until recently she had not been proud of her country and only now felt that emotion because of her husband's success in the primaries. Specifically, she told an audience, "People in this country are ready for change and hungry for a different kind of politics and...for the first time in my adult life I am proud of my country because it feels like hope is finally making a comeback."[39] The statement did not include the word "really," an addition that suggests that her pride in the country had not been generated, but rather augmented, by Obama's wins.

Later that day in Madison, Mrs. Obama repeated enough of the original statement to invite confusion between the two. The amended version substituted "really proud" for "proud" and avowed that her spouse's victories contributed to but were not the sole cause of her pride. "For the first time in my adult lifetime, I'm really proud of my country...not just because Barack has done well, but because I think people are hungry for change."[40] For a brief period, reveals ABC's Jake Tapper, the Obama campaign tried to persuade reporters that the Milwaukee statement was the only one made.[41] Thereafter, with noteworthy success, the campaign implied that the word "really" had appeared in the Milwaukee statement or deflected reporters to Mrs. Obama's second statement in Madison.[42] In short, before the gaffe could take hold outside the conservative blogosphere, talk radio, and Fox News, the Obama campaign had reconstructed it to minimize the likelihood that it would appear in general election attack ads. In July 2009, the only version that survives on YouTube is the amended one.

The Hazard Created for Obama by Reverend Wright

The danger posed by the March 2008 emergence of incendiary recorded statements made by Obama's Chicago mentor and pastor was that they would transform a healing candidacy into a polarizing one, and an even-tempered candidate into one perceived to have sequestered but not spurned the sentiments Wright voiced. The vulnerability was magnified by the fact that Wright had officiated at the Obama's marriage and baptized their children. Moreover, Obama had adopted a sermon title of Wright's for one of his books, praised Wright as his spiritual mentor, implied strongly that he was a regular churchgoer, hence presumably in the pews when at least some of the problematic comments had been made, and had evinced some awareness of Wright's controversial rhetoric by cancelling his minister's participation in the Illinois senator's announcement of candidacy.

In the simplifying world of political campaigning, there was no chance that Wright's words would be recontextualized. Instead, they were an attack ad waiting to happen. "No, no, no. Not God bless America. God damn America," the pastor had been recorded shouting to his enthralled congregation in 2003. An edited loop, which juxtaposed inflammatory statements from different sermons, broke into mainstream broadcast in mid-March.[43] Within days, the videos had been viewed by approximately half the country.[44] Both the impact of the Wright revelations on Obama and the effectiveness of the Democrat's response are reflected in our data (see figures 4.10 through 4.13).

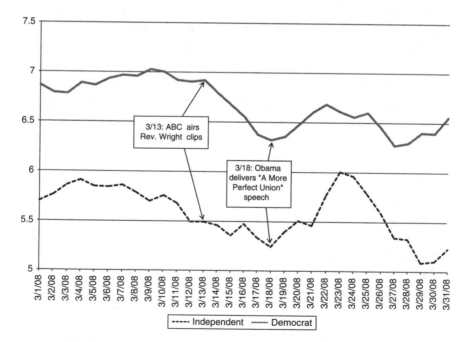

FIGURE 4.10 Perceptions of Obama as "Ready to Be President" among Democrats and Independents (10-point scale, 5-day PMA). *Source*: NAES08 telephone survey.

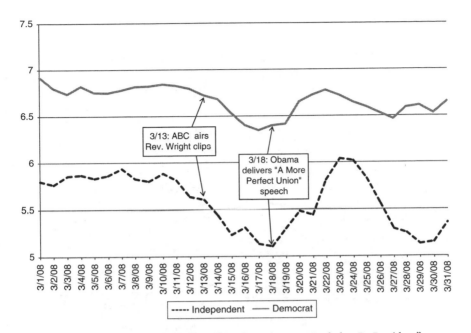

FIGURE 4.11 Perceptions that Obama "Has the Judgment Needed to Be President" among Democrats and Independents (10-point scale, 5-day PMA). *Source*: NAES08 telephone survey.

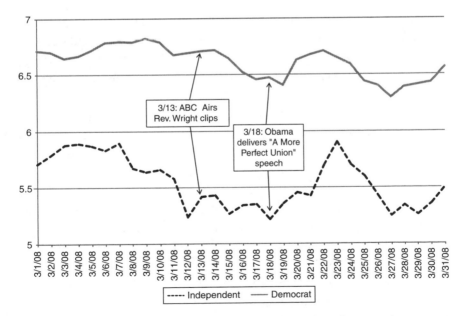

FIGURE 4.12 Perceptions of Obama as "Trustworthy" among Democrats and Independents (10-point scale, 5-day PMA). *Source*: NAES08 telephone survey.

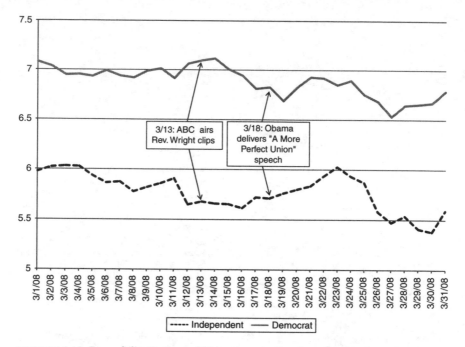

FIGURE 4.13 Favorability Ratings of Obama among Democrats and Independents (10-point scale, 5-day PMA). *Source*: NAES08 telephone survey.

Obama's March 18 Philadelphia speech on race halted the hemorrhaging occasioned by the Wright controversy. The 37-minute-39-second address also broke records by attracting more than 5.1 million views on YouTube, "marking," noted the *New York Times*, "YouTube's emergence as a vehicle for substantive discourse, not just silly clips."[45]

Speaking from a text he had completed the night before, the Illinois Democrat condemned his former mentor's sound bites as the expression of "a profoundly distorted view of this country—a view that sees white racism as endemic, and that elevates what is wrong with America above all that we know is right with America." At the same time, he rationalized Wright's views of race and America as a throwback to another time and place. "For the men and women of Reverend Wright's generation, the memories of humiliation and doubt and fear have not gone away; nor have the anger and the bitterness of those years. That anger may not get expressed in public, in front of white co-workers or white friends. But it does find voice in the barbershop or around the kitchen table. At times, that anger is exploited by politicians, to gin up votes along racial lines, or to make up for a politician's own failings. And occasionally it finds voice in the church on Sunday morning, in the pulpit and in the pews."

The speech cast the pastor as an eccentric uncle. "I can no more disown him than I can disown the black community. I can no more disown him than I can my white grandmother—a woman who helped raise me, a woman who sacrificed again and again for me, a woman who loves me as much as she loves anything in this world, but a woman who once confessed her fear of black men who passed by her on the street, and who on more than one occasion has uttered racial or ethnic stereotypes that made me cringe."

Wright's subsequent reiteration of the troubling sentiments at an April 28 performance at the National Press Club reopened the problem. Again Obama laid it to rest with rhetorical action, this time by resigning from the church Wright had until recently pastored and formally repudiating him on April 29.

Although Republican groups mined the pastor's image in independent expenditure ads we will discuss in a moment, the McCain campaign steadfastly refused to interject the Wright issue into the fall campaign even though the campaign's pollster had concluded that doing so might result in a win in the battleground and with it, in the electoral college, an outcome that he concluded would have undermined McCain's presidency. "Take our decision never to talk about Reverend Wright," recalled McInturff. "I said, 'If John McCain's going to win, we're going to lose the popular vote by three million votes. There will be an enormous potential for urban violence.' Imagine if we had done that and he'd been doing Reverend Wright and trying to actually serve as American president. It would have delegitimized his presidency."[46]

Invoking and Dispatching Stereotypes

Tying Obama to Angry Black Rhetoric: Uses of Reverend Wright

Nonetheless, in the fall campaign, a series of 527 and PAC ads associated Obama with Wright's seeming attacks on America and at the same time with the anger with which the pastor voiced them. The reverend was also a central figure in the message of a group that called itself Our Country Deserves Better, a label that forecast its view that Obama "seems to have different values from most Americans." One of this group's ads closed, "And who can forget these hateful sermons from Obama's pastor of 20 years?" At the ad's end, Wright is heard shouting, "God damn America."[47]

Assimilating Obama's identity into that of his former pastor, Our Country Deserves Better ran an ad on October 22 that tried to activate the stereotype of the angry, resentment-filled black man who is "Too radical. Too risky" and by implication un-American and anti-American. Although he had explicitly repudiated Wright's views, the spot implied that Obama shared them. "For

20 years, Barack Obama followed a preacher of hate," it began, as "hate, hate" appeared on a pictured film strip, followed by a picture of Wright preaching. Then a repetition of "hate." Obama "said nothing as Wright raged against our country," noted the spot. After Wright shouts "Not God bless America. God damn America," Obama is shown stating, "I don't think my church is particularly controversial." The ad then intercuts a clip of the pastor shouting, "U.S. of KKK-A." As it closes, the spot wraps these words around Obama's candidacy with the claim, "Wright was his mentor, adviser, and close friend. For 20 years, Obama never complained until he ran for president." The same set of associations was the subject of ads by a second Republican group calling itself the Republican Federal Committee of Pennsylvania[48] and by a Judicial Confirmation Network ad.[49]

However, where the Wright controversy dominated press coverage and percolated through the Internet from March through early June, the ads run in the final weeks of the campaign created only a minimal stir (figure 4.14).

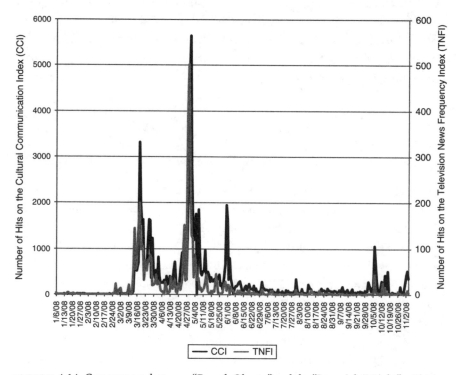

FIGURE 4.14 Concurrence between "Barack Obama" and the "Jeremiah Wright" within a Single Sentence. *Source*: Lydia News/Media Analysis System and Lexis Nexis.

Link to Suspected Misconduct or Crime Committed by Blacks

Although the McCain campaign refused to feature Reverend Wright's comments, it nonetheless implicitly primed negative associations tied to race. The move is a potent one because negative dispositions toward African-Americans affect opinions.[50] Moreover, as political science professor Tali Mendelberg argues, even as the "norm of equality" prompts some to reject explicit racial appeals, it may leave them susceptible to coded cues that they do not perceive as racist.[51] Consistent with this analysis, implicit visual[52] and verbal[53] racial cues have been found to heighten race-based negative responses.

Priming Race through Use of Franklin Raines

In 2008, Republicans tried to tie Obama to powerful men, some of them African-American, whom the ads alleged had engaged in misconduct or crime. The amalgamation both invited stereotypes and with them the question, can an African-American be trusted with the presidency?

When the *Washington Post* mentioned that Franklin Raines had "taken calls from Barack Obama's presidential campaign seeking his advice on mortgage and housing policy matters,"[54] the Republicans saw an opening. Raines, who is African-American, had headed the Federal National Mortgage Association (Fannie Mae) in the years prior to the meltdown (1999–2004) and had stepped down with a sizeable bonus in hand and under the shadow of questions about accounting errors during his time at the helm—errors that led to an out-of-court settlement of a civil suit against him. In mid-September, the McCain campaign linked Obama to the mounting financial crisis with an ad showing Raines' face while alleging that the former Fannie Mae CEO was an Obama advisor and noting, "Raines made millions and then left Fannie Mae while it was under investigation for accounting irregularities."[55] Raines responded by insisting that he had never been an Obama advisor.

In early October, a group calling itself RightChange.com picked up the theme in an ad saying, "McCain pushed regulatory reform, attacked the accounting corruption at Fannie under Franklin Raines, who advised the Obama campaign. McCain exposed [the] accounting fraud Raines used to pocket over 90 million dollars."[56] That spot included the picture of James Johnson, CEO of Fannie Mae from 1991–1998, whom Obama asked to head his vice presidential selection committee, and who had also been tied to accounting irregularities. Johnson, who is white, had resigned from the vice presidential team after the emergence of questions about a loan from Countrywide, a firm implicated in the subprime mortgage controversy. Raines and Johnson were also pictured in a second ad by

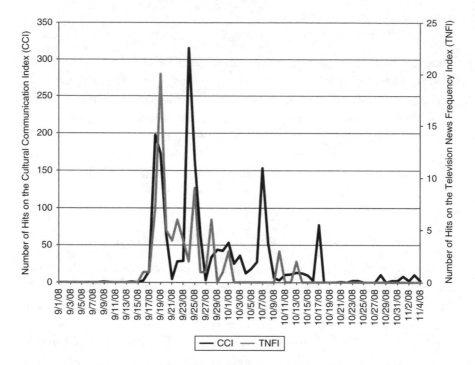

FIGURE 4.15 Concurrence between "Barack Obama" and "Franklin Raines" within a Single Sentence. *Source*: Lydia News/Media Analysis System and Lexis Nexis.

the group, saying, "Fannie and Freddie funneled more contributions to Obama than any politician. Now they're making taxpayers clean up their mess."[57] From mid-September to mid-October, the controversy over whether Raines had or had not been an Obama advisor spawned a flurry of broadcast television, blog, and Internet commentary.

Priming Race with Associations with Kwame Kilpatrick and Rev. Wright

Another ad associating Obama with misconduct by an African-American aired briefly in (Lansing) Michigan near the end of the campaign. By juxtaposing pictures of Obama with those of convicted former Detroit Mayor Kwame Kilpatrick, who is black, former Weatherman William Ayers, who is white, and Reverend Wright, the final ad by Our Country Deserves Better linked Obama to terrorism, anti-American rhetoric, and black crime all in one fell swoop. That spot alleged that "Barack Obama and his friends represent the wrong kind of change for Michigan and America."[58] In 2008, none of the independent expenditure ads secured the level of news attention and replay that in 1988 vaulted the National Security

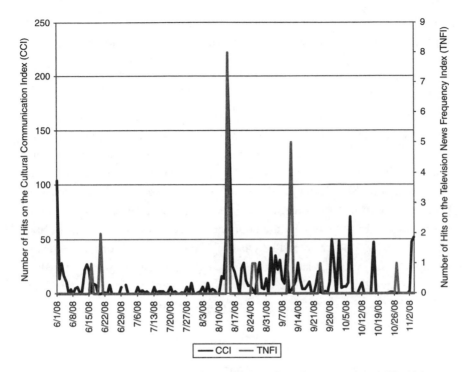

FIGURE 4.16 Concurrence between "Barack Obama" and "Kwame Kilpatrick" within a Single Sentence. *Source*: Lydia News/Media Analysis System and Lexis Nexis.

Political Action Committee's "Willie Horton" narrative into public consciousness; nor did they achieve the visibility of the 2004 anti-Kerry ads fielded by the Swift Boat Veterans for Truth.

Obama as Criminal

To these attempts to create guilt by association was added one Spanish and English language ad close in pedigree to the infamous Horton ads. Appearing in the last week of the election, that National Rifle Association Victory Fund spot showed a terrified woman in a bathrobe clutching a handgun in her darkened living room as the announcer intoned, "Imagine your child screaming in the middle of the night when a convicted felon breaks into your home." As a darkened home is shown on screen the voice over added, "Worse, he comes back a second time. You use a firearm. Unbelievably, Barack Obama voted to make you the criminal." The clearest racial cue came at the end of the ad, when a photo of Obama dressed in a suit and tie is superimposed on prison bars, a juxtaposition that suggests that he is a white-collar criminal protecting the unseen villain whom race-based fears would cast as black. "It's a true story and it gets worse," noted the announcer. "Obama voted four times to deny citizens the right of self-protection even in their homes."[59]

Welfare as a Code Word

In a move that we will explore in chapter 10, the McCain campaign tagged Obama's refundable tax credits, "welfare," a word so freighted with race that reporters assumed that she was black when Ronald Reagan spoke of an unnamed (and never located) "Welfare Queen's" misuse of the system.[60] Presumably mindful of the likelihood that a black candidate would be attacked if he championed any programs that could be construed as welfare, Obama signaled early in the postprimary season that he would aid the poor without resorting to it. In a spot titled "Dignity," an announcer noted that Obama "helped lift neighborhoods stung by job loss… [and] passed a law to move people from welfare to work, slashed the rolls by 80 percent…" On the screen, the concept was reinforced with the words, "The Obama Record: Moved People from Welfare to Work."[61] Obama's ads stressed parental responsibility as well.[62]

Unpatriotic and Supports Terrorists

Impugning Obama's patriotism by ascribing Wright's presumed views to him was only one of the moves Republican groups used to imply that the Democrat was un-American. A spot that began airing in mid-October opened with footage of the Democrat with his hands at his side as the national anthem is played. In the same scene, New Mexico Governor Bill Richardson and New York Senator Hillary Clinton hold their right hands over their hearts. The message then allied the Democrat with illegality and a series of tangential relations with suspect groups. "His supporters put up Cuban flags with the murderous leftist Che Guevara in the Obama campaign offices. Obama's campaign received $33,000 in illegal donations from Palestinians living in the Middle East. A top official of the terrorist group Hamas endorsed the Obama campaign."[63] After indicting Obama for not wearing a flag pin, Our Country Can Do Better attacked his patriotism with the line, "If America is not good enough for Barack Obama then Barack Obama is not good enough for America."[64] Another spot by that group intercut earlier indictments by Hillary Clinton with those of a woman identified as Deborah Johns, who reported that Obama "says he'll play nicey nicey with militants who want to kill Americans both here at home and abroad."[65]

The strongest attacks made by the McCain campaign on Senator Obama's patriotism came at the end of the first week in October, when vice presidential nominee Sarah Palin declared of Obama's passing association with former Weather Underground leader William Ayers, "I'm afraid this is someone [Obama] who sees

America as imperfect enough to work with a former domestic terrorist who had targeted his own country."[66] "This is not a man who sees America as you see it and how I see America,"[67] she noted. Obama "sees America, it seems, as being so imperfect that he's palling around with terrorists who would target their own country."[68] A McCain ad reinforced the anti-American theme by declaring that its candidate was the "American president America is waiting for,"[69] a formulation some heard to invite the inference that McCain's opponent was neither a prospective "American" president nor one worthy of belief.[70]

Palin was also the one who leveled a charge, repeated in a McCain attack ad, that Obama had said "that our troops in Afghanistan are just, quote, 'air-raiding villages and killing civilians.'" "I hope Americans know that is not what our brave men and women are doing in Afghanistan,"[71] added the Alaska governor. The same out-of-context allegation surfaced in the McCain/RNC ad titled "Dangerous." What Obama had actually said was, "We've got to get the job done there and that requires us to have enough troops so that we're not just air-raiding villages and killing civilians, which is causing enormous problems there."[72]

We find in our survey that the Democrat from Illinois was consistently seen as less patriotic than McCain (figure 4.17). But here, as with "trustworthy," both are

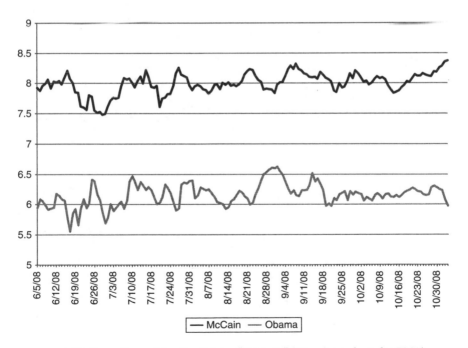

FIGURE 4.17 Perceptions of the Candidates: "Patriotic" (10-point scale, 5-day PMA).
Source: NAES08 telephone survey.

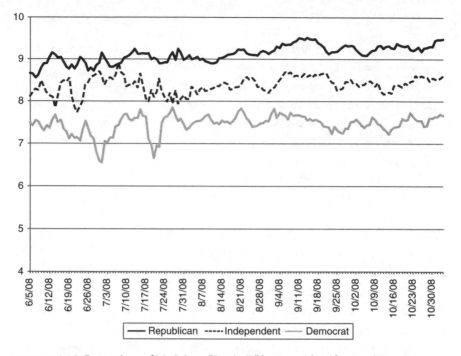

FIGURE 4.18 Perceptions of McCain as "Patriotic" by Party Identification (10-point scale, 5-day PMA). *Source*: NAES08 telephone survey.

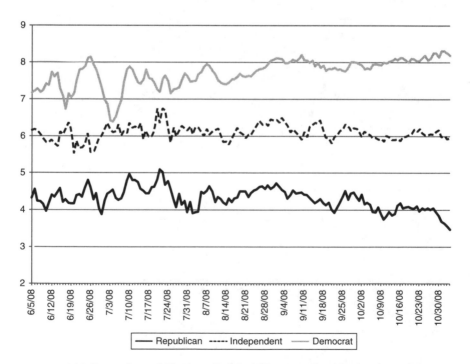

FIGURE 4.19 Perceptions of Obama as "Patriotic" by Party Identification (10-point scale, 5-day PMA). *Source*: NAES08 telephone survey.

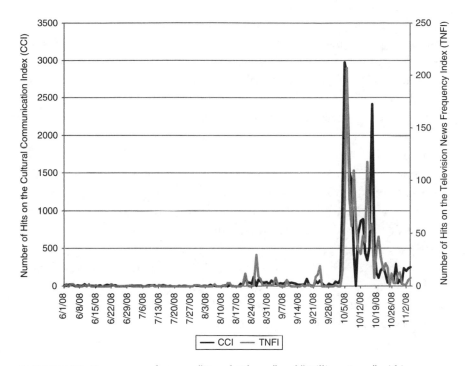

FIGURE 4.20 Concurrence between "Barack Obama" and "William Ayers" within a Single Sentence. *Source*: Lydia News/Media Analysis System and Lexis Nexis.

safely above the midpoint on a 0-to-10 scale. However, the breakdown by party iden-tification (figures 4.18 and 4.19) shows that there is less variation in perceptions of McCain than in those of Obama. In fact, Democrats gave Obama scores comparable to those they gave McCain. By contrast, Republicans and independents gave the Illi-nois senator a much lower rating than they did his Republican counterpart.

An analysis of the last three weeks of the campaign suggests that perceptions of Obama's and McCain's "patriotism" were associated with vote preference. The NAES data reveal that such beliefs were significant predictors of a preference to vote for Obama even when sociodemographic and political characteristics, news media exposure, and the presidential and vice presidential candidates' favorability ratings were taken into consideration. As preception that Obama was unpatriotic increased, the likelihood of voting for him dropped.[73*]

Linking Obama to Crime, Corruption, and Terror

Corruption was an inevitable theme in a campaign in which each side was affix-ing the other to as many lobbyists as it could locate; at the same time, Obama was stressing that his campaign was funded by small donors and, by implication, not big contributors seeking influence. The McCain attacks on Obama's associations first emerged in August with an ad on the 22nd that suggested that the Illinois senator engaged in special dealing with convicted felon Tony Rezko. "Barack Obama knows a lot about housing problems,"declared the ad. "One of his biggest fund-raisers helped him buy his million-dollar mansion, purchasing part of the property he couldn't afford. From Obama, Rezko got political favors, including 14 million from taxpayers. Now he's a convicted felon."[74] The allegation that Obama got his house as part of a special deal with Rezko was a mainstay of viral e-mail as well. (As fact checkers confirmed, Obama had paid market value for the home. Whether the owners would have sold the home without the sale of the adjoining property that Rezco purchased was another question.)

The combined set of messages took hold. In the Annenberg postelection Claims/Deception survey[75] 37.7 percent reported that the statement "Senator Obama was able to buy his house because a man named Tony Rezko purchased the lot next door at full price" was either "very" or "somewhat" truthful.

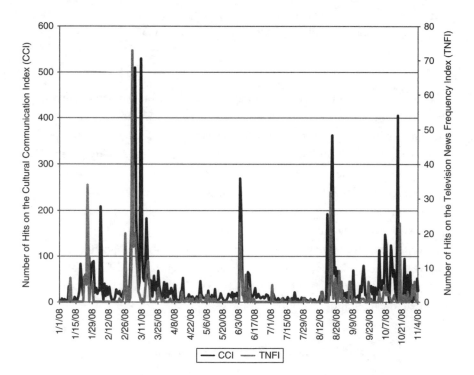

FIGURE 4.21 Concurrence between "Barack Obama" and "Tony Rezko" within a Single Sentence. *Source*: Lydia News/Media Analysis System and Lexis Nexis.

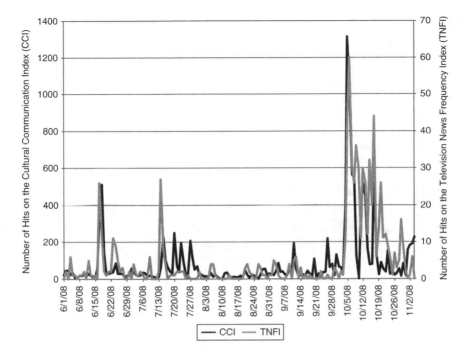

FIGURE 4.22 Concurrence between "Barack Obama" and "Terrorists" within a Single Sentence. *Source*: Lydia News/Media Analysis System and Lexis Nexis.

The RNC picked up the theme on October 10 with an ad that attempted to identify Obama with "The Chicago Way: Shady Politics." That spot cast Obama as the apprentice of Rezko, (a name introduced into the campaign by Hillary Clinton in the South Carolina primary debate)[76] as well as William Daley (mayor of Chicago and son of Chicago Mayor Richard Daley) and former Weatherman William Ayers:

> ANNOUNCER: His teachers? Tony Rezko, convicted of corruption, money laundering, aiding and abetting bribery. Rezko got Obama in on a shady land deal. William Daley, heir to the Chicago machine. A top Obama adviser. And William Ayers, leader of a terrorist group that bombed the U.S. Capitol. Obama's first campaign was launched at a gathering at Mr. Ayers' home.

"There's more you need to know," said the announcer at the end of the ad.[77]

The Annenberg Claims/Deception survey found that two-thirds (67%) said that they "heard or read about a controversy about the relationship of Senator Obama with a former member of the Weather Underground called William Ayers." Fifty-seven percent (56.9%) of those who knew of William Ayers said that his relationship with Obama was "somewhat" or "very close," a conclusion unsupported by evidence. Nearly 19 percent (18.7%) found the statement "Barack Obama pals around with terrorists" to be truthful.

Guilt by association was also the tactic of choice by an organization calling itself the National Republican Trust that visually associated Obama with 9/11 ringleader Mohammed Atta. "Nineteen terrorists infiltrate the U.S." noted the ad. As Mohammed Atta's photo appears on a driver's license on screen, the narration continued, "Thirteen got driver's licenses." The next person whose picture appears is the Democratic nominee. "Obama's plan gives a license to any illegal who wants one." The ad then shows Obama answering yes to a question not asked in the ad. The viewer is left to surmise that the question was about his plans as president, not, as was the case, about his agreement with a specific state plan. The spot closes, "Barack Obama: Too radical. Too risky."[78] Meanwhile, a group named Let Freedom Ring allied Obama with a "fiercely anti-American, radical and racist (Wright)," "a convicted criminal (Rezko)," a "radical extremist" (Louis Farrakhan),"[79] and a "terrorist" (Ayers)."[80]

The Viral Brew

Two viral arguments that did not explicitly appear in broadcast or cable ads bubbled throughout the campaign, the first alleging that Obama violated the Constitutional requirement that the president be a natural-born citizen; the second suggesting that he was a Muslim. Each was spread in e-mail and Web postings and repeatedly debunked by the fact checkers in the press. In our postelection Claims survey, 19 percent of respondents reported believing that Obama was a Muslim. Of those, 25 percent voted for him, while 63.9 percent supported McCain.[81]

Distortions about Obama's religion and citizenship emerged not just on the Web but in a riveting moment in the campaign, in which John McCain was taken aback by a female questioner in an audience who said:

> WOMAN: I don't trust Obama. I have read about him, and he's an Arab.

> SENATOR JOHN MCCAIN: No ma'am, no ma'am. He's a decent family man, citizen that I just happen to have disagreements with on fundamental issues. That's what this campaign is all about. He's not, thank you.[82]

Our postelection Claims survey found that 22 percent of respondents embraced the statement "Senator Obama is nearly half Arab."

Allegations such as these prompted concern in a prominent general whose endorsement of the Democratic ticket we treat in chapter 10. "I'm also troubled by, not what Senator McCain says, but what members of the party say," noted General

Colin Powell during his nationally televised endorsement of Obama and Biden on October 19. "And it is permitted to be said such things as, 'Well, you know that Mr. Obama is a Muslim,'" added Powell, "Well, the correct answer is, he is not a Muslim, he's a Christian. He's always been a Christian. But the really right answer is, 'what if he is?' Is there something wrong with being a Muslim in this country? The answer's 'no,' that's not America."[83] In an exchange with the press following the endorsement, Powell expressed disapproval of some of the rhetoric used to indict Obama. "To focus on people like Mr. Ayers, these trivial issues for purposes of suggesting that somehow Mr. Obama would have some kind of terrorist inclinations, I thought that was over the top," the former Secretary of State stated. "It's beyond just good political fighting back and forth.... And now I guess the message this week is 'we're going to call him a socialist.' Mr. Obama is now a socialist because he dares to suggest that maybe we ought to look at the tax structure that we have.... And there's nothing wrong with examining what our tax structure is or who should be paying more or who should be paying less. And for us to say that makes you a socialist I think is an unfortunate characterization that isn't accurate."[84] The fact-checking sites confirmed that Obama was both an American citizen and a practicing Christian. Still, viral e-mail persisted in stirring assertions to the contrary into a complex mix of extremist rhetoric:

> *Obama is the anti-Christ:* "[I]t is all stated in the Bible and it will happen sooner or later...This man fits every description from the Bible of the 'Anti-Christ!'"
>
> *A Muslim:* born to "a black MUSLIM from Nyangoma-Kogel, Kenya and Ann Dunham, a white ATHEIST form Wichita Kansas...Obama takes great care to conceal the fact that he is a Muslim."
>
> Was sworn into the Senate not on the "Holy Bible, but instead the Koran."
>
> *Is un-American:* "Barack Hussein Obama will NOT recite the Pledge of Allegiance nor will he show any reverence for our flag. While others place their hands over their hearts, Obama turns his back to the flag and slouches."

As scholars examine the record of the 2008 campaign, we suspect that they will wonder about two omissions in the stream of press commentary. Why was there so little discussion of the age stereotyping to which McCain was subjected and the racial coding used to attack Obama? And why did commentators so often assume that were Obama a Muslim, the fact would for practical purposes disqualify him from the presidency?

Analyses of the Annenberg Claims survey highlight the role of viral e-mail in predicting belief in the allegations that we have discussed in this chapter.[85]* Receiving e-mails about the candidates during the final weeks of the campaign increased the likelihood that a person reports believing that Obama is a Muslim, that he pals around with terrorists, and that he had a close relationship with William Ayres. Talk radio played the role one would expect of this overwhelmingly conservative medium. Exposure to it was significantly and positively related to thinking that Obama pals around with terrorists, that he and Ayres were close, and that he was able to buy his home because Tony Rezko purchased the lot next door at full price.

The Obama Rebuttal

The Person Who Lived Basic American Values Cannot Be a Person Who Would Destroy Them

Throughout most of the primary and general election season, Obama's biographical rhetoric telegraphed but did not dwell on his self-identification as African-American, a concept that uniquely signaled the nationality and race of his father and mother. To counter Republican attacks that he was a dangerous liberal and at the same time protect their candidate from insinuations that he was somehow un-American, the Democrats used Obama's biography to establish that he shared voters' values.[86]

Unlike the focus of *Dreams from My Father,* in which he told the story of his search for a racial identity, the narrative Obama unfolded in his ads subordinated his ancestry to an account of love of country and family. "I'm Barack Obama," the candidate stated in a June ad. "America is a country of strong families and strong values. My life has been blessed by both." The life history Obama then related told of admirable individuals who shaped the character and vision of a young man who worked hard and overcame the odds to achieve the American dream. "I was raised by a single mom and grandparents," noted Obama, who then identified with the Midwest (and hence not Hawaiian island or Indonesian) values of his white mother and grandparents. "We didn't have much money, but they taught me values straight from the Kansas heartland where they grew up." Where his white mother and her parents appear in pictures shown full screen, his black father, who walked out on Obama and his mother when the future senator was 2 years old, is shown instead in a framed photo. The values Obama espoused are ones integral to the American self-image: "Accountability and self-reliance, love of country, working hard without making excuses, treating your neighbor as you'd like to be treated." The ad closes with the pledge, "I approved this message because I'll never forget those values, and if I have the honor of taking the oath of office as president, it will be with a deep and abiding faith in the country I love."[87]

When race became an explicit topic of discussion in the Wright affair, the autobiography Obama presented focused not on rancor but on reconciliation. In the March 18 Philadelphia address, the Illinois Democrat made explicit what had been implicit in his rhetoric of "father from Kenya, mother from Kansas," to argue that his was a unique candidacy:

> I am the son of a black man from Kenya and a white woman from Kansas. I was raised with the help of a white grandfather who survived a Depression to serve in Patton's Army during World War II and a white grandmother who worked on a bomber assembly line at Fort Leavenworth while he was overseas. I've gone to some of the best schools in America and lived in one of the world's poorest nations. I am married to a black American who carries within her the blood of slaves and slave-owners—an inheritance we pass on to our two precious daughters. I have brothers, sisters, nieces, nephews, uncles and cousins, of every race and every hue, scattered across three continents, and for as long as I live, I will never forget that in no other country on Earth is my story even possible.
>
> It's a story that hasn't made me the most conventional candidate. But it is a story that has seared into my genetic makeup the idea that this nation is more than the sum of its parts—that out of many, we are truly one.

In her speech at the Democratic convention, Michelle Obama struck the same note by saying that her husband would govern by "bringing us together and reminding us how much we share and how alike we really are."[88]

Attacks on Obama's patriotism suggesting that he refused to wear a flag pin or pledge allegiance were rebutted by the appearance of a flag pin on his jacket and by the skillful use of biography. In an ad titled "Grandfather," the campaign opened by suggesting that Obama shared the same pride in moments of national achievement that other Americans did. In this ad, Obama said, "One of my earliest memories—going with my grandfather to see some of the astronauts being brought back after a splashdown, sitting on his shoulders, and waving a little American flag." As the screen showed a picture of Obama as a boy with his maternal grandfather, he added "And my grandfather would say, 'boy, Americans, we can do anything when we put our minds to it.'" Finally, an invocation of his mother introduced the word "American" and repeated the concept of American values for the third time in the ad. "My mother, she said to herself, you know, my son, he's an American (on the screen the young Obama is shown grinning as he swings a baseball bat) and he needs to understand what that means. She'd wake me up at 4:30 in the morning and we'd sit there and go through my lessons. And I used to complain and grumble. And she'd say, 'Well. This is no picnic for me either, Buster.'" After this exposition of American values, pride in country, patriotism, belief in hard work, the announcer closed, "His life was shaped by the values he learned as a boy." Obama concluded, "Hard work, honesty, self-reliance, respect for other people, kindness, faith. That's the country I believe in." In an ad aired in Ohio, Governor Ted Strickland reported that Obama "is a good and decent person. A loving father, a patriotic American, a sincere Christian."[89]

With backdrop visuals in ads showing that he was raised in a white household by a quintessentially American family, Obama also blunted attempts to tie him to the image of the angry Wright, the felon Kilpatrick, or the Weather Underground radical Ayers. In Obama's ads, his pictures of his father were incidental and photos of his mother and grandparents, central. "My mother died of cancer at 53," Obama recalls in one ad as the photo on the screen shows a smiling boy held by his mother.[90] Testifying to his path to the presidency were prominent white professors, organizers, elected leaders, and icons, including Laurence Tribe, Jerry Kellman, and David Kindler, who talked of his days as an organizer,[91] and newly elected Missouri Senator Claire McCaskill[92] and JFK heir Carolyn Kennedy.[93] In chapter 10, we will suggest that the strategy of reassurance was effective.

Where earlier we cited social psychologist Susan Fiske's important work on stereotype production and reduction, here we include her explanation for the failure of Republican efforts to "define Obama as 'other'":

> People grew accustomed to Obama.... [through] ... an accretion of evidence that Obama is a three-dimensional human being, closer to a smart middle-class professional with a nice family than to a one-dimensional bogeyman.... In the end, voters probably subtyped him as a Black professional, and given that the average American reports being proud of Black professionals, seeing them as competent, good people, this helped Obama's chances. In any event, people learned enough about Obama to complicate any initial stereotypes....
>
> To the extent that non-Black people found him alarming at first, their brain's amygdalae would have been on high alert, vigilant for danger. But they kept encountering him in the least alarming, most reassuring series of nonevents. He never lost his temper. He never appeared hostile.... Frequent exposure to an otherwise fear-inducing stimulus in a safe environment allows people to relax. And they evidently did.[94]

By the time of Wright's reappearance in the independent expenditure ads at the end of the campaign, the Democratic party nominee had succeeded in reassuring voters that his past associations did not bear on his prospective presidency. For practical purposes, by handling the Wright controversy in spring, Obama took it off the news agenda in fall. In the context of an economy in crisis, rehashing a warmed-over controversy devoid of new revelations neither attracted significant press coverage nor moved voters.

Did Race Matter?

On the NAES, we found evidence[95] that race-based perceptions played a role in the votes of some. But Obama's campaign boosted black turnout and white votes outside the Deep South enough to compensate for these anti-Obama ballots. And outside the Deep South, Obama actually gained white support beyond that garnered by John Kerry in 2004.

Since 1968, Republicans have carried a majority of voters who are white. They did so in 2008 as well. However, a comparison of the 2004 and 2008 exit polls suggests that Obama won a higher percentage of white voters (43 percent) than had John Kerry four years earlier (41 percent). Obama's gain is greater in the 2008 battleground states than the nonbattleground ones (figures 4.23 and 4.24).[96] In the states contested in 2008, Obama received 4.13 percent more white votes than had Kerry. In the nonbattleground states, Obama had a net advantage (2.24 percent) over Kerry as well.

In figure 4.25, we isolate the eight states in which Obama lost some white vote share. The greatest loss occurs in the Deep South in states such as Alabama, Louisiana, and Mississippi. He also lost a substantial percentage in Arkansas. Yet he made up for these lost votes in 34 other states and the District of Columbia (figure 4.26). In the remaining eight states, the percentages stayed the same (figure 4.27). Importantly Obama picked up white votes in greater proportions than Kerry in the upper south, an improvement tied in part at least to the organization Obama built in those states in the primaries and to increased black turnout. And the 2008 Democratic nominee drew 7 percent more of the African-American vote and 14 percent more of the Hispanic vote than his 2004 counterpart.[97]

What this all means is that even though race-based perceptions were at play with some voters, in net they did not diminish Obama's chances, because in the states whose delegates he needed to win, he gained white votes. At the same time, black participation rose, as did the percent of the black vote going to the Democrat.

In the exit polls, 7 percent described race as an important or somewhat important factor in their vote. Of white voters who did so, one-third voted for Obama and two-thirds for McCain. Based on their analysis of the exit polls, Todd and Gawiser surmise that "McCain's age may have been a bigger issue than Obama's race. Twice as many voters overall said the age of the candidates was a factor in their vote than those who said race was. And those concerned about age favored Obama by a two-to-one margin, 77 percent to 22 percent."[98] However, as our analysis suggests, the social pressure to suppress negative race-based comments is greater than that associated with dismissing a candidate as too old to meet the challenges of the nation's highest office.

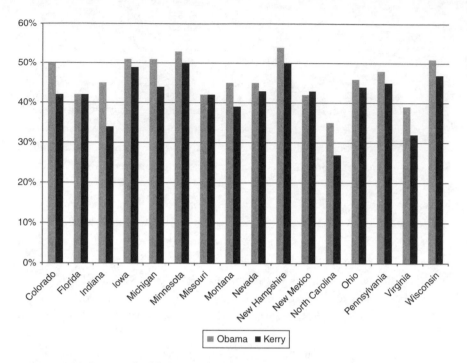

FIGURE 4.23 Percent of White Voters for Obama in 2008 and Kerry in 2004 by Battleground State. *Source*: CNN–Exit Poll Data.

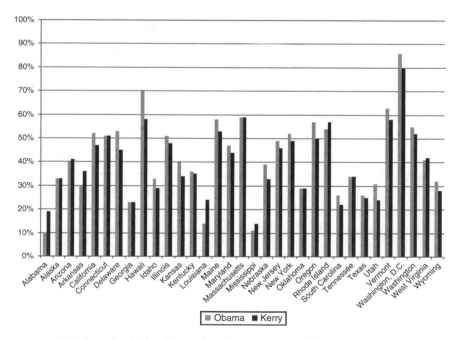

FIGURE 4.24 Percent of White Voters for Obama in 2008 and Kerry in 2004 by Nonbattleground State. *Source*: CNN–Exit Poll Data.

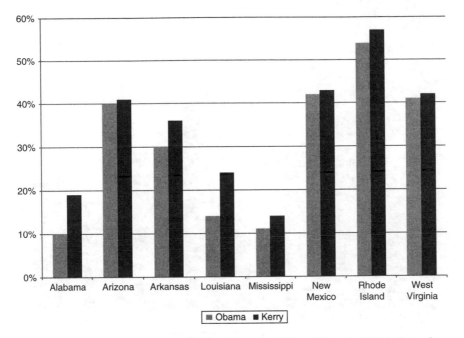

FIGURE 4.25 Percent of White Voters for Obama in 2008 and Kerry in 2004 in States in which Obama Lost Percentage of White Voters. *Source*: CNN–Exit Poll Data.

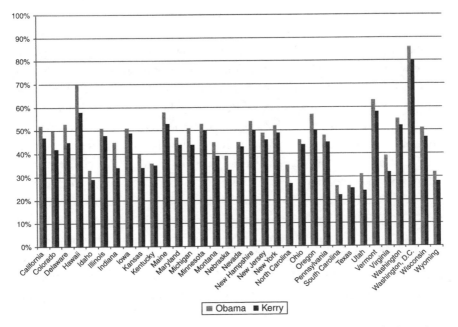

FIGURE 4.26 Percent of White Voters for Obama in 2008 and Kerry in 2004 in States in which Obama Gained Percentage of White Voters. *Source*: CNN–Exit Poll Data.

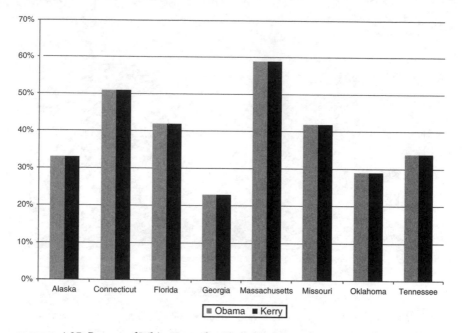

FIGURE 4.27 Percent of White Voters for Obama in 2008 and Kerry in 2004 in States in which there is No Change. *Source*: CNN–Exit Poll Data.

Conclusion

By the time voters balloted, the majority had concluded that McCain's age was more worrisome than Obama's background, however defined, and that the economic change they thought the country needed could better be delivered by the candidate perceived to share their values than by the one considered more experienced. How they arrived at that conclusion is the story to which we now turn. To tell it, we move from the account of the counterposed messages that pervaded the campaign, developed thus far, to the shifts in momentum that occurred in five months of the postprimary season. In service of that objective, we focus first on the advantage McCain gained on the energy issue during the preconvention weeks. Next, we explore the convention bounces for Obama-Biden and McCain-Palin. The Wall Street meltdown dominates our understanding of the early September through mid-October period, in which Obama's fortunes rose and McCain's plummeted. In period four, we track the short-term surge for McCain propelled by his exploitation of an Obama gaffe. We close our analysis of the turning points in the election with our explanation for the widening Obama lead in the campaign's final days.

PART II

Shifts in Momentum:
Five Periods

FIVE

Period One: McCain Gains Energy (June 7–August 22)

❧❧❧

THROUGHOUT THE LATE PRIMARY SEASON OF 2008, NETWORK NEWS translated rising prices at the pump into evocative images of disgruntled consumers. "I even stopped filling a much needed monthly prescription that costs $45 so I will have more money for gas," notes Rosaria Giamei in a mid-May account by ABC's Dan Harris. "[One person] told us the price of diesel fuel is putting her husband's excavating business in peril. 'We can't raise our hourly rates enough to break even,' she says. 'And realizing a profit is no longer an option.' When we tracked her down in Indiana today, she said they may simply close up shop after 32 years in business."[1]

During this period, news accounts fixed blame for the nation's economic woes in part on rising gas prices. "[T]he price of almost everything else seems to be going up, in part because the price of oil controls so much in this country," noted NBC's Brian Williams on February 27.[2] "A fresh wave of relentless bad news tonight, starting with inflation," reported the NBC anchor a month and a half later (April 15). "We all know about high gas and food prices already, but the inflation number that came out today was much higher than even the experts had predicted, with energy prices leading the way." "These record-high gas prices may really reduce the impact of the government's economic stimulus plan," declared Dan Harris on ABC News on April 28. "I would like to go out on a shopping spree to help boost the economy back up," a Connecticut mother of two is shown saying. "However ... I will have to invest in spending money in gas." "When millions of people like Moraima put their rebate checks in the tank," concluded Harris, "most of that money goes out of the country to Saudi Arabia, Russia and Venezuela, instead of to American companies like Apple and the Gap."[3] The implications for the election were clear. "And now what could be a huge issue in this coming November election," forecast NBC's Williams on April 21, 2008, "the cost of energy, oil, fuel, generally getting around and getting every product to market in this country...."

In this chapter, we argue that by championing drilling as a solution to the nation's energy crisis, McCain gained ground in summer 2008. In the world of what might have been, had skyrocketing gas prices dominated the discussion of the economy in the fall and had the Republican vice presidential nominee's argument that she was an energy policy expert enhanced the perception of her preparedness to be president, the contours, if not the outcome, of the general election campaign might have been more favorable to the Republican ticket.

As the last W-2s and 1099s were attached to tax forms on April 15, the presumptive Republican nominee tried to harness his campaign to the news agenda by advocating suspending the federal excise tax on gasoline from Memorial Day to Labor Day. By the end of the month, Democratic contender Hillary Clinton, who remained locked in a tight contest with Barack Obama, was championing the same idea. If, as lay logic but not economic theory suggested, the reduction in the gas tax meant lower prices for consumers, the move would reduce the cost per gallon of gas by the amount of the tax, about 18.4 cents for regular unleaded and 24.4 cents for diesel.

Barack Obama opposed the gas holiday as insistently as McCain and Clinton favored it. Doing so had three strategic advantages for the Illinois Democrat. First, it offered a clear issue difference with Clinton in a contest in which there were few. Second, it reinforced the notion that he was a principled leader able to tell voters things they did not want to hear. Finally, it invited attention to an issue other than his relation with Reverend Wright.

In taking the no-tax-holiday position, the Illinois Democrat was on the side of most economists. Indeed, when pressed, Senator Clinton could not name a single one of that elite class who considered the tax holiday a good idea.[4]

Even if it had an upside, the idea carried large liabilities. Experts reported that the suspension would cost the government upward of $10 billion in revenues—money that would otherwise be spent on improving the nation's transit system. In response to concerns that this shortfall would increase unemployment among road workers and delay needed highway repairs, Senator Clinton advocated a "windfall profits tax" on the oil companies to replace the lost revenue.[5] That tradeoff permitted her to recast the "gas tax holiday" as a plan to "let the oil companies pay the gas tax over the summer."[6] On the issue of lost government revenue, McCain was silent.

Obama had come to his position through experience. The state gas tax moratorium he had supported as a state senator had cost Illinois $175 million, with less of the foregone revenue passed to consumers than advocates had anticipated.[7] "It turned out to have a pretty small effect," reported a scholar who studied the moratorium. "Consumers were slightly better off, but the benefits were spread very thinly, and the government was a lot worse off."[8] Consistent with his posture as the candidate of change, the Democratic front-runner characterized the McCain-Clinton proposal as a typical Washington political scheme that would save drivers a pittance.[9] "Now, the two Washington candidates in the race have been attacking me lately because I don't support their idea of a gas tax holiday," he told an audience in Winston-Salem, North Carolina, on April 29. "This is an idea that, when all is said and done, will save you—at most—half a tank of gas over the course of the entire summer. That's about $28. It's an idea that some economists think might actually raise gas prices." Obama added, "[I]t's designed to get [Senator Clinton and Senator McCain] through an election."[10]

On May 2, 2008, Senator Clinton upped the ante with an ad that, like her earlier challenge to his "cling to guns" gaffe, painted Obama as "out-of-touch":

ANNOUNCER: What has happened to Barack Obama?

WOMAN: Right now we are living paycheck to paycheck.

ANNOUNCER: He is attacking Hillary's plan to give you a break on gas prices because he doesn't have one.

MAN: The price of gas is going up.

WOMAN: It's hard to fill up the tank.

ANNOUNCER: Hillary wants the oil companies to pay for the gas tax this summer—so you don't have to.

ANNOUNCER: Barack Obama wants you to keep paying; $8 billion in all. Hillary is the one who gets it.

MAN: Hillary Clinton is the candidate that is going to fight for working people.[11]

On the suspension, the expert consensus was clear. "More than 200 economists, including four Nobel Prize winners, signed a letter rejecting proposals by presidential candidates Hillary Clinton and John McCain to offer a summertime gas-tax holiday," noted Brian Faler writing for Bloomberg.com. Opposition crossed party lines:

Columbia University economist Joseph Stiglitz, former Congressional Budget Office Director Alice Rivlin and 2007 Nobel winner Roger Myerson are among those who signed the letter calling proposals to temporarily lift the tax a bad idea. Another is Richard Schmalensee of the

Massachusetts Institute of Technology, who was member of President George H.W. Bush's Council of Economic Advisers....

"Suspending the federal tax on gasoline this summer is a bad idea, and we oppose it," the letter says. Economist Henry Aaron of the Brookings Institution is among those circulating the letter. Aaron said that while he supports Obama, the list includes Republicans and Clinton supporters.[12]

Rather than taking on the economists, Senators McCain and Clinton dismissed their views. "I find people who are the wealthiest who are most dismissive of a plan to give low-income Americans a little holiday... Thirty dollars mean nothing to a lot of economists—I understand that. It means a lot to some low-income Americans," Senator McCain insisted.[13] When pressed by host George Stephanopoulos on ABC's May 4 *This Week* to name an economist who supported the gas tax holiday, Clinton responded, "I'm not going to put my lot in with economists."

The spring 2008 debate over the suspension merits a brief digression here because of the unique factors at play. Included in this single controversy were disagreements among political elites (Senator Obama versus Senator Clinton and Senator McCain), intraparty contention (Senator Clinton versus Senator Obama), an interparty contest (Senator Obama versus Senator McCain), and a clash between expert and political elite opinion (Senators Clinton and McCain versus the economists). Put these factors together, and you have a test of the scholarly consensus that: 1) Expert opinion can influence public opinion; 2) citizens use elite cues to form opinions, with the most politically attentive individuals adopting elite opinion; and 3) elite opinion has the greatest impact on public opinion when there is a consensus among elites.[14] Consistent with past scholarship, NAES data on the summer gas-tax holiday suggest that the public accepted elite economic opinion and with it the Obama view of the gas tax holiday.[15*]

Since on Capitol Hill the idea was dead on arrival, the significance of all of this for consumers was nil. "We're not going to interject ourselves in the presidential election," said Senate majority leader Harry Reid on May 6.[16] By contrast, House Speaker Nancy Pelosi unapologetically sided with Obama. "There is no reason to believe any moratorium on the gas tax will be passed on to consumers. That's first and foremost," she told the *Washington Post*. "'Second, it will defeat everything we've tried to do to lower the cost of oil,' noting that Democrats have been trying to shift the nation to alternative fuel sources, not promote gasoline consumption."[17]

What the economists thought the country needed was either an increased supply of energy or reduced demand. Although all three candidates championed alternative forms of energy, none of them—including the solar, wind, biofuel, and nuclear options—could fill that summer's empty gas tanks. Nor were more tankers heading to U.S. shores from the Middle East. In mid-May, George W. Bush's request to Saudi leaders to increase production was rebuffed, just as it had been in January. As news reports were quick to suggest, the rejection was a lesson in the prevalence of political posturing and limits of political rhetoric:

MARTHA RADDATZ (ABC News): (*voiceover*) President Bush made a similar plea last January, back when oil was just over $91 a barrel. Telling ABC's Terry Moran...

PRESIDENT GEORGE W. BUSH (United States): I will say to him that if it's possible, your majesty, you know, consider what high prices is doing to your— one of your largest customers.

MARTHA RADDATZ (ABC News): (*voiceover*) The president was publicly turned down then. Especially hard to take given that, as candidate Bush, he once boasted...

PRESIDENT GEORGE W. BUSH (United States): The president of the United States must jawbone OPEC members to lower the price.

GRAPHICS: OIL PRICES[18]

Although he said he didn't think it would affect prices, on May 19, the president marginally increased supply when he signed legislation putting a six-month hold on filling the Strategic Petroleum Reserve. If the energy source were oil and the solution increased supply, an alternative those concerned about global warming found worrisome, two other proposals were potentially on the table: drilling in the Arctic National Wildlife Refuge, a proposal both McCain and Obama opposed (but which Governor Sarah Palin favored) and lifting the federal and Congressional moratoria on new offshore drilling. While tantalizing, the latter held long-term but not short-term prospects. The Department of Energy estimated in 2008 that "there may be 18 billion barrels of oil in coastal waters, but they also say that drilling for it would not have a significant impact on production or prices until 2030."[19]

For decades, the country's elected leaders had been on the same page on offshore oil drilling. Contributing to that consensus were memories of the 1969 Santa Barbara oil spill that hemorrhaged 200,000 barrels of crude oil across an 800-square-mile region, leaving one of the nation's lovelier beaches soaked in tar and the ecosystem struggling with dying or hobbled sea life. Accordingly, in 1982 Congress enacted and, until 2008, kept renewing the moratorium on exploration of most of the country's outer continental shelf. Underscoring that ban was an executive order issued by President George H.W. Bush in 1990 instructing the Department of the Interior not to lease areas covered by the congressional ban. In effect, unless overridden or extended by his successor, President Bush's leasing ban was in place until 2000. In 1998, his Democratic successor advanced that date to 2012.[20] In practical terms, these decisions meant that a combination of presidential action and congressional inaction would be required to permit drilling from 300 to 200 miles off most of the U.S. coast.

In a sign that the energy problem was worsening, on June 6 the price of a barrel of oil reached $134 a barrel, double that of a year before and up 42 percent since New Year's. "Oil Prices Take a Nerve-Rattling Jump Past $138" read the *New York Times* headline.[21] At the same time, "the Dow dropped 394.64 points to 12209.81. Two days later, the average price at the pump reached four dollars for the first time. Gas prices had jumped 29 percent in a year."[22]

Meanwhile, the political process had produced two presumptive major-party nominees. On June 4, Barack Obama had mustered enough delegates to effectively end the Democratic contest, a fact acknowledged by Hillary Clinton on June 7, when she threw her support to her former rival. Already in general election mode was Arizona Senator John McCain, who had wrapped up his party's nomination fight in March.

As summer approached, bringing with it the year's peak driving times, oil prices remained the filter through which the economy was screened in news.

BRIAN WILLIAMS: The worst fear is that there's a kind of economic perfect storm brewing, and it's heading right for American consumers and workers. Unemployment went up today at a rate we haven't seen since 1986. The big news, the bad news, was the oil market. Oil rocketed up $10.75 a barrel, one day, up more than 8 percent in this one day, to close at $138.54 a barrel. That, we need not tell you, is a new all-time high. That's coming soon, by the way, to a gas pump near you. Then there's Wall Street. The Dow plunged almost 395 points.[23]

By comparison, in January 2001, oil was trading at $32 a barrel.

Until mid-June 2008, the presumptive nominees of both major parties supported the moratorium. So too had Senator John McCain in his unsuccessful presidential bid in 2000. However, with upwardly spiraling oil prices dominating the news and 80 percent in a *Washington Post*/ABC poll reporting that high gas prices were causing them financial hardship, McCain reversed course on June 16 in the name of eliminating "our dependence on foreign oil."[24] This turnabout created a clear divide between the nominees of the two major parties and elicited a radio attack ad by the Sierra Club in Ohio.

Days later, incumbent President George W. Bush endorsed lifting the part of the moratorium under presidential control, a move that placed both the unpopular president and the prospective Republican nominee on the winning side of an issue. In July, Bush followed up by rescinding the executive ban on leasing.

For more than two weeks after McCain's about-face, Obama held to his unpopular position. "When I'm president, I intend to keep in place the moratorium here in Florida and around the country that prevents oil companies from drilling off Florida's coasts," the Illinois Democrat told reporters in Jacksonville in late June. "That's how we can protect our coastline and still make the investments that will reduce our dependence on foreign oil and bring down gas prices for good."[25]

From June through election eve, McCain hammered the Democratic nominee first on his opposition and later on his tepid, calibrated "consideration" of drilling. Beginning in late June and ending October 19, Republican TV ads identified McCain's position with the country's national security and economic interests. Although there was no credible evidence that permitting drilling would yield a short-term increase in supply, some of these ads blamed the Democrats for $4.00 a gallon gas. Aired between June 26 and July 30 at a cost of just under $3 million, a Republican broadcast spot called "Purpose" promised that John McCain "will call America to our next national purpose—energy security. A comprehensive bipartisan plan to lower prices at the pump, reduce dependence on foreign oil through domestic drilling, and champion energy alternatives for better choices and lower costs."[26]

Picking up the refrain for the last three weeks in July, a second broadcast ad backed by a buy of just over $9.5 million contended, "Gas prices. $4. $5. No end in sight because some in Washington are still saying no to drilling in America. No to independence from foreign oil. Who can you thank for rising prices at the pump?" For its answer, the ad cuts to a crowd chanting. "Obama, Obama..." The announcer continues, "One man knows we must now drill more in America and rescue our family budgets." Playing off the Obama mantra of "hope," the ad closed by contrasting empty aspiration with action, "Don't hope for more energy, vote for it."[27]

Couching their bets, the Republicans cradled the drilling attack in a traditional argument about Democratic dispositions to tax. With a total air price of over $3.6 million, a televised spot titled "Celeb" (first discussed in chapter 2) reinforced the message from July 30 to election eve. Amplifying the theme "he's the biggest celebrity in the world, but is he ready to lead?" and using footage of the crowd of 200,000 that gathered in Germany to hear his July 24 speech, "Celeb" stated, "With gas prices soaring, Barack Obama says no to offshore drilling and says he'll raise taxes on electricity. Higher taxes. More foreign oil. That's the real Obama."[28] In its earlier incarnation, the ad raised a rush of press discussion for its inclusion of hotel heiress Paris Hilton and pop music star Britney Spears in its opening pantheon of celebrities. Lost in that talk were the ad's claims about energy, one of which, that Obama would increase taxes on electricity, was called false by FactCheck.org.

After the press buzz about the heiress subsided and Hilton herself parodied the celebrity claim in a Web ad by dismissing McCain as an old man and championing her own energy policy, the McCain team quietly scuttled the images of Spears and Hilton while retaining the rest of the original.

The Obama campaign began its counterattack on July 8 with a TV spot named "New Energy"[29] that aired just under 5,000 times between July 8 and 28 with a price tag of just over $2 million and another called "New Energy-Revised" that carried his message just over 8,000 times from the end of July to the middle of October and cost just under $3.5 million. The first argued that, "On gas prices, John McCain's part of the problem. McCain and Bush support a drilling plan that won't produce a drop of oil for seven years. McCain would give more tax breaks to big oil. He's voted with Bush 95% of the time. Barack Obama will make energy independence an urgent priority: raise mileage standards, fast-track technology for alternative fuels, a $1,000 tax cut to help families as we break the grip of foreign oil. A real plan and new energy." The cornfield pictured in the ad offered farmers in Minnesota, Iowa, and Wisconsin a subtle reminder that, unlike McCain, Obama supported the federal subsidy of ethanol.

The second spot reiterated the first's claims about energy independence, mileage standards, alternative fuels, and a tax cut for families, while linking McCain not to Bush but to Washington. "John McCain," said the announcer. "He's been in Washington for 26 years. As gas prices soared and dependence on oil exploded, McCain was voting against alternative energy, against higher mileage standards." Although one of the two ads attacked McCain's support of drilling, neither indicated Obama's position on that issue.[30]

On drilling and its precursor, lifting the federal moratorium, Obama was on the wrong side of public opinion. As "Celeb" made its first appearances on national cable and in 11 swing states and increased its visibility with no-cost play in cable discussion, a CNN poll in late July found 69 percent of respondents favoring such drilling, with only 30 percent opposed.[31] In the NAES, 66.1 percent of respondents favored the lift on the federal ban.*

With one eye on environmentalists whose opposition he did not want to rouse, the Democrat pirouetted to a position open to some offshore exploration under some circumstances in an August 1 statement in which he insisted that any drilling would be "careful" and "carefully circumscribed." "My interest is in making sure we've got the kind of *comprehensive* energy policy that can bring down gas prices," Obama said in an interview with the *Palm Beach Post*. "If, in order to get that passed, we have to compromise in terms of *a careful, well thought-out drilling strategy that was carefully circumscribed to avoid significant environmental damage*—I don't want to be so rigid that we can't get something done" (emphasis added). The Illinois senator then added, "I think it's important for the American people to understand we're not going to drill our way out of this problem."[32] "It's also important to recognize if you start drilling now you won't see a drop of oil for ten years, which means it's not going to have a significant impact on short-term prices. Every expert agrees on that."[33]

"Obama Shifts on Offshore Oil Drilling," reported an *Associated Press* story.[34] "Shifting from his previous opposition to expanded offshore drilling, the Illinois senator told a Florida newspaper he could get behind a compromise with Republicans and oil companies to prevent gridlock over energy," noted the report.

The next day, the Democrat argued that he had not taken a new position after all. "I made a general point about the fact that we need to provide the American people some relief and that there has been constructive conversations between Republicans and Democrats in the Senate on this issue," he said during a press conference in Cape Canaveral. "What I will not do, and this has always been my position, is to support a plan that suggests this drilling is the answer to our energy problems."[35]

In a separate set of exchanges on past energy votes, McCain deflected Obama's attempts to link him to Bush-Cheney by arguing that on the major energy bill passed during Obama's time in the Senate, it was the Illinois senator who sided with the administration and McCain who opposed Bush's energy plan. Where McCain objected to the bill's "giveaways" to big oil, Obama touted its subsidies for green energy. In news accounts, such as this one on NBC, McCain gained a rare concession that he did not vote in lockstep with the Bush administration, even as he lined up with Bush on lifting the moratorium on offshore drilling.

ANDREA MITCHELL: ... touring a nuclear power plant today, McCain pointed out Obama voted for the Bush-Cheney energy bill three years ago.

SENATOR JOHN MCCAIN: When the energy bill came to the floor of the Senate full of goodies and breaks for the oil companies, I voted against it. Senator Obama voted for it.

With the public supporting drilling, news accounts that suggested McCain's wholehearted and Obama's tepid support advantaged McCain, even when the stories implied that the candidates' changed positions were borne of calculation rather than conviction.

MITCHELL: In fact, as energy prices climb this summer, both candidates have shifted with the political winds. McCain is now a true believer in offshore drilling, which he once opposed....

MITCHELL: ... in recent days, Obama also endorsed offshore drilling as a last resort. And after opposing taking oil from the strategic petroleum reserve to lower prices, Obama now favors it, along with rebates for lower-income people paid for by taxes on oil company profits. Still, experts say the real solution is to use less energy, not more.[36]

Meanwhile the Democrats in Congress scrambled to remove the drilling issue from the national debate and the fall elections with a House-passed compromise bill that permitted some drilling under some circumstances in some places. The process that led to passage in the House provided cover for the presumptive Democratic nominee. "Sen. Barack Obama today [August 4] softened his opposition to new offshore drilling, saying in a speech at Michigan State University that he is 'willing to consider' allowing additional drilling in a limited number of offshore areas if it helps Congress pass energy legislation," stated *U.S. News and World Report*.[37]

With drilling a popular solution, news accounts that primed energy prices and framed them as a cause of the country's dyspeptic economy benefitted McCain. That is precisely what news was doing in the days leading up to the August 16 Saddleback forum:

> SCOTT COHN REPORTING: It is the biggest jump in the prices we pay in more than 17 years. Leading the way: the cost of energy, up more than 29 percent from last year, and food prices up nearly 6 percent overall, bananas up 20 percent, potatoes up nearly 18 percent, rice up 35 percent....

> MR. MICHAEL DARDA (MKM Partners Chief Economist): Households really are caught in a vise here between high inflation on the one hand and falling real wages and falling net worth on the other.

Even as this sort of story shored up McCain's short-term political prospects, its concluding lines warned of a longer-term complication for the Republican campaign. In the foreseeable future, the link between energy prices and the faltering economy would break.

> COHN: But many economists do think this may be the worst of it. Prices have gone up so much that people are starting to cut back. Oil prices are already falling. Trouble is, a slowdown in spending could stall the nation's economy even more. Scott Cohn, CNBC, New York (August 14, 2008).[38]

At Pastor Rick Warren's forum at Saddleback that weekend, McCain forcefully reiterated his position on drilling, while Obama avoided doing so. The importance of the issue is evident in the fact that each worked energy policy into his answer to a question from Warren about something else.

A charting of public opinion across this period suggests that during the month of August, McCain was able to distance himself from Bush (see figure 5.1). Moreover, a snapshot of the electorate before the Democratic

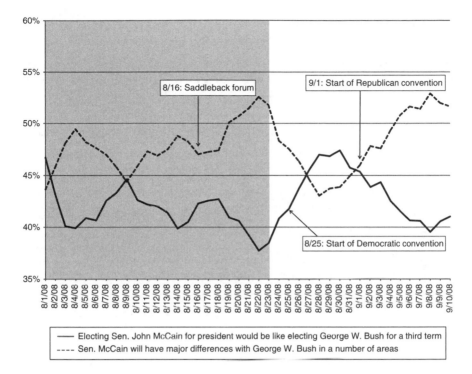

FIGURE 5.1 Perceptions of McCain-Bush Similarity between August 1 and September 10, 2008 (5-day PMA). *Source*: NAES08 telephone survey.

convention reveals that, despite the fact that Bush and McCain were on the same page on drilling, those who supported lifting the ban were more likely to perceive differences between McCain and Bush, even when controlling for a host of factors.*

In our postelection debriefing, the Democrats acknowledged that McCain gained an advantage from the back and forth on energy. "We mishandled the drilling issue," admitted Obama's chief strategist David Axelrod. "Any time you could do something to make yourselves the candidates of change against the status quo politics of Washington, you were helping your candidate. In that one, we walked into a trap.... [Y]ou were willing to do the courageous thing [and] break with the status quo on this issue. And we were not. [W]e stood with the Washington interest group—on this issue. [I]t took us some time to work through that issue. We shifted the discussion to the long term versus the short term. And we made some headway. But we lost 17 points. We had a 17 point lead on energy, when you started the drilling initiative. We went down to zero. And we lost some standing in the polls overall as a result of that."[39]

For the Republicans, the issue was a twofer. Here was a position that gave Senator McCain standing not simply in his area of strength, national security, but also on Obama's natural territory, the economy. It did so in a way that overcame a traditional conservative handicap. "It's difficult for the conservative party's candidate to offer prescriptions," McCain advisor Steve Schmidt notes. "What the energy issue allowed us to do is to be active on an economic issue by calling for an action that the Democrats were opposed to... [F]our dollar gasoline gave us an opportunity on an economic issue to be interventionist, to be active... That was an issue that had resonance and gave us currency all through the summer as well."

The different levels of enthusiasm that Obama and McCain brought to the prospect of drilling were palpable throughout the remainder of the campaign. In the final debate, Obama sounded cautious:

> And I think that we should look at offshore drilling and implement it in a way that allows us to get some additional oil. But understand, we only have three to four percent of the world's oil reserves and we use 25 percent of the world's oil, which means that *we can't drill our way out* of the problem (emphasis added).[40]

By contrast McCain's position was can-do and categorical:

> Well, you know, I admire so much Senator Obama's eloquence. And you really have to pay attention to words. He said, we will look at offshore drilling. Did you get that? Look at. *We can offshore drill now. We've got to do it now.* We will reduce the cost of a barrel of oil because we show the world that we have a supply of our own. It's doable. The technology is there and we have to drill now (emphasis added).[41]

The rolling cross-sectional NAES telephone survey suggests McCain's position on drilling was a factor helping him gain traction against Obama in August, an effect magnified by his defense of that position at Saddleback. Just under one in five (19.4 percent) of our sample reported watching the question-and-answer session between Pastor Rick Warren and Senators Obama and McCain.[42] A regression analysis suggests that watching the forum and favoring lifting the ban on offshore drilling each predicted a favorable rating of McCain in the presence of controls. The interaction between watching Saddleback and favoring lifting the drilling ban also predicted higher McCain favorability ratings. In other words, those who were in favor of offshore drilling *and* watched Saddleback were more likely to think highly of McCain than were those who did not watch the forum or did not favor lifting the moratorium.*

The compromise energy package that provided the Democrats with cover effectively died in September for want of the needed votes in the Senate. Meanwhile, the congressional moratorium on new drilling was lifted by inaction when

Congress failed to authorize its renewal. As these events were unfolding, the entire debate over drilling was being sidetracked as a collapsing economy and reduced demand drove oil prices down and out of the headlines.

The falling price per barrel of crude oil plots the demise of drilling as an issue. Throughout late spring and early summer, the issue had legs. The day before the fireworks of the Fourth of July, at the height of the summer vacation season, oil prices hit a record high. But in a harbinger of difficulty for McCain, by July 10 news accounts indicated that "U.S. drivers [had] cut back their use of gasoline to levels not seen in five years."[43] The effects of the decline in demand were compounded by the disorienting drops in the Dow. As the Wall Street crisis escalated, oil fell to $95.71 on September 16, its first close below $100 a barrel since March. Although on September 23, oil prices surged to $120.92 a barrel, "the biggest–ever one day jump," the figure was an aberration. On October 16, crude was trading at $74.54 a barrel, "down nearly half from its record close in July." With OPEC responding by curtailing production, the trading price had dropped by an additional $10 on October 25.[44] In effect, McCain's first successful argument of the postprimary season was sidetracked on the national issue agenda by the law of supply and demand, the roiling markets, and the heart-stopping anxiety that pervaded a country transfixed by the Wall Street free fall. But for a time in summer, drilling seemed an issue McCain could ride, if not to victory, to a close election.

However, as we argue in the next chapter, one of the effects of McCain's presumed advantage on this topic was its heightened importance in the selection of a vice presidential running mate. The energy issue "was very much alive as we made the vice presidential selection" recalls McCain campaign director Steve Schmidt. "I went back and looked at what was happening in the campaign at the time we made the decision," reported McCain advisor Nicolle Wallace.[45] "A lot of people forget that the top domestic issue, at least in the press, was energy prices, gas prices. We were obviously running on the Lexington Project which was John McCain's initiative to create a path toward true energy independence in America ... [H]e sought a running mate who had done some of the same things he had done, had stood up to special interests, had stood up to her own party, had taken a stand against corruption and was really a doer and a player on the national energy scene."[46]

If the election were an interactive novel in which a campaign could select a plot trajectory and then script its logical conclusion, the energy-framed economy would have been the Republicans' choice. Of the two-thirds of those surveyed in the exit polls who reported supporting expanded offshore drilling, 59 percent voted for McCain and 39 percent for Obama.[47] However, as we argue in chapter 8, the novel the electorate was reading from September 6 through Election Day focused not on energy but on candidate response to the financial sector's meltdown. Before exploring that period, we turn to the conventions and the impact of vice presidential nominees Joe Biden and Sarah Palin.

SIX

Period Two: Impact of the Vice Presidential Selections and Conventions (August 23–September 9)

A S DEMOCRATIC DELEGATES BOARDED PLANES TO THEIR PARTY'S convention, the divinations of Gallup and RealClearPolitics.com suggested that the race was tightening. In the last two Gallup snapshots before the Democrats gaveled their gathering to order, the contest fell within the margin of error. Contrary to the expectations of the pundits and scholarly prognosticators, McCain had taken the lead by the end of the Republican convention in early September. In the following pages, we explore the dynamics created over the two-week period from the Biden pick, August 23, to September 9, a few days after the end of the Republican convention, when a so-called convention bounce was still evident.

In this chapter and the one that follows, we also account for the shifts in perception of the readiness of Biden and Palin to be president from their nominations through the rest of the general election, and ask what difference, if any, their selection made in the outcome. To make sense of the role of the vice presidential nominees in the 2008 election, we have parsed this chapter into four parts: the Biden announcement, the Democratic convention, the Palin pick, and the Republican convention.

The Biden Announcement

In the predawn hours of Saturday, August 23, with the Democratic convention scheduled to open in two days, the Obama campaign sidestepped the press by notifying its supporters electronically that Delaware Senator Joseph Biden had gotten the Democratic vice presidential nod. Minutes after the Obama message landed in inboxes, at 2:22 A.M. the McCain campaign reminded the insomniacs in the press of Biden's past doubts about Obama. "There has been no harsher critic of Barack Obama's lack of experience than Joe Biden," said the Republican cyber-release. "Biden has denounced Barack Obama's poor foreign policy judgment and has strongly argued in his own words what Americans are quickly realizing—that Barack Obama is not ready to be President."[1]

By afternoon, a Republican TV ad had repackaged Biden's earlier assertions that, unlike McCain, Obama was not ready for the Oval Office:

ANNOUNCER: What does Barack Obama's running mate say about Barack Obama?

GEORGE STEPHANOPOULOS (ABC): You were asked, "Is he ready?" You said, "I think he can be ready but right now, I don't believe he is. The presidency is not something that lends itself to on-the-job training."

SENATOR BIDEN: I think that I stand by the statement.

ANNOUNCER: And what does he say about John McCain?

BIDEN: I would be honored to run with or against John McCain, because I think the country would be better off.[2]

That last valentine to the Arizona senator came on Comedy Central's *Daily Show with Jon Stewart,* a venue in which John McCain appeared more often than any other presidential contender.[3] In his interview with Biden, host Jon Stewart posited a scenario in which "You may end up going against a Senate colleague, perhaps McCain, perhaps Frist?" Biden responded: "John McCain is a personal friend, a great friend, and I would be honored to run with or against John McCain...." Seemingly astonished by the answer, Stewart stuttered: "Did I hear, did I hear *with?*" (emphasis added).

BIDEN: You know, John McCain and I think—

STEWART: Don't become cottage cheese my friend. Say it.

BIDEN: The answer is yes.[4]

With McCain and Obama virtually tied in the polls, reporters surmised that the Democratic standard-bearer had both rationalized those earlier admissions by Biden and tasked his senior senatorial colleague from Delaware with blunting them. "Mr. Obama's choice of Mr. Biden suggested some of the weaknesses the Obama campaign is trying to address at a time when national polls suggest that his race with Senator John McCain, the presumptive Republican nominee, is tightening," noted an article in the *New York Times*.[5] "The decision to go with Biden, 65, a Washington insider, over a younger politician with a lesser-known national profile, such as Obama's friend Virginia Gov. Tim Kaine, reflects how tight the contest is between Obama and Republican John McCain," said a write-up in the McClatchy papers.[6]

Where Obama was 47, a three-and-a-half year Senate veteran and identified with change, Biden was a 65-year-old, 36-year Senate veteran and Washington insider whose aborted first run for president in 1988 was derailed by the revelation that he had plagiarized part of a speech by British Labor Party leader Neil Kinnock. "Obama is running on the slogan change we can believe in," pointed out ABC's Jake Tapper, "but the freshman senator selected as his running mate a six-term Senate institution...."[7] "The candidate of change went with the status quo...," concluded the Associated Press's Ron Fournier. "He picked a 35-year veteran of the Senate—the ultimate insider—rather than a candidate from outside Washington...."[8] As blogger Kyle Trygstad observed, Biden "was elected in 1972, the year Barack Obama turned eleven...."[9]

Where Obama had been in the Senate for a bare two years before starting his run for the presidency, by 2008 the long-serving Biden had advanced through the seniority system to the rank of chair the Senate Foreign Relations Committee. Data from the 2008 NAES suggest that the pick marginally boosted public perception that Obama had the experience and judgment needed to be president and was ready to be Commander-in-Chief (see figures 6.1, 6.2, and 6.3). Specifically, positive perceptions of Obama on these traits began to rise on the day Biden was selected and continued to move upward as they were reinforced throughout the Democratic National Convention. By contrast, McCain's selection of Palin did not have the same immediate effect on perceptions of his experience and judgment to be president; however, perceptions of him on these traits did increase after the Republican convention.[10]

The Biden pick brought political plusses. By naming the chair of the Senate Foreign Relations Committee, Obama compensated for his lack of experience in international affairs, a weakness on display in the Democratic primaries when he agreed to meet without preconditions within his first year with rogue foreign leaders, including Iran's Mahmoud Ahmadinejad,[11] a gaffe from which he retreated with the sleight of tongue that said "without precondition" did not mean "without preparation."[12]

A Catholic with working-class roots who had not parlayed his Senate career into personal wealth, the Delaware senator presumably also would appeal to the blue-collar ethnics Hillary Clinton had claimed in the primaries, including those in Pennsylvania, the state that was Biden's childhood home. In a year in which biographical narrative was king, the Senate Foreign Relations Committee chair also

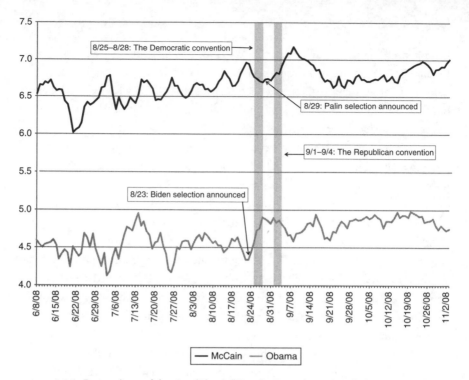

FIGURE 6.1 Perceptions of the Candidates: "Has the Experience Needed to Be President" (5-day PMA). *Source*: NAES08 telephone survey.

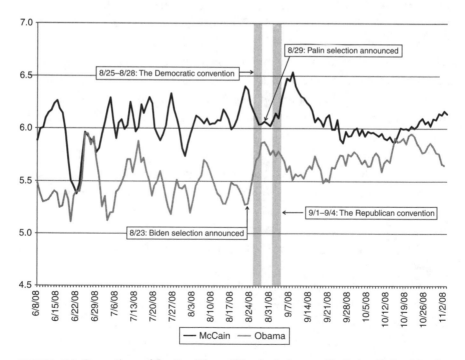

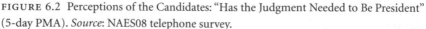

FIGURE 6.2 Perceptions of the Candidates: "Has the Judgment Needed to Be President" (5-day PMA). *Source*: NAES08 telephone survey.

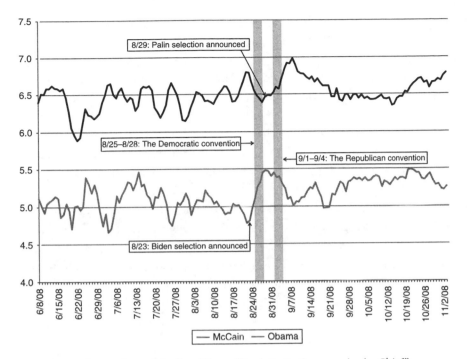

FIGURE 6.3 Perceptions of the Candidates: "Ready to Be Commander-in-Chief" (5-day PMA). *Source*: NAES08 telephone survey.

starred in a compelling story, poignantly detailed by his son at the convention, of raising two young children after the death of his wife in an auto accident.

Biden "turned out to be a great pick for us," recalled David Axelrod. "Barack Obama was more than enough change for people. And they wanted to see him surround himself with some folks with a few gray hairs, and a long résumé... [T]hey wanted to know that there would be people around him to help him implement that change. And Biden really fulfilled that. He also was someone from Scranton, Pennsylvania who had a great profile with middle class voters and spoke to them in a compelling way. We gained some ground after Biden's appointment...."[13]

Still, the Biden candidacy came with baggage beyond the digital record of comments reprised in the McCain attack ad. Where Obama brandished his opposition to the Iraq war to certify that he had the judgment to be president, the senior senator from Delaware, like the junior senator from New York, had voted to authorize the intervention. Biden's defense of that vote was indistinguishable from Hillary Clinton's. Both argued that they had authorized the incumbent Republican to use the threat of war to force inspectors back into Iraq to determine whether the feared "weapons of mass destruction" were hiding there, an explanation Obama ridiculed in the primary debates. Other notable differences lurked in the public record as well, including Biden's disagreement with the Democratic standard-bearer about meeting with disreputable heads of state without preconditions.

Moreover, if the 72-year-old McCain was disqualified by age, what of the 65-year-old Biden, who would turn 73 in the last year of a second term? "As you know, John McCain is an older white-haired man who has been in the Senate over 20 years, voted for the Iraq war, and said Barack Obama did not have the experience to be president," joked Jay Leno, putting the case concisely. "I'm sorry, that's our intro for next week when Joe Biden is on. I'm sorry, I got confused."[14]

In early 2007, reporters dusted off the word "logorrhea" to characterize Biden's[15] patronizing observation to the *New York Observer* that Barack Obama was a "storybook" candidate because he was "the first mainstream African-American who is articulate and bright and clean and a nice-looking guy."[16] Not only did this castor-oil-coated compliment call the intelligence, attractiveness, linguistic facility, centrist political tendencies, and personal hygiene of past presidential aspirants Shirley Chisholm, Reverend Jesse Jackson, Reverend Al Sharpton, and Alan Keyes into question, it also raised the possibility that troubling race-based perceptions lingered, even in unexpected places.[17] Nothing Biden said about the event that occasioned the interview, the launch of his presidential exploratory committee, had the staying power of that self-indicting sound bite. The comment also lit up the phones of conservative talk-radio hosts. "If Biden thinks that Obama is clean, then he has to think that others are not clean," riffed Rush Limbaugh, who asked his audience to imagine the brouhaha had a Republican made such a statement. "... Once [liberals] get off script... they expose their prejudice."[18]

As reporters noted at the time, Biden's remark about Obama was one in a growing list of ill-considered comments. In June 2006, the once and future Democratic contender had said of the increase of Indian immigrants in his state of Delaware, "You cannot go into a 7–Eleven or a Dunkin' Donuts unless you have a slight Indian accent. Oh, I'm not joking."[19] Later in the year, he described his home state as a "slave state that fought beside the North. That's only because we couldn't figure out how to get to the South. There were a couple of states in the way."[20]

In short, the risk from a Biden pick was that, in a foot-in-mouth moment, the VP nominee would call either his own readiness to be president or that of Obama into question. The picture reporters sketched of this facet of Biden's biography was not flattering. "[A] shoot-from-the-lip running mate,"[21] said one reporter. "[A] motormouth who veers wildly off message," observed another.[22] "He can't keep his mouth shut," noted *Newsweek*'s Howard Fineman. "Sometimes he talks before thinking. He is not always a systematic thinker. He loves to hear himself talk."[23] "The central mystery for those who have watched Biden over the years is this," commented *Time*'s Mark Halperin. "[H]ow could someone so smart, experienced, and articulate be his own worst enemy by saying just the wrong thing at just the wrong moment?"[24]

The premise in Halperin's comment explains why the indictments expressed in words such as "motormouth," "talkative," "garrulous," and "loquacious" did not translate into conjecture about competence. The well-known and well-regarded Delaware senator whom Halperin had watched "over the years" was "so smart, experienced and articulate" that it was difficult to understand how he could say the wrong thing at the wrong time. Set in that context, Biden's troubling comments did not register as a window into the candidate's prospective conduct as vice president or president but rather as a sign of unchecked but innocent ebullience. Moreover, although a number of his preprimary comments evoked controversy, they did not undercut his competence as a vice presidential nominee because senior reporters, respected by their peers, took his abilities, and in particular his command of foreign affairs, for granted, a presupposition the little-known Palin did not garner. At the same time, Obama's youth made questions of the qualifications of his second-in-command less central than they would be for the 72-year-old melanoma survivor heading the other ticket.

Moreover, long-windedness had not proven lethal for the only Democrat re-elected to a second presidential term in Biden's lifetime. Joe Biden's interminable questions on the Senate Judiciary Committee recalled Bill Clinton's seemingly endless keynote speech at Michael Dukakis's 1988 convention. Both elicited late-night humor. "Have you watched any of these confirmation hearings for Supreme Court nominee Sam Alito? Senators are given 30 minutes to question the guy: 30 minutes exactly," Leno had observed long before the primary season began. "Senator Joe Biden's question took 23 and a half minutes. His question took 24 minutes. And Alito is smart. He's brilliant. Do you know what he said? 'I'm sorry, could you repeat the question?' "[25]

Biden's vice presidential prospects were bolstered and worries about his tendency to veer off message countered by his concise, competent responses in the 2007 and early 2008 Democratic debates. The would-be vice presidential nominee's most effective rebuttal occurred after debate moderator Brian Williams summarized conventional wisdom about Biden by quoting an *LA Times* editorial that said, "In addition to his uncontrolled verbosity, Biden is a gaffe machine." The NBC moderator then handed Biden a gift-wrapped question, "Can you reassure voters in this country that you would have the discipline you would need on the world stage, Senator?" Not since Ronald Reagan was asked in a general election debate of 1984 whether he was too old to be president had a candidate been handed a question he needed to answer as badly or could respond to as readily. "Yes," replied the senator from Delaware. As the audience realized that that was the full extent of his reply, it broke into laughter.[26]

If Biden's job was providing foreign policy credentials and luring home the nearly 18 million voters who had helped Hillary Clinton dent the glass ceiling, McCain's included reminding voters that Biden wasn't the only prominent Democrat who, in primaries now past, had found the Obama candidacy wanting. Accordingly, 24 hours after the Biden announcement was made, the Republicans moved onto the air a TV ad called "Passed Over" that said:

ANNOUNCER: She won millions of votes. But isn't on his ticket. Why? For speaking the truth. On his plans:

HILLARY CLINTON: "You never hear the specifics."

ANNOUNCER: On the Rezko scandal:

HILLARY CLINTON: "We still don't have a lot of answers about Senator Obama."

ANNOUNCER: On his attacks:

HILLARY CLINTON: "Senator Obama's campaign has become increasingly negative."

ANNOUNCER: The truth hurt. And Obama didn't like it.[27]

The verbal discipline Biden marshaled in the primary debates did not prophesy comparable control in the general election. Later in the campaign, in one of a string of mangled responses with which we will deal in a moment, Joe Biden raised the eyebrows of grammarians and the hormone levels of story-starved reporters when he said: "Hillary Clinton is as qualified or more qualified than I am to be vice president of the United States of America. Quite frankly, it might have been a better pick than me."[28]

The Democratic Convention

The 2008 convention season was the most tightly compressed in recent memory. In just under a fortnight, the Democrats and Republicans named their vice presidential choices, nominated vice presidential and presidential candidates, and applauded the acceptance speeches of the contenders. Consistent with the high levels of public attention paid to politics during the year, viewers tuned in for the key convention speeches in numbers that handily surpassed the totals for 2004. In a sign that the race was not over by any means, Republican John McCain attracted an even larger viewing audience than did his Democratic opponent; Palin outdrew Biden as well.

McCain—38.9 million

Obama—38.3 million

Palin—37.2 million

Biden—24 million[29]

By contrast, in 2004, George W. Bush's acceptance address was seen by 27.6 million TV and cable viewers and John Kerry's by 24.4 million.[30]

Custom dictates that the party peering at the White House through its wrought-iron gates holds its convention first. Accordingly, the Democrats gathered at the Pepsi Center in Denver, Colorado, from August 25–28, with Senator Obama's acceptance speech held before an audience of 84,000 at Invesco Field on the last evening; the Republicans opened their convention on September 1, Labor Day, in St. Paul, Minnesota, and wrapped it up with McCain's acceptance speech on September 4. The unusually late convention dates reflected the campaigns' desire to avoid competing with the Beijing Summer Olympics.

Both campaigns and influential journalists declared the two events a success, a Republican accomplishment made more remarkable by the fact that a hurricane was bearing down on New Orleans as their gathering opened. The Democratic convention "was something we had always counted on as a place to fill in the Obama biography," noted Axelrod. "To make people more comfortable with him." The first day focused on Obama's biography, with the candidate's spouse delivering the final address of the evening. "She had a spectacular speech," noted Axelrod. "Increased her favorables by 12 points in one night. And never looked back after that. The convention accomplished that objective."[31] NAES data confirm that Obama benefitted from his convention. His favorability and, as we noted a moment ago, positive perceptions of key attributes rose during that celebration (see figure 6.4).

The remaining Democratic objective was getting the message out. "The second night we drove the economic message, and the economic contrast," Axelrod notes. "The change versus more of the same message. Hillary Clinton anchored that for us. And she was great."[32] Consistent with the Democratic strategy, NAES data show an increase during the convention of perceptions that electing McCain meant a third Bush term (see figure 6.5).

On the convention's third night, the goal was burnishing Obama's national security credentials, a task ably discharged by recent convert Bill Clinton and newly nominated Joe Biden. "Barack Obama is ready to lead America and to restore American leadership in the world. Ready to honor, to preserve, protect, and defend the Constitution of the United States. Barack Obama is ready to be president of the United States," declared Bill Clinton, who then cleverly suggested that it was the addition of Biden to the ticket that explained the past president's own about-face. "With Joe Biden's experience and wisdom, supporting Barack Obama's

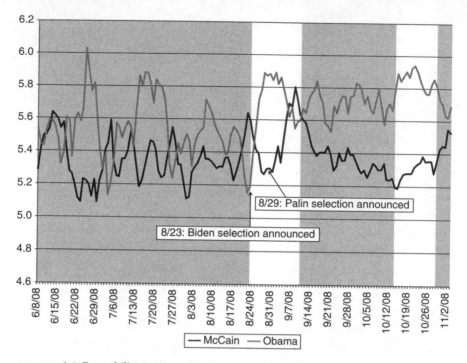

FIGURE 6.4 Favorability Ratings of McCain and Obama (5-day PMA). *Source*: NAES08 telephone survey.

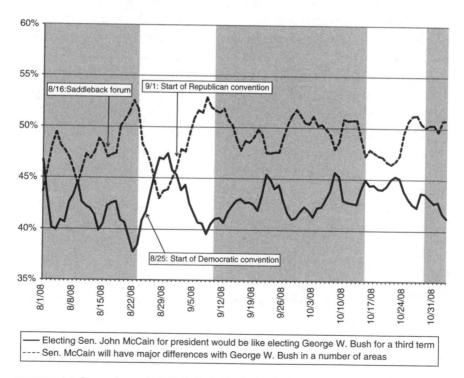

FIGURE 6.5 Perceptions of McCain-Bush Similarity (5-day PMA). *Source*: NAES08 telephone survey.

proven understanding, insights and good instincts, America will have the national security leadership we need."[33] In that statement, Hillary Clinton loyalists could hear that it was only because a person with Biden's experience was on the ticket that the former president considered Obama up to the job.

Biden's Acceptance Speech

Where Clinton's speech was cogently delivered, Biden ad-libbed enough odd comments to subvert major sections of his otherwise well-crafted address. The Delaware senator's extemporaneously delivered add-ons probably would have elicited parody if the order of the conventions been reversed. Had Palin's nomination already raised questions about the competence of the vice presidential nominees, the commentary might have concentrated on the implications of Biden's tendency to misspeak. Instead, the pundits centered their analysis on the strength and sincerity of Bill Clinton's endorsement of the Democratic nominee.

A few of the strange moments in the speech should be sufficient to highlight Biden's problem. Early in the address, for example, the Democratic vice presidential nominee seemed to reveal doubts about his own ticket's ability to deliver the change it promised:

> It's an honor to share the stage tonight with President Clinton, a man who I think brought this country so far along that I only pray we do it again....[34]

Where the prepared text credited Obama with providing health insurance to 150,000 children and parents in Illinois, somewhere between teleprompter and spoken word Biden lost more than 149,000 of them:

> Because Barack Obama—because Barack Obama made that choice, 150 more children and parents have health care in Illinois. He fought to make that happen....[35]

Moreover, read literally, at one point Biden questioned the believability of one of his own indictments of his admitted friend John McCain:

> You know, John thinks—John thinks that, during the Bush years, quote, "We've made great economic progress." I think it's been abysmal. And in the Senate, John has voted with President Bush 95 percent. And that is very hard to believe....[36]

When Biden promised that Obama would "change the change" that we need, one could be forgiven for hearing the statement as a reprise of a widely circulated Web parody by a group called JibJab, in which a "cartoon rendering of Obama" bounds about on a unicorn singing, "The change we must change to the change we hold dear. I really like change, have I made myself clear?"[37] What Biden said was:

> The choice in the election is clear. These times require more than a good soldier. They require a wise leader. A leader who can change, change—the change that everybody knows we need....[38]

Moreover, in a declaration with more than a passing similarity to some for which George W. Bush was pilloried in 2000, Biden asked:

> Should we trust John McCain's judgment when he says—when he says we can't have no timelines to draw down our troops from Iraq?...[39]

"Not the silky orator that Obama is, Biden frequently stepped on his lines and ad-libbed awkward changes to his prepared text," concluded the *Boston Globe*. "But he maintained a clear-eyed sense of outrage directed at the Republican administration, casting himself as the advocate for average folks who've lost ground in recent years and who have seen an alarming decline in American prestige."[40]

And Biden had done that convincingly with passages capturing his bond with ordinary folks:

> Almost every single night—almost every single night, I take the train home to Wilmington, Delaware, sometimes very late. As I sit there in my seat and I look out that window, I see those flickering lights of the homes that pass by, I can almost hear the conversation they're having at their kitchen tables after they put their kids to bed.
>
> Like millions of Americans, they're asking questions as—as ordinary as they are profound, questions they never, ever thought they'd have to ask themselves.
>
> Should Mom move in with us now that—now that Dad's gone? Fifty, sixty, seventy dollars just to fill up the gas tank, how in God's name, with winter coming, how are we going to heat the home? Another year, no raise. Did you hear—did you hear they may be cutting our health care at the company?
>
> Now—now we owe more money on our home than our home is worth. How in God's name are we going to send the kids to college? How are we going to retire, Joe?
>
> You know, folks, that's the America that George Bush has left us.

What ensured that the Bidenisms in the address did not evoke the tag "big, blowhard doofus" that Karl Rove had ascribed to the Delaware senator[41] was the empathy with which Biden conveyed middle-class anxiety. Instead of shouting "doofus," this identification with working-class America transformed his fumbles into a charming sign of authenticity. Biden's off-message meanderings were the antithesis of the "Red Sea-parting" grandiloquence of the Republican parodies of Obama. The audience could overlook "regular–guy" stumbles from a fellow rail commuter who drank his beer from the bottle and remembered what it was like to grow up in a blue-collar household that struggled to make ends meet.

Although, the Democratic vice presidential nominee's speech may have been marred by oddities and eclipsed by the 42nd president, data from the 2008 NAES suggest that it did have a detectable impact on viewers. In the presence of stringent controls, those who watched Biden accept his party's nomination were significantly more likely to hold favorable perceptions of him than nonviewers.[42*] The evidence from the NAES suggests that Biden's speech indirectly affected vote preference by influencing Biden's favorability ratings, which in turn increased our respondents' disposition to vote for the Democratic ticket. Our demographic, party identification, ideology, news media exposure, and candidate favorability ratings controls increase our confidence in the conclusion that the effect of Biden's speech was not merely the byproduct of selective exposure. Taking various factors into account, Biden's speech enhanced the public's favorability ratings of him, which then heightened support for the Democratic ticket.

Obama's Acceptance Speech

On Thursday the 28th, Obama's 42-minute acceptance speech at Invesco Field attacked John McCain's alliance with and allegiance to George Bush, argued that McCain was out of touch with concerns of the middle class, and reiterated the Obama agenda of change. "On November 4th, we must stand up and say: 'Eight is enough,'" said the Democrat. In terms that permitted the campaign to argue that it was doing no such thing, the speech also reinforced the assumption that McCain was too old to be president. "It's not because John McCain doesn't care. It's because John McCain doesn't get it," said Obama.[43]

The flag-pin-wearing nominee also reframed the McCain slogan "Country First" by declaring, "I love this country, and so do you, and so does John McCain. The men and women who serve in our battlefields may be Democrats and Republicans and independents, but they have fought together and bled together and some died together under the same proud flag. So I've got news for you, John McCain: We all put our country first." At the convention's end, the public rated Obama more highly on the trait of patriotism than it had before the convention had begun.[44] NAES data reveal that those who watched some or all of Obama's speech gave the Democratic nominee a rating of 7.2 on a 10-point "patriotic" scale; those who did not watch his speech gave him a rating of 5.2.[45]

The Invesco speech took on the "celebrity" charge as well, with accounts about those, including his seriously ill grandmother, who had shaped the nominee's life. "I don't know what kind of lives John McCain thinks that celebrities lead," said the Democratic nominee, "but this has been mine."

The same evening, McCain aired a gracious ad:

> JOHN MCCAIN: Senator Obama, this is truly a good day for America. You know, too often, the achievements of our opponents go unnoticed. So I wanted to stop and say, congratulations. How perfect that your nomination would come on this historic day. Tomorrow, we'll be back at it. But tonight Senator, job well done. I'm John McCain and I approved this message.[46]

NAES data collected in the six days after Obama's speech reveal that those who watched the Illinois senator accept his party's nomination were more favorably impressed by him than those who did not view the speech. The impact was significant, even when controlling for a host of demographic variables and ideological predispositions. Watching Obama's speech also increased vote preference for the Democratic ticket.*

The Palin Pick

A half day later, the Republicans hijacked news coverage of the Obama's acceptance speech and convention with McCain's announcement of his vice presidential nominee. The statement touting the appointment of the 44-year-old first-term governor of Alaska who was the mother of five, including an infant, telegraphed both that she was like McCain in significant ways and different from Obama and Biden in others. Moreover, unlike any other candidate on the two major-party tickets, she was cast as an energy expert with executive experience. Like McCain, she was a bipartisan leader who had taken on her own party, had a son in the military, and was a deficit hawk. As evidence of her fiscal conservatism, the McCain camp touted Palin's role in stopping a bridge proposed for federal funding by Republican Senator Ted Stevens (R-Alaska) that McCain had pilloried as a boondoggle.[47]

The Republican's choice of Palin caught the Obama team by surprise. In a misstep, its first response was both condescending and counterproductive. "Today, John McCain put the former mayor of a town of 9,000 with zero foreign policy experience a heartbeat away from the presidency," it read.[48] The last thing the Democrats needed was a debate about whether McCain's VP choice had as much experience in foreign policy as the top of the Democratic ticket. Moreover, ignoring the fact that Palin was a governor and instead stressing the limits of her job as mayor was akin to depriving Obama of his time in the U.S. Senate to locate his credentials in his time as a community organizer, a move that Palin used as a rebuttal in her acceptance speech. There she said:

> I was mayor of my hometown. And since our opponents in this presidential election seem to look down on that experience, let me explain to them what the job involved.
>
> (*applause*)
>
> I guess—I guess a small-town mayor is sort of like a community organizer, except that you have actual responsibilities.
>
> (*applause*)
>
> I might add that, in small towns, we don't quite know what to make of a candidate who lavishes praise on working people when they're listening and then talks about how bitterly they cling to their religion and guns when those people aren't listening.[49]

Rather than retreating from the experience issue, the Republicans embraced it. The day before Palin's acceptance address, Steve Schmidt told Katie Couric that Palin "is more experienced and more accomplished than Senator Obama," adding, when pressed, "Barack Obama was in the United States Senate for one year before he took off...to run for president full time. He was a state senator, he had no executive decisions. And 130 times [on] tough votes [as a state senator in Illinois], he took a pass and voted present. Leaders have to make decisions. Governor Palin makes decisions."[50]

Trouble began brewing for the Palin candidacy even before her nomination. Before the first speech was delivered in St. Paul, the Republicans reluctantly revealed that Palin's unmarried teenage daughter, Bristol, was pregnant, a strategic move required to rebut bloggers' insinuations that the governor's four-month-old son, Trig, a child with Down syndrome, was actually Bristol's child. Even before Palin delivered her acceptance address, the campaign was contending with false Internet-flung charges that, as mayor, the Alaskan had removed books from the town library and, as governor, cut special needs funding. "Sliming Palin" was the headline on the FactCheck.org article correcting the viral slurs.[51] Contrary to those e-mails, Palin was Trig's mother, had not removed books from the Wasilla library and had not cut special needs funding in Alaska. However, this onslaught of attacks may explain why the Palin selection did not immediately enhance people's perceptions of McCain's judgment and experience, a finding that we noted earlier.

The McCain team responded to these allegations with the rejoinder that challenges to Palin's qualifications were sexist and press preoccupation with her infant son, evidence of both gender discrimination and liberal elite media bias. "Today, Katie," said Schmidt, "I've been asked questions that are outrageous by the national media. I've been asked questions about when her amniotic fluid started to leak with regard to her last birth. I was asked whether we would make the genetic tests available because she had a Down syndrome child. Members of this campaign went to off-the-record lunches with reporters today, and they were asked if she would do paternity tests to prove paternity for her last child. Smear after smear after smear, and it's disgraceful, and it's wrong, and the American people are going to reject it overwhelmingly when they see her tomorrow."[52]

Palin would make a related argument in her acceptance speech. "And I've learned quickly, these past few days, that if you're not a member in good standing of the Washington elite," she noted, "then some in the media consider a candidate unqualified for that reason alone. But here's a little news flash for all those reporters and commentators: I'm not going to Washington to seek their good opinion—I'm going to Washington to serve the people of this country."[53]

Not all of the rumblings about Palin proved unfounded, however. On the first day of the Republican convention, PolitiFact challenged the veracity of her claim to have stopped the Bridge to Nowhere.[54] In fact, she had favored the bridge before opposing it. As serious for Palin's credibility was the allegation that the Alaska governor had abused her office by firing a public safety commissioner who reported being pressured by the governor to ax Palin's about-to-be-ex-brother-in-law from his job as state trooper. Tagged "Troopergate" by pundits and bloggers, the charges and state investigations of them dogged Palin for the rest of the campaign. Where the Alaska legislature concluded that she had abused her power,[55] the Alaska Personnel Board concluded on election eve that she had not.[56]

With Hurricane Gustav barreling down on New Orleans and bringing with it memories of the incumbent president's inept response to the devastation of Katrina three years earlier, the Republicans decided to abbreviate the first night of the Republican convention. As a result, George W. Bush did not appear in person as originally planned. Meanwhile, on that same evening Obama stumbled seriously by again depriving Sarah Palin of her governorship and comparing his experience to hers:

ANDERSON COOPER: And, Senator Obama, my final question—your—some of your Republican critics have said you don't have the experience to handle a situation like this. They in fact have said that Governor Palin has more executive experience, as mayor of a small town and as governor of a big state of Alaska. What's your response?

SENATOR OBAMA: Well, you know, my understanding is, is that Governor Palin's town of Wasilla has, I think, 50 employees. We have got 2,500 in this campaign. I think their budget is maybe $12 million a year. You know, we have a budget of about three times that just for the month.

So, I think that our ability to manage large systems and to execute, I think, has been made clear over the last couple of years. And, certainly, in terms of the legislation that I passed just dealing with this issue post-Katrina of how we handle emergency management, the fact that many of my recommendations were adopted and are being put in place as we speak, I think, indicates the degree to which we can provide the kinds of support and good service that the American people expect.[57]

There was nothing the Democratic contender could gain either by pointing to experience as a category of evaluation or by comparing the head of the Democratic ticket's experience to that of the Republican vice presidential nominee. Judged by the length of his résumé, Obama was a weak candidate; however, his campaign argued that the prescience evident in his speech against war in Iraq warranted stronger inferences about his readiness to assume the nation's highest office. If his candidacy could be built on one farsighted speech, why couldn't hers be sustained by the decision to take on her own party in Alaska? Moreover, his indictment of Palin sinned by omission. Palin was no longer mayor. Nor did comparing his responsibility as putative manager of his campaign and hers as governor work to Obama's advantage. As governor, she headed a bureaucracy larger than that of the Obama campaign, with a total state budget exceeding it as well. That interview marked the last time that Obama addressed Palin's experience. Instead, for the remainder of the campaign his team stood by contentedly as the press and pundits tested Palin's credentials and responses in interviews against their own expectations of a vice president.

But even as it invited a politically advantageous comparison with Obama's relatively short time in office, the Palin selection undercut McCain's argument that his experience meant that he, and not Obama, was ready to lead. If Palin and Obama's levels of experience were comparable, and the Democrat was unready to be president, then why had McCain placed someone with as limited a résumé as the Democratic nominee's a heartbeat away from the presidency of a 72-year-old melanoma survivor?

As we argued in chapter 3, McCain's age was a well-known fact reinforced by news accounts about a person identified as "Senator John McCain, 71" during the primaries and, following an August birthday, "Senator John McCain, 72" in the general election. Bundle the realities and stereotypes of age together with fears of the melanoma for which he had been repeatedly treated, and the qualifications of his VP pick became more salient. "So let us ask the question that should be on the mind of every thinking person in the world at this moment," noted the founder of Project Reason, Sam Harris, in the *Los Angeles Times* the day of Palin's acceptance speech: "If John McCain becomes the 44th president of the United States, what are the odds that a blood clot or falling object will make Sarah Palin the 45th?"[58]

To make his case, Harris turned to statistics on average longevity:

> The actuarial tables on the Social Security Administration website suggest that there is a better than 10% chance that McCain will die during his first term in office.... Should President McCain survive his first term and get elected to a second, there is a 27% chance that Palin will become the first female U.S. president by 2015. If we take into account McCain's medical history and the pressures of the presidency, the odds probably increase considerably that this bright-eyed Alaskan will become the most powerful woman in history.

To quash the spiraling concerns fed by fears of an unprepared vice president assuming the presidency, a convincing case needed to be made for Palin's readiness. What McCain needed was the 2008 equivalent of Lloyd Bentsen, who had prompted commentators to say that the Democratic vice presidential nominee was even more qualified than the person at the top of his own ticket. But where Dukakis could accomplish this by selecting a senior statesman, McCain had no choice but to go with a younger running mate. Still comparative youth did not necessarily signal either inexperience or lack of preparedness.

The problem for Palin was establishing competence in a 10-week period, when it had taken the skillful Obama more than a year to do the same. The Democratic nominee himself doubted that Palin could manage it. "He told his aides," reported Todd S. Purdum, "that it had taken him four months to learn how to be a national candidate, and added, 'I don't care how talented she is, this is really a leap.'"[59] Where she had a single debate in her foreseeable future, Obama had stood the test of comparison against more experienced alternatives in a fiercely fought primary season, a grueling marathon of debates and repeated no-holds-barred interviews in venues such as *Meet the Press*. Moreover, on primary election night after night, the Illinois senator had delivered victory or concession speeches that increased public familiarity with him and his message. In Obama's case, as we argue in chapter 10, exposure bred not concerns but confidence in his competence.

Although Biden had dropped out of the primaries after the Iowa caucuses, he had by that point participated in more than 10 debates. By requiring that he prepare concise answers to reporters' questions of the day and affording him the opportunity over a more than six-month period to respond to the carefully crafted answers of his peers, that process gave him practice Palin lacked. By contrast, the time between Palin's selection and first major network interview was two and half weeks. With the exception of energy policy, Palin had no reason to be up to speed on the issues facing either Congress or the country as a whole. Finally, as an attractive former beauty pageant winner and sportscaster, she shouldered stereotypes over and above those attached to women in or seeking power. To some, she was "Caribou Barbie," to others a woman reduced to sexualized Photoshopped Internet images. Where Hillary Clinton was cast as a dominatrix by her Internet detractors, Palin was a MILF or WILF, a characterization that surprisingly was mentioned in a *Saturday Night Live* skit.

The Alaska governor's dilemma was plain: since Biden's competence, particularly in foreign policy, was assumed and hers questioned, how could she avoid having every minor misstatement confected into the conclusion that she was not ready to be president? And how in a matter of weeks could she master what Joe Biden had learned in more than three decades on the national scene?

Unlike Palin, a virtual unknown inserted on short notice into the narrative of the 2008 campaign, the senior senator from Delaware also had advantages derived

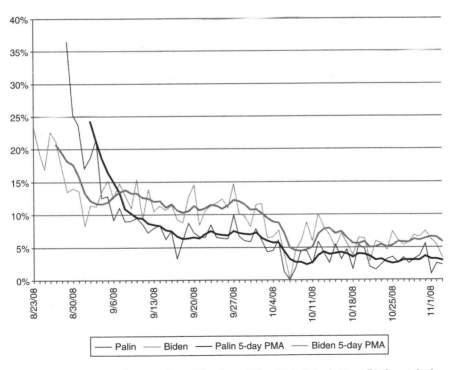

FIGURE 6.6 Percent of Respondents Who Stated That They "Don't Know" When Asked to Rate the Favorability of the Vice Presidential Candidates. *Source*: NAES08 telephone survey.

from decades of contact with national reporters. Introducing a new player guaranteed scrutiny from the press and at the same time increased the influence of media coverage on those voter opinions that were otherwise unanchored in experience with the candidate.

Data from the 2008 NAES indicate that the public quickly formed opinions about Sarah Palin. Figure 6.6 shows the across time percentages of NAES respondents who said that they "didn't know" how to rate the two vice presidential nominees. The day the nation was formally introduced to McCain's running mate, over 35 percent did not know what to think of her; by contrast, less than 15 percent could not express their opinion of Senator Biden in numerical terms. However, the percentage who felt they could rate her accelerated at mach speed. Within 10 days of her announcement, the percentage of NAES respondents saying they did not know how favorably they felt about Palin was lower than the percent indicating the same about Biden.

Palin's Acceptance Speech

In her well-received September 3 acceptance address at the Xcel Energy Center in St. Paul, Minnesota, the self-described hockey mom showed her talents as a campaigner by forcefully defending McCain's positions and stressing her own credentials as an energy expert. Indeed, one might plausibly argue that she was as effective on a teleprompter as Obama. And unlike Biden's speech and despite the fact that her teleprompter was working poorly, hers was fumble-free.

Moreover, she had expertise on an issue still integral to perceptions of the economy. If foreign policy was Biden's calling card, Palin's speech cast energy as her all-purpose issue. Among its other virtues, it certified her bona fides as a maverick:

> And despite fierce opposition from oil company lobbyists, who kind of liked things the way that they were, we broke their monopoly on power and resources. As governor, I insisted on competition and basic fairness to end their control of our state and return it to the people. (*applause*)[60]

Indeed, her convention speech suggested that her actions were already part of the nation's solution to the energy shortage:

> I fought to bring about the largest private-sector infrastructure project in North American history. And when that deal was struck, we began a nearly $40 billion natural gas pipeline to help lead America to energy independence. (*applause*)[61]

The issue also bolstered her national security credentials:

> That pipeline, when the last section is laid and its valves are open, will lead America one step farther away from dependence on dangerous foreign powers that do not have our interests at heart.[62]

And it tied to domestic economic concerns:

> The stakes for our nation could not be higher. When a hurricane strikes in the Gulf of Mexico, this country should not be so dependent on imported oil that we're forced to draw from our Strategic Petroleum Reserve. And families cannot throw more and more of their paychecks on gas and heating oil.[63]

At the same time, her credentials on the issue were stretched to encompass foreign policy expertise:

> With Russia wanting to control a vital pipeline in the Caucasus and to divide and intimidate our European allies by using energy as a weapon, we cannot leave ourselves at the mercy of foreign suppliers. (*applause*)
>
> To confront the threat that Iran might seek to cut off nearly a fifth of the world's energy supplies, or that terrorists might strike again at the Abqaiq facility in Saudi Arabia, or that Venezuela might shut off its oil deliveries of that source, Americans, we need to produce more of our own oil and gas. And...(*applause*)
>
> And take it from a gal who knows the North Slope of Alaska: We've got lots of both. (*applause*)[64]

Having argued that energy policy was what bound the national issue agenda into a coherent reason to consider her ready to be president, Palin then used her newly polished credentials to attack Obama:

> Our opponents say again and again that drilling will not solve all of America's energy problems, as if we didn't know that already. (*laughter*)
>
> But the fact that drilling, though, won't solve every problem is no excuse to do nothing at all. (*applause*)
>
> Starting in January, in a McCain-Palin administration, we're going to lay more pipelines, and build more nuclear plants, and create jobs with clean coal, and move forward on solar, wind, geothermal, and other alternative sources. We need...(*applause*)
>
> We need American sources of resources. We need American energy brought to you by American ingenuity and produced by American workers.[65]

In the days before the Republican convention, news of Palin's selection blunted Obama's convention bounce. After a shaky launch, her widely praised speech at the convention boosted positive perceptions of her with the pundits, the press, and the public. "Tonight [Governor Palin] makes a very auspicious debut as the vice presidential candidate before this hall and a national television audience," noted NBC's Tom Brokaw.[66]

Laced throughout the press comments were evaluations shaded by gender, however. Palin was "charming," "winning," "warm yet tough," even "dazzling," comments a male governor would have been unlikely to garner. "She could not have been more winning or engaging," noted Brokaw.[67] "They loved every minute of her speech," reported ABC's George Stephanopoulos, "...she was funny, she was warm at times, very, very tough at times as well..."[68] Palin was "absolutely dazzling" declared Chrystia Freeland of the *Financial Times*.[69] "[A]n appealing combination of charm and bite befitting her description of a hockey mom as a pit bull in lipstick," observed an editorial in the *Washington Post*.[70] Such characterizations opened the question, would gender play a role in perception of her qualifications to lead?

Interestingly, Hillary Clinton's run increased perceptions among Democrats that the country was ready for a woman president, and Sarah Palin's did the same among Republicans, suggesting that although neither was on the ticket that won in November, their candidacies nonetheless may have broken down stereotypes among those who shared the candidates' ideological dispositions (see figure 6.7).

Where Joe Biden's speech had essentially gotten lost on a night that included an address by Bill Clinton, Palin's elicited both attention and accolades. "Well, let's just start with an obvious point that I don't think anyone has made yet," stated CNN analyst Jeffrey Toobin. "This speech was a heck of a lot better than Joe Biden's speech."[71]

After suggesting that her address "energized" and "electrified" the Republican Party's conservative base, commentators concluded that the Palin pick provided the McCain campaign with a shot in the arm. "[W]hat Governor Palin achieved is something that a lot of Republicans who are here and who are watching didn't think was necessarily possible," commented MSNBC's David Gregory. "And that is that there could be a very energized and enthusiastic base of the Republican Party."[72] By comparing her to the Gipper, *Associated Press* writers paid Palin the ultimate compliment a Republican aspirant can receive. "[T]he former TV sportscaster spoke in calm, TV-friendly tones reminiscent of Ronald Reagan. Like the former GOP president, Palin warmed the crowd with quips and jokes."[73]

The Alaska governor's convention debut left little doubt that like the hockey moms to whom she affectionately applied the label, Palin was ready be the ticket's "pit bull with lipstick," whose presence on the ticket "should scare Democrats,"[74] and

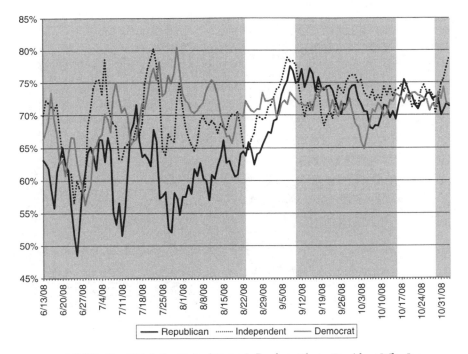

FIGURE 6.7 "Do You Think the United States Is Ready to Elect a President Who Is a Woman, or Not?" by Party Identification (5-day PMA). *Source*: NAES08 telephone survey.

who was "a force to be reckoned with,"[75] who landed "some pretty good zingers,"[76] "tagged Democratic candidate Barack Obama as an elitist"[77] and "wowed the Republican convention using wit, sarcasm, charm and ridicule in a full scale assault on a now familiar cast of GOP targets: an elitist adversary, biased media and high taxes."[78]

Data from the NAES indicate that, like Biden's speech, the Republican vice presidential nominee's address improved people's general impressions of her. Those who saw Palin's national debut gave her significantly higher favorability ratings than those who did not see her speech. This finding was detected even when demographic characteristics, party identification, ideology, news media exposure, and people's favorability ratings of McCain, Obama, and Biden were taken into consideration. As with Biden's remarks, Palin's did not directly affect vote preference but did so indirectly by increasing people's favorable impressions of her, which in turn influenced their vote choice.*

Although the press's effusive reception of Palin's convention speech went part of the way toward vindicating McCain's choice, news accounts also noted the presence of concerns about the first-term governor's readiness to be president.

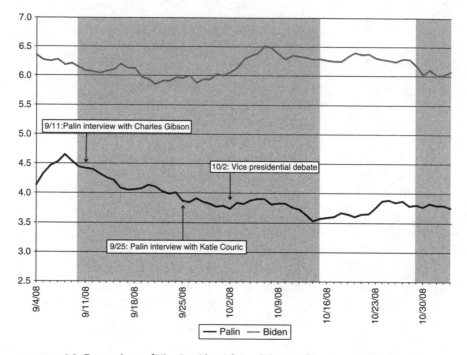

FIGURE 6.8 Perceptions of Vice Presidential Candidates as "Ready to Be President" (5-day PMA). *Source*: NAES08 telephone survey.

"Ms. Palin's appearance electrified a convention that has been consumed by questions of whether she was up to the job, as she launched slashing attacks on Mr. Obama's claims of experience," noted Elisabeth Bumiller and Michael Cooper in the *New York Times*.[79] Despite the fact that her acceptance speech increased the public perception that she was ready to be president, from the time of her announcement through the general election Palin's perceived readiness never exceeded Biden's in our rolling cross-sectional telephone survey (figure 6.8).[80]

McCain's Acceptance Speech

Palin's speech wasn't the only one that was well received at the Republican convention. The success of John McCain's acceptance address was reflected in news accounts as well. "McCain spoke movingly about his years as a prisoner of war in Vietnam," noted an article in the *Boston Globe*, "and how it changed him from a selfish and brash young man to a mature 'servant' of his country. 'I've never lived a day, in good times or in bad, that I don't thank God for that privilege,' he said."[81]

Both Barack Obama and John McCain filled out their life stories in their acceptance addresses. In an account that CNN's David Gergen called "moving,"[82] McCain recounted his experiences in the Hanoi Hilton and then translated that biography into a pledge of future service. "Sen. John McCain of Arizona completed a long and often improbable journey to the Republican presidential nomination Thursday night," noted the report in the *Washington Post*, "offering himself as an 'imperfect servant' who will never surrender in his fight to change Washington and the country."[83]

Where Barack Obama linked McCain to Bush and claimed the mantle of change, McCain distanced himself from the unpopular incumbent by stressing his record of bipartisan reform. Reporters also took note of the fact that the Arizonan spoke "bluntly and at length of the economic concerns of middle-income Americans—directly taking on the theme Sen. Obama increasingly has made the centerpiece of his campaign."[84]

In St. Paul, the candidate who in the past seemed to be at war with a teleprompter and confounded by text delivered the best speech of his campaign. "Through it all," David Brooks observed in the *New York Times*, "he communicated his burning indignation at the way Washington has operated over the last 12 years.... And this passion for change, combined with his proven and evident integrity, led to the crescendo of raw energy that marked this convention's conclusion."[85]

The McCain speech even elicited favorable comparisons to the one delivered by his counterpart a week earlier. CNN's Anderson Cooper, for example, noted that from John McCain, "we heard in his acceptance speech, a lot of specifics, arguably more specific than we heard in Barack Obama's acceptance speech."[86]

NAES data show that McCain's favorability ratings rose among those who watched his convention speech. His speech indirectly influenced people's vote preference by positively affecting favorability ratings of him.*

Like the Democrats, the Republicans concluded that their convention had done what it needed to do. "We had succeeded—in what our goal was," recalled Steve Schmidt. "We distanced ourselves from the unpopular administration [and] restored McCain's maverick appeal, his reform appeal. We had made significant incursions into the middle of the electorate, and we had excited the base."[87] As figure 6.5 suggests, the Palin pick, McCain speech, and Republican convention undid much of the work the Democrats had done to that point in tethering McCain to George W. Bush. The Republican convention also managed to swing momentum in the Republican ticket's direction when it came to the public's vote preference (see figure 6.9).

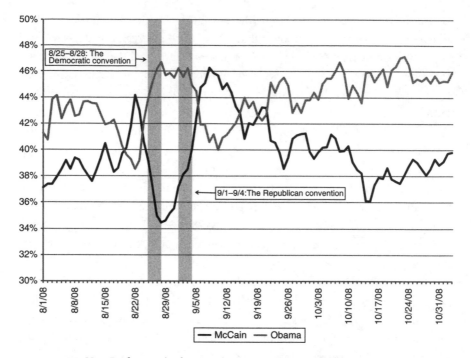

FIGURE 6.9 Vote Preference (5-day PMA). *Source*: NAES08 telephone survey.

Conclusion

Both tickets benefitted from their conventions. Vote preference for Obama increased during the Democratic gathering and for McCain during the Republican one. After the convention period, the gap in vote preference that had opened in Obama's favor during the Democrat's celebration had once again closed. For the second time in a two-month period, the polls seemed to be confounding the forecasters' models. Indeed, the Republicans appeared to have gained momentum coming out of their convention, with enthusiasm for Palin driving part of that gain. But where at the beginning of September the public perception of Biden's readiness to be president was securely in place, Palin's perceived preparedness was the weakest of any of the four on the two major-party tickets. And it would fall in the coming weeks.

In the next period, September 10–October 14, Republican hopes were dashed by the unanticipated economic crash and McCain and Obama's dissimilar responses to it. Before exploring those dynamics, we pause in our analysis of the five periods into which we have segmented the election to ask, "What impact, if any, did the vice presidential nominees have on the general election and its outcome?" It is to that question that we turn in the next chapter.

SEVEN

The Impact of Sarah Palin
and Joseph Biden

❧

V ICE PRESIDENTIAL CANDIDATES ARE SELECTED FOR A VARIETY
of reasons, among them, helping the nominee carry the running mate's
home state or region,[1] creating ideological balance in an effort to shore
up a vital constituency,[2] and compensating for the presidential candidate's limitations in background, temperament, or expertise. A vice presidential pick can also
be designed to unify factions within a party and broaden the appeal of the ticket.[3,4]
"If it is impossible to find one person who combines within his or her heritage,
personality, and experience all the virtues allegedly cherished by American voters,"
wrote Nelson Polsby and Aaron Wildavsky, "the parties console themselves by
attempting to confect out of two running mates a composite image of forward-
looking-conservative, rural-urban, energetic-wise leadership that evokes hometown, ethnic, and party loyalties among a maximum number of voters. That, at
least is the theory behind the balanced ticket."[5]

In the last chapter, we telegraphed some of the reasons for the two major party's vice presidential picks. Securing home state electoral votes wasn't a factor in
either selection. There was little doubt that the Democrats would carry Delaware's
electoral votes and the Republicans, Alaska's. However, each pick did balance the
ticket, although in different ways. Delaware Senator Joseph Biden added foreign
policy experience and Washington know-how to the Democratic ticket. Governor
Sarah Palin shored up the Republican Party's conservative base and, Republicans
hoped, would appeal to at least some of the women who flocked to Hillary Clinton's candidacy. Like McCain, she was a reformer with a reputation for reaching
across the aisle. At the same time, at the end of a summer dominated by concerns
about gas prices, she carried energy credentials developed while governing an

oil-rich state. And, as McCain's leadership team stressed in the Annenberg debriefing, the Palin pick was meant to serve as "a game changer."[6] In short, Biden helped Obama establish that he was ready to lead, while Palin boosted McCain's argument that the Republican ticket consisted of mavericks who represented a break with Bush and Washington-based "politics as usual."

At the same time, as we argued in the last chapter, each pick opened vulnerabilities. Palin's scant résumé undercut the 72-year-old melanoma survivor's argument that the country required leadership forged by experience. Compounding the challenge facing the Alaska governor was the fact that what background she had was secured in a state far from the centers of national discussion and power. Where in the eyes of the Washington press corps, Biden's Congressional record and his early primary season debate performances confirmed his competence, the country's top reporters raised suspicions about hers when the Republican campaign initially put off their requests for interviews with Governor Palin. The Democratic vice presidential choice wasn't problem-free either. In Biden's case, the prospect that one of his off-handed remarks would derail the campaign was the nightmare scenario.

Despite these risks and potential rewards, conventional wisdom shouts that because citizens vote the top of the ticket, the vice presidential selection doesn't usually affect the electoral vote tallies. The exceptions include JFK's selection of Lyndon Johnson in 1960, which helped him carry Texas and swung a close election to the Massachusetts senator, and Bill Clinton's 1992 choice of Al Gore, which helped the Democratic ticket carry Gore's native state of Tennessee.[7] However, as John Kerry learned in 2004, the calculus that says that home state votes follow a vice presidential nominee into that ticket's electoral column is iffy at best. (Indeed, it is not necessarily a given that the top of the ticket will accomplish that feat in his own state. After all, had Gore managed it in 2000, he would have won the electoral college as well as the popular vote.)

Although judiciously chosen running mates have occasionally carried a key electoral state, there is little evidence that those widely perceived as ill-qualified have decisively damaged their ticket's chances. The cases in which an underwhelming choice became vice president include 1972, when Richard Nixon tapped Maryland Governor Spiro Agnew, who resigned in the second term after pleading nolo contendere to corruption charges, and 1988, when Indiana Senator Dan Quayle's performance in the vice presidential debate introduced the metaphor "deer caught in the headlights" into the political lexicon. In each of those years, Democratic ads asked which of the two major-party vice presidential picks was "your choice" to be "a heartbeat away from the presidency," a question posed with confidence that the answer was neither "all of the above" nor "the Republican party's nominee." The corollary holds as well. Cases in which a ticket failed despite the presence of a vice presidential nominee whom the public regarded more favorably than either major party's presidential contender include 1968 and 1988. In those years, survey data suggest that voters considered Edmund Muskie (1968) and Lloyd Bentsen (1988) better presidential timber than those at the top of either ticket.[8]

In sum, there aren't ready instances in which a disparaged vice presidential contender cost his party the presidency. Pose a less stringent test, however, and it is possible that under some circumstances a vice presidential candidate can drive voter defection. Among those who prefer the presidential candidate on one ticket and the vice presidential on another, feelings about the second in command may create a net influence on votes. So, for example, when Wattenberg combined "all 824 cases of major-party voters with [such] split preferences in the American National Election Study data sets for the years 1968 through 1992," he found that "15.6% of voters defected from their presidential preference. By comparison, those voters with consistent presidential and vice presidential preferences defected only 2.9% of the time."[9] In a close election, that level of defection could swing an outcome.

Before trying to ascertain the effect, if any, of their presence in the race, we will highlight those moments in which something the vice presidential nominees said or something that was said about them may have mattered. To make sense of all this, we've parsed this chapter into a first and longer section devoted to analysis of Governor Sarah Palin's performance and a second focused on two gaffes by Democratic nominee Joseph Biden that were exploited by the McCain campaign. Aware that our examination of their October 2 debate doesn't fit neatly into this organizational structure, we arbitrarily assign that discussion to the portion of the chapter devoted to the Alaska governor.

Because both vice presidential nominees experienced ups and downs in the general election and each helped the top of the ticket in some ways and hurt in others, our argument in this chapter is not a simple one. Of interest to us here are the questions, "How and when did the vice presidential candidates have an effect on their tickets? And what ultimate effect, if any, did they have?"

To make sense of Governor Palin's postconvention candidacy, we concentrate on six events: the Gibson-Palin interview whose first part was aired on ABC on September 11, the Couric-Palin question-and-answer sessions whose initial segment was broadcast on CBS on September 25, the parodies of Palin that *Saturday Night Live* laced throughout the general election, attacks on Palin's competence from the Right, the vice presidential debate of October 2, and General Colin Powell's attack on Palin's readiness in his October 19 endorsement of Obama-Biden. Our examination of Biden centers on two of his comments exploited by the McCain campaign, the first on September 17 that the Democratic ticket did not support so-called clean coal, when in fact Obama did, the second his forecast on October 19 that within his first six months as president, Obama would be tested by a foreign power.

In this chapter, we draw on NAES data to argue Palin's presence on the Republican ticket was a mixed blessing that over time became a curse. On the plus side of the ledger, the Alaska governor generated enthusiasm among conservatives and helped propel McCain to his one postconvention lead in the polls. On the minus side, after that bounce dissipated, drops in her popularity predict a decline in support for McCain. One explanation for this finding is that Palin's fumbles provided a context for commentators to voice concern about McCain's age at the same time that McCain's age heightened discussion of her readiness. And, as we noted in chapter 2, the perception that McCain was too old to be president forecast a vote for Obama and against McCain.

Although she initially bolstered the prospects of the Republican ticket among high school-educated women earning less than $50,000 a year, Palin's ultimate impact on this key voting block was negative. The public's confidence in Palin's competence was eroded not by her performance in the vice presidential debate, where she held her own, but rather by her meandering nonresponses to some of the questions asked her by CBS's Katie Couric. Compounding Palin's problems was look-alike Tina Fey's *Saturday Night Live* send-up of Palin, a comedic routine that, among other moments, featured the Couric interview and included an appearance by Palin herself. Also harming the Alaskan's standing with voters was the indictment of her extremism that General Colin Powell incorporated into his October 19 endorsement of Barack Obama and Joseph Biden.

Meanwhile, Biden's perceived readiness was damaged by his observation that the country needed to prepare itself for the prospect that in his early months as president Obama would elicit a challenge from adversaries abroad. However, as we suggested in the last chapter, picking the Delaware senator also boosted perceptions of Obama's readiness to be president. Overall, the presence of Biden on the Democratic ticket had less effect on its chances one way or the other than did Palin's on the other side.

Where in earlier chapters in this section of the book we have focused on a limited number of weeks (or, in the case of period one, of months) at a time, here we range across the general election unconstrained by our period-based organizational structure. This cross-election analysis of the vice presidential nominees will free us in the following chapters to concentrate on the interplay between McCain and Obama.

September 11: The Gibson-Palin Interview

When the McCain campaign did not capitalize on its convention bounce by quickly making Governor Palin accessible for either a news conference or extended TV or print interviews by mainstream reporters, the decision fueled press speculation about her competence. The ABC interview segments that marked her break from the campaign's cocoon raised more questions about her than they answered.[10] "Now that we've seen the entirety of the Palin-Gibson tete-a-tete," wrote conservative Ross Douthat of the ABC segments aired early in September, "I concur with [fellow conservatives] Rich Lowry and Rod Dreher. The most that can be said in her defense is that she kept her cool and avoided any brutal gaffes; other than that, she seemed about an inch deep on every issue outside her comfort zone. .... [T]here's no way to look at her performance as anything save supporting evidence for the non-hysterical critique of her candidacy—that it's just too much, too soon—and a splash of cold water for those of us with high hopes for her future on the national stage."[11] On September 18, Republican senator from Nebraska Chuck Hagel joined the chorus of critics with the observation, "She doesn't have any foreign policy credentials. ... You get a passport for the first time in your life last year? I mean, I don't know what you can say. You can't say anything."[12]

The Gibson-Palin interview also revealed to an audience estimated at 9.7 million[13] that some of the expertise on energy on which the case for her nomination had been built was illusory:

> PALIN: Let me speak specifically about a credential that I do bring to this table, Charlie, and that's with the energy independence that I've been working on for these years as the governor of *this state that produces nearly 20 percent of the U.S. domestic supply of energy*, that I worked on as chairman of the Alaska Oil and Gas Conservation Commission, overseeing the oil and gas development in our state to produce more for the United States.[14] (emphasis added)

As FactCheck.org noted, "It's simply untrue that Alaska produces anything close to 20 percent of the U.S. 'energy supply,' a term that is generally defined as energy *consumed*. That category includes power produced in the U.S. by nuclear, coal, hydroelectric dams and other means—as well as all the oil imported into the country."[15] "Palin Exaggerates Alaska's Energy Role" read the headline in the *Washington Post*.[16]

NAES data reveal that watching the interview had a significantly negative effect on white women's perceptions that the Alaska governor was ready to be president.* Since the Palin pick was intended in part at least to appeal to women, the fact that her mainstream media debut instead seemed to dissuade them was a problem for the Republicans.

As one would expect, party identification affected one's response to the interview. Viewing the Gibson-Palin exchange had no impact on Democrats, presumably because they were already predisposed to discount her credentials and competence. However, after watching it, Republicans were somewhat more likely to believe that she was ready to be president.* Also, independents who tuned in were marginally more likely to believe that she was ready. However, since only one-third of independents believed that she was up to the job to begin with, this slight improvement in perception didn't help much.

The Couric-Palin Interview

Palin's command of policy in the Gibson interview seems masterful compared with the level on display in the exchanges with CBS's Katie Couric that began airing September 25. Some of the Alaska governor's nonanswers were problematic in part because viewers could so easily imagine themselves responding to them.[17] For example, Palin replied to a question about "what newspapers and magazines" she regularly read by saying, "I've read most of them again with a great appreciation for the press for the media, I mean…" and when pressed, "Um, all of 'em, any of 'em that um have been in front of me over all these years, um…I have a vast variety of sources where we get our news too. Alaska isn't a foreign country where it's kind of suggested it seems like, 'wow how could you keep in touch with what the rest of Washington, D.C., may be thinking and doing, when you live up there in Alaska.' Believe me, Alaska is like a microcosm of America."

Sensing vulnerability and verifying the axiom that humor works by reinforcing what is already believed, comedians lambasted Palin by likening her to Bush. "Critics are still analyzing Sarah Palin's interview with Katie Couric last week, and they're saying she was halting, repetitive, and stumped on basic questions. Yeah, in other words, Palin appeared very presidential," said NBC's Conan O'Brien.[18] "Have you been watching the Sarah Palin interview with Katie Couric on the *CBS Evening News?*" asked CBS's David Letterman. "Pretty interesting. Sarah Palin could not remember the name of a newspaper or a magazine that she reads. And I was thinking, wow, we could possibly have a leader of the country who doesn't read. And then I thought, well, hell it's worked pretty good for George Bush."[19] "Sarah Palin, she's getting ready for tomorrow's debate. I understand she now knows all three branches of government," added NBC's Jay Leno.[20] These comedic riffs added a new line of argument to the Democratic one that McCain would extend Bush's policies. Where the Obama campaign was arguing that, like Bush, McCain was out of touch, these jokes suggest that Palin is like Bush because neither was firing on all cylinders.

Although the effects of the attacks by conservative critics and the caricature by Tina Fey are difficult to separate from exposure to the Couric interview, our data show that people who reported being more likely to see information about the 2008 presidential campaign on CBS than on other broadcast or cable television outlets were more inclined to rate Palin negatively on our "ready to be president" question than were people who did not report CBS as their most often seen broadcast or cable source about the campaign, a finding circumscribed by the fact that CBS's viewers tend to be less conservative and more Democratic than those who rely on other channels for news.[21]*

The Palin Parody on *Saturday Night Live*

In a lethal caricature, former *Saturday Night Live* "weekend anchor" Tina Fey returned to the show to import whole passages from the Couric-Palin exchange into a farcial re-creation. The similarity between Palin's actual answers and Fey's reprise of them was so marked, and the fact that Fey's version was the more coherent of the two, so obvious, that MSNBC's liberal provocateur Keith Olbermann simply juxtaposed them to indict Palin:

SARAH PALIN: Every American I'm speaking with were ill—

TINA FEY (*Saturday Night Live*): Like every American I'm speaking with, we are ill.

PALIN: But ultimately, what the bailout docs is help those who are concerned about the health care reform that is needed—

FEY: But ultimately, what the bailout does is help those that are concerned about the health care reform that is needed to help shore up our economy.

PALIN: Helping the   it's got to be all about job creation.

FEY: It's got to be all about job creation, too.

PALIN:—to shoring up our economy and putting it back on the right track.[22]

FEY: Also to shoring up our economy and putting Fannie and Freddie back on the right track.[23]

When at a loss for an answer, Palin had told Couric that she'd have to get back to her, a moment Fey morphed into the catchphrase contestants use in a popular television game show:

FEY (as Palin): Katie, I'd like to use one of my lifelines.

AMY POELER (as Couric): I'm sorry?

FEY (as Palin): I want to phone a friend.[24]

"I'd like to use one of my lifelines" was one of two of Fey's comments that entered popular culture as emblems of Palin's cluelessness. The second was a recasting of her statement that the proximity of Russia to Alaska established her foreign policy credentials. One blogger, Chris Weigant, gave Fey his award for best political theater for her riff on the line. What Palin had said was, "As Putin rears his head and comes into the airspace of the United States of America, where do they go? It's Alaska. It's just right over the border."[25] "Palin's own words needed no satirizing, they were ridiculous enough on their own, and they needed a very light comedic touch in order to make them even more hilarious," noted Chris Weigant. "And Fey uttered the immortal line (which got quoted more than anything Palin actually said)—'I can see Russia from my house!'"[26]

The Palin parodies attracted a sizeable broadcast and Internet audience. Overall, the online tracking service Visual Measures reported that *SNL* Palin skits drew more than 63 million views. A representative of that firm observed that online sharing of the *SNL* segments meant that it was effectively the "top TV show on the Web."[27] Especially popular in that venue was Fey as Palin in the Couric interview. Although a tally of hits doesn't translate into a measure of discrete numbers of viewers, the Internet segment attracted more than 10 million views.

The *SNL* skits increased the show's audience and with it the potential damage to Palin. On the night it aired, that program's parody of the Palin-Couric interview drew 10 million viewers.[28] An even larger audience of 15 million, *SNL*'s largest audience in 14 years, tuned in for the Fey-Palin joint appearance on October 18.[29]

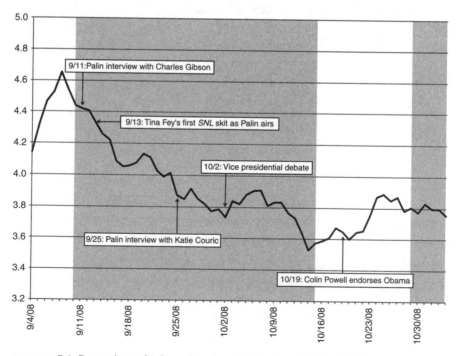

FIGURE 7.1 Perceptions of Palin as "Ready to Be President" (5-day PMA).
Source: NAES08 telephone survey.

NAES data suggest that exposure to the *SNL* caricatures hurt Palin's prospects. Those who regularly watched *Saturday Night Live* were more likely to contend that she was not ready to be president.* The relationship between *SNL* watching and the conclusion that Palin was unready for the presidency was especially pronounced with independents, a group whose support McCain had to draw to win the election. As audiences processed her faltering responses to the Couric interview and as the effects of Tina Fey's impersonation of Palin as cheerily clueless set in, perceptions of her readiness to be president dove (figure 7.1).

Palin Is Attacked from the Right

Some conservatives were as unsympathetic to Palin as was Fey's portrayal. Right-of-center columnist Kathleen Parker even called on the Alaskan to withdraw from the race. "Only Palin can save McCain, her party and the country she loves," wrote Parker. "She can bow out for personal reasons, perhaps because she wants to spend more time with her newborn. No one would criticize a mother who puts her family first."[30] "Palin's recent interviews with Charles Gibson, Sean Hannity and now Katie Couric have all revealed an attractive, earnest, confident candidate. Who Is Clearly Out Of Her League," Parker argued. "Palin filibusters. She repeats words, filling space with deadwood. Cut the verbiage, and there's not much content there." The week before the vice presidential debate, conservative columnist George Will lobbed a hand grenade by telling an audience that Palin is "obviously not qualified to be president," and calling her CBS interview with Katie Couric a "disaster."[31]

Following a time-honored rule that says, "don't intervene when your opponent is self-destructing," and fearful than any attack could be cast as sexist, the Democrats laid low.

Palin Recovers Somewhat in the Vice Presidential Debate

If basement-level expectations advantage a contender in a debate, Sarah Palin entered the arena on October 2 with a distinct edge over Joe Biden. ABC's introduction to the face-off in St. Louis included George Stephanopoulos's morning news report that 6 out of 10 Americans say that Governor Palin "does not have the experience it takes to serve as president."[32] In dramatic evidence that the readiness question was wrapped around Palin but not Biden, the former Clinton-staffer-turned-Sunday-host offered no polled perceptions of Biden's perceived qualifications.

CBS's preview of that night forecast that Palin was ill-prepared for the evening ahead. When asked in back-to-back segments with Couric for examples of

Supreme Court decisions with which each disagreed, Biden responded with an eye to bolstering his bona fides with a key voting bloc for which Palin was vying. To do so, he argued passionately and in detail that the Supreme Court was wrong when it held his Violence Against Women Act unconstitutional. By contrast, as conservatives awaited her denunciation of *Roe v. Wade,* her condemnation of cases outlawing school prayer, an attack on a decision permitting flag burning, or even her reflexive rejection of the Exxon Valdez decision[33] that reduced Exxon's obligations[34] to those affected by the Alaska oil spill, Palin failed to name even one decision she would have decided differently.[35]

The networks weren't the only ones playing the expectations game. In a losing gamble that Biden would say something self-destructive, the McCain campaign released a Web ad inviting reporters to expect a "foot in mouth" moment from Biden in the debate. Remarkably, here was a campaign lowering expectations about an opponent!

ANNOUNCER: What might Joe Biden say at tonight's debate? Anything's possible.

JOE BIDEN: "I think I probably have a much higher I.Q. than you do....What am I talking about?"

ANNOUNCER: We know he has impeccable tact.

JOE BIDEN: "You cannot go to a 7-Eleven or a Dunkin' Donuts, unless you have a slight Indian accent. I'm not joking....What am I talking about?"

ANNOUNCER: Maybe he'll send Hillary in his place?

JOE BIDEN: "Hillary Clinton is as qualified or more qualified than I am. Might have been a better pick than me....What am I talking about?"

ANNOUNCER: And what might he say about his vote to raise taxes on those making just $42,000 a year?

JOE BIDEN: "It's time to be patriotic Kate, time to jump in, time to be part of the deal."

ANNOUNCER: We know he'd never embarrass himself.

JOE BIDEN [speaking to a man in a wheelchair]: "Stand up Chuck. Let them see you! Oh, God love you, what am I talking about?"

ANNOUNCER: Ready to gaffe? Yes. Ready to lead? No.[36]

In the face-off between the two vice presidential contenders, Palin exceeded low expectations and Biden looked stately when compared to the performance forecast by the McCain Web ad. Moreover, as he had at his convention, the Delaware senator connected with middle-class concerns.

Although both Biden and Palin danced around some questions, what made the Republican's deflections noteworthy was their artlessness. At a critical moment, for example, she invited attention to her nonanswer by proclaiming, "And I may not answer the questions the way that either the moderator or you want to hear, but I'm going to talk straight to the American people and let them know my track record also." That assertion came in the context of a statement by Biden that Palin had failed to address a series of earlier charges:

> BIDEN: …if you notice, Gwen, the governor did not answer the question about deregulation, did not answer the question of defending John McCain about not going along with the deregulation, letting Wall Street run wild. He did support deregulation almost across the board. That's why we got into so much trouble.
>
> MODERATOR GWEN IFILL: Would you like to have an opportunity to answer that before we move on?
>
> PALIN: I'm still on the tax thing because I want to correct you on that again. And I want to let you know what I did as a mayor and as a governor. And I may not answer the questions the way that either the moderator or you want to hear, but I'm going to talk straight to the American people and let them know my track record also. As mayor, every year I was in office I did reduce taxes….Now, as for John McCain's adherence to rules and regulations and pushing for even harder and tougher regulations, that is another thing that he is known for though. Look at the tobacco industry. Look at campaign finance reform.[37]

The final part of that response suggests that Palin doesn't know or isn't interested in addressing McCain's stance on deregulation of Wall Street. At the same time, she missed the chance to argue that it was Biden who voted for the Gramm-Leach-Bliley Act[38] and Bill Clinton who signed the bill dismantling the barriers among financial sectors. Instead, she noted that McCain "adheres to rules and regulations," hardly the description of a maverick. She then contorted a question about deregulation of the financial sector into an answer that said that McCain had pushed for tougher regulation of tobacco and campaign finance, neither a subject of obvious relevance to the economic meltdown.

Biden also was more responsive than Palin to a question whose answer could have advantaged the fiscal conservative at the top of the Republican ticket.

> IFILL: …I want to get—try to get you both to answer a question that neither of your principals quite answered when my colleague, Jim Lehrer, asked it last week, starting with you, Senator Biden.
>
> What promises—given the events of the week, the bailout plan, all of this, what promises have you and your campaigns made to the American people that you're not going to be able to keep?

BIDEN: Well, the one thing we might have to slow down is a commitment we made to double foreign assistance. We'll probably have to slow that down...[39]

After offering that single example, Biden produced a list of expensive promises Obama planned to keep and specified the proposals of McCain's they would not implement.

Instead of addressing the question, as Biden had (if only briefly), Palin offered a soliloquy on Obama and McCain's records on the 2005 energy bill and her own history of taking on the oil companies in Alaska. This tack prompted Ifill to repeat her original question:

> So, Governor, as vice president, there's nothing that you have promised as a candidate that you would—that you wouldn't take off the table because of this financial crisis we're in?[40]

In fairness to Palin, the question is phrased as what "you (not John McCain and you) have promised as a candidate." Still, an intellectually nimble surrogate would have responded with an account of McCain's past efforts to slow governmental growth and his proposal to freeze Federal discretionary spending. Instead, Palin said:

> There is not. And how long have I been at this, like five weeks? So there hasn't been a whole lot that I've promised, except to do what is right for the American people, put government back on the side of the American people, stop the greed and corruption on Wall Street.
> And the rescue plan has got to include that massive oversight that Americans are expecting and deserving. And I don't believe that John McCain has made any promise that he would not be able to keep, either.[41]

When we compared the attitudes of debate viewers and nonviewers in the presence of controls, we found evidence that the vice presidential debate upped Biden's favorability ratings, without affecting Palin's one way or the other.*

While watching the vice presidential encounter improved perceptions of Biden, 6 in 10 viewers (59%) felt that the Alaska governor's performance exceeded their expectations.[42] Confirming that expectations affect evaluation, those holding that view gave her higher favorability ratings than those who did not feel that she had done better than expected. By contrast, debate expectations had no effect on impressions of Biden.* Although watching the vice presidential debates improved Biden's favorability ratings and not Palin's, winning the expectations game was important for Palin because it had the potential to dampen negative press commentary about her competence in the coming days.

The take of the pundits was that although she was not hurt by the debate, her performance failed to allay questions about her competence. In postdebate commentary, talking heads interpreted the Republican vice presidential nominee's disposition to dodge as a worrisome sign. "I must say," noted CBS's Bob Schieffer, "I found it a little disconcerting, time and again, Governor Palin would just choose not to answer the question and launch into some dissertation, sometimes talking points, and not really address what Gwen Ifill had asked her."[43] "She didn't answer the questions," observed Andrea Mitchell on MSNBC. "And, in fact, she would say, I want to talk about taxes, which hadn't even come up."[44]

Because the press frame on the event asked, "Is Palin ready to be president?" not, "How qualified are they?" Palin's digressions, deflections, and errors were mentioned in press commentary more often than Biden's. For example, although each made factual errors, it was Palin's misstating the last name of the commander of the NATO International Security Assistance Force in Afghanistan, (General McKiernan, not, as the Alaska governor said, General McClellan) that drew press attention. Not so Biden's erroneous location of the executive branch in Article I rather than II of the Constitution.

There was method to Palin's relentless redirection from the question to the answer she wanted to give: the strategy was designed to brand Obama and Biden as tax raisers and establish that, unlike either, she was an energy expert. So preoccupied with energy issues was the Republican vice presidential nominee that she turned a question about bankruptcy legislation into an answer on energy.[45]

Nonetheless, the Alaska governor's performance in the vice presidential debate may have helped her to reclaim a bit of the luster lost in the Gibson and Couric interviews. Although the postdebate polls called the debate a win for Biden, our survey suggests that after it Palin had a short-term boost in favorability, even as Biden's upward trend accelerated (see figure 7.2). Since the comparisons of debate watchers to those who did not tune in to the event show that viewing did not significantly change people's evaluations of Palin, the improvement in her trend lines may have been a result of the media reports that she had exceeded expectations.

Nonetheless, her performance failed to override the concerns of some key conservative opinion leaders. "[W]e have seen Mrs. Palin on the national stage for seven weeks now, and there is little sign that she has the tools, the equipment, the knowledge or the philosophical grounding one hopes for, and expects, in a holder of high office," wrote Reagan and Bush 41 speechwriter and *Wall Street Journal* columnist Peggy Noonan on October 17.[46] In that essay, Noonan concluded, as General Colin Powell would two days later, that Palin's candidacy "is a mark against John McCain, against his judgment and idealism." Still we see no change in people's perception of McCain's judgment in this period.[47]

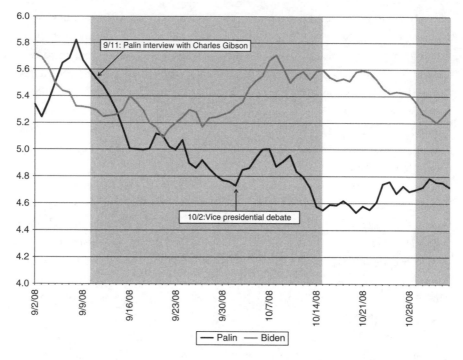

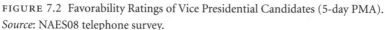

FIGURE 7.2 Favorability Ratings of Vice Presidential Candidates (5-day PMA). *Source*: NAES08 telephone survey.

Colin Powell Attacks Palin's Qualifications: October 19

In the early primaries of 2000, Colin Powell had supported McCain over George W. Bush. The admiration was mutual. In that contest, the Arizona senator had forecast that, were he elected, he would name the general his secretary of state.[48] This fact and Powell's credibility with voters meant that his endorsement of Obama was a body blow to McCain. (We explain the effect on perceptions of the Republican nominee in chapter 10.)

Because in his endorsement, the 71-year-old general and former secretary of state under George W. Bush indicted Governor Palin's preparedness and touted Senator Joe Biden's, here we focus on its effects on the perceptions of the vice presidential nominees' readiness to be president. Specifically, on *Meet the Press*, Powell told Tom Brokaw, "She's a very distinguished woman, and she's to be admired. But at the same time, now that we have had a chance to watch her for some seven weeks, I don't believe she's ready to be president of the United States, which is the job of the vice president. And so that raised some question in my mind as to the judgment that Sen. McCain made." To this assessment the general added, Joe

Biden "is ready to be president on day one." And he indicted Palin's role in his party's move to the right.[49]

Powell's repudiation of his own party's ticket and embrace of the Democratic one created a flurry of favorable news coverage for Obama. "The description of Mr. Obama, the Democratic nominee for president, as a 'transformational figure' by Mr. Powell, a Republican who directed the first Iraq war, could lift Mr. Obama among some independents, moderates and Republicans and neutralize concerns about his experience," hypothesized the *New York Times*.[50]

Polls promptly suggested that the former secretary of state's embrace of Obama had registered a small but potentially significant effect. "While 80% of registered voters are aware of former Secretary of State Colin Powell's endorsement of Barack Obama for president," reported Gallup two days later, "only 12% of this attentive group say the endorsement makes them more likely to vote for Obama, while 4% say it makes them less likely to vote for the Democratic nominee."[51] "Two in 10 independent voters said they are more inclined to vote for Obama because of Powell's backing; 4 percent said they were nudged the other way," reported the *Washington Post*.[52] Unanswered were the questions we address here: did the Powell endorsement affect perceptions of Palin or Biden, and did it alter views about McCain's judgment in placing the Alaska governor a heartbeat away from the presidency?

Of 1,035 NAES respondents interviewed between October 19 and October 22, 65.6 percent correctly identified Barack Obama as the candidate whom Powell had endorsed. When all were told that Obama was the one endorsed, 17.4 percent responded that that fact made them more likely to vote for Obama, 4.1 percent said that it made them less likely to vote for him, 75.8 percent said that it made no difference, and 2.8 percent did not know or refused to respond.[53] On the surface, it appears that the endorsement gave Obama a small boost. Taking several demographic, political attitudinal variables, and news consumption into account, our results suggest that the Powell attack hurt Palin's favorability ratings and perceptions of her readiness "to be president" but did not directly affect feelings about Obama. Nor did it affect ratings of McCain. The endorsement of Obama also helped Biden's favorability ratings and perceptions of his readiness "to be president."*

Is Biden Ready to Be President?

As we noted a moment ago, on the evening of the vice presidential debate, a Republican Web ad reminded reporters that Biden had had his share of ill-considered campaign utterances, among them asking a man in a wheel chair to "stand up. Let the people see you." Another (unnoted by the Web ad) was telling Katie Couric that when the stock market crashed the country into the Great Depression, FDR's words of comfort reached American homes over TV, a statement wrong on two counts. The medium available at the time was radio, and the crash occurred before FDR took office.

More worrisome for the Democratic ticket were two Biden flubs that opened the party's standard-bearer to attack. The first misstated the ticket's position on so-called clean coal; the second seemed to warn the audience of the risks involved in electing a president with comparatively little experience in foreign affairs.

Does the Democratic Ticket Support "Clean Coal"?

Biden stumbled into the "clean coal" blunder on September 17, when from a rope line a voter asked in an accusatory tone, "Why are you supporting clean coal?" The Democratic vice presidential nominee responded categorically, "We're not supporting clean coal. Guess what? China's building two every week. Two dirty coal plants. And it's polluting the United States. It's causing people to die....No coal plants here in America. Build them, if they're going to build them over there, make 'em clean because they're killing you."[54] The Delaware senator's attack on "clean" coal was not only blatantly at odds with the position espoused by the person at the top of that ticket but also political poison in parts of vote-rich coal- producing states, such as West Virginia, Kentucky, and Pennsylvania, a fact that may explain Obama's reiteration of his position in his 30-minute ad aired October 29, "And to further reduce our demand for foreign oil," proclaimed the Democratic aspirant in that nationally televised program. "I'll tap our natural gas reserves, invest in clean coal technology, and expand domestic production of oil."[55]

In the vice presidential debate on October 2, Biden seemed to reveal that his statement on the rope line was not a slip of the tongue. Perhaps he and the person who had tapped him as a running mate were not on the same page on this issue after all. "The way in which we can stop the greenhouse gases from emitting," said the Delaware senator, "we believe—Barack Obama believes—by investing in clean coal and safe nuclear, we can not only create jobs in wind and solar here in the United States, we can export it" (emphasis added).

Moderator Gwenn Ifill followed up:

IFILL: Let me clear something up. Senator McCain has said he supports caps on carbon emissions. Senator Obama has said he supports clean coal technology, which I don't believe you've always supported.

BIDEN: I have always supported it. That's a fact.

Remembering reports of the Biden exchange in the rope line, Palin pounced:

PALIN: I was surprised to hear you mention that because you had said that there isn't anything—such a thing as clean coal. And I think you said it in a rope line, too, at one of your rallies.

IFILL: We do need to keep within our two minutes. But I just wanted to ask you, do you support capping carbon emissions?

PALIN: I do. I do.

IFILL: OK. And on the clean coal issue?

BIDEN: Absolutely. Absolutely we do. We call for setting hard targets, number one...

IFILL: Clean coal.

BIDEN: Oh, I'm sorry.

IFILL: On clean coal.

BIDEN: Oh, on clean coal. My record, just take a look at the record. My record for 25 years has supported clean coal technology. A comment made in a rope line was taken out of context. I was talking about exporting that technology to China so when they burn their dirty coal, it won't be as dirty, it will be clean.[56]

"After the McCain campaign jumped on his remarks last week, the Obama campaign responded by reiterating Mr. Obama and Mr. Biden's support of clean coal technology," noted a *New York Times* posting after the debate, "but they were not able to fully explain the contradiction between that position and Mr. Biden's remarks to the voter on the rope line."[57]

Despite the fact that Biden told his accuser, "We're not supporting clean coal" and "no coal plants here in America," the Delaware Democrat was accurate in saying that he had supported clean coal technology in the past. Still, he suffered no serious penalty for distorting what he had told the woman. The reasons are various. Energy was no longer a central campaign issue. The press was diligently assessing Palin's, but not Biden's, competence. And in the debate, Biden responded in terms of his voting record, the actual focus of Ifill's question. As a result, the exchange in the rope line and the Delaware senator's subsequent about-face in the debate did not resurrect concerns in the press that Biden was prone to speak before thinking. Perceptions of his competence remained intact.

As a hypothetical, however, imagine both that energy remained a dominant issue in September and October and gas prices remained high. Among other things, when the Delaware senator came out against "clean coal" before he was for it, the vice presidential dynamic might have shifted to pair questions about Palin's competence with those about Biden.

Obama Will Be Tested

With a bit more than two weeks to go to the end of the election, Biden, who chairs the Senate Foreign Relations Committee, handed the Republicans a far more lavish gift than the gaffe about clean coal. Speaking at a closed-door Seattle fund-raiser on October 19, the Democratic vice presidential nominee forecast that if Obama were elected he would be tested with an international crisis.[58] Like the Obama "bitter" comment, Biden's remark was recorded by a member of his audience. The impact of the Biden gaffe was magnified by news reports:

> RON CLAIBORNE (ABC News): (*voiceover*) But the McCain campaign believes Joe Biden handed them a real opening this past weekend with comments he made at a fund-raiser, Sunday in Seattle.
>
> GRAPHICS: BIDEN COMMENT
>
> SENATOR JOE BIDEN (Democratic vice presidential candidate): Mark my words, it will not be six months before the world tests Barack Obama, like they did John Kennedy. Watch, we're gonna have an international crisis, a generated crisis to test the mettle of this guy.
>
> RON CLAIBORNE (ABC News): (*voiceover*) Today, McCain and his running mate, Sarah Palin, campaigning in Colorado, jumped all over Biden's remarks, claiming that Biden was warning that a foreign country would challenge a new, inexperienced President Obama.[59]

The McCain campaign memorialized the Biden stumble in an ad that its team rushed onto the air. From October 25 through Election Day, TV viewers in battle-ground states were bombarded by "Listen to Biden" 5,899 times at a cost to the McCain campaign of almost $2.5 million.[60]

> ANNOUNCER: Listen to Joe Biden talking about what electing Barack Obama will mean.
>
> JOE BIDEN: Mark my words. It will not be six months before the world tests Barack Obama. The world's looking. We're going to have an international crisis to test the mettle of this guy. I guarantee you it's gonna happen.
>
> ANNOUNCER: It doesn't have to happen. Vote McCain.[61]

Biden's statement that "It will not be six months before the world tests Barack Obama. I guarantee you it's going to happen" was also included in a spot by the independent group calling itself Let Freedom Ring. From October 28 to Election Day at a cost of just over $400,000, that spot aired a combined total of 281 times in Colorado, Nevada, Ohio, Pennsylvania, Virginia, and Washington, D.C.

In it, former Reagan Assistant Secretary of Defense Frank Gaffney played on the assumption that Democrats are "weak on defense" to allege that Obama was determined not to use military force, a claim belied by the Democrat's insistence on increasing the U.S. military presence in Afghanistan. "When we see candidates taking positions that [sic] unmistakably convey determination neither to use military power, nor to ensure that they have it at their disposal, should it be necessary," said Gaffney, "they are conveying to our enemies weakness, and weakness invites aggression."[62]

The Delaware senator's slip-up provided attention-grabbing evidence against Obama. People found Biden's admission convincing, argued Republican pollster Bill McInturff. "Joe Biden's not a Republican. And Joe Biden says he's [Obama's] going to be tested."

In a TV ad titled "Audio Tapes," the Democrats condemned the Republicans for selectively editing Biden's remarks. "Here," said the message, as it engaged in selective editing of its own, is "what Biden actually said about Barack Obama: "They're going to find out this guy's got steel in his spine." Making the campaign's signature move, the ad then tied the Republican nominee back to Bush.

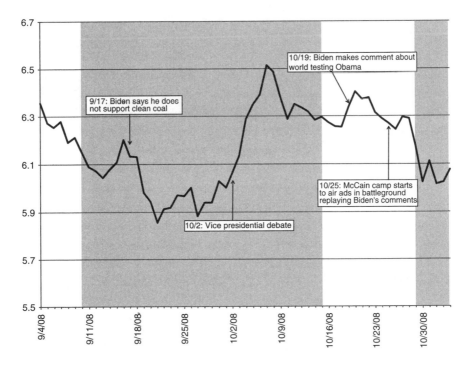

FIGURE 7.3 Perceptions of Biden as "Ready to Be President" (5-day PMA).
Source: NAES08 telephone survey.

"His policies, 'following in Bush's footsteps.' And that's the risk we can't afford to take." A still photo of the incumbent president nodding his approval at a smiling McCain served as the spot's closing photo.[63]

NAES data suggest a possible effect of the Republican advertising not on views of Obama but on those of his running mate (figure 7.3). Although his assertion that Obama would be tested by foreign nations was made on October 19, declines in public perception of Biden's readiness to be president didn't start in earnest until the McCain camp tied the gaffe to its argument that Obama was a risky unknown candidate not ready to lead in a time of national crisis. However, even at their low point, ratings of Biden's readiness safely topped the midpoint on a 10-point scale and handily bested Palin's.

Net Effect of Palin-Biden

To understand the extent to which Palin and Biden helped or hurt their tickets, we examined how presidential and vice presidential candidates' favorability ratings related to vote preference. Table 7.1 provides a glimpse into the relationship over two time periods. As expected, voters' presidential favorability ratings were more

TABLE 7.1. Relationship of Candidate Favorability to Vote Preference

	Group 1 Like President, Like Vice President	Group 2 Like President, Dislike Vice President	Group 3 Dislike President, Like Vice President	Group 4 Dislike President, Dislike Vice President
September 5 through October 14				
Obama-Biden	83.8%	63.4%	7.1%	2.9%
N	3,515	369	241	1,990
McCain-Palin	83.5%	25.6%	17.6%	2.2%
N	3,514	525	184	2,420
October 15 through November 3				
Obama-Biden	84.3%	53.4%	13.4%	3.1%
N	2,008	166	124	1,164
McCain-Palin	81.3%	27.3%	16.2%	1.6%
N	1,708	379	71	1,355

Data: NAES08 telephone survey; percentages are based on weighted data.

important than those of the vice presidential nominees. These results suggest that people are strongly guided by the top of the ticket.

Nevertheless, when voters are concerned about a vice presidential candidate, those worries can translate into ticket choice. In 2008, Palin's favorability ratings affected vote preference more so than did Biden's. According to NAES data, in the last three weeks of the campaign, a 1-unit increase in Palin's favorability reduced the odds of voting for the Obama-Biden ticket approximately 22 percent, after taking demographic and political attitudinal variables into consideration.* In contrast, a 1-unit increase in Biden's favorability ratings reduced the odds of voting for the McCain-Palin ticket approximately 8 percent.* In other words, impressions of Palin mattered more than impressions of Biden in predicting vote preference. Since Palin's favorability ratings were significantly lower than those of the Democratic vice presidential nominee, the push and pull of these peceptions on vote netted out strongly in Biden's favor, a point on which we will elaborate in a moment.[64]

Although Palin initially attracted voters to the Republican side, lack of familiarity with her meant that those initial dispositions were susceptible to change. And change they did. To make this case, we break out favorability ratings of the vice presidential candidates by key demographic groups in two periods: the first from September 5 to October 14, the second from October 15 to November 3 (see table 7.2). The results show that for a majority of the demographic and political groups, Biden held an advantage on favorability. Palin received higher ratings from only a few categories of voters. During both time periods each of only three audiences rated her more highly than Biden: those who attend church more than once a week, Republicans, and conservatives ($p < .001$ for each of the three groups and both time periods).

Between September 5 and October 14, whites, who made up 78.8 percent of our sample, gave her slightly higher ratings than they gave Biden ($p < .05$). However, her ratings in this population fell during the latter part of the general election campaign. Biden received slightly higher ratings than Palin among these individuals between October 15 and November 3 ($p < .05$). The change is particularly dramatic among one of the demographics Palin was tasked with attracting: non-college-educated white women making less than $50,000, a group that makes up 9.4 percent of our weighted sample (see figure 7.4) and a demographic Hillary Clinton commanded in the primaries. NAES data suggest that of the Democrats and independents who were part of this group, 56 percent supported Clinton, 22.2 percent favored Obama, and the remainder didn't know or didn't vote.[65] Where in the week after the Republican convention, Palin's favorability exceeded that of McCain, Obama, and Biden's with this group, by mid-October she was trailing the other three (see figure 7.4).

TABLE 7.2. Mean Comparisons of Vice Presidential Nominee Favorability Ratings by Demographic and Political Groups

	September 5 to October 14			October 15 to November 3		
	Biden Favorability	Palin Favorability	Difference[a]	Biden Favorability	Palin Favorability	Difference[a]
Total[b]	5.31	4.98	.33 ***	5.43	4.65	.78 ***
Female	5.50	4.80	.70 ***	5.55	4.62	.93 ***
Male	5.10	5.16	−.06	5.30	4.68	.63 ***
18 to 29	5.33	4.48	.85 ***	5.81	4.27	1.53 ***
30 to 44	5.21	5.12	.09	5.30	4.65	.65 ***
45 to 64	5.32	4.87	.45 ***	5.47	4.62	.85 ***
65 or older	5.42	5.36	.06	5.26	5.01	.25
White	5.10	5.30	−.20 **	5.17	4.94	.23 *
Black or African-American	6.83	2.88	3.96 ***	7.23	2.67	4.57 ***
Hispanic	5.29	4.86	.43 *	6.05	4.30	1.75 ***
Non-Hispanic	5.31	4.99	.32 ***	5.37	4.69	.68 ***
High school or less	5.17	5.15	.03	5.33	4.86	.47 ***
Some college or post-high school training	5.23	5.10	.13	5.25	4.75	.50 ***
College four-year degree or more	5.54	4.65	.88 ***	5.73	4.30	1.44 ***
Household income below $35K	5.46	4.76	.70 ***	5.62	4.42	1.20 ***
$35K to below $75K	5.35	4.95	.40 ***	5.50	4.70	.80 ***
$75K plus	5.29	5.05	.24 *	5.34	4.70	.64 ***
Church attendance more than once a week	4.66	6.03	−1.37 ***	4.66	5.97	−1.31 ***
Once a week	5.08	5.52	−.44 ***	5.17	5.13	.04
Once or twice a month	5.42	5.07	.35 *	5.56	4.64	.92 ***
A few times a year	5.58	4.53	1.05 ***	5.67	4.46	1.22 ***
Never	5.63	4.05	1.58 ***	5.87	3.42	2.45 ***
Republican	3.74	7.43	−3.70 ***	3.55	7.27	−3.72 ***
Democrat	6.72	3.03	3.68 ***	7.01	2.63	4.38 ***
Independent	5.20	5.00	.20 *	5.34	4.64	.70 ***
Conservative	4.06	6.73	−2.67 ***	4.10	6.40	−2.31 ***
Moderate	5.77	4.44	1.33 ***	5.98	3.99	1.98 ***
Liberal	6.62	3.00	3.62 ***	6.82	2.81	4.02 ***

[a]Significant differences between Biden and Palin measures were determined by paired-samples t tests. The favorability ratings were measured on a 10-point scale.

[b]The overall sample size for the September 5 to October 14 paired-samples t test was 8,540; for the October 15 to November 3 sample, it was 4,586.

Data: NAES08 telephone survey; means are based on weighted data.

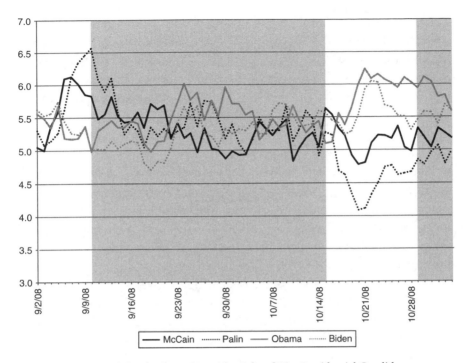

FIGURE 7.4 Favorability Ratings of Presidential and Vice Presidential Candidates among Non-College-Educated White Women with Household Income Less than $50,000 (5-day PMA). *Source*: NAES08 telephone survey.

Palin also lost ground with those attending church once a week, a group that made up 11.5 percent of our September 5 through October 14 sample. Between those dates, she had statistically higher favorability ratings than did Biden among once-a-week church goers ($p < .001$). During the postdebate period, that is, after October 14, however, her ratings were statistically comparable to those of Biden with this demographic. In short, Biden gained support among Palin's core constituencies. Attitudes favorable to the Alaska governor's candidacy also eroded among some populations that gave each of the two vice presidential contenders comparable ratings during the first of our two periods. Those whose disaffection with Palin increased in the second period include: males, 30-to-44-year-olds, those with high school degrees or less, and those with some college or post-high school training. Members of each of these subgroups compared Biden favorably to Palin during the last three weeks of the campaign.

Across the campaign, the Alaska governor held her ground with senior citizens (65 years old or older), a demographic that McCain carried in the election. But so too did her counterpart. Palin and Biden had statistically comparable favorability ratings with seniors in both of the two analyzed periods.

In order to win, McCain needed to not only energize conservatives but also draw independents and crossover voters. As the data in chapter 1 indicated, the percentage of the electorate calling itself Republican was too small to ensure his victory. If independents broke evenly and McCain-Palin carried all of those who self-identified as Republicans, they would still lose unless they also obtained significant numbers of crossover votes from Democrats.

Palin failed to help the Arizonan reach that goal. When we compared those who considered themselves independents with those identified with either of the two major parties, we found that Biden had a statistically significant 0.2 point edge on the 10-point favorability scale between September 5 and October 14. This gap widened to 0.7 points during the last three weeks of the campaign. On the liberal, moderate, conservative grid, Biden also had a decisive advantage with moderates ($p<.001$ for both time points). Among these individuals, positive evaluations of Biden rose and those of Palin fell between time one and two.

During the last few weeks of the campaign, Palin was rated at or above the neutral mid-point by only five demographic groups: those 65 years old and older (rating of 5.01), those who attended church more than once a week (5.97), those who attended church once a week (5.13), Republicans (7.27), and conservatives (6.40). As we noted, assessments by those 65 years old and older gave neither vice presidential nominee an edge. Although those who attended church once a week rated Palin favorably on average, she lost ground with them toward the end of the campaign.

By contrast, in the campaign's final weeks, Biden was placed above the neutral point by all but those who attended church more than once a week (4.66), Republicans (3.55), and conservatives (4.10). Since the percentage of voters identifying as Republican had dropped since the 2004 election, it was not particularly consequential that they did not hold Biden in high regard. Importantly, both women and men gave him higher ratings than they gave Palin.

These changes matter because overall they increased our pool of respondents' disposition to express support for the Democratic rather than the Republican ticket. What all of this meant was that Palin's declining favorability over the course of the general election[66] (figure 7.2) created a drag on the Republican ticket.[67]

The extent to which regarding Palin favorably affected the vote varied across the general election campaign, however. As figure 7.5 suggests, the odds ratio of Palin's favorability rating on the McCain-Palin vote increased in mid-October, meaning that her influence was increasing during that time frame. Assessments of Palin had their strongest association with vote preference during the two weeks following the third presidential debate and in the last three days of the campaign. The peak point of Palin's influence on the vote was October 22. From that date

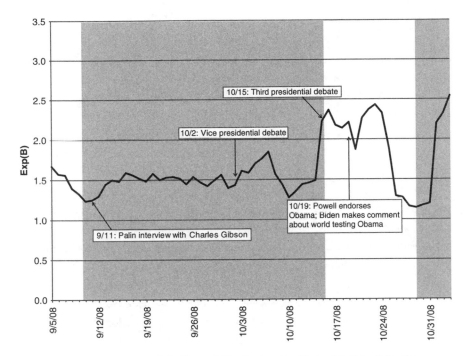

FIGURE 7.5 Odds Ratio of Palin Favorability Ratings Predicting McCain-Palin Vote Preference across Time (5-day PMA). Note: The logistic regression model from which the Exp(B)s were obtained included gender, age, race, ethnicity, education, income, religious attendance, party identification, ideology, and the favorability ratings of the presidential and vice presidential candidates. *Source*: NAES08 telephone survey.

to the end of October, it decreased. It spiked again during the last few days of the campaign, suggesting that those who had not voted absentee drew on their evaluations of her in making their final decision. Because Palin's favorability ratings dropped substantially over the course of the campaign, they acted as a weight on the Republican ticket's prospects. From the last week of September through Election Day, Palin's average favorability ratings remained below the neutral point (5) on our scale.

In net, the presence of the Alaska governor on the Republican ticket had a greater effect on the final vote than did Biden's on the other side for two reasons: Palin elicited significantly lower favorability ratings than did her Democratic counterpart from the last week of September through Election Day, and she quickly lost favor with non-college-educated women making under $50,000 and independents, regardless of gender.

Even when we take a host of demographic and political variables into account, the favorability ratings of the major-party vice presidential candidates affected vote preferences.* Responding favorably to Biden increased the chances that someone would vote for the Democratic ticket, and thinking highly of Palin did the same for the Republican one. Assuming a 50 percent baseline probability of voting for Obama-Biden, a 1-unit increase in Biden's favorability ratings would have increased voters' likelihood of voting for the ticket by 2.1 percent. In contrast, assuming a 50 percent baseline probability of voting for the McCain-Biden, a 1-unit increase in Palin's favorability ratings would have netted the Republican ticket an extra 6.1 percent of the vote. Because voters overall thought better of Biden than Palin, the net effect was higher for the Democratic than for the Republican ticket.

Examining the vice presidential candidate's favorability ratings across time using data from the NAES, we detected a one-day lagged effect of Palin's favorability ratings on vote preference for the McCain-Palin ticket. In essence, this suggests that feelings toward Palin on a given day influenced people's vote preferences the following day.[68] When Palin's competence eroded, doubts about her readiness to assume the presidency hurt the Republican ticket's chances.* In a finding consistent with ours, on election eve, 44 percent of likely voters in a *Washington Post*/ABC News poll said that the Palin pick had decreased their likelihood of voting for McCain.[69]

Conclusion

The challenges facing the McCain-Palin ticket included an unpopular incumbent, a poor economy for which the Republican party was blamed, and fewer GOP identifiers than had been in the electorate when George W. Bush secured his first and second term. While Palin ran well with Republicans, the McCain-Palin ticket needed to draw Democratic crossover and independent votes in order to win. The Palin candidacy failed to help with either. Instead, concerns about her readiness hurt the Republican ticket. When her adequate though unimpressive favorability ratings at the start of the general election eroded, that decline further depressed the Republicans' chances of winning the presidential election in 2008.

None of that was on the table at the end of the Republican convention, however. Buoyed by her nomination, the Republicans left their gathering in Minneapolis ahead in the polls. For another half week, the bounce lingered. But in a portent of things to come, the morning after McCain's acceptance speech, new unemployment figures suggested that the economy was becoming unhinged. And even as energy prices were starting to come down, foreclosures continued to rise. The ground under the election was about to shift dramatically, and with it, Obama and McCain's prospects. In the next chapter, we tell the story of the candidates' responses to the economic collapse that occurred in September 2008.

EIGHT

Period Three: The Campaigns Confront the Economic Collapse (September 10–October 14)

B Y RELENTLESSLY BINDING THE REPUBLICAN NOMINEE TO BOTH President George W. Bush and the faltering economy, in period three the Obama campaign met the expectations of the forecasting models.[1] Easing that process were missteps by Senator John McCain and his surrogates. So it is unsurprising that voters' assessments of the Republican nominee plummeted in this time frame (see figure 6.4). At the same time, with a reassuring response to the financial meltdown and steady performances in both the first debate, September 26, and in nationally televised two-minute mini-speeches, Senator Barack Obama undercut a key McCain attack by increasing the public's confidence in his trustworthiness.

The Democratic rhetoric cast the amalgam of McCain/Bush/Republicans as the real problem and electing Barack Obama as the remedy. With the economy central to the agenda of the White House, Congress, the public, and the media, the Obama campaign translated this problem-solution narrative into three interconnected arguments: (1) Republican deregulation, incestuous relations with lobbyists, tax cutting, and job outsourcing had jeopardized the financial security of middle-class Americans; (2) like Bush, McCain was out of touch with the concerns of the country; and (3) electing McCain would mean more of the same. By contrast, the Democrats' messages of reassurance posited Obama as the candidate of change, in touch with middle-class concerns, and the person best prepared to clean up the mess created by deregulation and lobbyist-run Washington.

For their part, the Republicans attacked Obama on two fronts: instead of making conditions better, Obama's tax-and-spend liberalism would worsen them, and the real Obama was both an old-style Chicago pol and (an idea we explored in chapter 4 and to which we will return in period five) an intimate of suspect individuals. Specifically, Obama's past associations reeked of corrupt politics as usual, while his inspiring rhetoric camouflaged a person not ready to lead.

In the contest between these disparate views of the world, the Democrats' version benefited from the troubled economy. At the same time, even as news concentrated on the country's Wall Street-induced woes, the Obama campaign's bankroll ensured that even his noneconomic messages would be heard in the battleground states. Meanwhile, McCain's rhetorical impact was limited by fewer dollars to buy media time and a resulting reliance on hybrid ads, messages jointly funded with one's political party with the proviso, in the case of attack ads, that half their content be devoted to the opponent and half to his party mates in Congress.

The Economy as the Most Pressing Issue Facing the Nation

From mid-January 2008 through Election Day, the economy was at the front, middle and back of voters' minds. The percentage seeing it as the country's most important issue rose steadily from September 14 through mid-October. As figure 8.1 suggests, the short-lived period-four increase in McCain's favorability that we will treat in the next chapter coincides with a drop in the percentage labeling the economy the most important issue and a drop in the perception that the country was on the wrong track. But even then, the percentage viewing it as the top issue and believing that the country was on the wrong track remained securely above 50 percent. As figure 8.2 indicates, the view that the country was on the wrong track also increased during period three, as did the perception that one's own economic circumstances had worsened over the past year.

Throughout the five periods into which we have parsed the postprimary season, Obama retained his lead on dealing with the economy. As Labor Day approached, the Illinois senator bested his Republican counterpart by almost 20 points on that indicator. However, the gap separating the two on what every major survey cast as the most important problem facing the nation started to close after the Republican convention. Even then, however, Obama's advantage was significant. In period three, as figure 8.3 shows, Obama did not appreciably increase the perception that he would better handle the economy; instead, on this key indicator, McCain lost ground. If the election was decided on the economy, it was Obama's to lose. (The reason that the percentages do not total to 100 percent is that some respondents said that they "did not know," indicated "neither candidate," or simply refused to answer the question.)

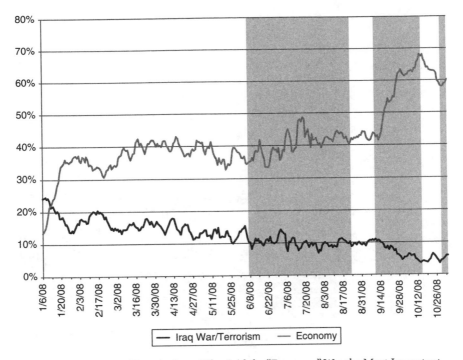

FIGURE 8.1 Percent of Respondents Who Said the "Economy" Was the Most Important Problem Compared to the Percent of Respondents Who Said "Iraq War/Terrorism" (5-day PMA). *Source*: NAES08 telephone survey.

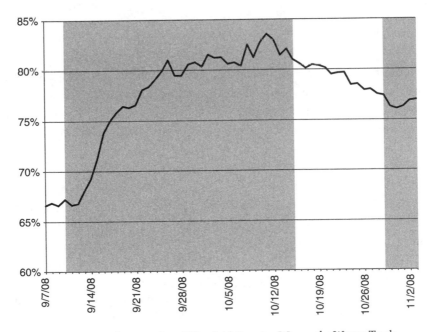

FIGURE 8.2 Percent of Respondents Who Said Country Was on the Wrong Track (5-day PMA). *Source*: NAES08 telephone survey.

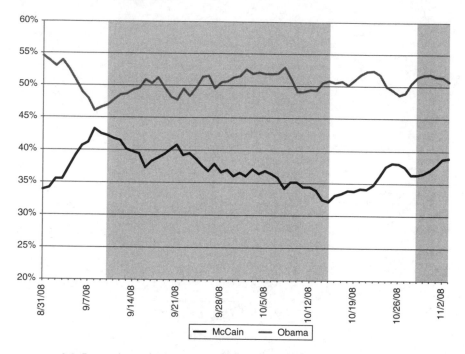

FIGURE 8.3 Perceptions of Which Candidate Would Better Handle the Economy
(5-day PMA). *Source*: NAES08 telephone survey.

The Media Primed the Belief That the Economy Was in Crisis

In the postconvention period, daily media accounts ensured that anyone who was
not comatose would know that housing foreclosures were up, the Dow down, and
401(k)s in a slide toward what some wags labeled 201(k)s. When news concentrates laser-like on an issue such as the economy in extremis, agenda setting, framing and priming theories predict that that focus will magnify the likelihood that
news watchers will see the economy as the central issue, conclude that it is in crisis,
and evaluate candidates on their ability to fix it. And this press focus underscored
the story Barack Obama was telling the electorate. "September 15 is a killer for
the following reasons," recalled McCain's pollster Bill McInturff. "First and most
importantly, it fed into a narrative which is, 'That's it. I've had it. The Republicans
and George Bush have helped the rich. This doesn't work. Everything's broken.'
And by the way, that's a rational response."[2]

The most trauma-freighted fall election season in memory began on the day
after the close of the Republican convention (September 5) when the nation awoke
to the news that the August jobless rate had risen to 6.1 percent, a figure that
translated into nine and a half million people out of work. The economic news

worsened from September 8–14 with reports of the federal takeover of mortgage giants Fannie Mae and Freddie Mac. According to the Pew Project for Excellence in Journalism, "[t]hat event was the second-biggest newspaper story of the week..."[3] We set the beginning of period three at September 9 because we see our trend lines changing there. But for practical purposes, the bad economic news was escalating from the 5th onward.

From September 14 through October 12, the economic collapse dominated the news.[4] Not until the week of October 13–19 did that topic slide to second place behind reports on the October 15 presidential debate. The economic crisis "had other real consequences," notes McInturff. "We stopped having a campaign. The daily press report wasn't reporting, 'He said, he said, back, forth, this story, this story.' It was instead, 'Today America's economy is falling apart. Here's how awful everything is. Here's the candidates' reaction to it.' ...Despite Republicans liking to claim 'press bias,' who among you can call up a reporter and say, 'You should get rid of those banner headlines about how awful the economy is.' It was a huge story. It was the most important story. And it's an important story that blew us off the front pages."

Even before the tsunami of dire indicators and accompanying headlines, public attention to the campaign, measured as "close following," had been high. After the first week in September, that indicator spiked into the stratosphere (figure 8.4).

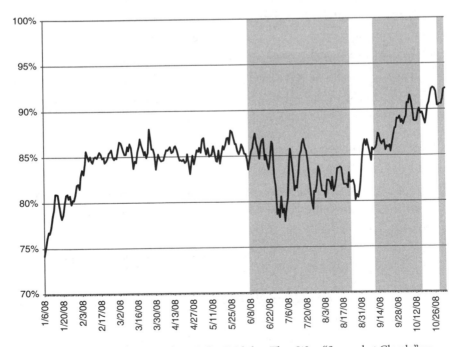

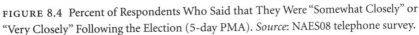

FIGURE 8.4 Percent of Respondents Who Said that They Were "Somewhat Closely" or "Very Closely" Following the Election (5-day PMA). *Source*: NAES08 telephone survey.

This heightened level of attention magnified the agenda setting, framing, and priming effects of news consumption. Unsurprisingly, heavy news consumers were more likely than those who paid less attention to see the economy as the country's most important problem. Those closely following the election increasingly saw the economy as the more important problem facing the nation, with habitual TV and print news consumers the most likely to harbor that conclusion.* Although most still regarded the economy as the most pressing issue, not all the media produced a detectable agenda-setting effect. In a finding for which we have no good explanation, Internet use was one exception. The other was talk radio exposure, where conservative hosts presumably provided avid listeners with reassurance.

The Democratic Argument: Election of McCain Means More of the Same Economic Philosophy

In period three, the Obama campaign harnessed news, ads, and debates to drive the message that McCain was a Bush replica on economic matters. Press accounts on September 15, the day of the Lehman Brothers collapse, suggest that the Democrats were successful. On ABC, Jake Tapper reported:

> JAKE TAPPER (ABC News): (*voiceover*) In Grand Junction, in western Colorado this afternoon, Barack Obama said the economic philosophy John McCain subscribes to is behind what he called "the most serious financial *crisis* since the Great Depression." (emphasis added)

> SENATOR BARACK OBAMA (Democrat): It's the same philosophy we have had for the last eight years, one that says we should just stick our heads in the sand and ignore economic problems until they spiral into crisis.[5]

On the same day, McCain moved aggressively to separate himself from the toxic incumbent. CBS news correspondent Nancy Cordes reported:

> NANCY CORDES (CBS): Senator John McCain wasted no time putting some distance between himself and President Bush in the wake of today's financial news.

> SENATOR JOHN MCCAIN (Republican presidential nominee): We'll put an end, as I said, to running Wall Street like a casino.[6]

As we noted in chapter 2, the Democratic strategy allied Bush and McCain in an attack slogan that pervaded the Obama attack ads: "We can't afford more of the same."[7] For example, on October 10 the Democratic campaign aired a message featuring a worker named Barney Smith, who called for electing a president who puts Barney Smith before Smith Barney. Reprising a key indictment offered by Democratic party nominee John Kerry against incumbent George Bush in 2004, Smith reported supporting Obama because McCain "voted to give tax breaks to companies that export jobs…We can't afford more of the same." A second message that began airing the 10th criticized the Republican party nominee for wanting taxpayers to buy up bad home loan mortgages. As a Wall Street intersection sign telegraphed the answer, that ad asked, "Who wins [under McCain's plan]?" "The same lenders that caused the crisis in the first place." The ad closed with a picture of McCain and Bush side by side as the announcer intoned, "We can't afford more of the same."

The Democratic Argument: Like Bush, McCain Is Out of Touch with the Economic Concerns of Real People

By mid-September, the Obama campaign had honed the economic theme that it would deploy for the remainder of the election: where the Democrat would solve the financial crisis, McCain neither could nor would. The building blocks of the new arguments were in place in earlier Democratic attacks, specifically, allegations that McCain had both admitted to not being well versed in economics and lacked empathy for the concerns of ordinary Americans.

In period three, Obama was able to turn the "not ready to lead" argument against his rival in large part because the Arizona senator made three mistakes: saying parenthetically on September 15 what was heard as "the fundamentals of our economy are strong," calling for a commission to study the crisis, and suspending his campaign to broker a deal and then failing to deliver either Republican votes or a better rescue plan. Meanwhile, McCain's surrogate Carly Fiorina, a former Hewlett-Packard CEO, seemed to question both her candidate's credentials and those of his running mate by suggesting that neither was qualified to run a large corporation.[8] At the end of this chapter, we will hypothesize that fumbles such as these, reinforced in Democratic ads and magnified in news, contributed to an erosion of the perception that McCain "shares my values" and has "the judgment needed to be president."

The Fundamentals of Our Economy Are Strong

September 15 wasn't the first time John McCain professed his faith in the underlying resilience of the economy. For the Vietnam veteran, that expression of confidence was a commonplace that had some of the characteristics of a verbal tic.

In mid-August, the Obama campaign exploited McCain's earlier reassurances by stitching together a series of statements, some seriously out of context,[9] suggesting that the Republican candidate was more sanguine about the nation's financial well being than was the public.[10] Indeed, the Democrats had indicted his August 20 statement about fundamental economic strength in an earlier ad.

Since the statement had been turned against him before, McCain's reiteration of it on the day that the Dow plummeted by 500 points was surprising. As contextualized by Obama and the press, it raised the question, "Did he recognize that the country's economy was in dire straits?" If not, the Democratic rhetoric insisted, then he was out of touch, perhaps because he was a "country club" Republican,[11] the wealthy owner of so many houses he couldn't recall the exact number, a kindred spirit of George W. Bush, a proponent of the philosophy that had gotten the country into this mess, or simply too old to know better.

Lost in all of this was what the senator from Arizona had actually said on September 15 and the context in which he said it:

> You know that there's been tremendous turmoil in our financial markets and Wall Street, and it is—it's—people are frightened by these events. Our economy, I think, still the fundamentals of our economy are strong, but these are very, very difficult times. And I promise you we will never put America in this position again. We will clean up Wall Street. We will reform government.[12]

The word "still" in the inopportune sentence looks back to the predicating one, "You know that there's been tremendous turmoil in our financial markets and Wall Street and…people are frightened by these events." In the clause that the Obama campaign confected into the contention that McCain was either callous or clueless, "still" means "despite these factors." As the Arizonan's three concluding statements make clear, the "fundamentals" assertion is not an act of denial but reassurance situated within a diagnosis that included "tremendous turmoil," "people frightened," "very difficult times," and a vague proposed remedy, Wall Street reform.

Since consumer confidence shores up the economy, there is a plausible explanation for McCain's insistence on its fundamental economic strength. Put plainly, confidence in the fundamentals counterbalances his own dire rhetoric to ensure that he is not seen as "talking the economy down." Nor was the statement foolish on its face. How different, after all, is it from the suggestion that, "There are a lot of individual families who are experiencing incredible pain and hardship right now. But if we are keeping focused on all the fundamentally sound aspects of our economy, all the outstanding companies, workers, all the innovation and dynamism in this economy, then we're going to get through this. And I'm very confident about that."[13] When President Barack Obama offered that rhetoric in mid-March, 2009, the Dow was dramatically lower and unemployment higher than their September 15 level. Yet the president's pronouncement did not elicit ridicule, nor was it taken as evidence that the Democratic incumbent was out of touch with reality or with the experience of Middle America. Instead, President Obama's statement was interpreted as "part of an accelerating campaign to project confidence that the nation can pull out of the downturn...."[14]

Setting the frame for McCain's remark were reporters' perceptions that economic matters weren't his strong suit. "Were McCain known as a student of the economy...[his] statement would matter little," noted Dan Balz in the *Washington Post*. "Because he is known as someone who is not, it matters plenty. McCain has responded by ratcheting up his rhetoric about cracking down on Wall Street and Washington."[15]

Within hours of McCain's stumble, Obama was indicting it as a revealing gaffe. In a speech that same day, the Democrat tied it to the notion that the Republican nominee was insensitive to Middle America's pain, "It's not that I think John McCain doesn't care what's going on in the lives of most Americans. I just think he doesn't know. He doesn't get what's happening between the mountain in Sedona where he lives and the corridors of Washington where he works. Why else would he say that we've made great progress economically under George Bush? Why else would he say that the economy isn't something he understands as well as he should? Why else would he say, today, of all days, just a few hours ago that 'the fundamentals of the economy are still strong?'" As it replayed in news, Obama's concise, scripted response invited voters to question both McCain's credibility and his capacity for empathy. "This morning he said that the fundamentals of the economy are still strong. Senator McCain, what economy are you talking about?" asked the Democratic candidate.[16,17]

Within 24 hours of McCain's muddled acknowledgement of turmoil and difficult times but strong fundamentals, news accounts were cementing the Obama version of that moment in public memory by showing McCain uttering the "fundamentals" statement, with the reporter simply paraphrasing the rest of what he'd said if they mentioned it at all. Other moves by reporters magnified the Republican standard-bearer's difficulties. So, for example, an ABC segment quoted a statement the Arizonan made later in the day to suggest that McCain had finally recognized the crisis, a juxtaposition of statements helpful to the Obama's campaign's efforts to characterize McCain as erratic:

JAKE TAPPER (ABC News): (*voiceover*) Obama seized on remarks McCain made in Jacksonville, Florida, this morning to paint his opponent as out of touch. McCain said these are difficult times, but he also said this.

SENATOR JOHN MCCAIN (Republican presidential candidate): The fundamentals of our economy are strong.

SENATOR BARACK OBAMA (Democratic presidential candidate): Senator McCain, what economy are you talking about? What's more fundamental than knowing that your life savings are secure and that you can retire with dignity?

JAKE TAPPER (ABC News): (*voiceove*r) Hours later, at a rally in Orlando, McCain changed his tone.

SENATOR JOHN MCCAIN (Republican presidential candidate): The American economy is in a crisis. It is in a crisis.[18,19]

Within days, news accounts were routinely suggesting that on the day of the Lehman Brothers collapse and the Dow's headlong rush toward 9,000, McCain had declared "the fundamentals of our economy are strong." A search by Annenberg researcher Jackie Dunn for that statement in Lexis Nexis from September 15 through November 4 produces 668 hits in newspapers and 303 in news transcripts. When the search is broadened to include "difficult times" within the same paragraph, the newspaper mentions drop by more than half to 320 in newspapers and 43 news program citations. A search for the entire sentence McCain uttered (which we conducted by adding "turmoil" to the search) produced only 15 broadcast uses and 12 newspaper accounts.[20]

If McCain's statement were taken to mean that he did not recognize the seriousness of the crisis, then it revealed that he and voters resided in different galaxies. After all, from mid-January 2008 onward, more than 50 percent of the public thought the economy was worse than it had been a year ago. After some improvement in perception from late July, on September 14, the day before the McCain statement, we see a steep rise in belief among our NAES phone respondents that the country was on the wrong track (figure 8.2).

Within a day of the McCain remark, the Democrats began reinforcing the truncated version of it in an ad called "Fundamentals." In screaming capital letters, the resulting indictment juxtaposed "SEPTEMBER 15, 2008: JOB LOSSES AT 605,000 FOR THE YEAR" and "SEPTEMBER 15, 2008: FORECLOSURES AT 9800 A DAY" with McCain saying, "Our economy I think, still, the fundamentals of our economy are strong." The ad closes, "HOW CAN JOHN MCCAIN FIX OUR ECONOMY…IF HE DOESN'T UNDERSTAND IT'S BROKEN?" In the final frame, McCain and Bush are shown side by side as the Arizona senator, in a voice-over, is heard saying, "The fundamentals of our economy are strong." For the remainder of the campaign, Democratic ads showcased the abbreviated version of the McCain statement.[21]

The same week, McCain slipped up again, this time in a way that called his understanding of presidential powers into question. Shortly after the Republican nominee decisively declared that were he president he would fire SEC chairman

Christopher Cox,[22] news accounts carried the coda that firing an SEC chair was not within a president's prerogatives.[23]

On October 9, the Democrats added another verbal lapse from the McCain camp to their buffet of spots, with an attack ad reporting that "McCain's own campaign admits that if the election is about the economy, he's going to lose."[24] That spot concludes, "But as Americans lose their jobs, homes, and savings, it's time for a president who will change the economy, not change the subject." The same Republican operative's anonymously voiced admission took center stage in a message moved on air the next day that attacked John McCain for "smears and false attacks." "With no plan to fix our economy," says the ad, "smears are all McCain has left."

On September 15, Obama had urged the electorate to judge the nominees by their response to the financial crisis. "Sen. Barack Obama, D-Ill., told voters [that if they] want to understand [how] he and Sen. John McCain, R-Ariz., differ they should look at how they have responded to the housing and financial crisis," reported ABC News on September 15.[25]

Central to that process was branding McCain with a scarlet E for "erratic." At the Annenberg Public Policy Center's 2008 election debriefing, his chief adviser David Axelrod told the McCain high command in the room, "Obviously you [the McCain campaign] required a course correct for 'the fundamentals of the economy are strong.' When Senator McCain moved from that position to one of crisis pretty quickly, it created a sense of inconsistency. We used the word 'erratic' a lot during that period. Then you [the McCain campaigners] suspended your campaign [to go to Washington to work on pending legislation to address the crisis]. Our feeling was that there was a herky-jerky nature to what was going on [in your campaign] at the time and it played well against our solidity. And I think that was reflected in the numbers."[26]

Bush/McCain and the Republicans Are to Blame
for the Economic Free Fall

For decades, Democrats have morphed the GOP into the party of Wall Street and allied their own with Main Street. According to the logic of these paired associations, if Wall Street failures precipitated an economic meltdown, then it was the Republican party that deserved blame. Following this line of thought, a bailout of Wall Street must be benefitting those in business suits wearing Bush/McCain buttons. By initially casting their initiative as a "Wall Street bailout" rather than a "middle-class rescue plan," President George W. Bush and Federal Reserve chair Ben Bernanke embraced language that both undercut their own efforts and weighted down the McCain campaign.

The Republicans and McCain/Bush Deserve the Blame for the Crisis

The Obama team annotated its arguments about McCain's inadequate grasp of the economy with the notion that the Republican philosophy of deregulation and Republican nominee's close association with financial sector lobbyists either caused or exacerbated the crisis crippling Main Street America. At the same time, in speeches whose sound bites migrated to news, the Democratic standard-bearer alleged that McCain's solutions, including a commission to study the crisis's causes and remedies, were a typical and hence flawed Washington insider's response. The implication was that the Republican nominee was well meaning but out of touch. "I certainly don't fault Senator McCain for these problems. But I do fault the economic philosophy he subscribes to," argued the Democratic standard-bearer on September 15.[27]

Obama then upped the ante by blaming the Republican philosophy of deregulation for the convulsions on Wall Street. Without mentioning Bush or McCain by name, the first of Obama's two-minute national ads both emphasized economic distress and invited voters to incorporate the earlier Democratic attacks on Bush-McCain into this indictment of Washington politics:

> In the past few weeks, Wall Street's been rocked as banks closed and markets tumbled. But for many of you—the people I've met in town halls, backyards, and diners across America, our troubled economy isn't news. 600,000 Americans have lost their jobs since January. Paychecks are flat, and home values are falling. It's hard to pay for gas and groceries, and if you put it on a credit card, they've probably raised your rates. You're paying more than ever for health insurance that covers less and less.
>
> This isn't just a string of bad luck. *The truth is that while you've been living up to your responsibilities Washington has not.* That's why we need change. Real change (emphasis added).[28]

The assault on Washington serves as a subtheme in Obama's positive spots as well. In late September, one advised viewers that Obama had a health care plan "to cut costs and cover everyone." The Illinois senator closed, by saying, "I approve this message because to fix health care, we have to fix Washington." Included in the ad's appeals was a plea to "stop the bickering and the lobbyists."[29]

Obama's second nationally aired two-minute message debuted September 30. In it, the Illinois senator explicitly indicted the Bush economic philosophy. "For eight years," said the candidate speaking in a medium shot, "we've been told that the way to a stronger economy was to give huge tax breaks to corporations and the wealthiest Americans. And somehow prosperity would trickle down. Well, now we know the truth. It didn't work." The Democratic nominee then catalogued the drop in family income, loss of jobs, and deficits before contrasting his tax plan with McCain's and concluding "The old trickle-down theory has failed us. We can't afford four more years like the last eight."[30]

The Obama campaign carried its indictment of Republican economic theory into news coverage as well. "Reacting to the financial crisis, the Democratic party nominee repeatedly cast John McCain as a champion of the deregulation...faulted for the current turmoil on Wall Street in a 40 minute address today that focused heavily on the economic crisis," reported Nick Timiraos in the *Wall Street Journal*.[31] Similarly, on the *CBS Evening News*, Obama is shown saying, "John McCain cannot be trusted to reestablish proper oversight of our financial markets for one simple reason: he has shown time and again that he does not believe in it."[32]

McCain's Message Was Diluted by Hybrid Ads

Before recounting McCain's period-three messages, it is important to note that the playing field on which the campaigns jousted was anything but level. As we observed in chapter 1 and will treat in greater detail in chapter 12, Obama outspent McCain. In an attempt to diminish that Obama advantage, the McCain team turned to hybrid advertising, an FEC-approved form that split the cost of ads with the RNC. Doing so required that the resulting spots bifurcate their attack with half of each ad assaulting Obama and the other half generically attacking the Democrats. The McCain 30-second hybrid titled "Dome" illustrated the resulting problems. At a cost of just under $8 million, this was the second-most-broadcast message of the McCain campaign. In it, the Republicans deployed traditional attacks by arguing that Obama and his allies were liberals whose election would bring bigger government, wasteful new spending, and increased taxes.

> ANNOUNCER: When our economy's in crisis, a big government casts a big shadow on us all. Obama and his liberal congressional allies want a massive government, billions in spending increases, wasteful pork. And we would pay—painful income taxes, skyrocketing taxes on life savings, electricity, and home heating oil. Can your family afford that?[33]

The most aired McCain ad was also a hybrid. At a cost of almost $8 million in air time, throughout September, "Expensive Plans" said:

> ANNOUNCER: Take away the crowds, the chants. All that's left are costly words. Barack Obama and out-of-touch congressional leaders have expensive plans. Billions in new government spending, years of deficits, no balanced budgets, and painful tax increases on working American families. They're ready to tax, ready to spend, but not ready to lead.[34]

One of the least coherent hybrid ads appeared October 10. Its message indicted Obama's "blind ambition." "When convenient, he worked with terrorist Bill Ayers," says the ad. "When discovered, he lied. Obama. Blind ambition. Bad judgment." Then the non sequitur, "Congressional liberals fought for risky subprime loans...."[35]

So incomprehensible were some of the McCain-RNC hybrids that Republican operative and CNN commentator Alex Castellanos emailed McCain ad-maker Chris Mottola with the suggestion, "If you have any time left at the end of the [hybrid]spot, you need to say, 'If anyone has any idea what this spot is about, call 1–800-McCain-Palin.'"[36]

"When you create hybrid ads, you have to involve lawyers who say you need to have 30 words for McCain and 30 for the RNC," explained Mottola. "You've got to equal those out. So you've got lawyers rewriting spots. Our lawyers were great, and they were trying to protect the campaign and John McCain and everybody from liability, but the list of great political spots written at 8:00 at night by lawyers with FCC training is zero." Believing them ineffective, the McCain campaign ultimately abandoned this blended form of message. "[Finally] in October, we made a decision to stop doing the hybrid ads and to ship all the remaining money to the RNC," recalls McCain campaign manager Steve Schmidt. "[We made that decision] on the simple basis that the hybrid ads that the campaign was producing made no sense."[37]

Democrats Are Responsible for the Economic Meltdown

The fact that McCain's ads were often tacitly or explicitly reacting to Obama's charges reflects the Republican campaign's struggle to grab hold of the campaign agenda. Responding to the omnibus Obama claim that his opponent was out of touch with the economy, one Republican spot tried to turn the tables by saying, "Obama has no background in economics." The ad, which we discussed in chapter 4, then pivoted to indict supposed Obama adviser Franklin Raines as a Washington insider responsible for the economic meltdown.[38]

Where Obama tagged the Arizona senator with an alliance with Washington lobbyists, as we noted earlier McCain responded by tying Obama to Jim Johnson, the former Fannie Mae head. Like others, this ad links the notion that Obama's rhetoric is either empty or suspect to a specific issue claim. In the attack ad titled "Jim Johnson," Obama is shown saying, "It would be unacceptable for executives of these institutions to earn a windfall" with the overlay, "What Obama says...is not what he does." "Meet Jim Johnson, former Fannie Mae CEO," notes the announcer as a picture of Johnson appears under a quotation from the *Washington Post,* saying, "Fannie Mae Lobbies Hard to Protect its Tax Break." "Fannie cooked the books and Johnson made millions" said the ad. "Then Obama asked him to pick his VP and raise thousands for his campaign. Barack Obama. More empty words."[39]

Obama and McCain each blamed the other's party for the economic melt-down. Challenged for supporting the outsourcing of jobs,[40] McCain fielded an ad in Michigan (shortly before the campaign pulled its resources from that state) saying, "Michigan manufacturing jobs are going overseas. Barack Obama and his liberal allies are to blame." The reason? Democrats had voted against "mak-ing health care more affordable," against "reduce[d] energy costs," against "lower taxes."[41] Short of funds, the Republicans decided on October 2 to withdraw from that electoral-vote-rich state in order to reallocate resources.[42] The reason given by McCain's pollster was the vulnerability created by McCain's statement in the Michigan primary season that "the [auto industry] jobs aren't coming back,[43] a conclusion President Obama himself offered without a hint of irony as "a hard truth" on July 14, 2008.[44]

After airing ads castigating Democrats, McCain inexplicably put up a spot in early October in which he said, "What a week. Democrats blamed Republicans. Republicans blamed Democrats. It shouldn't take a crisis to pull us together. We need a president who can avert crisis...." The bipartisan rhetoric was short-lived. On October 10, a hybrid McCain/RNC ad alleged that "Congressional liber-als fought for risky sub-prime loans. Congressional liberals fought against more

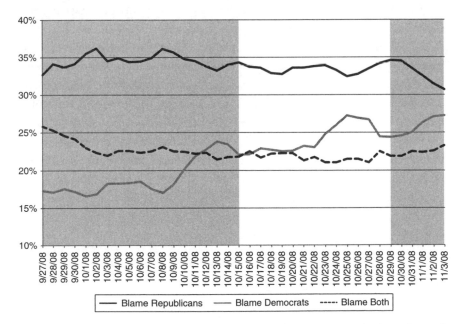

FIGURE 8.5 Attribution of Blame for "Current Financial Crisis Facing the United States" (5-day PMA). *Source*: NAES08 telephone survey.

regulation. The housing market collapsed, costing you billions." The spot closed by attacking "judgment," the trait on which Obama had built his candidacy. "We need leadership," it said, "not bad judgment."[45]

Although the percentage of voters blaming the Democrats for the economic mess rose from the end of September to Election Day (see figure 8.5), in the contest over which party should shoulder responsibility, more of our respondents affixed the blame to the Republicans. Pointing fingers at the Republicans predicted an Obama vote; indicting the Democrats did the same for support for the Republican ticket. Presumably aware of this dynamic, the Republicans tried to associate Obama with Democrats in Congress.*

Electing a Tax-and-Spend Liberal Would Make Matters Worse

As we forecast in chapter 2, in this period, McCain's ads linked his prospective presidency to "change" and allied Obama with a discredited liberal past tied to big government, massive spending increases, and tax hikes. In one McCain/RNC hybrid ad, the words "MASSIVE GOVERNMENT" appear over a picture of a smiling Obama superimposed on the Capitol dome. That spot makes explicit its assumption that bigger government would exacerbate the crisis. "Obama and his liberal congressional allies want a massive government. Billions in spending increases, wasteful pork." The announcer then repeats the single-most-often aired deception of the McCain campaign, the notion that Obama would raise taxes on everyone. "And *we* would pay painful income taxes, skyrocketing taxes on life savings, electricity, and home heating oil. Can *your* family afford that?" (emphasis added). Over McCain's picture, the tag proclaims, "Change is coming."[46] From early September through mid-October, the McCain campaign rotated two tags on its ads: "Change is coming" and "The original maverick" and occasionally reprised its spring and summer theme, "Experience and Leadership," with the addition of the words, "in a time of crisis."[47]

The Republicans' efforts to increase perceptions that Obama was a liberal had little effect in period three (see figure 8.6). By October 14 that perception had returned only to its set point after the Republican convention.

Obama Is Not Ready To Lead

September 15 was a circled date in the McCain calendar as well. It was during that week that the Republican team had planned to lay in place pieces of Obama's

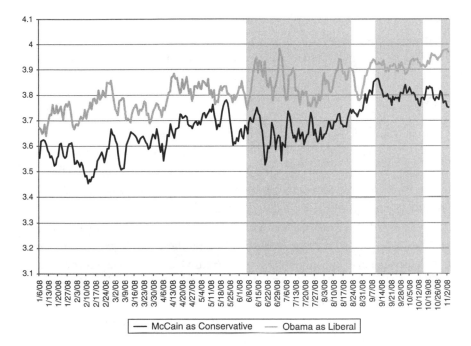

FIGURE 8.6 Perceptions of Candidate Ideology (5-day PMA). *Source*: NAES08 telephone survey.

biography that would build on the celebrity ads of summer to underscore the notion that the Democratic nominee was not ready to lead. Unlike the earlier foray into this argument, which in August attracted substantial cable news attention, in October, press preoccupation with the economic crisis wiped out the possibility that these McCain themes would garner much media attention. Instead, the news on the economy featured the blunders by McCain and his surrogates we discussed earlier.

All of this frustrated the Republican campaign's plans. "People say, 'Why didn't you run a campaign against Obama?'" recalled McCain pollster Bill McInturff. "We had a campaign against Obama. It started in September…with the Chicago ad. That's the start of what was going to be a six- or seven-week narrative saying, 'He's not quite the guy you think he is. He's not quite ready.'" These ads raised such questions as, "Is he really going to be president? What's he really done? Is he experienced enough?" McInturff reasoned, "There're a lot of fundamental questions. You can feed into that by saying, 'In fact, there's more about him you need to know. He's not the reformer you think he is. He's part of this Chicago machine. We have these concerns.'…We were going to start with the Chicago story, because in fact the guy did have a layer of protection. If you started with the issues, people said, 'No, that doesn't fit. Doesn't fit.…That's not the guy I'm seeing.' We had to raise fundamental questions about the guy they were seeing." But instead of focusing on the attacks, he added, the press focused on "what's happening to the economy. And our typical campaign stuff gets blown off the air."[48]

Where the Democrats hammered home the notion that McCain was McSame, the Republicans struggled to break through with their central attack on Obama's unreadiness to be president. One ad tying Obama to a discredited presumed adviser closed by charging, "Barack Obama. Bad advice. Bad instincts. Not ready to lead." "Not ready to lead" is also the tag on an ad associating him with Tony Rezko, the Chicago political machine and convicted felon we discussed in the fourth chapter. "Too risky for America," an allied notion, is the closing line in the October 6 ad that took Obama's words out of context to say, "He says our troops in Afghanistan are 'just air-raiding villages and killing civilians.' "[49]

A series titled "Who is Barack Obama?" was added to the McCain mix in early October. In an attack on Obama's trustworthiness, these ads alleged that the Democrat's messages had knowingly mischaracterized McCain's stances on Social Security, health care, and stem cell research. "Barack Obama. He promised better," said one of them "He lied."[50] Another answered the question, "Who is Barack Obama?" with "The National Journal says he's the Senate's most liberal. How extreme."[51]

McCain vs. Obama as Reassuring Leader

In the period on which we are focusing here, McCain worked aggressively to overcome the negative framing of his comments on the economy that we treated earlier. Before offering reassurance that he knew how to turn around the economy, the Arizonan needed to convince the public that, contrary to the Obama allegations, he understood that the country was in crisis. To address the "fundamentals" gaffe, the Republicans aired declarations that the state of the economy was dismal. For example, the hybrid "Dome," with which we dealt a moment ago, overlaid a shot of the nation's capitol with the words "Our Economy in Crisis" as the announcer offered a statement that made little sense: "When our economy's in crisis, a big government casts a big shadow on us all." If there was a shadow, the giant casting it was known by names such as Lehman Brothers and AIG. Moreover it was not big government's intrusion in the market that was the culprit in the media's stories of what went wrong, but rather decisions to reduce governmental power through deregulation. And as we will show in a moment, McCain himself was calling for more, not less, regulation.

Hoping to dispatch the Obama characterization of McCain's response to the crisis as "erratic," Republican ads highlighted unambiguous but nonetheless abstract declarations about McCain's goals. "I'll meet this financial crisis head-on," declared the Arizonan in one. "Reform Wall Street. New rules for fairness and honesty. I won't tolerate a system that puts you and your family at risk."[52] In another, the Republican nominee affirmed, "I'll reform Wall Street and fix Washington. I've taken on tougher guys than this before."[53] Of course, these ads worked only to the extent that the viewer granted McCain's credibility on the issue, an attribute being undermined by the Obama campaign. As we will note in a moment, during this period as in those that followed, Obama counterbalanced his attacks on McCain with his own detailed rhetoric of decisive leadership and reassurance.

Period three is not simply the story of a drop in McCain's favorable ratings but the tale as well of a rise in the perception of Obama's credentials, an increase that in the short-term at least did not substantially improve his favorability rating. Two factors are at play in this second narrative: Obama's use of 60- and 120-second direct-to-camera ads and his successful performance in the first presidential debate on September 26.

Two-Minute Ads

When the charges being hurled against a candidate contain the words "unready" and "risk," one effective response is to offer reassuring exposure to the maligned candidate. On September 17 at a cost of just under $4 million, the Democrats reached into a bank account brimming with dollars raised outside the federal finance system to pay for a two-minute ad titled "Real Change." In it, their candidate comforted and counseled the country in a fashion designed to shore up national polls and battleground state votes:

> Here's what I believe we need to do. Reform our tax system to give a $1,000 tax break to the middle class instead of showering more on oil companies and corporations that outsource our jobs. End the "anything goes" culture on Wall Street with real regulation that protects your investments and pensions. Fast-track a plan for energy "made in America" that will free us from our dependence on Mideast oil in 10 years and put millions of Americans to work. Crack down on lobbyists—once and for all—so their back-room deal-making no longer drowns out the voices of the middle class and undermines our common interests as Americans. And yes, bring a responsible end to this war in Iraq so we stop spending billions each month rebuilding their country when we should be rebuilding ours.
>
> Doing these things won't be easy. But we're Americans. We've met tough challenges before. And we can again. I'm Barack Obama. I hope you'll read my economic plan. I approve this message because bitter, partisan fights and outworn ideas of the Left and the Right won't solve the problems we face today. But a new spirit of unity and shared responsibility will.[54]

The ad was successful in influencing perceptions of Obama's "trustworthiness." In a regression model predicting the difference in that scale (Obama minus McCain), the ad-buy data for the two-minute advertisement produced a significant and positive relationship in the presence of controls.*

On the same day, the Republicans countered with a half-million-dollar buy to air "Foundation." In this message, which was a quarter the length of the Obama's two-minute speech, the Republican nominee suggested, as we noted a moment ago, that all Obama offered was "talk and taxes," an argument undercut by the policy detail in the Obama two-minute soliloquy:

> JOHN MCCAIN: You, the American workers, are the best in the world. But your economic security has been put at risk by the greed of Wall Street. That's unacceptable. My opponent's only solutions are talk and taxes. I'll reform Wall Street and fix Washington. I've taken on tougher guys than this before.
>
> ANNOUNCER: Change is coming. John McCain.[55]

The First Debate—September 26, 2008

As important as the hair-raising news about the economy was the fact that the Dow Jones industrial average declined dramatically on three of the four days on which general election debates were held, losing more than 2,500 points between the first and last of these encounters. Moreover, between the first presidential debate on September 26 and the October 2 showdown between the vice presidential nominees, this key economic index crashed through the 11,000 floor. In the brief period between that vice presidential exchange and the second presidential debate, October 7, the Dow plunged through the 10,000 mark. In the week between the second and third presidential face-off, the 9,000 barrier was breached. On October 15, the day of that final debate, it plunged 733 points, its second-largest single-day drop ever (table 8.1).[56]

TABLE 8.1. Dow Closing on
Days of Presidential Debates,
2008

Date	Index
9/26/2008	11143.13
10/2/2008	10482.85
10/7/2008	9447.11
10/15/2008	8577.91

Downward drafts in the Dow matter in part because, as the Investment Company Institute reports, 55.3 million households own mutual funds, a number that means that nearly half of U.S. households have a stake in the stock market.[57] And the *Wall Street Journal*/NBC poll found in March 2009 that "Americans most likely to have stock investments—those with family incomes above $50,000—also are markedly more likely to say they are very dissatisfied with the economy."[58] Consistent with this finding, in September and October 2008 NAES respondents with family income over $50,000 were significantly more likely than those with lower incomes to report that the economy had gotten worse.

The first debate was the only one on which the Dow was up day-over-day (see figure 8.7). At the close of business on the September 26, the increase over the day before was 200 points on what Erin Burnett on NBC News called "the hopes of...a possible bailout."[59] However, even then the economic signals were, as Brit Hume reported on Fox News, "mixed." "The Dow was up a little more than 121. The Nasdaq dropped about three and a quarter, and the S&P gained just four."[60]

With Obama scheduled to appear at the first debate and the bailout unresolved, McCain had little choice but to rethink his pledge to forgo the nationally televised event, a decision he originally made in order to stay in Washington to

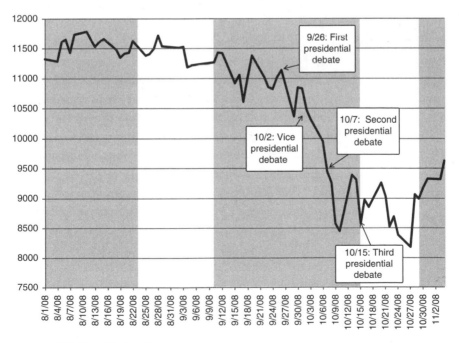

FIGURE 8.7 Dow Closing Average.

help resolve the legislative deadlock. But here too the economic collapse under-mined him. Where the candidates had agreed that the first debate would con-centrate exclusively on foreign affairs, this new climate dictated that half of the candidates' first encounter be devoted to the economy.

Throughout the debate, Obama reinforced his central theme by pinning the crisis squarely on Bush and McCain:

> We also have to recognize that this is a final verdict on eight years of failed economic policies promoted by George Bush, supported by Senator McCain, a theory that basically says that we can shred regulations and consumer protections and give more and more to the most, and some-how prosperity will trickle down. It hasn't worked. And I think that the fundamentals of the economy have to be measured by whether or not the middle class is getting a fair shake.[61]

At every opportunity the Democrat advanced his economic argument against the Republican nominee in ways that reinforced the Democratic ads and the cam-paign's sound bites that had infiltrated news:

> We've had years in which the reigning economic ideology has been what's good for Wall Street, but not what's good for Main Street... [It's impor-tant that we] look at some of the underlying issues that have led to wages and incomes for ordinary Americans to go down, the—a health care sys-tem that is broken, energy policies that are not working, because, you know, 10 days ago, John said that the fundamentals of the economy are sound.
>
> ....when you look at your tax policies that are directed primarily at those who are doing well, and you are neglecting people who are really struggling right now, I think that is a continuation of the last eight years, and we can't afford another four.
>
> ....John mentioned me being wildly liberal. Mostly that's just me opposing George Bush's wrongheaded policies since I've been in Congress.
>
> ....John, it's been your president who you said you agreed with 90 percent of the time who presided over this increase in spending. This orgy of spending and enormous deficits you voted for almost all of his budgets. So to stand here and after eight years and say that you're going to lead on controlling spending and, you know, balancing our tax cuts so that they help middle class families when over the last eight years that hasn't happened I think just is, you know, kind of hard to swallow.[62]

Conventional wisdom says that first presidential debates advantage the candidate being attacked for being inexperienced or risky. John Kennedy gained ground in the first Kennedy-Nixon debate. So too did John Kerry in his first debate with incumbent president George W. Bush in 2004. That was the case in 2008 as well. Viewing the first presidential debate predicted a significant increase in the perception that Obama would do a better job than McCain at handling the economy in the presence of controls.* As worrisome for the McCain campaign was the finding that viewing the debate also predicted a significant increase in the perception that electing McCain would in effect produce a third Bush term.*

These data are consistent with David Axelrod's belief that "this race was won between September 15th and September 26th." At the Annenberg debriefing, Obama's chief strategist argued, "I really think this race was over after the first debate. I think that the lines of demarcation were the first day of the Lehman Brothers collapse, the global crisis, and Senator McCain's comment that the fundamentals of the economy were strong, which just seemed completely discordant with everybody's perception of what was going on. It fed our narrative that he, like the president, was completely out of touch with the reality of the economy. We drove it hard in ads...." By contrast, Obama "was very measured throughout. I think he looked very presidential, and very thoughtful, and very focused, and consistent through that nine-day period."[63]

Nor did the environment improve for the Republican nominee in the following week. Instead it became clear that McCain's efforts to broker bipartisan support for the rescue plan had failed. "On September 29th, the Monday of the vote," Schmidt notes, "I was on a plane with Governor Palin and watching the split screen of the markets collapsing and the bill being voted down. Then the news conference when the Republicans said they did this because Nancy Pelosi gave a mean speech."[64] "I very rarely sleep on planes," notes Schmidt. "But I took off my headphones (it was a JetBlue charter) and fell asleep almost instantly, like I was being anaesthetized in a doctor's office."[65]

Nor did the ultimate passage of the bill [October 3] improve McCain's prospects. "After being larded up with an extra $150 billion dollars in what some considered pork and others saw as a process of quid pro quo needed to secure Republican votes," Schmidt adds, "the bailout finally passed...and contrary to what the public had been led to expect, in subsequent days the market dropped another 1,800 points."[66]

The Vice Presidential Debate and the Dow

The economic news on the evening of the October 2 vice presidential debate was anxiety-producing as well. The evening before, the "rescue package" had passed the Senate overwhelmingly. However, it failed in the House the first time it went to the floor. On October 2, it was not clear whether the bill would make it through on the second try. "The importance of tonight's debate might be overshadowed by the country's financial meltdown,"[67] observed David Gregory on MSNBC. On the evening of the debate, Charlie Gibson of ABC News attributed the 348-point drop in the Dow that day in part "to fears the economic rescue package pending in the House won't pass."[68]

The Second Debate—October 7, 2008 and the Dow

Unlike the "mixed" news from Wall Street on the night of the first presidential debate, on the evening of the second the message was clear. Where the day before the vice presidential debate the Dow dropped 350, on October 7, the day of the second presidential debate, it was in a free fall, closing 508 points down from the previous day's low. "For the first time in four years," noted Maggie Rodriguez on CBS, "the Dow was below 10,000, and at one point dropped 800 points."[69]

Coming into that debate, the press focus on horse race cast McCain, who was behind in the polls, in a negative light. So, for example, speaking from the Nashville, Tennessee site of the second presidential debate, MSNBC's Chris Matthews observed that, "Tonight's debate could be a last opportunity for John McCain to change the direction of the presidential race. McCain's poll numbers have been headed downward along with the economy, and he didn't get any help from Wall Street today. The Dow Jones fell more than 500 points today, bringing the total one-year decline to an awesome 5,000 points."[70]

Obama may have gained marginally from the second presidential debate as well. We find that watching it was positively related both to the view that he would handle the economy better and the perception that a McCain election would equal a Bush third, but these relationships do not reach conventional levels of statistical significance.*

More important is our finding that overall debate viewing was significantly associated with the favorability ratings for Obama but not McCain.* The more debates respondents reported watching, the more likely they were to report a more favorable assessment of the Democratic candidate. By contrast, none of the debate watching coefficients were significant predictors of the Republican candidates' favorability ratings. The limits of cross sections mean that we can't justify the strong causal claim that debate viewing produced an increase in favorability ratings for Barack Obama and Joe Biden. However, since these associations were

significant in the face of a robust set of controls, we think we can make a plausible
case for such an effect.

Overall, Obama's candidacy was helped and McCain's hurt in period three.
In this time frame, the gap separating them on judgment and "experience needed
to be president," two traits that had advantaged McCain, narrowed, and the spread
between the two on "shares my values" expanded, all to McCain's disadvantage
(see figures 8.8, 8.9, and 8.10). Aggregate-level correlation between these trait variables and the date of survey shows that in period three the changes outlined in the
following charts are statistically significant. In each case, McCain lost more than
Obama gained.

In our model, the beliefs that the country is on the wrong track, the economy
is the most important issue, and Republicans should be blamed for the crisis predict the notion that electing McCain equals a Bush third term and also increase
the likelihood of a favorable rating of Obama. A series of regression analyses
indicate the interrelations among these variables.* TV and newspaper use and
the perception that the country is on the wrong track are significantly related to
economic concerns, a conclusion consistent with the agenda setting and priming
effects forecast earlier. Concern about the economy is significantly and positively

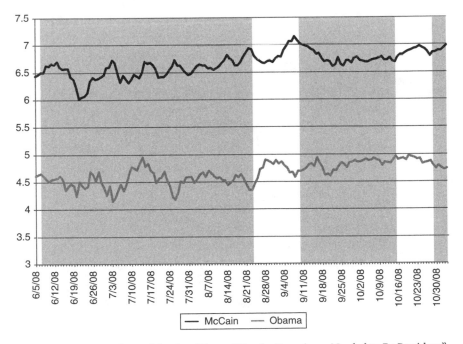

FIGURE 8.8 Perceptions of the Candidates: "Has the Experience Needed to Be President"
(5-day PMA). *Source*: NAES08 telephone survey.

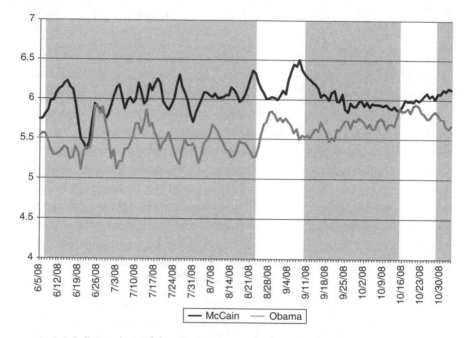

FIGURE 8.9 Perceptions of the Candidates: "Has the Judgment Needed to be President" (5-day PMA). *Source*: NAES08 telephone survey.

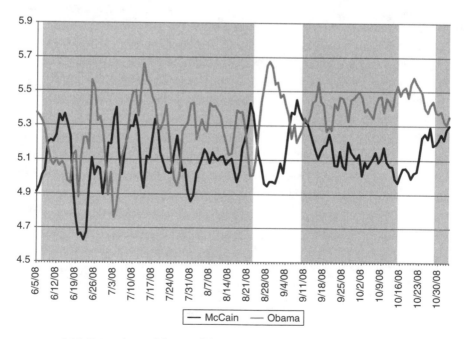

FIGURE 8.10 Perceptions of the Candidates: "Shares My Values" (5-day PMA). *Source*: NAES08 telephone survey.

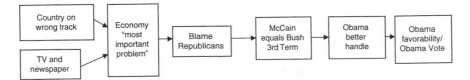

FIGURE 8.11   Theoretical Progression to Obama Vote through Economic Concerns.

related to the belief that the Republicans are responsible for the economic melt-down. Blaming the GOP significantly predicts the belief that electing McCain is the same as electing Bush for a third term. These variables are significantly and positively related to the belief that Obama can handle the economy better than McCain, which in turn predicts Obama favorability and an Obama vote. Figure 8.11 illustrates our logic.

In period three, belief that the country is on the wrong track rises and, with it, the perception that the economy is the major issue facing the country. At the same time, perception that the Republicans are to blame for the crisis remains high, and the rope tying McCain to Bush is tightened. Each independently predicts an increased likelihood of indicating a vote preference for Obama.

As important is the fact that the plummeting economy unnerved a key Republican constituency (figures 8.12 and 8.13). McCain lost support among educated white men, a reliable part of a Republican candidate's base. Where in the 2000 general election, 60.5 percent of educated white men supported Bush, in 2004 that percent was 56.7 percent,[71] according to the 2000 and 2004 NAES. By contrast, McCain's margin was in single digits.

For college-educated white males, the model we just sketched works in the same way that it does for the population as a whole. Perception that the country is on the wrong track, the belief that the Republicans are responsible for the economic crash, and that view that electing McCain will in effect produce a third Bush term all independently predict an increased likelihood that educated white men will say that they prefer Obama for president.*

Taken together, this analysis suggests that period three dramatically circumscribed McCain's chances and significantly boosted Obama's as well. This sort of movement is of course consistent with the notion that in the face of an unpopular Republican incumbent and faltering economy, voters will increasingly do what the models suggest and move to the Democrat. Surprisingly, in period four, that forecast did not hold true. Instead, after the third and final presidential debate on October 15, McCain began to move up in vote preference. To explain this turn in fortune, the next chapter will argue that an infelicitous utterance by the Democratic nominee opened his candidacy to charges some found compelling.

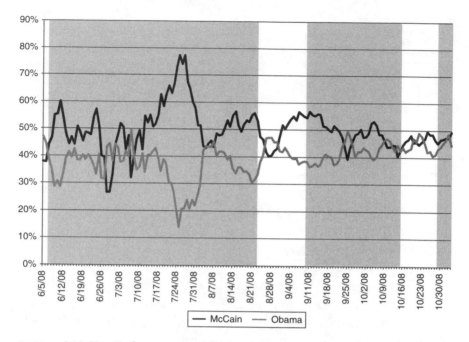

FIGURE 8.12 Vote Preference among White Males with at Least 4 Years of College (5-day PMA). *Source*: NAES08 telephone survey.

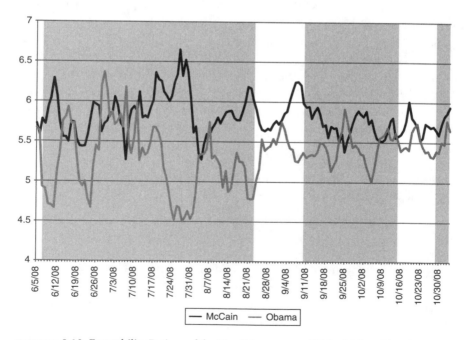

FIGURE 8.13 Favorability Ratings of the Candidates among White Males with at Least 4 Years of College (5-day PMA). *Source*: NAES08 telephone survey.

NINE

Period Four: The McCain Surge (October 15–28)

I N THE FINAL WEEKS OF OCTOBER, THE MCCAIN CAMPAIGN CLAIMED the offensive on the tax issue and, by so doing, gained a fingers-clinging-to-a-ledge hold on the possibility that its candidate could use it to regain momentum in a contest that seemed otherwise to have slipped from McCain's grasp. In this chapter, we account for the resurrection in the Republican ticket's favorability in the two weeks following the October 15 presidential debate (see figure 9.1).

What improved McCain's prospects was his campaign's use of a chance encounter between Obama and a voter that happened a few days before the final debate of 2008. On October 12, in a rare lapse, the Harvard-educated Democrat reprised his professorial past by instructing a typecast blue-collar worker in the merits of "sharing the wealth." The protagonist in the resulting Republican-scripted morality play was "Joe the Plumber" in the role of average person and "share the wealth," a window into the soul of a patronizing tax-and-spend liberal. If the Republicans succeeded, "share the wealth" would also telegraph that its promulgator was "out of touch," as surely as had Democratic recasting of McCain's ill-timed assertion roughly a month earlier that "the fundamentals of the economy are strong." In short, Senator Barack Obama's apparent eagerness to "share" what he mistakenly thought was Joe the Plumber's "wealth" was an answer to Republican prayers. In one of the ironies of the 2008 election, the Democratic nominee's statement, like McCain's, was taken out of context.

In the stage-managed world of politics, some extemporaneous utterances are polished by opponents and the media into mirrors reflecting the Dorian Gray beneath the veneer of the candidate's scripted self. So, for example, in summer

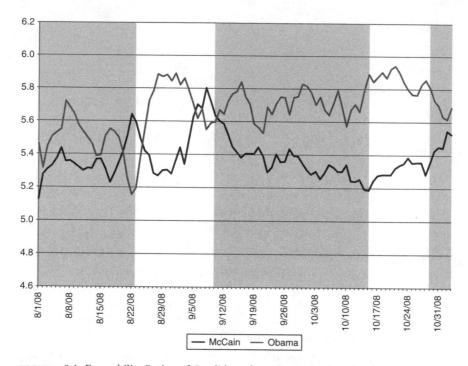

FIGURE 9.1 Favorability Rating of Candidates from the Beginning of August 2008 to Election Day (5-day PMA). *Source*: NAES08 telephone survey.

2004 Senator John Kerry's prospects of delivering a presidential inaugural plummeted when he rationalized his vote for continued funding for the war in Iraq by saying, "I actually did vote for the 87 billion before I voted against it."[1] Similarly, in the 2008 primaries, Senator Hillary Clinton's odds of winning her party's nomination were lengthened when she inaccurately recalled "landing under sniper fire"[2] when she visited Tuzla, Bosnia, in 1996; central to the resulting attacks was footage of the landing showing Senator Clinton being greeted with a hug by a little girl who read the first lady a poem. Along the same lines, Senator Barack Obama's blue-collar appeal dissipated in the Pennsylvania primary as press focus heightened awareness of a recording of him saying that when those in small towns experienced economic problems "it's not surprising then they get bitter, they cling to guns or religion or antipathy to people who aren't like them or anti-immigrant sentiment or anti-trade sentiment as a way to explain their frustrations."[3]

John McCain recognized the significance of his opponent's mid-October stumble. "You know [when] we look back on political campaigns," he told Sean Hannity on Fox. "[We see] 'I paid for this microphone, Mr. Breen.' Ed Muskie crying outside the *Union Leader....* [T]here are moments when something happens.

And clearly Senator Obama going to Joe the Plumber's driveway and him [Joe] getting an answer that clearly he didn't like [was one of those moments]."[4]

In the postelection debriefing, McCain strategist Steve Schmidt remarked that "[t]he [Obama] encounter...before the third debate defined the tax issue...in a way that we had been unable to define it for the entire campaign."[5] The electorate found the notion that Obama had said he wanted to share the wealth "convincing," added McCain pollster Bill McInturff. "[A]fter having lost the tax message, we got it back."[6] Fortunately for the cash–strapped Republican campaign, the Obama slip occurred before the third presidential debate, an event whose audience exceeded 56 million viewers.

In the following pages, we argue that during the period of October 15–28, Senator McCain effectively exploited inconsistencies in the Democrats' explanation of their taxation plans and Obama's injudicious exchange with Joe the Plumber. If these moves succeeded, the public would conclude that the Democratic nominee would raise taxes in order to benefit the undeserving. In order to make sense of that Republican assault on the Democratic ticket, we need to begin by mapping the candidates' give-and-take on the tax issue in the months leading up to the third and final presidential debate.

The Democrat as Tax Cutter and the Republican as Tax Raiser

For most of the general election, the Democrats made inroads on the tax issue by persistently arguing that Obama offered greater reductions for the middle class than did McCain. The gospel according to the Illinois senator included a tax cut for 95 percent of a group sometimes cast broadly as "Americans" and at other times more narrowly as "working Americans" or "working families."[7] If believed, this promise undercut the Republican mantra that Democrats are congenitally disposed to raise taxes and Republicans to cut them. To underscore his argument, Obama reiterated that he would only increase taxes on those (sometimes referred to as couples or households but occasionally implied to be individuals) making more than $250,000 and individuals making more than $200,000. As part of the package, he would reduce federal taxes for 95 percent of Americans.[8] Underlying the Democratic proposal was an ingenious political calculation. If everyone advantaged by the Obama plan were to vote for him, he would win in a landslide.

Meanwhile, from October 1 through the election, the Obama team hammered home the misleading assertion that McCain pollster Bill McInturff characterized as a "rip your heart out health tax" claim[9] that, if elected, the Republican presidential contender would raise most people's taxes by making employer-provided health benefits taxable for the first time. That frequently aired deception capitalized on the Democrat's ownership of the health care reform issue.

In contrast with decades of campaigns in which the Republicans comman-deered the tax issue, a mid-October *New York Times*/CBS News poll found 51 percent of respondents thinking that McCain would raise taxes, compared with 46 percent saying the same of the Democrat.[10] Our survey, as well as others, con-firmed that McCain's focus on this issue in the final weeks of October paid off. On October 31, the *New York Times*/CBS News poll reported that "[f]orty-seven percent of voters said Mr. McCain would not raise taxes on people like them, up from 38 percent who said so two weeks ago."[11]

These end-of-October polling numbers suggest that, although his message was beginning to get through, it still had a long way to go to undo the damage inflicted by the Democratic attack. After all, McCain insisted that he didn't intend to raise taxes on anyone,[12] a promise that only made sense if one assumes that his proposed tax would drive employers and employees to drop high-dollar plans. Should that forecast prove faulty, his campaign contended that the numbers cov-ered by "Cadillac plans" were in any event small. Of course the Democrats con-tested both of these assertions. "For us to have been able to diffuse and neuter the tax issue was an important thing to have accomplished," observed Obama media director Jim Margolis.[13] "We figured if [the Republicans]…were going to come after us, it was going to be on taxes," noted chief Obama strategist David Axelrod at the Annenberg election debriefing. "So we wanted to inoculate against that early. We had a middle-class tax cut from a year earlier. We pushed that issue hard." "The Obama campaign did a masterful job of stealing the tax issue from the Republi-cans," reported Axelrod's counterpart, Steve Schmidt.[14]

The McCain campaign responded to the neutering of their signature attack by arguing deceptively that Obama's plans called not only for raising everyone's taxes but also for imposing new ones, for example, on electricity and small businesses making less than $250,000. From Michael Dobbs at the *Washington Post* to Bill Adair at PolitiFact and Brooks Jackson at FackCheck.org, the fact police called the Republican campaign on these false tax charges.

The distortions were spread in appearances, in candidate stump speeches, in ads, and by campaign surrogates in news and cable talk shows. As we noted earlier, a McCain-RNC ad called "Dome" used an image of the Capitol dome and alleged that under Obama and "his liberal allies" "we would pay painful income taxes, skyrocketing taxes on life savings and home heating oil." The spot, which, as we discussed earlier, was the second-most-aired message from McCain and the Republicans, closed with the question, "Can your family afford that?"

In the final month of the campaign, the McCain tax charge against Obama gained traction. NAES data suggest that a majority of middle-income

Americans making between $35,000 and $150,000 believed, contrary to Obama's pledge, that with him as president their taxes would go up, not down. An even larger number of people from households in the $150,000–$249,999 income range (whose taxes would remain unchanged if the Democrat kept his word) foresaw an Obama tax increase. Those making over $250,000, however, had gotten the message that a tax increase was in their future under an Obama administration.

Obama had consistently stated that only those couples and businesses making more than $250,000 would see a tax increase. And, as we noted earlier, he had repeatedly declared that 95 percent of Americans would see a tax cut, without being as clear about the income levels to which that cut would apply, leading some to conclude that those under $250,000 would see a reduction.

The Republican attack on proposed Democratic tax increases assumed that Obama's voting record exposed dispositions denied in his campaign rhetoric. In ads aired as early as July, the McCain campaign argued that "Obama voted to raise taxes on working Americans making just $32,000 a year," an allegation based on a vote by Obama for a nonbinding budget resolution. Had the resolution had force, it would have "sunset" the provisions of the 2001 and 2003 Bush tax cuts and, as a result, increased taxes on those making more than $41,500 in gross income.[15] Whatever the implications of that vote, Obama's 2008 proposals preserved all of the Bush tax cuts for those in the lower income brackets. Because past action is a generally reliable indicator of future performance, the question the Republicans in effect were raising was, which was more reliable, the rhetoric or the record? In the final weeks of the campaign, when Obama and Biden gave them an opening to argue that Obama's promised tax cuts were a ruse, the Republicans reprised the $42,000 argument.

The Democratic Argument on Taxes against McCain

In the contest over health care reform in general and his proposal in particular, McCain faced a serious hurdle. Specifically, on that hotly contested topic, public belief in Democratic competence was overwhelming. From 1992 to the end of 2007, Gallup surveys found the Democrats trouncing their counterparts in handling it. The fleeting exception occurred in 1994, the year in which the Clinton health care reform effort crashed.[16] Although his lead was not as decisive as the 30-point advantage that the Democrats had on the issue in late 2007, Obama bested McCain on handling health care throughout the closing month of the general election. The Republicans responded by putting into play another reliable, party-based assumption: Obama's plan was a big-government takeover of health

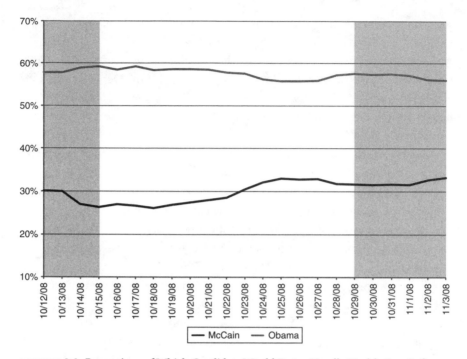

FIGURE 9.2 Perceptions of Which Candidate Would Better Handle Health Care Reform
(5-day PMA). *Source*: NAES08 telephone survey.

care, an allegation the Democrats challenged by arguing that Obama's program
preserved the private insurance model, even as it opened increased access to a
federal program.

Because McCain's health care plan was complicated, it all but invited simplifying attacks. The cost an employer pays in health benefits is currently not
counted as employee income and hence is not subject to income tax. By contrast, an individual who goes into the market to purchase insurance does so with
post-tax funds. McCain planned to tax employees for the insurance cost paid by
their employers on their behalf and then counteract the effects of that tax for
all but those with very high-value plans by providing an offsetting tax credit.
The tax credit would have been $5,000 for employer-insured families, $2,500
for insured individuals. By ignoring the tax credit, the Obama allegation that
McCain planned to tax "your health benefits" sinned by omission. Since most
of those with health insurance in the United States receive it as an employee
benefit, and comparatively few among them have very high-dollar health care
plans, the overwhelming majority would not only see no net tax increase as a
result of the McCain plan but instead would have some of the offset left over
to place in a health savings account for otherwise uncovered medical needs.[17]

For the uninsured, that $5,000 ($2,500 for an individual) would be available to purchase insurance. (In an irony not lost on McCain, as president, in winter 2010 Obama endorsed a Democratic bill containing a tax on high-value health insurance plans.)[18]

The Democrats' ability to mislead voters about McCain's intent was abetted by inept Republican communication about the plan. So confusing was the campaign's rollout that major newspapers mistakenly reported that the Republican ticket intended to remove the tax deductions *employers* take for providing the benefit, when instead it was *employees* who would see the benefit taxed. Complicating the confusion, a widely read AARP publication misstated the McCain proposal as well.[19]

McCain's convoluted explanations didn't help matters. By sometimes talking about the refundable tax credit but not his plans to tax existing employer-provided benefits and at other times muddling the details of the plan, he often in effect let the Obama allegations stand.[20]

At the same time, a poorly written explanation on his campaign's Web site handed the Democrats an opening when it said that for those without insurance the $2,500 or $5,000 refundable tax credit would be paid to insurance companies. Capitalizing on this communications blunder, Obama's advertisers featured a shot of the quotation nestled on the Web page to imply that the funds were a subsidy for insurers and not a benefit for individuals. Omitted both from the Republican Web site and the Democratic attack was the rationale for this payment structure. Direct payment to insurance companies not only guaranteed that the subsidy was used to purchase insurance but also ensured that it wasn't taxed.

The flaw on the McCain Web site was grist for an Obama ad titled "Tax Healthcare," which was aired almost 22,000 times and backed by a purchase of air time larger than any buy behind a single McCain advertisement. The spot alleged that "John McCain talks about a $5,000 tax credit for health care. But here's what he's not telling you. McCain would make you pay income tax on your health insurance benefits. Taxing health benefits for the first time ever. And that tax credit? McCain's own Web site says it goes straight to the insurance companies, not to you. Leaving you on your own to pay McCain's health insurance tax. Taxing health care instead of fixing it. We can't afford John McCain."[21]

Just as they had with the McCain tax charges, the fact checkers weighed in to condemn this set of claims. Since the money would pay for insurance, it would of course go to an insurance company, they noted; for those retaining their employer coverage, it would offset the tax, leaving most people with a net amount available for placement in a health savings account.

On this issue, Obama benefitted not only from his campaign's ability to outspend McCain but also from fliers and ads distributed by Planned Parenthood and the labor unions, all making the same charge. Unsurprisingly, the number

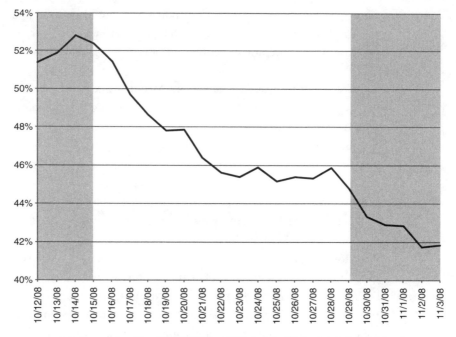

FIGURE 9.3 Perception That Federal Taxes Will Go Up if John McCain Is Elected President (5-day PMA). *Source*: NAES08 telephone survey.

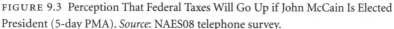

of people saying McCain would raise their taxes increased by mid-October to the point that more people believed that McCain would bleed taxes from them than would Obama (figure 9.3). However, as the notion that Obama would "share the wealth" took hold, the percentage of the public thinking their federal taxes would go up under McCain began to fall.

Obama's case against the McCain plan was unexpectedly reinforced by presumed Republican soul mates when on October 7, the morning of the second presidential debate, the *New York Times* reported that, "American business, typically a reliable Republican cheerleader, is decidedly lukewarm about Senator John McCain's proposal to overhaul the health care system by revamping the tax treatment of health benefits, officials with leading trade groups say." The article listed organizations and named names:

> The officials, with organizations like the U.S. Chamber of Commerce, the Business Roundtable and the National Federation of Independent Business, predicted in recent interviews that the McCain plan, which eliminates the exclusion of health benefits from income taxes, would

accelerate the erosion of employer-sponsored health insurance and do little to reduce the number of uninsured from 45 million....

"To some in the business community, this is very discomforting," said R. Bruce Josten, executive vice president for government affairs at the Chamber of Commerce. "The private marketplace, in my opinion, is ill prepared today with an infrastructure for an individual-based health insurance system."[22]

In the debate that evening, Obama brandished that article to indict McCain's proposal. "In fact, just today," the Democrat noted, "business organizations like the United States Chamber of Commerce, which generally are pretty supportive of Republicans, said that this plan would lead to the unraveling of the employer-based health care system."[23] Not until October 27 did the *Times* focus on what businesses thought of the Democratic alternative. When it did, the resulting article ran under the headline, "Businesses Wary of Details in Obama Health Plan."[24]

The Inaccurate Tax Claims on Both Sides Were Believed

Both sets of false charges worked. Our postelection Claims survey of 3,000 respondents suggests that just as McCain's messages magnified public belief in the false argument that the Democratic ticket would raise taxes on more than those specified in his plans, Obama's persuaded 20 percent of both Democrats (20.5 percent) and independents (19.6 percent) to embrace the false implication that McCain's tax on employer-provided health benefits meant that he would in fact ratchet up their pain on April 15 of each year.

Three of the central Republican claims against Obama also took hold: he would increase everyone's taxes, he would increase the taxes on most small businesses, and he had voted to increase taxes on those making more than $42,000.

McCain made his case that most small businesses would be affected by Obama's plans by focusing on the total amount of their collective revenue that would be taxed. To make his argument that few would see a hike in taxes, Obama focused instead on the percent of small businesses that would be affected. In the second debate, for example, Senator McCain noted, "Senator Obama's secret that you don't know is that his tax increases will increase taxes on 50 percent of small business revenue." Senator Obama countered, "Now, Senator McCain talks about small businesses. Only a few percent of small businesses make more than $250,000 a year. So the vast majority of small businesses would get a tax cut under my plan."[25] If a few small businesses earned much more than $250,000 apiece, it was of course possible that both claims were correct. To assess whether respondents believed Obama, we centered our question on business owners, not total small business revenue.

As we noted earlier, the McCain charge that Obama would raise everyone's taxes also stuck. Where at the beginning of the chapter we used NAES data from the last month of the election to document the belief that Obama would raise middle-class taxes, here we use postelection cross-sectional data to suggest that many agreed that the Democrat proposed to raise everyone's taxes.

Since in the postelection survey we were concerned not with the belief about what Obama would do but on whether people knew what he had proposed, we phrased our question to foreclose the possibility that respondents knew Senator Obama's stated position but didn't believe that it expressed his actual intent. As a result, this question asks not what the respondent thinks Obama will actually do if elected but rather what he has proposed to do.

In our final question, we clearly asked whether Obama voted for legislation *that passed and increased taxes,* phrasing that captures the implication of the McCain campaign's inaccurate charge that Obama voted to raise taxes on such individuals. More independents found the statement truthful than untruthful.

What Changed for McCain in Mid-October?

In the aftermath of the last debate, the McCain campaign gained a foothold with its contention that Obama would raise taxes more than would McCain (figure 9.4). At the same time, the Republicans expanded their tax-and-spend allegations with the assertion that Obama's plans alternately constituted welfare, a government handout or check for those who paid no federal income taxes. Scaffolded on those redefinitions was the notion that the refundable tax credits in the Democratic standard-bearer's proposal were a form of socialism.

Obama Would Tax Joe the Plumber

In Barack Obama's exchange with the man cast by McCain as "Joe the Plumber," the Ohio blue-collar worker argued that Obama's tax proposals could reduce the profitability of a plumbing business he aspired to own:

MR. WURZELBACHER: I'm getting ready to buy a company that makes about $250,000, $270,000, $280,000 a year.

SENATOR OBAMA: All right.

MR. WURZELBACHER: Your new tax plan is going to tax me more, isn't it?"[26]

Mistakenly accepting Joe's premise about the business's income, Obama answered by justifying increased taxes on those of higher means. The problematic

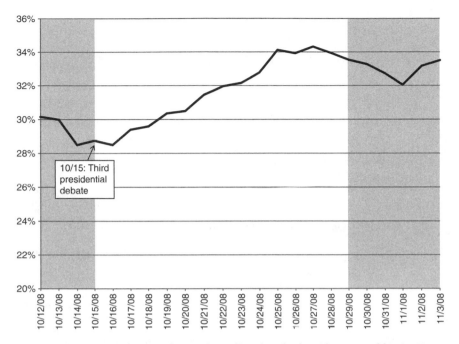

FIGURE 9.4 Percent of Respondents Who Believed Both That Obama Would Raise Taxes *and* That McCain Would Not Raise Them. Note the increase after the third presidential debate (5-Day PMA). *Source:* NAES08 telephone survey.

phrase "spread the wealth" came in response to another of Wurzelbacher's questions, this one about support for a flat tax, a context lost in subsequent discussion of the exchange. "I don't mind paying just a little bit more than the waitress who I just met over there who…can barely make the rent," Obama replied defending progressive taxation. "Because my attitude is if the economy's good for folks from the bottom up, it's going to be good for everybody. If you've got a plumbing business, you're going to be better off if you've got a whole bunch of customers who can afford to hire you. And right now, everybody's so pinched that business is bad for everybody. And I think when *you spread the wealth around, it's good for everybody*" (emphasis added).[27]

As later media accounts revealed, Wurzelbacher's income fell well below $250,000 and would not rise enough to reach the threshold at which Obama's tax increase kicked in even if he found a way to buy the business. As a result, the Democrat's tax plan was actually in the aspiring small business owner's economic self-interest. Still, the unlicensed Ohio plumber, whose given name was Sam and not Joe,[28] initially appeared on news arguing that he would be hit with the Obama tax increase. Before the final presidential debate, the GOP's newest celebrity told Fox News's Neil Cavuto: "I resent the government or Obama's plan to take more away from me."[29] Once it was clear that it would not, McCain's new-found champion changed his story to say that he resented the prospect of a tax hike were he to break into that higher income range. In the October 15 debate itself, McCain repeated the false premise about "Joe's" economic circumstances:

> Joe wants to buy the business that he has been in for all of these years, worked 10, 12 hours a day. And he wanted to buy the business but he looked at your tax plan and he saw that he was going to pay much higher taxes. You were going to put him in a higher tax bracket which was going to increase his taxes, which was going to cause him not to be able to employ people, which Joe was trying to realize the American dream.[30]

The next day, Wurzelbacher conceded to ABC's Diane Sawyer that the $250,000 income figure reflected aspiration, not actuality:

> SAWYER: "To get straight here, you're not taking home $250,000 now, am I right?"
>
> WURZELBACHER: "No. No. Not even close."
>
> SAWYER: "And you were asking about the prospect, the hope that someday you would make $250,000, and you were saying you didn't want that to be taxed."
>
> WURZELBACHER: "Well, exactly. Exactly…

Within days of the debate, the facts of Wurzelbacher's case were widely known.[31] "ABC News reports Wurzelbacher wants to buy the business for roughly $250,000," noted conservative columnist Rich Lowry on October 17, "but doesn't expect to make that much in income right away. In the meantime, he might be eligible for the Obama smorgasbord of middle-class tax credits. Ninety-five percent strikes again!"[32]

Joe the Plumber and "Share the Wealth" in the Third Presidential Debate

"Joe the Plumber" was a refrain heard nine times through the October 15 presidential debate. With "Joe's" help, McCain both pushed Obama to the defensive and asserted control over the tax discussion. "I think the fact that John McCain was able to make Joe Wurzelbacher a character in this campaign…shows…why this was his [McCain's] best debate so far," observed ABC's George Stephanopoulos. "He was able to set the agenda on a lot of issues like taxes, especially with Joe Wurzelbacher."[33] After the debate, the *AP* headline read, "McCain Puts Obama on the Defensive."[34] "McCain Presses Obama in Last and Pointed Debate" said the front page headline in the *New York Times*.[35]

For decades, social psychologists have known that repetition has persuasive power in its own right. In the third debate, "Joe the Plumber" and "share the wealth" became for McCain what "95 percent" had been for Obama—brightly flashing and sometimes annoying neon signs encapsulating core campaign themes. In their final joint appearance, the Arizonan returned doggedly to the contrast implied by the phrases: Obama will raise Joe's and your taxes and I won't, my opponent wants to share the wealth by taking money from people like Joe and having government give it to someone else, and, perhaps most damning, Obama is going to make the shell-shocked economy worse by raising taxes:

MCCAIN: And I will not have—I will not stand for a tax increase on small business income. Fifty percent of small business income taxes are paid by small businesses. That's 16 million jobs in America. *And what you want to do to Joe the plumber and millions more like him is have their taxes increased* and not be able to realize the American dream of owning their own business.

OBAMA: *I want to provide a tax cut for 95 percent of working Americans,* 95 percent. If you make more—if you make less than a quarter million dollars a year, then you will not see your income tax go up, your capital gains tax go up, your payroll tax. Not one dime. And 95 percent of working families, 95 percent of you out there, will get a tax cut. In fact, *independent studies have looked at our respective plans and have concluded that I provide three times the amount of tax relief to middle-class families than Senator McCain does.*

MCCAIN: You know, when Senator Obama ended up his conversation with Joe the plumber—we need to *spread the wealth around. In other words, we're going to take Joe's money, give it to Senator Obama, and let him spread the wealth around.*

I want Joe the plumber to spread that wealth around. You told him you wanted to spread the wealth around.

The whole premise behind Senator Obama's plans are class warfare, *let's spread the wealth around.* I want small businesses—and by the way, the small businesses that we're talking about would receive *an increase in their taxes right now.*

Who—why would you want to increase anybody's taxes right now? Why would you want to do that, anyone, anyone in America, when we have such a *tough time,* when these small business people, like Joe the plumber, are going to create jobs, unless *you take that money from him and spread the wealth around.*[36] (emphasis added)

The pattern persists throughout the debate:

MCCAIN: And of course, I've been talking about the economy. Of course, I've talked to people like Joe the plumber and tell him that *I'm not going to spread his wealth around. I'm going to let him keep his wealth.* And of course, we're talking about a positive plan of action to restore this economy and restore jobs in America … *I'm not going to raise taxes the way Senator Obama wants to raise taxes in a tough economy.* And that's really what this campaign is going to be about.[37] (emphasis added)

In the final debate, Obama and McCain's strategies differed. Where the Democrat assumed an audience that tracked debate arguments as a judge would at moot court, the Republican spoke to the family unfamiliar with the issues and eager for a few simple reiterated points. Unlike McCain, Obama seemed to presuppose that once a charge had been rebutted there was no advantage in driving another stake into it when McCain resurrected it. This move left two of the Democrat's rebuttals in the debate's rearview mirror instead of its headlights: He had promised tax cuts for 95 percent of working families and independent groups agreed that his plan gave more to the middle class.

By contrast, McCain treated Obama's responses as confirmation that Joe the Plumber would suffer under the Democrat's plans. After a first rebuttal, Obama should have responded to McCain's repetition by either deepening his argument or by reiterating his core themes. Instead, in a tone bordering on exasperation, he made a tactical error by justifying higher taxes without specifying on whom.

OBAMA: So, look, nobody likes taxes. I would prefer that none of us had to pay taxes, including myself. But ultimately, *we've got to pay for the core investments that make this economy strong and somebody's got to do it.*

MCCAIN: Nobody likes taxes. Let's not raise anybody's taxes. OK?

OBAMA: Well, I don't mind paying a little more.

MCCAIN: The fact is that businesses in America today are paying the second highest tax rate of anywhere in the world. Our tax rate for business in America is 35 percent. Ireland, it's 11 percent.

Where are companies going to go where they can create jobs and where they can do best in business?

We need to cut the business tax rate in America. We need to encourage business. *Now, of all times in America,* we need to cut people's taxes. We need to encourage business, create jobs, not spread the wealth around).[38] (emphasis added)

The Democratic nominee faltered as well when John McCain deployed Joe the Plumber to undercut an Obama reference about the ability of his billionaire supporter Warren Buffet to pay more in taxes. That exchange allied Obama with the wealthiest man in the U.S., known as the Oracle from Omaha, for whom extra taxes were pocket change, while at the same time associating McCain with a just-trying-to-make-ends-meet blue-collar worker.

> OBAMA: If I can answer the question. Number one, I want to cut taxes for 95 percent of Americans. Now, it is true that my friend and supporter, Warren Buffett, for example, could afford to pay a little more in taxes in order...
>
> MCCAIN: We're talking about Joe the plumber.
>
> OBAMA: ...in order to give—in order to give additional tax cuts to Joe the Plumber before he was at the point where he could make $250,000.[39]

In the second debate, Obama had tied McCain to tax cuts for the wealthy "that would give the average Fortune 500 CEO an additional $700,000 in tax cuts." By contrast, in their final face-off the Democrat anchored his own argument in the experiences of a billionaire, who in late September had invested a spare $5 billion in Goldman Sachs.[40] Where McCain championed the chances of the middle class to live the American dream, Obama reminded viewers that he and a billionaire were buddies. Interestingly, in the second debate Obama had cast McCain's tax cuts as the very wealthy "not sharing a burden," a framing favorable to the Democrat's position but one that was a precarious noun away from the "sharing the wealth."

When he wrested control of the tax agenda from the Democrat, McCain created a dilemma for Obama. By repeating the original charge, refutation risks reinforcing the argument being debunked. In the context of talk of high taxes, the exchange about the truth about Obama's [nonbinding] vote to raise taxes tacitly reinforced the link between Democrats and big government coveting middle-class paychecks.

> MCCAIN: Senator Obama talks about voting for budgets. He voted twice for a budget resolution that increases the taxes on individuals making $42,000 a year.
>
> OBAMA: Now with respect to a couple of things Senator McCain said, the notion that I voted for a tax increase for people making $42,000 a year has been disputed by everybody who has looked at this claim that Senator McCain keeps on making.
>
> Even Fox News disputes it, and that doesn't happen very often when it comes to accusations about me.[41]

For McCain, Joe the Plumber personifies the effects of the Obama tax plan. Where Obama moves to statistics (95 percent will receive a tax cut) and authority (independent experts certify that he gives more in tax cuts), McCain translates Obama's plan into pain for plain-talking Joe:

MCCAIN: *Now, Joe,* Senator Obama's plan, if you're a small business and you are able—and your—the guy that sells to you will not have his capital gains tax increase, which Senator Obama wants, if you're out there, my friend, and you've got employees, and you've got kids, *if you don't get—adopt the health care plan that Senator Obama mandates, he's going to fine you.*

MCCAIN: Now, Senator Obama, I'd like—still like to know what that fine is going to be, *and I don't think that Joe right now wants to pay a fine when he is seeing such difficult times in America's economy.*

OBAMA: And this is your plan, John. For the first time in history, you will be taxing people's health care benefits.

By the way, the average policy costs about $12,000. So if you've got $5,000 and it's going to cost you $12,000, that's a loss for you.

MCCAIN: *Now, Joe, you're rich, congratulations, and you will then fall into the category where you'll have to pay a fine if you don't provide health insurance that Senator Obama mandates, not the kind that you think is best for your family, your children, your employees, but the kind that he mandates for you.* That's big government at its best...." (emphasis added).[42]

In these exchanges, Obama did score once. Responding to McCain's charge that Wurzelbacher's business would be fined if it failed to provide health insurance for its employees, the Illinois Democrat assured Joe that he would pay no fine. Since his plan exempted small businesses, explained the Democrat, the amount of the fine was "zero." There was nothing of the nuanced college professor in the monosyllabic "zero." Still, talk of fines reinforced the notion that the Democratic plan contained an unpalatable mandate or alternative penalty.

Moreover, as those attentive to the give-and-take may have realized, Obama had failed to define a key term. Neither he nor his campaign had revealed what constituted a small business, a fact that explains the incredulous look on McCain's face when he heard Obama say "zero." Pressed by ABC's Gregory Wallace and Teddy Davis in early August, Obama's director of economic policy, Jason Furman, refused to indicate who would be covered by Obama's small business exemption. "We haven't put out a specific number," said Furman at the time.[43] Then on September 22, 2008, JoNel Aleccia reported on msn.com, "The campaign has not said how large the tax would be for businesses that opt not to offer insurance, or how small a business would have to be to be excluded."[44] The day after the final debate, the Obama campaign confirmed that it had no intention of specifying the size of the fine. "Obama officials say the campaign has no plans to answer that question

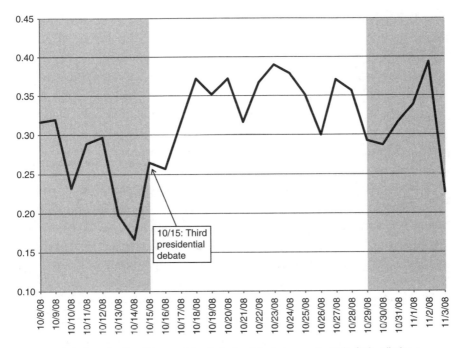

FIGURE 9.5 Standardized Betas of the Relationship between the Belief That "Obama Would Raise Taxes and McCain Would Not" and McCain Favorability across Time (5-day PMA). Note: Early voters were not included in the analysis. Daily regression analyses include controls. *Source*: NAES08 telephone survey.

before Election Day on November 4," reported Laura Meckler in the *Wall Street Journal*.[45]

Employing the combined wisdom of postelection surveys and pundit consensus, many of the professional opiners in the press declared the final debate a win for Obama. Still, we see evidence that it marked a turning point for McCain on the tax issue. NAES analyses showed that the belief that Obama will raise taxes and McCain won't was significantly related to higher favorability scores for McCain,* and the strength of this relationship increases directly after the third and final debate (figure 9.5). In the presence of controls, watching the October 15 debate significantly predicted the belief that Obama would raise taxes and McCain would not.*

Spread the Wealth with a Government Check to Those
Who Pay No Federal Income Taxes

In the Republican playbook, "spread the wealth" recast an increase in the rate of progressive taxation as snatching money from those who worked hard to earn it in order to hand it to those who hadn't. GOP surrogates then played the ball forward by magnifying a theme McCain had hinted at but did not develop in the debate: the redistribution would be conducted by individuals not to be trusted ("politicians") on behalf of "big government," not to benefit deserving workers but instead to line the pockets of either politicians or their "cronies" or those who pay no taxes. The allegation apparently resonated with debate watchers, who were significantly more likely than nonviewers to believe that Obama's proposed tax plan would provide a government check to millions of people who pay no federal income taxes.*

Within two days of the last debate, former Republican Speaker of the House Newt Gingrich had fine-tuned McCain's argument. On October 17 on *Good Morning America,* Gingrich characterized the controversial Obama remark as a "Freudian slip" and added, "he [Obama] basically said, 'Look, we've got to spread the wealth.' But who's he talking about? The 'we' here is politicians. Now…the fact is the average American doesn't believe—it doesn't matter who you're raising taxes on. The average American doesn't believe that it's a right thing for America to have politicians deciding to spread the wealth to their cronies."[46]

In a sound bite that travelled quickly into cable and broadcast news, McCain ramped up his attack on Obama's proposal by casting it in the racially coded term "welfare":

MCCAIN: His plan gives away your tax dollars to those that don't pay taxes.

CROWD: (*booing*)

MCCAIN: That's not a tax cut. That's welfare! America didn't become the greatest nation on earth by redistributing the wealth. We became the greatest nation by creating new wealth.[47]

In their editorials backing McCain, conservative papers advanced the argument that those not paying income taxes would benefit from Obama's plan. "Obama promises a tax cut for 85 percent of households," argued the *Tampa Tribune,*" even though only 62 percent of households pay any income tax now."[48] "Even the one-third of all American working families who pay no income taxes now will receive a government check under Obama's proposal," argued the *Pittsburgh Times Review.*[49] "Obama touts his economic policies as providing tax cuts for 95 percent of Americans," noted the editorial endorsement in the *San Diego Union-Tribune.* "In truth, he would achieve this only by refunding the Social Security taxes of the millions of Americans who don't make enough to pay income taxes, while imposing even higher rates on wage earners who already pay a disproportionate share of income taxes. Thus, Obama's 'share the wealth' thrust would penalize the most productive, job-creating elements of society in order to reward the least productive."[50] "It

Doesn't Compute: Obama's Tax Plan a Ruse" headlined an editorial in the New Hampshire's *Union Leader* that asked, "What makes you so sure that you will wind up on the right side of that equation once an Obama administration begins making up the difference between the massive number of benefits it promised to deliver and the tiny amount of pain it promised to inflict to finance those benefits?"[51]

The Republican "welfare" charge threw the otherwise unflappable Obama campaign onto the defensive. In the process, the Democratic nominee conceded that his plans would give a check to those paying no federal income taxes. He repeatedly added, however, that these individuals were taxed in other ways.

JAKE TAPPER (ABC): (*voiceover*) Obama disputed John McCain's charge that his tax proposal is welfare or socialist because some recipients receive a cut even if they do not make enough to pay income taxes.

OBAMA: What he's confusing is the fact that even if you don't pay income tax, there are a lot of people who don't pay income tax, you're still paying a whole lot of other taxes.

You're paying payroll tax, which is a huge burden on a lot of middle income families. You're paying sales taxes. You're paying property taxes.[52]

Even reporters who took issue with the allegation that Obama's plan constituted welfare acknowledged the truth in the charge of redistribution. On CBS, Wyatt Andrews noted:

McCain calls it one of the biggest differences between him and Barack Obama, the claim that most of Obama's tax cuts are actually government giveaways.

SENATOR JOHN MCCAIN (Republican presidential candidate): Senator Obama's plan to raise taxes on some in order to give checks to others—it isn't a tax cut. It's just another government giveaway...

On this claim, McCain has a point. Obama has proposed four new refundable tax credits, which are different from tax cuts or deductions. The refundable designation means that millions of taxpayers who don't normally owe income taxes would get refund checks from the government.[53]

Whose Tax Policies Benefit Whom?

In news accounts in the closing days of October, the McCain and Obama salvos on taxes took the form of competing sound bites:

MCCAIN: Mr. Obama's plan gives away your tax dollars to those who don't pay taxes. That's not a tax cut, that's welfare.

OBAMA: McCain is so out of touch with the struggles you are facing that he must be the first politician in history to call a tax cut for working people welfare.[54]

Who Will Get the Obama Tax Cut?

In the Republican script, the debate about redistribution focused on the implications of taxation (it would hurt the economy in tough times) and on what would be done with the increased revenue (it would be given to the undeserving). A final line of attack asked who would really receive a tax cut and tax increase under the Obama plan? In one fell swoop, this assault suggested that Obama was perhaps a traditional Democrat, after all, and at the same time called his trustworthiness into question. Distrust of a Democrat's promises to cut taxes drew plausibility from memories of the 1992 election, where challenger Bill Clinton ran on middle-class tax relief that never materialized.

Whose Taxes Would Be Raised?

Among the cognitive shortcuts that voters carry with them are assumptions about the intrinsic instincts of the two political parties. Although not always reliable, these primal beliefs are confirmed often enough to prove serviceable in the absence of conflicting evidence. Although, as we suggested in chapter 4, the public perception of which party nominee would better handle taxes was not a slam dunk for either one in the decade preceding the 2008 election, the notion that Democrats are disposed to raise taxes on upper-income earners and Republicans to cut them for that same group was borne out in the rhetoric of the major-party nominees in 2008. Moreover, the presidency of George W. Bush had revivified the idea that, left to their own devices, Republicans pared down taxes with the higher dollar benefits going to those assessed the most to start with. If "share the wealth" meant "take from those who have and give to those who have less," the only question was, into which category does an individual fall?

The exchange between Obama and Joe the Plumber provided scaffolding from which Republicans could build their case that the Democrat was disposed to raise not just taxes on the wealthy but on others as well. Joe framed the premise as a question in his October 16 interview with Diane Sawyer on *Good Morning America*: "I mean, $250,000 now. What if he decides, well, you know, $150,000, you're pretty rich too. Let's go ahead and lower it again. You know, it's a slippery slope. When's it going to stop?"

Whose Taxes Would Be Cut?

Until mid-October, the Republicans hadn't made much of the shifting tax-cutting thresholds Obama had offered.[55] Nor had the press. "[N]ailing down Sen. Obama's various tax proposals is like nailing Jell-O to the wall," McCain observed in the second debate. "There have been five or six of them, and if you wait long enough, there will probably be another one. But he wants to raise taxes." But without specifics, the charge conjured up not a vacillating Democrat but a gooey wall.

However, in October the Republicans cobbled the Democrats' varying statements together to charge that Obama's 95 percent mantra was bogus. Backing the argument were missteps by Democratic surrogates and the campaign. These stumbles opened Obama to the charge that his tax-cut rhetoric was actually a shell game.

As followers of prime-time crime shows know, self-indicting admissions spike attention and lend credibility to the arguments they back. To support their bait-and-switch charge, the Republicans knit together an Obama statement from summer, another from an October ad, and an offhand comment made by Joseph Biden in a radio interview. Republican archivists located the first in a statement made by the Democratic standard-bearer in Powder Springs, Georgia, on July 7, 2008, promising, "If you make *$250,000 a year or less,* we will not raise your taxes, *we will cut your taxes*" (emphasis added).[56] The second came from Obama's statement in a two-minute TV ad titled "Defining Moment" aired October 25. In that spot, the candidate promised, "If you have a job, pay taxes, and *make less than $200,000 a year,* you'll get a tax cut."[57] The following day, the Democratic vice presidential nominee served up the third in an interview with WNEP radio in his hometown of Scranton Pennsylvania. Responding to a question about Obama's defense of sharing the wealth, Biden said, "Spreading the wealth was not—he was talking about is all of the tax breaks have gone to the very, very wealthy.... It [Tax breaks] should go to middle-class people—*people making under $150,000 a year.*"[58]

In a Fox News interview with Sean Hannity, McCain laid out the Republican premise:

> Remember, it was $250,000. Then, quietly, his campaign came out and said, Well, now it 's $200,000. Then somebody figured it out in the

Wall Street Journal that it's $140,000-some. Then we go back into history, and Senator Obama has voted to raise taxes on individuals making $42,000.[59]

"It's interesting how their definition of rich has a way of creeping down," McCain told an audience in Hershey, Pennsylvania. "At this rate, it won't be long before Senator Obama is right back to his vote that Americans making just $42,000 dollars a year should get a tax increase. We won't let that happen."[60]

The presumed tax hike permitted McCain to grab hold of the economic crisis that was dominating both the news and voters' concerns, to argue, as two pages-full of McCain-supporting economists had on October 7 and as the Arizonan had in the second and third debates, that Obama's tax-and-trade plans would worsen the recession, perhaps leading to a depression. "It was exactly such misguided tax hikes and protectionism, enacted when the U.S. economy was weak in the early 1930s," surmised the economists whose statement was packaged for press distribution by the McCain campaign, "that greatly increased the severity of the Great Depression."[61] "This is pretty funny," responded progressive blogger Matthew Yglesias. "The McCain campaign's letter of 100 economists warning of the dire impact of Barack Obama's policies on the economy is only signed by ninety people. Note that the American Economic Association has over 17,000 members."[62]

For McCain, the number of economists was less important than the argument they endorsed. In a climate rife with fear, the notion that any plans might catapult a recession into a depression had rhetorical power. In his radio address in mid-October, McCain even revived a name from the Republican past to castigate Obama's plans: "History shows us if you raise taxes in a bad economy, you hurt the economy and—there was a president named Herbert Hoover, a Republican. They raised taxes. They practiced protectionism. And we went from a serious recession into a deep depression." John McCain reiterated that appeal in an op-ed in the *Wall Street Journal* on November 3: "Senator Obama wants to raise taxes and restrict trade. The last time America did that in a bad economy it led to the Great Depression."[63]

The timing and content of the Democratic two-minute ad that aired October 26 suggest that the Obama campaign was aware of the power of this new McCain charge. Prior to that point, Obama had kept open the possibility that he might postpone his proposed tax hikes but had avoided actually promising such a delay. Asked on CNBC's *Your Money: Your Vote* on June 10, 2008 "[I]s there reason, because of the situation we're in, to delay the implementation of any of those [tax increases] to avoid having a negative effect on job creation?" Obama responded "Well, there's no doubt that any policies I implement are going to be based on the economic situation that I inherit from George Bush."[64] Similarly, when ABC's George Stephanopoulos asked on September 7 about postponing the tax increases "if we're in a recession next January," Obama responded, "I think we've got to take a look and see where the economy is."[65] When challenged by McCain in the second debate to forgo his tax increases, Obama refused to take the bait. "You know," said McCain, "he said some time ago, he said he would forgo his tax increases if the economy was bad. I've got some news, Senator Obama, the news is bad. So let's not raise anybody's taxes." When his turn came, Obama instead insisted, "If you make less than a quarter of a million dollars a year, you will not see a single dime of your taxes go up. If you make $200,000 a year or less, your taxes will go down."[66] His silence in response to McCain's challenge spoke volumes. Even with the country in an economic freefall, in early October the Democratic party's standard-bearer was unwilling to either delay of forsake the tax increases he had consistently forecast.

Not so at the end of October when, speaking directly to camera in a two-minute ad, the Democratic nominee came out instead for letting the Bush tax cuts simply expire. After listing his priorities to address "this defining moment in our history," Obama asked in that brief address, "How will I pay for these priorities?" His list of answers includes, "I'll let the temporary Bush tax cuts for the wealthiest 2 percent expire...."[67] That changed position meant that rates for upper-income earners would not, as his earlier rhetoric had implied, increase as soon as President Obama could secure the required legislation but rather would return to their 1990s pre-Bush level when they were set to do so at the end of 2010.

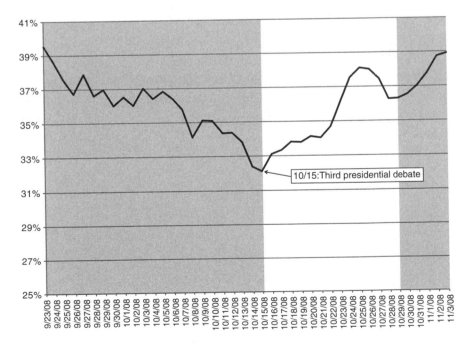

FIGURE 9.6 Percent Believing McCain Would Be Better than Obama at Handling Economy (5-day PMA). *Source*: NAES08 telephone survey.

One sign that the McCain storyline on taxes resonated with voters was increased numbers of respondents reporting that he would do a better job than Obama on the economy, the issue voters considered paramount (figure 9.6).

Socialism

The first campaign surrogate to equate the Obama plan with socialism was not Sarah Palin but Joe Wurzelbacher, who told Diana Sawyer on *Good Morning America* the day after the last presidential debate, "Because you're successful, you have to pay more than everybody else? We all live in this country. It's a basic right. And Obama wants to take that basic right and penalize me for it, is what it comes down to. That's a very socialist view and it's incredibly wrong."

Insulating herself somewhat from the charge that her rhetoric had become extreme, Palin initially attributed the inflammatory charge to Wurzelbacher. Specifically, in Springfield, Missouri, on October 24, 2008 she noted, "Senator Obama says that he wants to spread the wealth, which means...government takes your money, [distributed]...however as a politician sees fit. Barack Obama calls it spreading the wealth, and Joe Biden calls higher taxes patriotic. And yet to Joe the Plumber...it sounded like socialism. And now is not the time to experiment with socialism." After quoting that statement, PolitiFact observed that, "She has repeated the line in Nevada, New Mexico, Colorado, and most recently in Leesburg, Virginia, on October 27, 2008."[68]

When the Republican nominee first included the socialism charge in an October 18 radio address, he, like his running mate, did so by crediting it to the now ubiquitous plumber. "You see, he [Obama] believes in redistributing wealth, not in policies that help us all make more of it," McCain said of Obama. "Joe, in his plainspoken way, said this sounded a lot like socialism. And a lot of Americans are thinking along those same lines." However, McCain then embraced the allegation as his own. "At least in Europe, the socialist leaders who so admire my opponent are up front about their objectives," McCain added.[69]

Attacks suggesting that the Democrats' plans constituted socialism built on the presupposition that those on the Left favor government intervention in the market, while those on the other side of the ideological continuum do not. Still, tagging Democratic plans with that label seems a bit strange coming from a Republican nominee who, like his opponent, supported the $700 billion "rescue package" or "bailout" that gave taxpayers a $250 billion share of major U.S. banks. McCain's decision to back that bill angered the same fiscal conservatives who applauded his subsequent attacks on Obama's redistributionist tendencies.

Being called on one's inconsistency wasn't the only risk raised by bandying about a charge of socialism. Among those who both commanded the term and rejected the assumption that socialist and Democrat were synonyms, such histrionics invited the conclusion that the speaker was playing to his party's right wing. For those unfamiliar with its meaning, suggesting that Obama's views were socialist may have seemed an odd way to praise his affability.

To parry the charge that he was a practicing socialist, Obama marshaled the endorsements of former Secretary of State Colin Powell and billionaire Warren Buffet. "It's kind of hard to figure out how Warren Buffet endorsed me and Colin Powell endorsed me, and I'm practicing socialism. John McCain thinks that giving these Americans a break is socialism. Well, I call it opportunity," said Obama.[70]

Citing the Republican nominee's words, the *Washington Post* on October 19, 2008, carried the headline "McCain Assails Obama's Plans as Socialist."[71] The same McCain radio address reiterated the attack on the 95 percent figure that stood at the heart of the Obama tax argument:

> In the best case, "spreading the wealth around" is a familiar idea from the American Left. And that kind of class warfare sure doesn't sound like a "new kind of politics." This would also explain some big problems with my opponent's claim that he will cut income taxes for 95 percent of Americans. You might ask: How do you cut income taxes for 95 percent of Americans, when more than 40 percent pay no income taxes right now? How do you reduce the number zero? ...Since you can't reduce taxes on those who pay zero, the government will write them all checks called a tax credit. And the Treasury will cover those checks by taxing other people, including a lot of folks like Joe.[72]

In the final weeks of October, the Republicans wove "spread [or share] the wealth," "welfare," and "socialism" into their tax messages. At McCain rallies, partisans shouted their approval of these charges. At one, noted the *Washington Post*, audience members responded to McCain's castigation of Obama for planning to "share the wealth" by crying out "Socialist!" That same speech included the lines, "Obama's tax plan 'is not a tax cut—it's just another government giveaway."[73] Unspoken by the McCain campaign but spotlighted by the Democrats was the hypocrisy in these Republican attacks on Obama's refundable tax credits. After all, to offset the cost of his proposed tax on employer-provided benefits or facilitate the purchase of insurance by the uninsured, McCain's health care plan provided the same kind of credits. Hence, the GOP's nominee was planning the same government handouts, welfare, and socialism as his Democratic opponent.

Nonetheless, the Republican offensive had a number of advantages for the Arizonan's candidacy. It shouted "liberal" at Obama while at the same time insinuating the racially tinged concept of "welfare" into the debate. In the Republican's narrative, Obama was plotting to siphon additional taxes from the salaries of workers in order to subsidize those whose identity as nonworkers was implied by the phrase "those who pay no taxes." The Obama campaign responded by insisting that he would provide a tax cut to 95 percent of *working* Americans, an argument that captured the fact that the proposed beneficiaries who did not pay federal income taxes nonetheless were workers who paid payroll taxes.

Reporters picked up the distinction, even as they advantaged McCain by replaying the welfare claim:

MCCAIN: This plan gives away your tax dollars to those that don't pay taxes. That's not a tax cut, that's welfare.

JAKE TAPPER (ABC News): (*voiceo ver*) That's false. Obama's tax cuts only go to people who work, so by definition, it's not welfare. Some working people eligible for Obama's tax cut make so little they do not pay income taxes, but they do pay payroll taxes and other taxes.[74]

As the campaign moved into the final weeks of October, the Arizona senator pounded away at Obama's tax-cut proposal by accusing the Democrat of adding a work requirement to sidetrack the allegation that he was creating a new kind of welfare. "He changed his tax plan because the American people learned the truth about it, and they didn't like it," McCain told an enthusiastic crowd of several thousand, who packed a lumber yard in Ormond Beach, a suburb of Daytona Beach.... "It's another example that he'll say anything to get elected."[75]

Throughout the campaign, both sides secured news time and space with ads disseminated only on the Web. Called "press ads" by those inside the campaign, these messages were a low-cost attempt to fill cable news time and set the news agenda. So, for example, the day after the last presidential debate, the McCain campaign alerted reporters to its posting of a Web ad titled "Joe the Plumber." The ad opened with the Wurzelbacher-Obama exchange that culminated in Obama praising the value of "spread[ing] the wealth around":

ANNOUNCER: Americans are catching on.

JOE: Your new tax plan is going to tax me more.

OBAMA: It's not that I want to punish your success...I think when you spread the wealth around, it's good for everybody.

ANNOUNCER: Everybody? Leading papers call Obama's taxes 'welfare'...'government handouts.' Obama raises taxes on seniors, hardworking families to give 'welfare' to those who pay none. Just as you suspected. Obama's not truthful on taxes."

Unrevealed, of course, was that the newspapers using the language of "welfare" and "government handouts" were doing so not in news space but in editorials in outlets such as the *Wall Street Journal* and *New York Post* with conservative editorial pages.[76]

The Web ad succeeded in driving the Republican message into news. "McCain says the cash payments to these earners would be tantamount to welfare," noted the *LA Times*. "A recent campaign Internet ad charges: 'Obama raises taxes on seniors, on hard-working families, to give 'welfare' to those who pay none.'"[77] Political spots by third-party groups reinforced the message: A full-page ad placed in the *New York Times* on Election Day by IncomeTaxFacts.org pictured the moderator of the last debate, CBS's Bob Schieffer. "Bob, you forgot to ask the question at the final debate!" Captioning the photo was the question, "How do you cut income taxes for people who don't owe them?" The ad went on: "32% of all working Americans pay zero federal income taxes. Doesn't 'returning' money that was never paid sound like a scam?"

In the period of time on which we have been focusing, a high-cost TV ad and a low-cost Web ad summarized the claims on which the Republicans bet the election in the closing days. The McCain message moved into paid air time on October 21 with a spot that then aired through the rest of the election at a cost of just over $5.7 million. By final CMAG count, "Sweat Equity" was broadcast more than 12,750 times. This closing argument quoted Senator Obama telling Joe the Plumber, "I think when you spread the wealth around, it's good for everybody." Multiple speakers then affirmed, "I'm Joe the plumber." "Spread the wealth?" asks the incredulous announcer. Individual speakers added, "I'm supposed to work harder just to pay more taxes. Obama wants my sweat to pay for his trillion dollars in new spending?" "I'm Joe the plumber" repeated a young woman. As an unflattering picture of Obama captioned *more spending* appeared, the announcer intoned, "Barack Obama, higher taxes, more spending, not ready." To reinforce the "Sweat Equity" message, the individuals featured in the spot then made the rounds of conservative radio and TV shows. So, for instance, on Neil Cavuto's *Your World* on Fox, small-business owner April Byrd insisted that Obama's commitment to share the wealth "goes against the grain of the American dream..."

The "Joe the Plumber" theme persisted in the election's final week. Posted in the hope of replay in cable and broadcast news, a final ad brought together the campaign themes on which the McCain team had settled. To increase the likelihood that the message would secure free airtime, the Republicans spent a little over $6,000 for 20 airings of "McCain Your Choice." As pictures of Obama crossed the screen, an announcer contrasted the programs of the Republican and Democratic nominee from McCain's viewpoint: "Your choice. For higher taxes. For working Joes. Spread your income. Keep what's yours. A trillion in new spending. Freeze spending; eliminate waste. Pain for small business; economic growth. Risky; Proven. For a stronger

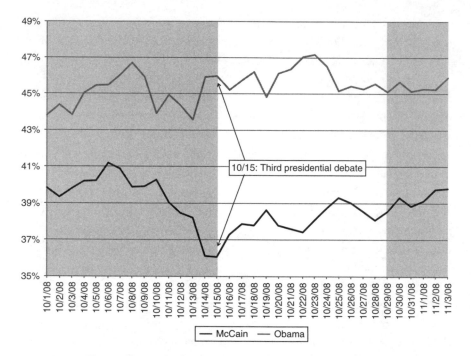

FIGURE 9.7 Vote Preference (5-day PMA). *Source*: NAES08 telephone survey.

America: McCain." In a news environment focused on economic issues, this bid to garner unpaid airing in cable talk and on network news failed.

NAES data show that believing that Obama will raise your taxes and McCain won't and thinking that Obama proposed a tax-cut plan that would provide a government check to millions of people who pay no federal income taxes were positively related to beliefs that 1) the Obama plan is socialist, 2) black elected officials will favor blacks, and 3) Obama is liberal.* Two of these three, the exception being the belief that black officials will favor blacks, predict a report that McCain will be better at handling the economy than Obama.*

The finding that believing the redistribution claim correlates with a belief in black favoritism suggests, although it doesn't establish, that the McCain argument also may have activated race-based concerns. Since we put the question on the telephone survey late in the campaign, we cannot track changes in the measure across time in a fashion that would permit us to suggest that one belief precedes the other.

Conclusion

In the weeks after the final presidential debate, McCain's tax message seems to have changed perceptions of his ability to handle the economy and also affected his favorability ratings. Capitalizing both on Obama's statement to "Joe the Plumber" and on inconsistent Democratic rhetoric on the Obama tax plan, the Republicans gained some ground with the charge that the senator from Illinois was a tax raiser. This period four jump (figure 9.7) in support for McCain runs counter to the expectations of those who see campaigns as mere activators of existing partisan dispositions. The activation model has trouble accounting for the lead McCain briefly claimed after the Republican convention as well. However, as we noted in chapter 1, Obama did win with the spread predicted by the modelers.

In the next chapter, we explain how in the final days of the election the Democratic ticket opened its lead back up to produce the final national vote spread. That story involves a national television program, a national two-minute spot, an effective ad linking McCain to Bush, a commanding presence in battleground radio, and a resurfacing of concerns about McCain's age and Palin's qualifications. And as we will argue in a later chapter, in key battleground states Obama had locked up an early voting advantage before the McCain surge.

TEN

Period Five: Be Very, Very Afraid/ Be Reassured (October 29–November 4)

I N PERIOD FIVE, OBAMA'S ADS CONTINUED TO HAMMER MCCAIN ON both the economy and his links to the incumbent president. Meanwhile, the Republicans kept up their attack on Obama as a tax-and-spend liberal whose proposals would deepen the recession. But with Election Day in sight, Obama also ramped up his rhetoric of reassurance with detailed descriptions of his plans, while the Republicans raised the decibel level on their allegation that the Democratic nominee was ill-prepared to deal with a crisis. It is on these new elements of fear and reassurance that we focus here.

From them we will construct our answer to the question, "Why, after McCain began closing in on Obama in period four, did the gap between them widen again in the final days?" Our answer is both complex and simple. We attribute Obama's upward swing to his rhetoric of reassurance, which blunted McCain's fear-based attacks. At the same time, the Democrats burnished perceptions that their standard-bearer shared voters' values.

Our account of the McCain drop in the final days is more complex. We believe that the Arizonan's viability was undercut when voters drew two conclusions: first that Obama was better prepared to handle the troubled economy and second that electing McCain meant a continuation of the failed policies of George W. Bush. One other factor constricted the Arizonan's prospects. As we argued in an earlier chapter, his vice presidential nominee acted as a net drag on the Republican ticket. In this chapter, we explore those dynamics.

The Republicans' Closing Argument: Fear-Based Attacks on Obama's
Readiness to Deal with Crisis

With the Iowa caucuses of 2008 on the horizon, there was one ray of sun for
McCain in the otherwise overcast polling data. In late 2007, the Republican party
held a 10-point advantage over the Democrats in handling terrorism, a figure
down from 30 percent in January 2004. A February 2008 Pew poll showed a more
modest lead for the Republicans on this issue (45–38 percent).[1] Still, one promising combination for McCain was the link between terrorism and the ability to
manage a crisis.

Another was the possibility that the wars in Afghanistan and Iraq would
retain center stage and thereby heighten McCain's advantage in public perception
as a prospective Commander-in-Chief. As we noted in an earlier chapter, Obama's
inexperience in foreign policy and lack of military experience, and McCain's service and championing of the surge meant that throughout the general election the
Republican nominee also held the advantage on handling Iraq. Although Obama

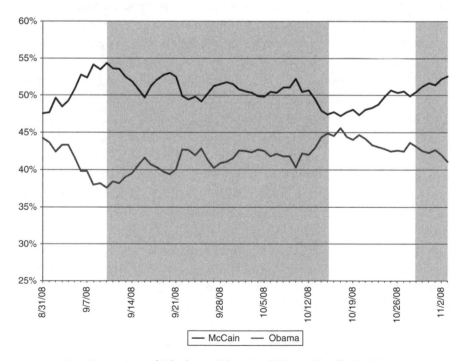

FIGURE 10.1 Perceptions of Which Candidate Would Better Handle the War in Iraq
(5-day PMA). *Source*: NAES08 telephone survey.

narrowed McCain's lead on the question of which candidate could better deal with the war, McCain controlled this territory to the end (figure 10.1). Had the election been fought not on the economy but on handling terrorism or the country's two-front war, McCain's odds would have been less forbidding.

Weak on Defense

Nonetheless, Republicans could draw solace from the assumption that the public would be disposed to tag a Harvard-educated liberal former professor as "weak on defense." That attack has not only been a mainstay of recent Republican rhetoric but has also been the genesis of some of the modern presidency's more notorious oppositional TV ads. In one that depicted toy replicas being swept from a table, Democrats for Nixon argued in 1972 that McGovern would undercut military readiness by making substantial cuts in the numbers of troops, tanks ships, and planes. In another from the 1988 campaign, allegations that Dukakis would gut the country's military preparedness scrolled across the screen, as the helmeted Democrat was shown grinning from the hatch of an M1 tank.

In times past, Democratic attempts to counter the advantage Republicans had on military matters proved largely futile. So, for example, in 2000, Democratic nominee Al Gore proposed an increase in the military budget twice the size of the one advocated by Governor George W. Bush. "Why did that not make a difference in perception of strength on the issue?" Bush strategist Karl Rove was asked at the 2000 Annenberg election debriefing. Bush "owned" that issue was the strategist's response.

The 2004 election fit the rule as well. In that contest, the Republicans turned Democratic standard-bearer Vietnam War hero John Kerry's infelicitous statement that "I was for the 87 billion before I was against it" into an indictment of his ability to manage the military engagements in Iraq and Afghanistan and superintend the so-called war on terror as well.

In the closing days of 2008, the RNC particularized its argument that Obama was a risky choice with appeals to key battleground states. In Virginia, for example, its ads asserted that the Democrat would cut defense jobs vital to the Virginia economy. The Obama campaign volleyed with an attack on McCain's desperation and testimony from the Republican's "own military advisor, Robert Kagan," who is pictured as print from the *Washington Post* quotes him saying, "Obama wants to increase defense spending." "Barack Obama knows," said the announcer, "a stronger military means a safer America."

To neutralize the Democrats' traditional vulnerability on all things military, Obama also used tough language about diplomacy and tried to turn his opponent's area of greatest strength into a weakness. In his convention speech, the Illinois senator even cast the military veteran McCain as weak-willed. "When John McCain said we could just 'muddle through' in Afghanistan, I argued for more resources and more troops to finish the fight against the terrorists who actually attacked us on 9/11, and made clear that we must take out Osama bin Laden and his lieutenants if we have them in our sights. John McCain likes to say that he'll follow bin Laden to the gates of hell—but he won't even go to the cave where he lives."[2] In the same speech, Obama pledged, "I will rebuild our military to meet future conflicts. But I will also renew the tough, direct diplomacy that can prevent Iran from obtaining nuclear weapons and curb Russian aggression."

The Democratic nominee also attacked McCain's defense priorities. "[I]t is not true you have consistently been concerned about what happened in Afghanistan," he told McCain in the first debate. "At one point, while you were focused on Iraq, you said, well, we can 'muddle through' Afghanistan. You don't muddle through the central front on terror and you don't muddle through going after bin Laden. You don't muddle through stamping out the Taliban. I think that is something we have to take seriously. And when I'm president, I will."

Obama also explicitly repudiated the assumption that as a Democrat he would be reluctant to use force even when the country's security requires it. "I think the lesson to be drawn is that we should never hesitate to use military force," said the Democratic nominee in the first general-election presidential debate, "and I will not, as president, in order to keep the American people safe. But we have to use our military wisely. And we did not use our military wisely in Iraq."[3]

In language purloined from the Republicans, Obama's messages strafed McCain's candidacy. "But I do believe that we have to change our policies with Pakistan," said the Illinois senator in the second debate. "We can't coddle, as we did, a dictator, give him billions of dollars and then he's making peace treaties with the Taliban and militants." He paired this move with the suggestion that his opponent would casually dispatch the U.S. military. "Senator McCain, this is the guy who sang, 'Bomb, bomb, bomb Iran,' who called for the annihilation of North Korea. That I don't think is an example of 'speaking softly.' This is the person who, after we had—we hadn't even finished Afghanistan, where he said, 'Next up, Baghdad.' "[4]

As we noted earlier, Iraq was not on a fall campaign agenda dominated by economic concerns. For practical purposes McCain's ability to garner electoral credit for the Iraq surge dissipated and the likelihood that the election would center on the candidates' credentials as potential holders of the title "Commander-in-Chief" dropped, when the surge's success pushed that war onto the back pages.

The February Pew survey did find "marked improvement in perceptions of the situation in Iraq…"[5] However, underlying these changes was a fundamental problem for the Republicans. Specifically, the view that progress was being made did not carry with it an increase in the belief that the war was worth fighting. "[T]he balance of opinion about the decision to take military action in Iraq is about the same now as it was a year ago," reported the Pew Center. "A majority (54%) says the war was the wrong decision, while 38% say it was the right decision...nearly identical to what it was in February 2007."[6] This meant that Obama could readily set the surge's success in the context of larger failures of Bush and McCain's making.

Three other roadblocks challenged Republican use of McCain's perceived ability to handle both terrorism and the role of Commander-in-Chief. In 2008 no major news events reinforced fears of a recurrence of 9/11. By contrast, in 2004, memories of that national tragedy were still fresh. Additionally, Kerry's prospects were hurt when the salience of terrorism was magnified by not only the suspiciously-timed Wall Street terror alert the day after the close of the Democratic convention but also by the attack in a Beslan school in North Ossetia-Alania in early September and by the Osama bin Laden tape aired in the final week of the campaign. By contrast, as we have repeatedly noted, throughout fall 2008, headlines and the events they reflected primed the economy, an issue owned by the Democrats.

The second barrier blunting the effective Republican use of the "crisis management" argument was McCain's uneven performance during the early days of the Wall Street meltdown. Consistent with the rhetoric of the Obama campaign, that conduct called into question the Republican nominee's capacity to deal with unexpected challenges at the same time as Obama's responses reassured. Finally, the Democratic campaign had the financial wherewithal to attack McCain while also building a case for Obama's temperament, judgment, and values.

Still, in mid-October the Republicans grabbed the possibility that concerns about Obama's limited executive experience could be coupled with confidence in McCain's to create a lifeline for the Republican ticket. In doing so, however, the Republican National Committee opened on the economy, territory commanded by Obama both by party affiliation (see chapter 4) and by performance in the preceding weeks. To make this move, an ad titled "Chair" reprised a Carter attack on Reagan in 1980 to note, "Meltdowns, foreclosure, pensions, savings wiped out. And now our nation considers elevating one of the least experienced people ever to run for president." The spot then made an assertion about Obama that, unless one counted heading a squadron decades before as executive experience, was equally true of McCain. "Barack Obama. He hasn't had executive experience." As an empty chair in the Oval Office is shown, the announcer adds, "This crisis would be Obama's first crisis in this chair."[7]

As evidence that their concerns were warranted, the Republicans also touted Joe Biden's ad-ready comment, explored in chapter 7, that "it will not be six months before the world tests Barack Obama." By situating the hypothetical crisis in the international domain, Biden had done what "Chair" had failed to do. The visuals in the resulting McCain attack ad showed tanks prowling a desert setting and a menacing photo of Iranian President Mahmoud Ahmadinejad. In an ad titled "Storm," the RNC embellished the theme. With roiling seas on screen, that spot asked, "But what if the storm does get worse with someone who's untested at the helm?" The same message was carried in a Spanish-language version of the ad. In response, the Democrats set the Biden statement in the context of his affirmation of Obama's "spine of steel," accused the Republicans of selective editing, and slammed McCain as both erratic and as "following in Bush's footsteps."[8]

How Will Obama Deal with Domestic Crises?

On October 29, the McCain campaign wrapped its "celebrity" motif into its crisis theme. In an effort to underscore the themes that had resonated for the Republicans in the two weeks after the last debate, another McCain ad integrated the "celebrity attack" into the tax-and-spend allegation. "Behind the fancy speeches, grand promises, and TV specials lies the truth," said the ad. "With crisis at home and abroad, Barack Obama lacks the experience America needs, and it shows. His response to our economic crisis is to spend and tax our economy deeper into recession. The fact is Barack Obama is not ready… yet."[9]

The problem with McCain's assault wasn't its focus on taxes but its indictment of spending. Few economists thought raising taxes in a recession made much sense. By contrast, increased government spending was high on their lists of needed actions. By simply attacking Obama for spending, rather than suggesting that his proposed programs were ill-suited to stimulate recovery, McCain may have inadvertently signaled that he was indeed out of touch with the economy's needs. Also problematic for the Republican was the fact that increased spending did not in and of itself differentiate the two nominees. If the fact checkers had it right, both candidates' plans required a substantial net increase in governmental outlays.[10]

By October 29, the Republicans' "fear of the unknown" scenario had found its ultimate expression not in assertions but in questions. "Would you get on a plane with a pilot who has never flown?" asked the announcer. "Would you trust your child with someone who has never cared for children? Would you go under with a surgeon who has never operated? Can you hand a nation to a man who has never been in charge of anything? Can you wait while he learns?" One problem for McCain was that each of these questions could have been asked of his candidacy as well.

The difficulty for the Republicans was not the nature of their attack on Obama but its timing. Before he pivoted from Senate duties to presidential campaigning, Obama had spent two years as a member of the Senate Foreign Relations Committee, his sole foreign policy experience. Those two years did not brim with accomplishments. His novice status was on display in the debates in the primaries. As we noted earlier, when asked in the YouTube debate on July 23 whether he would meet without preconditions with the leaders of Iran, Syria, Venezuela, Cuba, and North Korea, he had agreed that he would. His answer to a question in the April 26, 2007 Orangeburg, South Carolina, debate was also problematic. Queried about the United States' three most important allies, he responded, the European Union, NATO, and Japan. Because his answer omitted Israel from the list, the answer was impolitic. Moreover, NATO and the EU would probably not have scored an A in most quiz books because each is composed of multiple nations and the United States is part of NATO!

However, by the final week of the election, months of Democratic reassurance had allayed the concerns on which the Republican ads were premised. So, for instance, when the McCain campaign attacked with the celeb ads in August, the Democrats responded in part with the rhetoric of reassurance. The strategy continued throughout the fall. When the McCain campaign moved the Franklin Raines attack onto the air, for example, the Democrats undercut the attack with messages in which Obama empathized with the nation's problems, blamed them on Bush and the Republicans, and detailed his solutions.

The Democratic Closing Argument: Be Reassured about Obama (and Afraid of Palin)

The Democratic team responded to the Republicans with comforting rhetoric, endorsements by a general, and with a pointed albeit low-cost attack on Sarah Palin, who had to that point been largely ignored by the Obama campaign.

Trying to Prime Palin

In a minuscule buy of under $5,000, the Democrats attacked Palin, tweaked McCain over his selection of the Alaska governor, and poked back at the Republicans for their reprise of Biden's forecast that Obama would be tested. With the economy dominating the news, the press failed to give the ad the press coverage and hence free airtime it sought.

A second Republican ad titled "McCain's Own Words" silently offered text after text of the Republican nominee downplaying his economic expertise. "I'm going to be honest. I know a lot less about economics than I do about military and foreign policy issues. I still need to be educated." "The issue of economics is not something I've understood as well as I should." Building on that foundation, the ad offered a final McCain observation. "I might have to rely on a Vice President that I select for expertise on economic issues." "His choice?" asked the announcer. On the screen, Governor Palin is shown speaking and then slyly winking at the camera. As data from the NAES that we included in chapter 7 suggest, the ad makers' assumption that voters were uncomfortable with Palin's readiness to be president was a safe one.[11]

Raising the Prospect of One-Party Rule

By allying Obama and Democratic party leaders, including Senate leader Harry Reid and House Speaker Nancy Pelosi, the Republican hybrid ads we discussed in earlier chapters hinted at the dangers of one-party rule. In late October, McCain tried to move that argument into news with a speech in Ohio forecasting a spending spree by that "dangerous threesome." The same address reduced the distinction between the nominees to a sound bite that separated both from the incumbent president. "This is the fundamental difference between Senator Obama and me. We both disagree with President Bush on economic policy. The difference is that he thinks taxes have been too low and I think that spending has been too high."[12] Unstated was the conclusion: were the Democrats to control both Congress and the White House, there would be no check on the spending impulses of either branch.

The exit polls suggest that this final argument didn't sell with voters. Where 61 percent reported that McCain would raise taxes, 71 percent thought Obama would. Among the 63 percent in the exit polls who considered the economy the most important issue facing the country, Obama topped McCain 53–44 percent. Thirty four percent believed that change was the most important candidate attribute. Of them, 89 percent backed Obama.[13]

Obama's Rhetoric of Reassurance

Ronald Reagan's effective use of five-minute straight-to-camera ads and his calm performance in his one debate with incumbent Jimmy Carter in 1980 suggest that familiarity, a calm demeanor, and a detailed agenda are powerful rebuttals to charges that an individual is scary or would not know what to do in an unanticipated crisis. When Obama calmly tried on the presidency with detailed reassurances expressed in nationally aired two-minute speeches and a half-hour program, voters concluded, as they had in the Gipper's case, that the fit was good.

McCain could not afford either two-minute ads or a half-hour of national time to lay out his own plans. In the final week of the campaign, his forecast of his own policies took the form of simple exhortation. No details. No identification with struggling middle-class families. "We can grow our economy, we will cut government waste," said McCain in a final RNC ad. "Don't hope for a stronger America. Vote for one."

The Two-Minute Obama Advertisement

As the election drew to a close, the Democrats added general exhortations, multiple types of reassurance, and sustained national advertising to their menu. The exhortation took the form of enjoinders evoking common purpose[14] and telling voters, "We can choose hope over fear and unity over division."[15] One important ad that we discussed in the last chapter reminded voters of Obama's widespread appeal by using the endorsements by businessman and philanthropist Warren Buffett and former Secretary of State General Colin Powell to tacitly undercut the Republicans' attacks on the Democrat's economic and military plans.[16]

The use of longer-form advertising was a staple of Obama's endgame. On each day of the last week of the election, at a cost of just over $5 million, the two-minute direct-to-camera ad titled "Defining Moment" aired on national television. From October 28 to November 4, its message gained additional exposure with airings in Colorado, Florida, Iowa, Indiana, Montana, North Carolina, Ohio, and Virginia. In Michigan, Missouri, New Mexico, Nevada, and Pennsylvania, the spot aired from October 28 through November 3. From October through election eve, it was shown in some, but not all, of the markets in Wisconsin as well.

In "Defining Moment," Obama opened by recasting the question that Ronald Reagan had famously asked in 1980. "At this defining moment in our history, the question is not, 'Are you better off than you were four years ago?' We all know the answer to that. The real question is, 'Will our country be better off four years from now?' 'How will we lift our economy and restore America's place in the world?'" The ad then recapped the central promises of the campaign, from a "tax cut for 95 percent of working Americans" to its more specific incarnation, a tax cut for those who "have a job, pay taxes, and make less than $200,000." Obama also forecast reallocating tax breaks from those companies that "ship our jobs overseas" to those "that create jobs here in America." For small businesses, he promised "low-cost loans," for all Americans a reduction in "the cost of health care, breaking our dependence on foreign oil and making sure that every child gets the education they need to compete." He then answered the question, "How will I pay for these priorities" with a series of artful dodges. "First," he said, "we've got to stop spending 10 billion dollars a month in Iraq while they run up a surplus." How much we should spend in Iraq was left unanswered.

Next, Obama promised, "I'll end this war responsibly so we can invest here at home." With an agreed-upon date for withdrawal already in hand, ending the war "responsibly" would not change the administration's cost forecasts. Nor did the promise to "monitor the Wall Street rescue plan carefully, making sure taxpayers are protected and CEOs don't game the system" explain how doing so would pay for his spending priorities. Letting the "temporary Bush tax cuts for the wealthiest 2 percent expire" didn't increase projected revenue, since they were set to expire anyway, while funding the extension of those cuts for those making less would increase costs over those in the Bush projections. So would the tax cuts for 95 percent of working Americans. Moreover, closing "corporate loopholes the lobbyists put in" and ordering "a top-to-bottom audit of government spending" and eliminating "programs that don't work" are empty rhetoric without the specifics indicating which loopholes and programs were on the table.[17]

His litany of specifics suggested that Obama had explored available options and developed a detailed plan, while at the same time his demeanor exuded a low-key sense of confidence, comfort and competence. The campaign then followed up with a half-hour program whose message was that of "Defining Moment" writ large.[18]

Before examining that infomercial in detail, we pause here to note an interesting effect it may have produced. Specifically, watching the Obama half-hour decreased perceptions of Governor Palin's readiness to be president.* If that finding is not a statistical fluke, one explanation may be that a program that never mentioned either member of the Republican ticket nonetheless primed questions about preparedness and experience. The two candidates who had been the objects of speculation about readiness were Palin and Obama. At the end of this chapter we will argue that exposure to the speech boosted belief in Obama's competence. It is possible that when thoughts of president preparedness were activated they carried with them the question, "What of the other candidate whose experience was at issue?" If the often replayed moments of Palin's answers in the Couric interview or the Fey parody of them were recalled and then set against Obama's performance throughout the general election, perceptions of Palin would, for most, have come out diminished by the comparison.

A Half-Hour of Empathy and Presidential Reassurance

On October 29, the Wednesday before the election, the Democrats revived a strategy warehoused since 1992, when independent Ross Perot had employed eight half-hour infomercials to instruct the nation on the dangers of the deficit and the deficiencies of the incumbent. At a cost of over $3 million, the Obama campaign purchased time to identify with the concerns of the middle class, reprise his campaign themes, and permit him to try on the presidency. Carried on NBC, CBS, Univision, BET, TV One, Fox, and MSNBC, the film included flags, anxiety-ridden families, and familial reassurance from the Democratic nominee.

At its core, the piece linked the stories of struggling Americans to solutions offered by the nominee. "For the past 20 months," said Obama, "I've traveled the length of this country. And Michelle and I have met so many Americans who are looking for real and lasting change that makes a difference in their lives. Their stories are American stories, stories that reflect the state of our union. I'd like to introduce you to some of these people tonight. I will also lay out in specific detail what I'll do as president to restore the long-term health of our economy and our middle class and how I'll make the decisions to get us there."[19] The graphics interspersed throughout the film highlighted specific promises whose precision implied command of the issues:

Cut Taxes for Families Making Less than $200,000
Tax Credit for Hiring New Employees in U.S.
Eliminate Tax Breaks for Shipping Jobs Overseas
Freeze Foreclosures for 90 Days
Low Cost Loans for Small Businesses
$15 Billion per Year in Energy Efficiency and Renewables
Creating 5 Million Clean Energy Jobs
Help Auto Companies Retool for Fuel Efficient Cars
Tap Natural Gas Reserves
Invest in Clean Coal Technology
Expand Domestic Production of Oil
Tax Credits to Cover Tuition
Coverage for Preventive Care and Pre-Existing Conditions
Lower Cost for Families by $2500
Rebuild Our Military
Renew Tough Direct Diplomacy
Refocus on Al Qaeda and Taliban

We recognize a president in part by the rhetoric he issues. In inaugurals, State of the Union addresses, and presidential farewells, our head of state acts as the conservator of the national narrative who helps the country make sense of its past, the challenges it is confronting, and its future. In this final national presentation to the nation, Obama played that role. "Earlier this year, we already knew our country was in trouble," he said. "Home foreclosures, lost jobs, high gas prices. We were running a record deficit and our national debt had never been higher. But then a little over a month ago, the bottom fell out."

The Democratic nominee then moved to an indirect indictment of the failed Bush presidency. "What happened in the financial markets was the final verdict on eight years of failed policies. And we're now going through the worst economic crisis since the Great Depression." Next, the speech shifted to reassure. "A few weeks ago, we passed a financial rescue plan. It's a step in the right direction, and as president I'll ensure that you, the taxpayers, are paid back first." As McCain was driving the message that Obama was a tax-and-spend liberal, the Democrat instead forecast that his first presidential act would be one that returned money to the taxpayers. As McCain was arguing that Obama's policies would make the recession worse, the Democrat said, "But we also need a rescue plan for the middle class, starting with what we can do right now that will have an immediate effect. As president, here's what I'll do...."

In the speech, Obama played a second presidential role by serving as the conservator of the stories of struggling Americans. "Mark Dowell and his wife, Melinda, have worked at the local plant for most of their adult lives," recounted the Democratic nominee. "Recently, the plant cut back Mark's work to every other week. Now they are struggling to make ends meet." By intercutting accounts of hard-pressed middle-class voters, Obama linked his proposals to them and through them to the viewing audience.

Interlaced into the seams of the half-hour was rhetoric of refutative reassurance. If voters had heard McCain's charges, the rhetoric functioned as rebuttal. If they hadn't, it stood nicely on its own. To the notion that he was advocating socialism or welfare, Obama responded, "Americans, they don't expect government to solve all their problems. They're not looking for a handout. If they're able and willing to work, they should be able to find a job that pays a living wage." To the charge that he would actually raise middle-class taxes, the ad responded with a testimonial by the governor of the key battleground state of Ohio. "Think of this—Barack Obama is going to be a Democrat in the presidency who actually cuts taxes. But he's going to cut taxes for the people who really need a tax cut. He's going to cut taxes for the struggling families, and he's going to do that while holding accountable those companies that take advantage of tax breaks in order to send jobs offshore and to other countries." Countering the allegation that he was a big-spending liberal, Obama offered the assurance that "for my energy plan, my economic plan and the other proposals you'll hear tonight, I've offered spending cuts above and beyond their cost..." The argument drew credibility from an opportune piece of evidence which Obama repeated from August, when the GAO first reported the possibility, through the end of the election. "We are currently spending $10 billion a month in Iraq when they have a 79-billion-dollar surplus. It seems to me that if we're going to be strong at home as well as strong abroad, that we've got to look at bringing that war to a close." Of course, as oil prices plummeted, so did Iraq's projected surplus.[20]

In the half-hour, surrogates took on the McCain claim that Obama lacked experience. The Democrat's Illinois colleague Senator Dick Durbin testified that "as a state legislator," Obama "was a clear leader in Springfield on so many important issues that really made a difference." Missouri Senator Claire McCaskill told viewers that, "He changed the rules in Washington. Gone are the free gifts from lobbyists, gone are the fancy airplane rides for nothing. He did that." Running mate Joe Biden recounted that Obama "reached across the aisle to Dick Lugar, one of the leading guys in America for the past 20 years on arms control, to keep loose nukes out of the hands of terrorists." A retired general certified that Obama was prepared to be Commander-in-Chief. "As a retired general officer from the U.S. Army," said Brigadier General John Adams, "it makes a difference to me how a potential commander in chief thinks about war and peace...[H]e's going to be a great president."

The half-hour also reminded voters of convenient biographical vignettes played earlier in ads. One countered the viral campaign that was impugning the Democratic nominee's patriotism and the charge by Sarah Palin that he had been "palling around" with terrorists. "My mother," said Obama, "she said to herself, you know, my son, he's an American and he needs to understand what that means. And she was working, full time, so she'd wake me up at 4:30 in the morning. And we'd sit there and go through my lessons." From another speech came the account, also found in ads, of his grandfather's service in Patton's army in Europe and his grandmother's work on a bomber assembly line. Then, cutting to Obama, the ad rebutted the assumption that he would be reluctant to use military force, even when needed. "I learned at an early age from my grandparents how vital it is to defend liberty, and as commander in chief I will never hesitate to protect our country."

Finally, Obama took on the charge that his run was presumptuous, the act of a person driven by ambition or love of celebrity. "I'm reminded every single day that I am not a perfect man," said Obama in a segment from a speech delivered in New Hampshire. "I will not be a perfect president. But I can promise you this. I will always tell you what I think and where I stand." By reprising moments from past ads and speeches, as well as segments of interviews and debates, the half-hour program conveyed a sense that the persona Obama had offered was a consistent one, rooted in his life experiences.

To energize voters, the 28 minutes of taped programming cut live to a rally at which Obama was speaking to 20,000 fans. In those closing moments, the nominee said, "In six days, we can choose hope over fear and unity over division, the power of change over the power of the status quo."

The half-hour was the closing argument in a campaign that built on the biographical narratives of the primaries and the two-minute ads to dispatch the charges, some of them histrionic, leveled against Obama. The persona the Democratic nominee offered in this extended program was consistent with his steady albeit unspectacular performance in the debates.

At 33.55 million, the total network audience for the Obama half-hour topped that for the last game of the World Series, which, according to Nielsen, averaged 19.8 million viewers.[21] Black Americans were significantly more likely to view the show, as were those who said they were closely following the election and respondents who got their campaign information from television.* Conservatives and Republicans were significantly less likely to watch it.[22] In the presence of controls, those who tuned in for the half-hour program were significantly more favorable toward Obama than those who didn't and marginally less disposed toward McCain.* And viewing translated into vote preference. Our analysis reveals that even after including the candidate favorability measures as controls, a move that takes the effects of selective exposure out of the equation, those who watched the Obama infomercial were significantly more likely to report a vote preference for Obama than those who did not watch it.*

During the last few days of the election, those who saw the program also rated Obama significantly higher on traits such as experience, judgment, and "shares my values" than those who did not watch.* Viewing the program, however, was not related to respondents' assessment of McCain on that series of traits.

The fatal flaw in a strategy that asks the electorate to fear the newcomer is that elections provide ample opportunity for a novice to prove as capable as his opponent. In a change election, that's what Obama had to do to win. He succeeded. In the exit polls, 51 percent of respondents reported that the Democratic nominee had the right experience to be president; 59 percent said the same of McCain. On judgment, Obama's recasting of the experience criterion, he won with 57 percent reporting that he possessed the "right judgment to be president," Forty-nine percent thought the same of McCain.[23] (Our data do not reflect the same conclusion. As we showed in an earlier chapter, on the trait "judgment," McCain consistently bested Obama. Even at the close of the election, McCain has a slight edge over Obama.) The ultimate indication of the success of the Obama strategy of reassurance is evident in the shift across time in public perception of which candidate could better handle an unexpected crisis. *Washington Post*/ABC poll data indicate that at the end of the Republican convention, McCain had a decisive 51–42 percent lead on this question. However, by November 2, the candidates were in a statistical tie.[24] Where Obama's standing improved by 12 points (37 to 49 percent) from September 7 to November 2, McCain's dropped by 8 points (54 to 46 percent). This change suggests that the Obama campaign was unharmed by the onslaught of potentially fear-inducing Republican attacks. By the election's end, Barack Obama had passed the threshold test required to secure the votes needed to elect him the 44th president of the United States.

This chapter concludes our analysis of the five periods into which we parsed the election. Our goal in those pages was examining the effects of media, major events and messages, and the interplay among the three. In the next section, we turn from our focus on candidates and messages to scrutinize the role that both early voting and the Obama spending advantage played in the dynamics of the election. After completing that mission, we draw the arguments of the book into a summative analysis of the relative effects of the fundamentals, message, and media in 2008.

PART III

The New Campaign Landscape

ELEVEN

Absentee and Early Voting in the 2008 Campaign

O N OCTOBER 16, BARACK OBAMA CAUTIONED HIS SUPPORTERS NOT to be lulled into overconfidence by polls projecting a Democratic win. "For those of you who are feeling giddy or cocky or think this is all set, I just have two words for you: New Hampshire," he said. "I've been in these positions before, when we were favored and the press starts getting carried away and we end up getting spanked."[1] Powering the conventional wisdom that Obama had locked the race up were three facts: Even as he spoke, five out of six adults reported their vote preference was firm and unlikely to change. For some voters, Election Day had already come and gone. After all, in some areas of the country, balloting opened as early as September 15.[2] And as the presidential candidates neared the final debate, RealClearPolitics.com forecast that Barack Obama held a 119-vote electoral advantage over John McCain.[3]

In this chapter, we examine how state laws governing when citizens could ballot influenced the campaign. Specifically, we argue that Obama locked up votes not only by getting his base to vote early but also by urging voters with a tentative commitment to his candidacy to do the same. In doing so, he insulating his prospects from the negative effects of unforeseen events and a resulting surge by McCain. To develop our case, we address two questions. First, to what extent did Obama secure votes early? Second, did Obama use early voting to merely capture people who would have voted for him anyway or did he also convince "soft" voters to cast their ballots for him before Election Day?

Competitive States and Persuadable Voters: A Moving Target

If presidential elections were decided by the popular vote rather than the Electoral College one, Al Gore would have been the country's 43rd president.[4] As

TABLE 11.1. RealClearPolitics Electoral Count Projections on October 12, 2008

Obama/Biden 277				Toss-Up (103)		McCain/Palin 158		
Solid Obama (211)		Leaning Obama (66)		Toss-Up (103)		Leaning McCain (15)	Solid McCain (143)	
CA (55)	CT (7)	MI (17)	MN (10)	CO (9)	FL (27)	GA (15)	AK (3)	AL (9)
DC (3)	DE (3)	NM (5)	VA (13)	IN (11)	MO (11)		AR (6)	AZ (10)
HI (4)	IA (7)	WA (11)	WI (10)	NC (15)	NV (5)		ID (4)	KS (6)
IL (21)	MA (12)			OH (20)	WV (5)		KY (8)	LA (9)
MD (10)	ME (4)						MS (6)	MT (3)
NH (4)	NJ (15)						ND (3)	NE (5)
NY (31)	OR (7)						OK (7)	SC (8)
PA (21)	RI (4)						SD (3)	TN (11)
VT (3)							TX (34)	UT (5)
							WY (3)	

Note: Electoral votes at stake in parentheses.

Source: http://www.realclearpolitics.com/epolls/election_2008/presidential_elections_electoral_count-10-12-2008.html

table 11.1 suggests, at the end of period three, statewide polls showed that Obama and Biden were on course to secure at least 277 electoral votes, seven more than the number required to claim the White House. According to RealClearPolitics.com, 16 states and Washington, D.C., with their 211 electoral votes, were solidly supporting the Obama-Biden ticket. McCain had notable strength in 19 states, several with smaller populations and fewer congressional representatives. So despite a larger number of states, his tentative electoral tally of 143 electoral votes fell short of Obama's. Of the eight "toss-up" states, none had voted for the Democratic presidential ticket more than twice in the four previous elections. Missouri, Nevada, Ohio, and West Virginia had sided with the Democratic ticket in two of the four previous elections (1992–2004). Colorado and Florida had voted for the Democratic ticket only once in the four previous elections, and Indiana and North Carolina were zero for four.[5] In politics, past is not prologue however. People migrate. Demographics shift.

If McCain had won all of the states categorized at the end of period three as solid or leaning toward his ticket plus all of the toss-up states, he would have netted 261 electorate votes, nine shy of the 270 needed to capture the presidency. Dampening down the likelihood that he would capture the electoral votes of all eight toss-up states was the fact that Obama had outspent him in advertising by ratios of 1.98 to 1 in broadcasting, 1.40 to 1 in cable, and 4.81 to 1 in radio between October 8 and October 15 in the nation's top media markets.

The McCain strategy therefore required the Arizona senator to target states considered Democratic territory. In an October 24 article, Adam Nagourney of the *New York Times* explained the rationale:

> Mr. McCain's advisers said the key to victory was reeling back those Republican states where Mr. Obama has them on the run: Florida, where Mr. McCain spent Thursday; Indiana; Missouri; North Carolina; Ohio; and Virginia. If he can hang on to all those states as well as others that are reliably red, he would put into his column 260 of the 270 electoral votes necessary to win. Mr. McCain's advisers said they would look for the additional electoral votes they need either by taking Pennsylvania from the Democrats, or putting together some combination of Colorado, Nevada, New Hampshire and New Mexico.
>
> Mr. McCain's advisers are most concerned about Virginia, and understandably so. On the other side of the coin, Mr. McCain's advisers believe that if he wins or comes close in Pennsylvania, he will probably win in Ohio and Florida. Aides to Mr. McCain and Mr. Obama agree that Mr. McCain remains very much in the game in Ohio and Florida. Not easy, but not impossible either.[6]

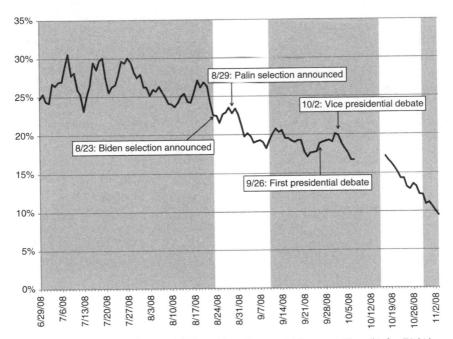

FIGURE 11.1 Percent of U.S. Adults Considered Persuadable across Time (5-day PMA). Note: The break in the line indicates dates when questions used to assess persuadability were not asked. *Source*: NAES08 telephone survey.

TABLE 11.2. Characteristics of Persuadable vs. Not Persuadable Voters

	September 11 to October 15			October 16 to November 3		
	Firm Vote	Soft Vote	Sig.[a]	Firm Vote	Soft Vote	Sig.[a]
Total	80.1%	19.9%		87.5%	12.5%	
Female	80.0%	20.0%		87.4%	12.6%	
Male	80.3%	19.7%		87.7%	12.3%	
18 to 29	79.1%	20.9%	*	81.1%	18.9%	**
30 to 44	77.8%	22.2%	*	86.9%	13.1%	**
45 to 64	81.3%	18.7%	*	88.3%	11.7%	**
65 or older	80.8%	19.2%	*	89.2%	10.8%	**
White	79.8%	20.2%	***	88.1%	11.9%	**
Black or African-American	90.9%	9.1%	***	90.1%	9.9%	**
Other	73.7%	26.3%	***	81.8%	18.2%	**
Hispanic	79.6%	20.4%		86.3%	13.7%	
Non-Hispanic	80.2%	19.8%		87.6%	12.4%	
High school or less	76.0%	24.0%	***	82.8%	17.2%	***
Some college or post-high school training	80.1%	19.9%	***	88.4%	11.6%	***
College four-year degree or more	83.4%	16.6%	***	90.9%	9.1%	***
Household income below $35K	77.2%	22.8%	***	84.3%	15.7%	***
$35K to below $75K	80.1%	19.9%	***	88.6%	11.4%	***
$75K plus	83.4%	16.6%	***	90.2%	9.8%	***
Republican	88.7%	11.3%	***	92.6%	7.4%	***
Democrat	85.6%	14.4%	***	91.1%	8.9%	***
Independent	70.9%	29.1%	***	81.7%	18.3%	***
Other	64.9%	35.1%	***	78.4%	21.6%	***
Conservative	84.4%	15.6%	***	88.6%	11.4%	***
Moderate	72.1%	27.9%	***	84.3%	15.7%	***
Liberal	86.2%	13.8%	***	91.9%	8.1%	***

[a] Significance based on chi-square results. * $p < .05$ ** $p < .01$ *** $p < .001$
Note: Row percentages given.

Data: NAES08 telephone survey.

Since voters had been firming up their vote preferences steadily since August, McCain's prospects looked bleak. While a large percentage of voters are die-hard party members who would never entertain voting for the other side, a sizeable percentage, largely independents, rely on campaign information to form judgments. In August, before the Democratic National Convention, one-quarter (25.6 percent) of adults in the United States were so-called soft voters, meaning that they either had not yet decided for whom they would vote or reported that they could change their declared vote preference, according to data from the NAES.[7] The proportions of persuadable voters did not differ between battleground and nonbattleground states. As shown in figure 11.1, the percentage with firm vote preferences declined steadily. By mid-October, the percentage of voters whose dispositions could be described as "soft" had shrunk to 14.4 percent; by contrast 48.9 percent could be classified as committed Obama voters, 36.2 percent as committed McCain voters, and 0.4 percent as committed to someone else.[8] For McCain to split the popular vote with his Democratic rival, he would have had to persuade 94 percent of the "soft" vote to ballot for him.

Several characteristics distinguished the "soft" voters from those with firm preferences. As table 11.2 indicates, individuals who had yet to form firm vote preferences in the campaign's final weeks were younger, not black, less educated, had lower household incomes, were not major-party identifiers, and described themselves as moderates. Ideology was not a significant predictor when other political and demographic variables were taken into account.* Contrary to popular belief but consistent with NAES research from 2000,[9] women did not constitute a disproportionate share of the "soft" vote.

The "Election Day" Misnomer

The last presidential debate of 2008 was held 20 days before Election Day. In years gone by, just less than three weeks may have seemed ample time to make one's case to the American public. After all, a number of major presidential contests, including Humphrey-Nixon in 1968, Carter-Reagan in 1980, and Bush-Gore in 2000 produced important shifts in public opinion in the final weeks of the campaign. But unlike these campaigns of seasons past, a sizeable part of the electorate was no longer in play as periods four and five inched toward the final days of the election. The NAES postelection telephone survey reveals that approximately one-third (34.3 percent) of voters reported having cast their ballots before Election Day.[10] These figures were up from 14 percent in 2000 and 20 percent in 2004.[11]

This increase in absentee and early voting is the byproduct of changes in state laws governing balloting before Election Day. Enacted by Congress in 1986, the Uniformed and Overseas Citizens Absentee Voting Act requires that all states and territories allow members of the United States uniformed services and merchant marine, their family members, and U.S. citizens residing outside of the United States to register and vote from their actual locations in elections for federal offices.[12] In addition, several states have adopted no-fault absentee and early voting procedures that allow registered voters to cast their ballots well before Election

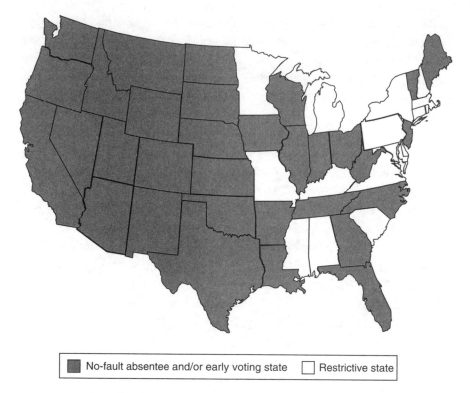

| ■ No-fault absentee and/or early voting state | ☐ Restrictive state |

FIGURE 11.2 Map Showing No-Fault Absentee and/or Early Voting States in the Continental U.S. Note: Alaska and Hawaii, not shown, are no-fault absentee and early voting states.

Day, without having to provide an excuse. By permitting unrestricted absentee voting from 1978 onward, California led the way. By 2000, 26 states offered no-fault absentee voting, unrestricted early voting, and/or vote-only-by-mail.[13] In 2008, 34 states had joined that bandwagon.[14]

No-fault absentee and early voting is particularly prevalent in the West. All of the states in the Pacific and Mountain regions allow registered voters to cast their ballots before Election Day, without providing an excuse (see figure 11.2).

The deadlines and details of absentee and early voting vary greatly by state. For example, in 2008 voting began in both North Carolina and Kentucky on September 15,[15] but in Kentucky an excuse was required for voting absentee, whereas in North Carolina none was needed. Other states offered no-fault absentee voting but waited until mid-October to begin such balloting (e.g., Kansas and Washington). Several give their citizens both no-fault absentee and early voting options. Oregonians don't ballot at the polls at all. Instead, they use a method called vote-only-by-mail, in which registered voters are sent and return ballots through the postal service. Voting terminology also varies. What is called "early voting" in one state may bear more than a passing resemblance to what is known as "in-person absentee voting" in another.

The procedures employed by states affect campaign organization and planning. For practical purposes, an individual's Election Day occurs when by casting a ballot that person loses the opportunity to change the recorded vote. The adoption of no-fault absentee and early voting procedures means that campaigns seek to elicit balloting from supporters and those leaning toward their side as soon as possible while continuing a stream of persuasion to those who have not yet voted.

As shown in figure 11.3 which profiles the voting patterns of respondents in our survey from September 22 to November 3, in 2008, absentee and early voting began well before Election Day. A small percentage of NAES respondents reported casting their ballots in September. However, the largest increases in absentee and early voting took place as Election Day neared. With four weeks of the campaign remaining, approximately 3 percent of adults said that they had already voted. Three weeks from Election Day, this percentage had doubled (6 percent). With two weeks to go, the percentage doubled again, with 12 percent of adults reporting that they had already cast their ballots. The week before Election Day, approximately 21 percent of adults reported having voted early, a little more than had done so

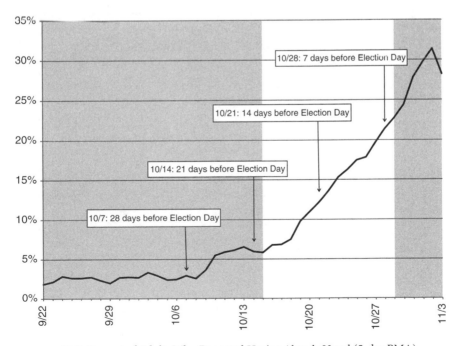

FIGURE 11.3 Percent of Adults Who Reported Having Already Voted (5-day PMA).
Source: NAES08 telephone survey.

in the 2004 presidential election when all was said and done.[16] And as mentioned previously, approximately one-third of voters cast their ballots early, according to the NAES postelection telephone survey.

A focus on the states that allow no-fault absentee and early voting reveals that when citizens were offered the opportunity to ballot early, they made use of it. According to data from the NAES postelection survey, nearly half of voters (49.8 percent) who lived in no-fault absentee and early voting states balloted before Election Day. A significantly smaller 15.3 percent who lived in states that required some kind of excuse cast their ballots early. As figure 11.4 indicates, at 3 percent, the percentage of those who lived in no-fault absentee and early voting states and cast their ballots early was comparable to the nation overall four weeks prior to Election Day. Three weeks before Election Day, the percentage of those who had already voted had more than doubled in no-fault absentee and early voting states (7 percent). Two weeks before Election Day, in these same states, about 16 percent of adults had cast their ballots. With one week left in the race, this rose to approximately 28 percent.[17] In short, the term "Election Day" has become a misnomer and the notion that American voters invariably cast their ballots on the first Tuesday in November, an anachronism.

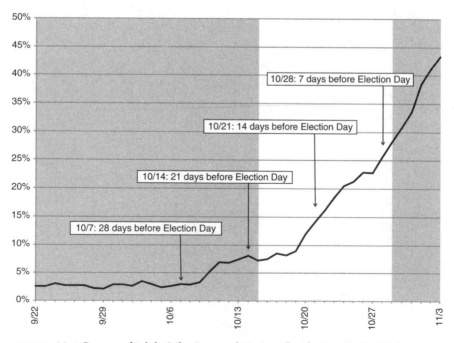

FIGURE 11.4 Percent of Adults Who Reported Having Already Voted in No-Fault Absentee and Early Voting States (5-day PMA). *Source*: NAES08 telephone survey.

Locking Up Votes Early

The contest for early votes had the potential to be consequential. Of the 15 states identified by RealClearPolitics.com as competitive in mid-October, all but four had no-fault and/or early voting (see table 11.3). With 133 electoral votes among them, the 11 that had absentee and early voting under way by then harbored the lion's share of the battleground's electoral votes. The other four (Michigan, Minnesota, Virginia, and Missouri) for whom Election Day actually would occur November 4 held only 51 electoral votes in total. In the competitive states, that is those still receiving campaign attention and ads, in the week leading up to the final presidential debate, approximately 6.7 percent of adults reported that they had already voted.[18]

Confident that their efforts had created a cushion in the key battleground states that allowed early balloting, the Democrats remained concerned about the almost three weeks between the candidates' last formal face off and traditional Election Day. "One of my concerns was there're 20 days between the last debate and the election," Obama campaign manager David Plouffe told us at the Annenberg election debriefing on December 5, 2008. "Now, in the early vote states, that's less of an issue. In North Carolina, Nevada, not an issue. But in the other states, and I think that's probably one of the reasons you guys [the McCain consultants] wanted Pennsylvania.There wasn't going to be much early voting there. So if things broke late, there weren't a lot of votes in the bank for us."[19]

While the worry about a McCain surge may have induced Democratic concern about some battleground states or the nonbattleground popular vote, if the focus were on three key Western battleground states, the Obama early voting campaign had all but locked them up. "[T]wenty days out from the election . . . ," wrote Plouffe in his best seller *The Audacity to Win*, "in [early voting] states like Colorado, New Mexico, and Nevada, we thought we were heading into Election Day with double-digit leads with over half the votes already cast. McCain would have to win Election Day by a massive margin to carry these critical states."[20]

The Democratic advantage in early voting persisted after the last debate. Between October 19 and October 23, 12.7 percent of adults in the NAES reported that they had already cast their ballots;[21] 48.3 percent of them for Obama and 32.8 percent for McCain.[22] Because it departs from precedent, this Democratic advantage in early voting is particularly notable. Republican George W. Bush captured approximately 60 percent of the early voters against both Al Gore in 2000 and John Kerry in 2004, creating the impression that Republicans owned the the world of early ballots.[23]

TABLE 11.3. Competitive States and Absentee/Early Voting Status

	No-Fault Absentee and/or Early Voting State
Leaning Obama States as of 10/12	
MI (17)	
MN (10)	
NM (5)	X
VA (13)	
WA (11)	X
WI (10)	X
Toss-Up States as of 10/12	
CO (9)	X
FL (27)	X
IN (11)	X
MO (11)	
NC (15)	X
NV (5)	X
OH (20)	X
WV (5)	X
Leaning McCain States as of 10/12	
GA (15)	X

Note: Electoral votes at stake in parentheses.

TABLE 11.4. Two-Party Vote Choice by When Ballot Was Cast

	Election Day	Day Before to About a Week Before Election Day	Two Weeks or More Before Election Day	Total
McCain	47.4%	42.1%	37.6%	44.9%
Obama	52.6%	57.9%	62.4%	55.1%
N	2,074	660	447	3,181
		chi-square = 16.954, df=2, $p<.001$		

Data: NAES08 postelection panel telephone survey

Looking at the two-party vote by when ballots were cast, the results from the NAES postelection survey show that Obama held a distinct advantage with those voting two weeks or more before Election Day. As Election Day drew near, the margin of the vote captured by Obama shrank considerably. Still, Obama captured a larger percentage of Election Day voters than did McCain (see table 11.4).[24] Consistent with this finding are the exit polls, which showed that Obama had barely edged ahead of McCain (49 percent to 48 percent) among those who had decided to vote within three days of Election Day but had a decisive lead with voters who had decided earlier than that (53 percent to 46 percent).[25]

Although campaigns make decisions on a state-by-state basis, as the goal is to capture electoral votes not the popular vote, an exploration into absentee and early voting rates for the country overall by vote preferences gives us a sense of how Obama banked votes early, giving him somewhat of a cushion before McCain's arguments gained traction during what we called the "surge" (chapter 9). Three weeks before Election Day, approximately 6 percent of the electorate had already cast ballots. According to the NAES postelection telephone survey, of people who reported voting two weeks or more before Election Day, 62.4 percent said they voted for Obama and 37.6 percent said that they voted for McCain, looking at the two-party vote (see table 11.4).[26] That means that approximately 3.7 percent of people in the electorate had cast ballots for Obama and 2.3 percent had cast ballots for McCain. The resulting projection suggests that Obama netted a lead of 1.4 percent of the eventual final vote over his Republican rival by the third debate. Using the same rationale for data collected two weeks before Election Day, when 12 percent of the electorate had already voted, 7.5 percent of the electorate had voted Obama's favor, while 4.5 percent supported McCain with their ballot. In short, with two weeks left in the presidential race, Obama had almost a 3 percent cushion of what would become the final vote.

On October 22, a *USA Today* headline proclaimed, "Dems Get Big Boost in Early Voting; Trend is a Reversal of Pattern Favoring GOP." Buried beneath the headline was the Republican argument that Democrats were "wasting their time pushing loyalists to the polls early."[27] Within the evidence available in our study, it is not possible to untangle the extent to which such positive Obama headlines may have contributed to a bandwagon effect. However, the Republican argument that the Democrats were merely marshaling die-hard supporters who would have voted for Obama anyway, rather than activating new support, can be examined with the NAES.

The Obama campaign team felt that it broke ground by persuading new or sporadic voters to cast their ballots for Obama before Election Day.

JON CARSON: [I]f we talked to people, and they were sporadic voters, 8 percent more of them turned out and voted early. We had slightly more marginal effect on likely voters. If you're a fired up 64-year-old grandmother, and we told you how to vote early, you're going to make sure your sporadic voting kids and grand kids are doing it too. So that was the strategy.

We do believe we turned out a lot more of our sporadic voters and new voters to vote early than the Republicans did. And that held across all the states that had significant early voting.

We had the ground to ourselves. For months, we were able to build an enormous organization. Those field operations we had in Oregon, Washington, Maine, Minnesota, who had no air cover, had no support, were getting the job done, were getting those ballots in, those vote by mail states, so that all the resources could be pushing the envelope out in those other states.[28]

Data from the NAES postelection survey suggest that it was Obama who convinced a greater number of unsure voters that he was the right candidate for the presidency. When asked if there was ever a time when the respondent thought he or she would vote for the other major-party candidate, 34.5 percent of Obama voters said yes, in comparison with 25.2 percent of McCain voters who said the same.[29] Of McCain voters who voted early, 19.1 percent said that they had thought of voting for Obama at some point. A larger 28.0 percent of McCain voters who voted on Election Day said that they had considered balloting for the Democratic ticket. Of Obama voters who voted early, 30.1 percent said that they had thought of voting for McCain; of Obama voters who voted on Election Day, 37.1 percent had planned to vote for the Republican nominee at some point. Taken together, the percentages suggest that Obama managed to persuade a greater number of "soft" voters overall to vote for him, and he managed to move more "soft" voters to vote early than McCain did.

However, perfervid partisans voted early as well. Our postelection panel suggests that those casting ballots before Election Day were more likely to claim having worked for one of the presidential candidates, in comparison to those voting on Election Day (10.3 percent to 6.0 percent). They were also much more likely to report having given money to a presidential candidate (27.9 percent to 18.6 percent). They weren't, however, any more likely than Election Day voters to talk to people and try to show them why they should vote for or against one of the presidential candidates (48.2 percent to 48.3 percent). Those casting ballots before Election Day reported having followed the 2008 presidential campaign "very closely," more so than their Election Day voting counterparts (68.8 percent to 60.7 percent).

The Obama campaign's efforts to motivate early voting worked. Individuals who balloted before Election Day were more likely to report having received an e-mail from the Obama campaign, in comparison to Election Day voters (16.7 percent to 12.6 percent).[30] When asked if they had gotten an e-mail from either the Obama or McCain campaigns, more respondents said that they had heard from the Obama campaign (13.4 percent) than the McCain one (7.7 percent). More than one in 10 (10.3 percent) said that they had received an e-mail from both campaigns.[31] Obama's Internet outreach appears to have encouraged voting before Election Day. Receiving an e-mail from the Obama campaign increased the odds of voting before Election Day 50 percent.* By contrast, getting e-mails from the McCain campaign did not yield a significant increase in the likelihood of early voting.

Changes to Campaign Strategy

By the campaign's end, several of the state electoral projections made in mid-October had changed (see table 11.5). McCain's anticipated count of 158 had plummeted to 132. Although Obama's projected count of 278 had remained the same, some of the states contributing to it had changed columns. Virginia, which was leaning toward Obama in mid-October, had become a toss-up state. The previous toss-up states of Colorado and Nevada had moved into the leaning-toward-Obama category. Recall that in mid-October, to win McCain had to claim all of the toss-up states, plus acquire nine votes from one of the states projected to choose Obama. As we noted earlier, in October, the McCain campaign decided that its best chances of picking up the needed votes resided in Pennsylvania, a state with 21 electoral votes and without early voting.

Since it was considered "solidly" for Obama in mid-October, Pennsylvania seemed an unusual pick. Although the Keystone State had not voted for a Republican presidential ticket since 1988 and was securely in the hands of a Democratic governor, it had supported Senator Hillary Clinton over Obama in the Democratic primary, no small feat for the New York senator since the Obama campaign outspent Clinton 3 to 1 on the air.[32] To win Pennsylvania, Clinton had assembled a coalition of blue-collar workers, seniors, and white men and women. On October

TABLE 11.5. RealClearPolitics November Electoral Count Projections

Obama/Biden 278				Toss-Up 128		McCain/Palin 132		
Solid Obama (228)		Leaning Obama (50)		Toss-Up (128)		Leaning McCain (14)	Solid McCain (118)	
CA (55)	CT (7)	CO (9)	MN (10)	AZ (10)	FL (27)	AR (6) SD (3)	AK (3)	AL (9)
DC (3)	DE (3)	NM (5)	NV (5)	GA (15)	IN (11)	WV (5)	ID (4)	KS (6)
HI (4)	IA (7)	PA (21)		MO (11)	MT (3)		KY (8)	LA (9)
IL (21)	MA (12)			NC (15)	ND (3)		MS (6)	NE (5)
MD (10)	ME (4)			OH (20)	VA (13)		OK (7)	SC (8)
MI (17)	NH (4)						TN (11)	TX (34)
NJ (15)	NY (31)						UT (5)	WY (3)
OR (7)	RI (4)							
VT (3)	WA (11)							
WI (10)								

Source: http://www.realclearpolitics.com/epolls/election_2008/electoral_count.html

25, an article in the *Economist* summed up the reasons that the state appealed to the Arizona senator:

> Mr. McCain has some solid things on his side. The Democrats' margin of victory has shrunk relentlessly from nine points in 1992 to four in 2000 to 2.5% in 2004. Pennsylvania's population is older than the American average, and more likely to be found in rural areas and small towns. Mr. McCain hopes that he can turn out enough Republicans and conservatives in small town Pennsylvania—particularly in the grim middle of the state—to offset Mr. Obama's advantage in the big cities.
>
> Mr. Obama has also had a lot of trouble connecting with working-class Pennsylvania. He lost the state to Hillary Clinton by nine points. He was ill at ease in the state's bars and bowling alleys. His problems in Pennsylvania inspired his famous remarks about "bitter" voters clinging to their guns and religion. Mr. McCain hopes that these bitter voters will add the Republican Party to the list of things that they cling to.[33]

To these advantages we add, as we noted a moment ago, that it was also a state that permitted neither no-fault absentee nor early voting, an important consideration in the McCain campaign's calculations.

Our analysis in this chapter suggests that no-fault absentee and early voting altered the chemistry of the 2008 general election by both by putting new voters in the Democratic column and by giving Obama a small but discernible cushion of votes in early voting states as insurance against a last-minute McCain comeback. Because Obama opened his national lead back up in the final days of the campaign, and even in the midst of McCain's period-four recovery maintained an edge, the Illinois senator's early voting advantage never had the potential to prove decisive. One can imagine circumstances in the future in which this change in voting rules could produce such an effect, however. And important to us as communication scholars is the fact that, unlike McCain's appeals, Obama's e-mailed messages seem to have mattered in increasing the disposition of recipients to not only cast a ballot early but to cast it for him.

TWELVE

Spending Differences and the Role of Microtargeting

Bruce Hardy, Chris Adasiewicz, Kate Kenski
and Kathleen Hall Jamieson

S CAN THE 2008 GENERAL ELECTION NEWS ACCOUNTS, REVIEW THE televised ads, listen to the candidates' speeches, and you would think that abortion and embryonic stem cell research were off the candidates' radar screens. Yet out of earshot of the press and the pundits, both camps were employing the targeting advantages inherent in radio to insistently whisper warnings about these hot-button social issues to women. So for example, to draw back the white women voters who moved to McCain in the aftermath of the Republican convention, a move motivated in part by enthusiasm about vice presidential pick Sarah Palin, the Obama campaign aggressively attacked McCain and Palin as opponents of a woman's right to choose. Rather than responding on abortion, the McCain campaign moved to certify his moderate instincts with ads reminding these voters that he supported federal funding of stem cell research. In this battle for the hearts of white women, Obama won the day by backing a microtargeted message with the significant audience delivery needed to shift votes. This chapter tells the story of money in service of such targeted messages.

Scholars have confirmed that outspending a presidential rival makes a difference. Bartels finds, for example, that "In five cases, their [Republican candidates] popular vote margin was at least four points larger than it would have been, and in two cases–1968 and 2000–Republican candidates won close elections that they very probably would have lost had they been unable to outspend incumbent Democratic vice presidents."[1] He also notes that, "Since Republican candidates spent at least slightly more money than their Democratic opponents did in each of those elections, it is not surprising to find that they did at least slightly better in every election than they would have if spending had been equal."[2] Although they disagree about the size of the effect, scholars also surmise that spending more on ads than one's presidential rival secures votes.[3] Importantly, in 2008 the spending gap was greater than in those studied campaigns in which both major-party contenders accepted federal funding. Also noteworthy in 2008 is the substantial spending on microtargeted radio and cable ads.

To explore the impact of the Obama campaign's marriage of money, extensive use of both cable and radio and microtargeting, we first document the Democratic ad advantage in spot radio and national, as well as spot broadcast and cable. We then demonstrate that those differences shifted votes. We close with a case study showing how targeted Obama radio affected perceptions of McCain.

The Dollar Differences

If money is the measure, the Obama and McCain campaigns resided in different galaxies. From the first of September to Election Day, the Democrats outspent their opponents in national broadcast and cable by over $20 million. In local, market-specific spot broadcast, the Democratic advantage was 42 million, in spot cable, over 9 million, and in radio, over 12 million. Put more starkly, Obama outspent McCain by almost as much as the total $84 million McCain received in general election federal financing. These dollar differences translated into an increased disposition to support Obama. Before beginning to offer charts and tables, we need to note that throughout our analysis the McCain totals include spending on his behalf by the Republican National Committee. The Obama totals do not include DNC figures because following the Obama campaign's wishes, the Democratic National Committee did not advertise on TV, cable, or radio for the national ticket.[4]

Impact of National Ad Buys

Figure 12.1 tracks the campaigns' differences in spending at the national level (including the 4 million dollars the Obama campaign spent on his 30-minute infomercial on October 29) against differences in favorability of the two candidates (Obama minus McCain) in nonbattleground media markets. In other words, the favorability difference reflects the views of respondents living in zip codes in which there was no local (i.e., spot) broadcast or cable spending by the two major party campaigns. In early September, the difference increases in Obama's favor

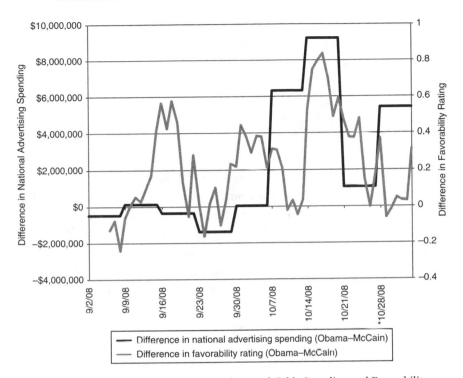

FIGURE 12.1 Differences in National Broadcast and Cable Spending and Favorability Ratings in Nonbattleground Media Markets. Note: The week of October 28 includes the $4 million the Obama campaign spent on the half-hour infomercial aired on October 29. *Source*: NAES08 telephone survey.

even as the McCain campaign is spending slightly more on national buys. As we argued in earlier chapters, the economic collapse, Sarah Palin, and McCain's suspension of his campaign worked in Obama's favor during this time as well. Overall, when we concentrate on respondents in the nonbattleground and control for demographics, political orientation, and media use, we find that weeks in which Obama outspent McCain on national ads are significantly related to an Obama vote "if the election were held today."*

Differences in Ad Spending Shifted Votes

Because a dollar spent on one channel at a particular time in one medium does not equal a dollar spent at a different time in the same venue, in this chapter we focus not on dollar differences in spot broadcast and cable but on the difference in an exposure measure known as gross ratings points (GRPs) that measures audience delivery. Media buyers and consultants assume that 100 GRPs on average would reach the targeted viewer one to two times during the time period for which the GRPs are purchased.

When deploying GRPs the media teams rely on two basic but important factors. The first is reach which estimates how many individuals within the target demographic will see the ad. This number is expressed as a percentage. The next is frequency which tells the consultants how many times on average the intended audience will see the advertisement. Reach times frequency equals gross rating points. A media schedule of 500 GRPs in a specific market could be constructed from a wide variety of combinations of reach and frequency (e.g., a 90 reach with a 5.5 frequency or a 65 reach with a 7.7 frequency). The reach and frequency vary based on the programs, networks, and time periods selected within a specific market. If a media team is only purchasing air time at 2 A.M. on Monday nights, the reach will be small compared to that accessed at a 9 P.M. time period on Thursday nights. So reach and frequency can vary within a given advertising schedule.

Because GRP captures exposure, we converted the advertising spending figures into them.[5] After doing so, we calculated spending-GRP ratios separately for McCain and Obama to account for any possibility that one campaign was more aggressive in negotiating lower ad costs than the other.[6]

Differences in GRPs in Spot TV, Cable, and Radio

Our data from CMAG, Nielsen, Media Monitors, stations, networks, and the campaigns themselves reveal that from early September through Election Day, Obama purchased a higher level of GRPs than McCain in spot broadcast, cable, and radio (see figure 12.2). Only in Iowa and Minnesota, both states carried by Obama, and possibly in New Mexico, did McCain air a higher level of GRPs than the Democratic ticket (figure 12.3). It is important to recall that the match between the radio, cable, and television markets and state boundaries is necessarily inexact. So, for example, television ads purchased in the Philadelphia market reach both New Jersey and Delaware. The possibility of spillover from or into a market in an adjoining state means that our figures by state are necessarily somewhat inexact.

Throughout the fall campaign, the McCain team felt cornered by the Democrats' capacity to spend whatever, wherever, and whenever they chose. "Whenever we'd get a grab, a little toehold in a state, you [the Obama campaign] would dump [something] like 5,000 points in [for example] Wilkes-Barre/Scranton and explode the whole thing out for us," recalled McCain media creator Chris Mottola at the Annenberg debriefing.[7] "We would desperately try to aggregate enough money

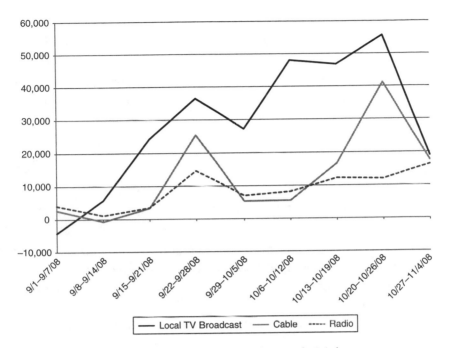

FIGURE 12.2 Obama Radio, Cable and TV GRP Advantage by Week.

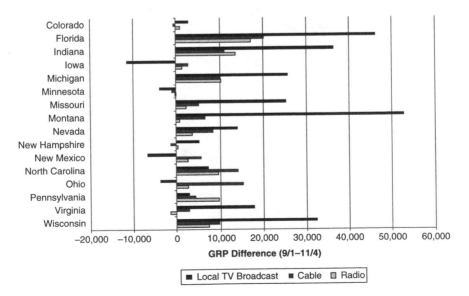

FIGURE 12.3 Obama General Election GRP Advantage in Battleground States.

to stay competitive in advertising," remembered McCain's pollster, Bill McInturff. "We'd be only $8 million behind this week or only $4 million behind when the Obama campaign would buy $10 million of two-minute spots. If you want to know what the key markets were, it isn't hard. [Look at the polling]. The campaign would say to me, 'Bill, what do you think he bought?' And I would say, 'Well, I tell you where they bought. They bought Orlando.' And they said, 'Gee, Bill, that's exactly the markets they bought.' It's not a secret why they dropped $10 million into those markets. Those markets were the key to who's left in this election."[8]

Did Differences in GRPs on Spot TV, Cable, or Radio Affect Vote?

In assessing the impact of differences in GRPs on vote, our main variable of interest is the sum of Obama GRPs (local broadcast television plus cable plus radio) minus the sum of McCain and the RNC's by zip code. Because the question of whether a decay rate should factor into this analysis will be of concern to political communication scholars, we have included a detailed methodological discussion in an appendix. Below we analyze the impact of ads on the day that they are aired. What this means is that we have decided not to factor in any cumulative impact or decay rate. Our technical justification can be found in the appendix. Our theoretical rationale is a simple one. During the 2008 general election, an Obama spending advantage backed a consistent stream of Democratic messages. We focus as a result on the spending differences in front of an all but continuous message stream. As the appendix shows, when we analyzed different decay rates, we found results consistent with those we report below.

Table 12.1 shows the influence of advertising in a logistic regression predicting an Obama two-party vote if "the election were held today." The interpretation of logistic regression models requires a little math and the awareness that messages will have less ability to persuade both those highly favorable to and highly opposed to Obama. To understand the impact of a net 100 GRP Obama advantage, start with a person whose baseline probability to cast an Obama vote is 50 percent. Turning this baseline probability into logodds, adding the coefficient (.079) to the logodds, and then turning this number back to a probability[9] gives us a new probability for this person which is 51.974 percent. This suggests that an Obama advantage of 100 GRPs has an impact around 2 percent on someone who does not lean one way or another. In short, a GRP difference has its greatest effect on those on the fence. By contrast, the same GRP difference will produce a 1.5 percent increased likelihood of voting for the Democratic ticket if the person has a low, 25 percent, baseline probability of voting for him in the first place. In this model, were our hypothetical individual a person disposed to vote for Obama with a baseline probability to cast an

TABLE 12.1. Logistic Regression Predicting Obama Two-Party Vote "If Election Were Held Today"

	B Coefficient		Standard Error	Odds Ratios
Intercept	2.613	***	.240	13.67
Female (1=yes, 0=no)	.061		.057	1.063
Age (in years)	−.003	#	.002	.997
Black (1=yes, 0=no)	2.845	***	.198	17.198
Hispanic (1=yes, 0=no)	.795	***	.118	2.214
Education (in years)	.039	**	.013	1.039
Household income (in thousands)	−.002	**	.001	.998
Republican (1=yes, 0=no)	−2.000	***	.077	.135
Democrat (1=yes, 0=no)	1.719	***	.068	5.577
Ideology (1=very liberal to 5=very conservative)	−.927	***	.030	.396
Average number of days heard or saw presidential campaign information in the past week across television, newspaper, talk radio, and Internet	.029		.019	1.030
2004 presidential vote margin by county (FIPS—Kerry percent of total vote minus Bush Percent of total vote)[a]	1.357	***	.116	3.883
Squared 2004 presidential vote margin by county	−.657	*	.327	.519
Difference in total GRPs by campaigns (Obama–McCain and RNC) (Per 100 GRPs)(Broadcast, Radio, & Cable)	.079	**	.023	1.082
N			11,612	
Percent Correct			85.0	
Cox and Snell R-Squared			.494	
Nagelkerke R-Squared			.659	

# $p < .10$ * $p < .05$ ** $p < .01$ *** $p < .001$

[a] Data for the county level election results were compiled by Dave Leip at Atlas of U.S. Presidential Elections, http://www.uselectionatlas.org

Data: NAES08 telephone survey. Dates: 9/1/08 to 11/03/08.

Obama vote of 75 percent, we'd also see a 1.5 percent increase in the probability that that person would report a disposition to cast an Obama vote (see figure 12.4).

In other words, the impact of paid broadcast, cable, and radio is both greatest for those who are undecided and dependent on a voter's baseline probability of pre-exposure support. If the electorate is completely polarized with equal numbers disposed (with the same probability on each side) toward McCain and Obama, and both sides air the same amount of advertising effectively targeted to them, then advertising would be unlikely to have a detectable impact.

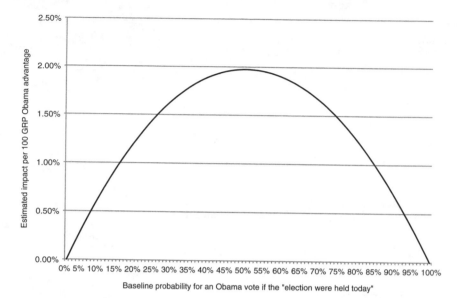

FIGURE 12.4 The Impact of 100 GRP Obama Advantage on a Vote for Obama if the Election were Held Today by Baseline Probability. *Source*: NAES08 telephone survey.

The next logical step in our analyses is to find the distribution of baseline probabilities in the 2008 general election. To do this, we estimated a probability for an Obama vote by subtracting McCain's favorability ratings from Obama's and transformed the values into percentages. For example, if a respondent gave McCain a score of "10" and Obama a "1" on each of the candidate's 10-point favorability scales, (where 1 anchors the negative side of the scale and 10 the positive) this respondent would receive a score of "−9" which translates into a 5 percent probability of voting for Obama. A respondent who gives Obama a "10" and McCain a "0" would have a 100 percent baseline probability. If a respondent gave both candidates the same score on their favorability measures he or she would receive a score of "0" which translates into a 50 percent baseline probability. This is not a perfect estimation, because someone giving both candidates the same score on the extreme low end of the favorability measures might not be someone who is conflicted and unsure. Someone scoring both candidates at "0" may have decided not to vote at all or is planning to cast a ballot for a third party candidate. That said, only 99 respondents included in these analyses gave both Obama and McCain an identical score of under "3." This means that only 7 percent of the respondents whose baseline probability we estimated to be 50 percent fell into this category. Figure 12.5 shows the distribution of the estimated baseline probability for the respondents included in the model above. Ten and half percent of NAES respondent are estimated to have 50 percent baseline. Sixty four percent of our sample falls between 25 percent and a 75 percent baseline probability for voting Obama. This distribution produces the impact of advertising that we outlined a moment ago.

The results from the logistic model are based on 100 GRP increments in Obama advantage. The impact of 100 GRPs on a voter who has a fifty percent baseline probability to vote for Obama is around 2 percent. Because our outcome variable—"vote for Obama if election were held today"—is a dichotomy and we are dealing with probabilities and not a linear relationship, we cannot double or triple the impact if we are interested in the effect of an Obama advantage of 200 or 300 GRP. The relationship between additional GRPs and estimated impact on an individual with a 50 percent baseline probability is outlined in figure 12.6.[10] As the figure shows, once you get to a 5,000 GRP advantage the impact starts to flatten. It is impossible for advertising to have a greater impact than 50 percent for someone with a 50 percent baseline because the probability of voting for Obama cannot be greater than 100 percent. The figure is of course positing a world in which none of us would agree to live. We strongly suspect that long before an individual watched the GRPs presupposed by this table, that person would have turned off the media channel, fled to a monastery, or been led away in a straight-jacket.

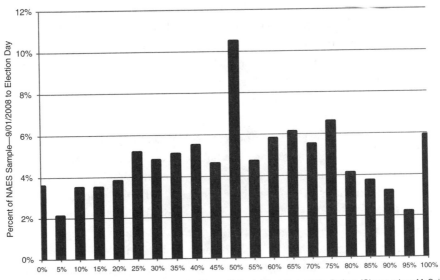

FIGURE 12.5 Estimated Distribution of Baseline Probability for Casting an Obama Vote.
Source: NAES08 telephone survey.

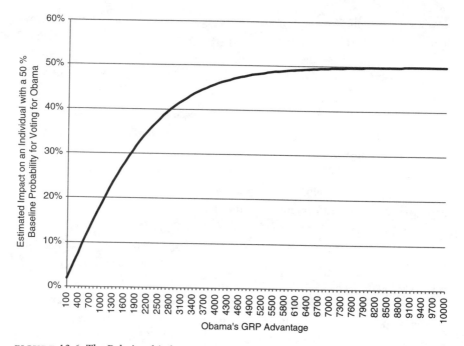

FIGURE 12.6 The Relationship between Obama's GRP Advantage and Estimated Impact. *Source*: NAES08 telephone survey.

Our examination of the impact of advertising in our three media shows that radio produces the strongest effect (table 12.2). We ran separate models for television, cable, and radio and also created a model that collapsed all three because the types of media are only moderately correlated.[11] Looking at the three models by individual medium, we see that the coefficients become greater as the medium permits higher targeting. A 100 GRP advantage for Obama in local TV advertising increases by 1.5 percent the probability that a person with a baseline probability of 50 percent will say that if the election were held on the day of interview she would cast an Obama vote, cable produces a 4.1 percent impact, and radio, a 5.5 percent one. When we put the three media's advertising GRP differences in the same model, only radio produces a significant coefficient.

One interpretation of these results is that radio is the only paid medium that had an impact during the 2008 general election. Logically, this doesn't make sense. Instead, what is happening here deals with size and specificity of targeted audience. Broadcast television has the largest coverage, cable is in the middle, and radio is the most highly pinpointed. This pinpointing allows radio to mask the impact of the other media in our model.

Media time buyers agree that all three media matter. "Each medium is very effective at what it does," notes Obama ad buyer Danny Jester. "But the effectiveness of each is magnified by a proper mix of the three."

TABLE 12.2. Logistic Regression Predicting Obama Two-Party Vote "If Election Were Held Today" By Paid Media

	Local Broadcast	Radio	Cable	All Three
Intercept	2.613***	2.568***	2.689	2.621
Female (1=yes, 0=no)	.059	.066	.063	.067
Age (in years)	−.003#	−.003	−.003#	−.003
Black (1=yes, 0=no)	2.842***	2.874***	2.784***	2.819***
Hispanic (1=yes, 0=no)	.793***	.802***	.805***	.814***
Education (in years)	.038**	.041**	.034*	.037**
Household income (in thousands)	−.002**	−.002**	−.002**	−.002**
Republican (1=yes, 0=no)	−1.998***	2.002***	−2.011***	−2.023***
Democrat (1=yes, 0=no)	1.715***	1.714***	1.720***	1.720***
Ideology (1=very liberal to 5=very conservative)	−.927***	−.927***	−.929***	−.930***
Average of number of days saw or heard presidential campaign information in past week across television, newspaper, talk radio, and Internet	.030	.026	.036#	.032
2004 presidential vote margin by county (FIPS–Kerry percent of total vote minus Bush Percent of total vote)	1.374***	1.334***	1.371***	1.322***
Squared 2004 presidential vote margin by county	−.665*	−.619#	−.667*	−.627#
Difference in Local Broadcast GRPs by campaigns (Obama–McCain and RNC) (Per 100 GRPs)	.059#	—	—	.028
Difference in Radio GRP by campaigns (Obama–McCain and RNC) (Per 100 GRP)	—	.225***	—	.203***
Difference in Cable GRPs by campaigns (Obama–McCain and RNC) (Per 100 GRPs)	—	—	.165#	.078
N		11,612		
Percent Correct	84.9	85.0	85.1	85.1
Cox and Snell R-Squared	.494	.494	.495	.496
Nagelkerke R-Squared	.659	.659	.661	.662

# $p < .10$ * $p < .05$ ** $p < .01$ *** $p < .001$

Data: Entries are logit coefficents NAES08 telephone survey. Dates: 9/1/08 to 11/03/08.

An Alternative Explanation?

There may be, of course, an alternative explanation for our findings. Specifically, our inference may be confounded by the possibility that the same targeting logic for paid media was at play in the ground campaign. Were that the case, then, what we see as an advertising effect may instead have been produced by other forms of microtargeting.

A thorough test of this alternative explanation would include a variable tapping Obama campaign contact for all of the 11,612 respondents in our model. We don't offer such a model because our "campaign contact" questions were asked of 2,200 individuals. However, a model on this subsample controlling for campaign contact produced similar results to those in the model we just offered. Specifically, a 100 GRP advantage produced a relationship of similar size to the one noted above.[12] Moreover, if the effect we found was produced by nonmediated campaign contact, zip codes with high Obama paid media spending would predict higher contact. However, the amount of GRP advantage held by the Obama campaign in a given zip code does not co-vary with the amount of contact from the Obama campaign.

We also need to explain why we have discarded a durable feature of earlier scholarship on political advertising. Past research has assumed that visits to a media market by a presidential or vice presidential candidate can stand in for nonadvertising pro-candidate communication in that market. Before the advent of satellite interviews between candidates and local media hosts, this assumption made sense. By appearing in a local market, a candidate would capture local news coverage and catalyze his troops. However, in a satellite era, candidates are able to gain local unpaid media time without setting foot on a local stage or studio. Nor does the arrival of the candidate's jet necessarily signal an increase in grassroots activity by his campaign. The on-the-ground mobilization that characterized efforts by Obama and the Democratic National Committee decoupled the level of local campaign activity from candidate presence in the market. For practical purposes, the Obama ground game was played 24–7 and at high intensity throughout the fall campaign. And we know from our election debriefing that both campaigns made extensive use of satellite interviews.[13]

Accounting for High Spending on Local Broadcast

McCain and Obama devoted more of their available funds to spot TV than to either cable or radio because broadcast is an efficient means of delivering large cross sections of the electorate. "Broadcast is also more effective at reaching low frequency TV viewers when compared to cable," says McCain buyer Kyle Roberts. Unlike national news viewers, those audience members are neither particularly partisan nor likely to be paying particularly close attention to the campaign, a profile that suggests that those among them who haven't tuned out politics are susceptible to persuasion. Consequently, it is unsurprising that Jamieson and Gottfried find that local news viewers were more likely than nonviewers to embrace Obama's most frequently broadcast attack, the notion that the Republican would create a net tax on employer-provided health care benefits. After all, not only did Obama outspend McCain, but the Republican nominee's ads did not rebut that Democratic distortion. Also consistent with past communication research, local broadcast news consumers did not disproportionately believe the McCain deception that Obama's plan would raise taxes on the middle class. Unlike McCain, Obama aggressively countered that McCain allegation in ads.[14]

But when the message is tailored to a specific subsection of the audience or to a specific geographic region, the move designed to win a battleground state, cable, and radio buys make sense. As we will suggest in a moment, a well-orchestrated campaign will layer its radio and cable messages into the context set in place by spot broadcast ads. Obama did just that by tying his radio attacks on McCain's supposed stem cell position and stand on abortion to the broader themes that pervaded his broadcast ads: McCain equals Bush, McCain doesn't share the voters' values and is out of touch.

Although a successful advertising campaign integrates all three media, some characteristics of cable and radio increased their desirability in recent years. Specifically, (1) some of broadcast's audience has shifted to cable, (2) cable and radio offer a wider range of options than local broadcast whose availability is concentrated in local news which reaches one block of individuals repeatedly in a cluttered ad environment, and (3) the capacity to microtarget is greater on cable and radio than broadcast.

The Shift from Broadcast to Cable

As cable multiplied the number of available channels, and audiences found new favorites among them, the newer medium's 50-plus menu of outlets lured viewers from broadcast. That trend continued in 2008. Overall, 37 "ad-supported cable networks enjoyed their best-ever primetime audience deliveries during a year in which the broadcast networks have lost more than 2 million viewers 18–49," noted *Variety,* quoting a cable analyst.[15] Where audiences tuned to three or four stations two or so decades ago, they now choose from over 50 networks. To reach people who have shifted some of their viewing time from broadcast to cable, advertising media buyers purchase time on that medium. Some of the effect we observe is probably related to the difficulty of efficiently locating the sought-after audience with broadcast buys. "It wasn't just that more people were watching Fox, CNN and MSNBC that we had to spend more on cable," reported McCain time buyer Kyle Roberts. "Networks like, FOOD, TNT, TBS, USA, Lifetime, HGTV, TLC and so many more allowed us to target to different segments of the voter population."[16]

To reach news viewers, media buyers must increasingly include spot cable as well because, as research by the Pew Research Center for the People & the Press suggests, more Americans regularly watch cable news than tune in to the three nightly broadcast newscasts.[17] Moreover, in major political moments the numbers for cable approach that of broadcast television. On election night 2008, for example, the audience watching the three major cable channels reached an average of 27.2 million, a figure not far from the average of 32.9 million drawn to the broadcast networks. "At the Democratic convention," notes the same Pew report, "the networks averaged 14.1 million viewers during the 10 P.M. hour, while the cable news channels averaged 10.1 million. During the Republican convention, the networks averaged 15.2 million and the cable news channels 11.3 million."[18] In response to these changes, local cable advertising became a more integral part of the time-buying mix in 2008. Where in the 2000 presidential campaigns, $2.3 million was devoted to cable buys, and in 2004, $4 million was spent to place ads in that medium, the dollar figure in 2008 was $61 million.[19]

The Impact of Broadcast Availabilities in Local News

Where cable provides a smorgasbord of ad-placement opportunities, a structural factor underlying local broadcast concentrates its available time in and around local news. As those who tuned to it in the battleground in 2008 know all too well, that venue was clotted with political messages, a factor that made it more difficult for any individual message to get through. In most markets, that tsunami of ad placements included those for members of Congress and, in some states, for the Senate. In 2008, North Carolina was a case in point. In that state, both the open senate seat and the gubernatorial contest were hotly contested, and the state was in play at the presidential level as well. At the same time, the availabilities that could be purchased on TV meant that local news viewers were more likely to encounter walls of political ads than were those turning to broadcast for soap operas, comedy, drama, or late-night comedy. In 2008, CMAG data suggest that half of the spot broadcast buys were tied to local news.[20] The reason is easy to explain. Where *NBC Nightly News with Brian Williams* sells either one minute-long or two thirty-second slots of adjacent time in a market, each local station offers up to 24 spots (12 minutes) of ad time per hour, or 22 spots (11 minutes) in a half hour. In short, one explanation for higher cable impact is that cable offers a higher proportion of its availabilities in less cluttered ad configurations.

At the same time, the concentration of availabilities in local broadcast news increases the amount of persuasion addressed to that audience, while minimizing the amount reaching those who watch nonlocal news programming on local broadcast stations.

The Capacity to Microtarget Using Cable and Radio

Audience fragmentation is a time buyer's dream come true. Because they are able to reach a more homogeneous audience than broadcast in general and broadcast news in particular, cable and radio have an advantage in reaching specific groups of persuadable voters. In short, radio and cable offer an efficient means of reaching a specialized audience with a message framed for it.

A skilled time buyer knows how to narrowcast messages to the various niche groups that gravitate to individual channels within the diverse cable and radio menu. So, for example, on cable, Lifetime skews heavily toward women and ESPN just as dramatically to men. BET attracts blacks and Univision, Hispanics. To reach independents 25–54 years of age, the buyer purchases Comedy Central, TLC, or Discovery; if women 25–54 are the key demographic, the networks of choice are E, HGTV, WE, Lifetime, and Oxygen. For news, conservatives prefer Fox; progressives, CNN and MSNBC. Drawing on Nielsen[21] data for age and gender, Mediamark Research & Intelligence (MRI)[22] for information on political ideology, and Scarborough Research[23] for party preferences, and voter data from campaign surveys, a time buyer can determine how likely the audience for a channel, such as CNBC, AMC, or AEN, is to be registered to vote, to actually vote, and to self-identify as Republican or Democratic.

It is, of course, possible to draw the same sorts of profiles of broadcast programs. But where broadcast casts a wide net, cable and radio have a greater capacity to microtarget. Where broadcast offers niche programs, cable presents niche networks that attract a specific type of audience throughout the day. With such information in hand, the campaign can determine both which programs and which networks will deliver the highest number of targeted voters per thousand dollars spent. So for example, where the Obama campaign purchased time on six broadcast networks in Charlotte, North Carolina, it bought time on 24 cable networks.

Cable and radio can narrowcast geographically as well. Broadcast markets are defined by the distance the signal is able to be transmitted, but "cable [is] developed on the local level with individual cable operators creating agreements with local municipalities to provide coverage for specific areas," notes Tim Kay, former Democratic political strategist and current executive at National Cable Communications (NCC).[24] As a result, the areas reached by cable are more tightly aligned to political boundaries, such as cities, counties, and states.

When selling soap or sodas, unless distribution is a factor, geographic targeting matters less than it does when hunting down votes that count toward an election in a battleground. So, for example, during the run up to the New Hampshire primary, voters in Massachusetts were bombarded with ads placed on Boston broadcast stations by those trying to reach voters in the state next door that was holding the nation's first 2008 primary. By one estimate, when a buyer purchases broadcast time in Boston to reach New Hampshirites, 90 percent of the messages reach those who can't vote in that primary election. Similarly in the general election, as McCain and Obama fought for votes in Pennsylvania, they wasted dollars also addressing residents in New Jersey and Delaware, bordering states that were already locked up. And money spent on D.C. broadcast channels to reach Virginia in the general election poured into reliably Democratic Maryland as well.[25]

The advantages of microtargeting were on display in St. Joseph County, a locale in Indiana that swung from Bush in 2004 to Obama in 2008. The difference was a Democratic pick-up of 16,000 votes. "In this market," noted the National Cable Communication's Tim Kay in a white paper prepared after the election, "the [Obama] campaign spent about $900 thousand dollars on broadcast, with an additional $136 thousand on cable advertising. What is interesting [is that] they bought the [cable] interconnect system which covered the whole DMA but reinforced the buy with an individual system that covered St. Joseph county only. This kept the overall message on the DMA with a specific message on cable targeted into a county of importance."[26] The purchase of St. Joseph County was a soft cable system buy, the most cost-efficient way to reach a specific geographic area. In 2008, the Obama campaign purchased 764 individual soft cable systems.

We suspect that we find the stronger spot cable and radio effect because like cable, the radio spectrum permits an ad buyer to micro-target swing voters, a process that increases the likelihood of persuasion. When the same audience is reached through two compatible media, the effect of each is magnified. Just as cable's network structure draws distinct subpopulations, radio's various formats attract their own demographics. Those over 65, for example, are more likely to listen to big band and easy listening formats, where those from 18–34 favor contemporary hits and alternative modern rock. Women gravitate toward classical, rhythmic oldies, and gospel, while men prefer classic rock, all talk (talk radio), all news, or sports. For Latinos, there are Hispanic radio stations and for African-Americans, black radio.

The format structure of radio makes it possible to match message to audience and audience to station. Use of radio to narrowcast in Pennsylvania, a state famously described as Pittsburgh and Philadelphia with Alabama in between, is illustrative. The NRA and National Right to Life ads would presumably find a sympathetic audience in Wilkes-Barre and Allentown but less so in the large urban centers that bracket the state. Nonetheless, the NRA aired its attacks on Obama on country radio station WOGF-FM in Pittsburgh, as well as WGGY-FM in Wilkes-Barre/Scranton, while National Right to Life aired its attacks on conservative talk stations WAEB-AM in Allentown and WILK-AM in Wilkes-Barre/Scranton but also WPGB in Pittsburgh. The explanation is an obvious one. Since in most states, Pennsylvania among them, electoral votes are decided by the statewide outcome, picking up conservative votes in more liberal bastions makes strategic sense. Doing so required speaking to the likeminded, without inviting a backlash from those on the other side of the debate. Hence both groups sought time on radio stations that attracted conservatives in an otherwise liberal media market.

Each side not only sought support from their candidate's soul mates as well as from swing voters who were playing the field. To reach moderate women in the Philadelphia suburbs with their competing messages on stem cell research, for example, both McCain and Obama purchased time in formats that disproportionately drew middle-aged moderate women. To explore the effects of targeted radio, we turn to the ad war over stem cell research and abortion crafted to swing women's votes.

Case Study on the Role of Radio in the Abortion and Embryonic Stem Cell Research Debate

"After the convention, our numbers with women skyrocketed," recalls McCain's Director of Strategy Sarah Simmons. "For the first (and only) time in the campaign, we led with women. [To rally women to his side] Obama ran a huge campaign [saying] Sarah Palin and John McCain were opposed to *Roe v. Wade* and would eliminate a woman's right to choose. As a response to the attacks on abortion, we ran ads stressing [McCain's support for] stem cell research in some suburban radio markets (Philadelphia, Detroit, Columbus Ohio, St. Louis, Denver, and Kansas City). Our strategic objective was to use those radio ads to blunt the impact of the abortion attack,...and to keep some share of women." Consistent with our NAES finding, Simmons concludes that although the McCain campaign "anticipated the attack on abortion [and] tried to blunt it," the McCain message was "overrun by the sheer volume of the attack by Obama."[27] "We hit the choice issue (and stem cell research) hard in the run up to the GOP convention on radio in about 20 select markets," recalls Obama ad director Jim Margolis. "The effort was focused on key battleground states and key markets within those states....We believed that we could move the needle on perceptions that McCain was a 'moderate.' In fact, on many issues, including choice, he was out of the mainstream." Margolis adds that throughout the general election "we had many tracks of advertising, in addition to aggressively responding to incoming attacks. On our women's track we made sure that thoughtful, swing, Independent and moderate Republican women knew his record."[28] We believe that we see the impact of the Obama campaign's "women's track" beginning in the last week of September (figure 12.7).

The reason that the narrowcasting of messages on abortion, in particular, was important is that knowing that Senator McCain favored overturning *Roe v. Wade* significantly increased the likelihood that moderates in general and moderate women in particular would vote for the Democratic nominee. However, it also increased the likelihood that conservative women would support McCain. Where the narrowcast battle increased the chances that moderate and conservative women knew his stand on abortion, it did not drive up the probability that they

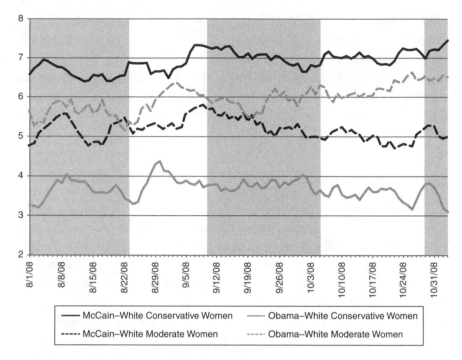

FIGURE 12.7 Candidate Favorability Ratings by Conservative and Moderate White Women (10-point scale, 5-day PMA). *Source*: NAES08 telephone survey.

knew his far more moderate position in support of federal funding of stem cell research, a finding suggesting that Obama's allegation that McCain opposed stem cell research blunted McCain's assertion that he was its champion.

The effects of suppositions about Republicans in general and the power of Obama's spending on ads presumably combine to explain why, even though McCain and Obama held the same position, most NAES respondents attributed a pro-stem cell stance to Obama only (figure 12.8) when asked "which candidate or candidates running for president supports federal funding for embryonic stem cell research?" And this attribution occurred regardless of the position on the issue held by the person surveyed.* Since we did not begin to ask the question until we spotted the radio attacks, we can't track changes over large swaths of time. What we do see nationally is an increase in accurate perception of Obama's stand in the last month of the campaign and no change in accurate perception of McCain's stand. Since the ads were airing only in the battleground, to explore effects we need to move from national data to a more specific analysis.

To do so we rely on our campaign ad-buy data and a logistic regression predicting the belief that Obama (not McCain or both candidates) supports federal

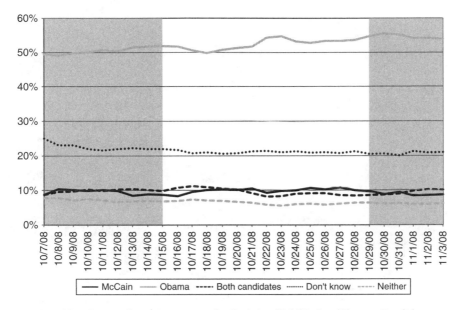

FIGURE 12.8 Respondents' Answers to the Question "Which Candidate or Candidates Running for President Supports Federal Funding for Embryonic Stem Cell Research?" (5-day PMA). *Source*: NAES08 telephone survey.

funding for embryonic stem cell research.[29] Our question gave respondents the option of picking "Obama," "McCain," "Both," or "Neither"—with the correct answer being "Both." Although the differential spending in Obama's favor produced relationships in the direction that could be interpreted as a pro-Obama effect, the relationship was not statistically significant.*

The Clash over Abortion

As the campaign progressed, more and more individuals identified McCain as the candidate who favored overturning *Roe v. Wade* (see figure 12.9). Using a logistic regression model parallel to the one we just described, we find an advertising effect driving this belief but only in radio and not cable and broadcast. This finding makes sense because radio was main channel carrying these messages. Furthermore, the effect only appears for moderate women. We know that both campaigns addressed moderate women and McCain targeted conservative ones with messages on abortion. This relationship was not significant for conservative and liberal women.

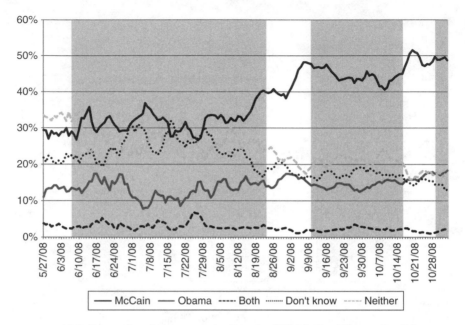

FIGURE 12.9 Respondents' Answers to the Question "Which Candidate or Candidates Running for President Favors Overturning *Roe v. Wade*, the Supreme Court Decision Legalizing Abortion?" (5-day PMA). *Source*: NAES08 telephone survey.

The effect of the Obama targeted radio buys can be best illustrated in a series of steps: (1) the advertising increased knowledge of McCain's opposition to *Roe v. Wade*, (2) as noted above, these ads also framed McCain as an out-of-touch conservative who would not protect the rights of women and did not share their values, (3) for moderate women, knowing McCain's position on this issue, thinking he is a conservative, and believing he does not share their values all predict an Obama vote.

Did Money and Microtargeting Matter?

We are not suggesting that Obama's expenditures on broadcast, cable or radio either altered or determined the outcome of the election. What we do know is that they shifted vote preference in his direction. Where that might have mattered is in narrowly decided states such as Indiana (1.03 percent)[30] and North Carolina (0.33 percent), and in states such as Florida (2.82 percent) and Virginia (6.31 percent), in which the Obama spending advantage over McCain was large (figure 12.3). However, even if McCain had taken those 66 electoral votes from Obama's 365 total, the Democrat would still have retained his hold on the Oval Office.

As the stem cell exchanges illustrate, the dollars and GRPs on which we focused here were placed in service of specific arguments and allegations. In the next chapter we turn to the question, what role did the campaigns' central messages play in the likelihood that a respondent would report planning to vote for one candidate or the other?

THIRTEEN

The Effect of Messages

❧❧❧

T HE OBAMA VICTORY HAS FOCUSED ON THE PROCESSES AT PLAY
in presidential elections, the factors that affect their outcomes, and the
mechanisms by which these effects occur. We did so as a framework for
understanding what part, if any, media, money, and message played in shaping the
2008 election. Our answer centers on the communication disseminated by the
campaigns, the media's treatment of it, the impact of the dollars spent to reach
voters, and voters' responses to the various forms of communication capable of
affecting their choice.

As part of this process, we laid out the argumentative terrain on which the
campaign was fought by examining the claims each campaign made about its
standard-bearer and exploring the attacks made to discredit the individuals on the
other side. In chapters 2 and 4, for example, we documented the Obama allegations that McCain should not be elected because he is too old, out of touch, and
too like the unpopular incumbent to address the challenges facing the country. In
chapters 3 and 5, we detailed the Republican contentions that Obama was a tax-
and-spend liberal, not ready to lead, and unpatriotic.

After making sense of these broad themes, in chapters 6 through 11 we chronicled the changes in the message dynamics across five postprimary periods from
early June to Election Day. Within them, we focused on the contest over energy in
the summer, the role of the conventions and the vice presidential picks, the economic plunge, a McCain surge in late October, and the final appeals in the last days
of the campaign. In chapter 11, we captured the advantage the Democrats gained
by locking up early votes. Chapter 12 made the case that Obama's financial advantage in the ad war translated into increased support for him and also explained

how paid media was used to target the audiences that strategists envisioned when they created these messages.

Our task in this chapter is marshalling the major messages of the campaign into a model that explores their relative impact on how people said they would vote on the day we surveyed them. To carry out this mission, we start by showing the interrelated ways in which media, money, and messages worked to tie McCain to the environmental factors we explored in the first chapter and then look at how messages about Bush and the economy played out in 2008. With these arguments in place, we chronicle the other communication effects we isolated to this point in the book. Finally, we construct a model that uses the fundamentals, sociodemographic variables, news media variables, and message variables to predict voting preference.

The Role of Media, Message, and Money in Linking McCain to the Fundamentals

Unpopular Incumbent

As we argued in chapter 2, the Obama campaign added George W. Bush to the 2008 Republican ticket by framing the election as a referendum on his presidency. By contrast, the Republicans cast the choice as one between McCain the Maverick and Obama the scary, unready, tax-and-spend liberal. To forecast the role communication played in public acceptance of one of these views, in the introduction we noted fluctuations across the postprimary period in the perception that electing McCain meant a third Bush term.

The linkage was consequential. Giving the incumbent president a higher job approval rating and reporting having cast a 2004 ballot for the Bush-Cheney ticket each predict a 2008 vote for McCain, as do Republican party identification and conservative ideology. (Alternatively, lower Bush approval ratings forecast support for Obama.) And identifying the Arizonan with the Texan prefigures a Democratic presidential vote over and above the effects of these basics. We take this to mean that communication strengthened the relationship between McCain and Bush beyond the natural level conveyed by the incumbent's approval rating and a vote for him four years earlier. Consistent with that view, in this chapter we show that as the spread between the number of gross ratings points purchased by Obama and McCain increased, so too did the likelihood of belief in this central Democratic ad claim. Advertising was not the only form of communication magnifying the association. The media affected the perception as well. The more one watched television news, read the newspaper, or went online for campaign information, the more likely one was to embrace the notion of McCain as McSame. Within the media landscape, there was one countervailing force, however. Drawing information from talk radio, a fortress of the conservative media establishment, produced the opposite effect.

At the campaign's end, McCain is more likely than before to be seen as McSame, in part because, abetted by the media, the Democrats scraped the maverick label from him and sutured the name and face of the Republican incumbent in its place. This blurring of identities is important because belief that, for all intents and purposes, electing McCain meant a Bush third term predicts a vote for Obama. Since both pro-Obama differences in ad GRPs and most forms of media exposure strengthened the McCain-Bush link, we wonder what would have happened had Bush approval and a past vote for the Texan remained a constant, but instead of priming McCain as "McSame" the media primed him as "maverick," and McCain held the GRP advantage.

Economy

On the campaign's central issue—the economy—the fundamentals interacted with money, media, and message as well. By unpacking the dynamic among them, we open a window into a box ordinarily sealed from scholarly view.

One dilemma for the senior senator from Arizona was that the success of the surge strategy that he championed moved the Iraq war out of the headlines and subordinated the question of which candidate would be the better Commander-in-Chief—one on which McCain consistently topped Obama—to the question on which McCain never held a lead: which was better at handling the economy? Initially, skyrocketing energy prices, then, foreclosures and unemployment, and, finally, the mid-September economic crash set the economy at the center of the nation's agenda, displacing Iraq as the issue of central concern early in the primary season.

Unsurprisingly, heavy news consumers were more likely than occasional ones to see the economy as the central national issue. Moreover, those closely following the election increasingly saw it as the more important problem, with habitual TV and print news consumers the most likely to report that conclusion. Although most individuals still regarded the economy as the most pressing issue, not all the media produced a detectable agenda-setting effect. In a finding for which we have no good explanation, Internet use did not. By contrast, our talk radio finding makes more intuitive sense. In that venue, listeners presumably heard reassurance about the economy from conservative talk-show hosts.

On handling the economy, the Democratic party had an advantage even before the primaries began. And throughout the postprimary season, Obama led McCain on which could better handle it. Throughout the postprimary season, the candidates made a series of arguments that framed their superiority on the issue. Where neither perceptions of one's personal economic condition nor raw economic indicators predict vote preference, judgments about which of the two candidates can better handle the economy do. There are changes across time in our respondents' evaluations, and not all of them increase support for the eventual victor. On this indicator, for example, McCain gains some ground in period four, the two weeks after the October debate. Overall, however, what the messaging on the economy did was not increase perceptions of Obama's prowess but depress McCain's.

The relationship between the belief that electing McCain meant a continuation of Bush policies and holding that the Arizonan should not be entrusted with handling the economy moves from "handling economy" to "Bush-McCain" on a conveyer belt propelled in part by media. The conclusions that the country is on the wrong track, the economy is the most important issue, and Republicans should be blamed for the crisis each predict the notion that electing McCain equals a Bush third term and also heighten the likelihood of a favorable rating of Obama. Turning to TV news and newspapers for political information and the perception that "the country is on the wrong track" are significantly related to economic concerns, a conclusion consistent with the agenda-setting and priming hypotheses.

At the same time, apprehension about the economy is significantly and positively related to the belief that the Republicans are responsible for the Wall Street meltdown. Affixing blame to the GOP, a central Obama message frame, significantly predicts the notion that electing McCain is the same as reelecting Bush. These variables are significantly and positively related to the conclusion that Obama can handle the economy better than McCain, which in turn predicts Obama favorability and a disposition to vote for him. In the end, we surmise that Obama won by convincing a majority that he shared its values and that McCain was not able to fix what ailed the economy. Where at the height of McCain's convention bounce, the two were each attracting about 45 percent saying he could better handle the economy, on election eve the gap was over 10 percent. At that point, Obama was securely above 50 percent and McCain below 40.

In recounting the process by which communication harnessed John McCain to both George W. Bush and the collapsing economy, we tell a familiar story. Communication did its job in linking the candidates to the conditions that political science considers important in voting decisions. But even after the effects of these fundamentals have been estimated, there is unexplained variance. Here the role of communication in setting the standards of evaluation and framing perceptions comes in. When deciding for whom to vote, it matters whether an individual thinks that Obama, rather than McCain, is the one who would better handle the economy. Believing that one is the bigger tax increaser makes a difference as well, as does the perception that one shares voters' values more so than the other. And surmising that Palin isn't ready to assume the presidency makes a difference too.

Messages and Moments That Mattered

Those who limit their search for communication effects to ads and news will miss a world of possibilities. In the periods into which we parsed the postprimary period, we found impact from a forum, speeches, interviews, debates, an extended parody, and an endorsement. Here we recap the campaign through the message effects that it produced, beginning with McCain's statement on offshore drilling at the mid-August Saddleback forum and moving to the late-August and early-September acceptance speeches of Biden, Obama, Palin, and McCain, the Gibson, and Couric interviews with Sarah Palin, the presidential and vice presidential debates, the Palin parodies on *Saturday Night Live*, the Biden statement that Obama would be tested, the late-October Obama endorsement by General Colin Powell, the Obama half-hour program, and two of the themes of the fall campaign: McCain was too old to be president and Obama too unpatriotic.

Saddleback Forum

Just under one in five (19.4 percent) of our sample reported watching the question-and-answer session between Pastor Rick Warren and Senators McCain and Obama. Turning to that forum and supporting lifting the ban on offshore drilling each predicted a favorable rating of McCain in the presence of controls. The interaction between watching Saddleback and favoring lifting the drilling ban also predicted higher McCain favorability ratings. In other words, those who supported offshore drilling *and* watched the forum were more likely to think highly of McCain than were those who did not watch the forum or did not favor lifting the moratorium.

Convention Speeches

Because the nominees' acceptance speeches reached a large swath of the public, it is unsurprising that they shaped voter perceptions. Taking various factors into account, Joseph Biden's acceptance speech enhanced the public's favorable ratings of him, which then heightened support for the Democratic ticket. In the presence of stringent controls, those who watched the Delaware senator accept his party's nomination were significantly more likely to hold favorable perceptions of him than nonviewers. Biden's speech indirectly affected vote preference by influencing his favorability ratings, which in turn increased our respondents' disposition to vote for the Democratic ticket.

In the six days after Barack Obama's speech, those who watched him accept his party's nomination also were more favorably impressed by him than those who did not view the speech. The impact was significant, even when controlling for a host of demographic variables and ideological predispositions. Watching Obama's address also increased vote preference for the Democratic ticket. The fact that we controlled demographics, party identification, ideology, news media exposure, and candidate favorability ratings increases our confidence that this effect was not merely the byproduct of selective exposure. Like Biden's speech, the Republican vice presidential nominee's address improved people's general impressions of her. Those who saw Governor Sarah Palin's national debut at the Republican convention gave her significantly higher favorability ratings than those who did not watch it. This finding persisted even when demographic characteristics, party identification, ideology, news media exposure, and people's favorability ratings of McCain, Obama, and Biden were taken into consideration. In the same pattern that we found in analyzing the effects of the Biden speech, Palin's did not directly affect vote preference but did so indirectly by increasing people's favorable impressions of her, which in turn influenced their vote choice.

The convention acceptance addresses of both McCain and Obama increased their favorability ratings among viewers. McCain's speech indirectly influenced people's vote preference by positively affecting his favorability assessments. Obama's speech not only improved his favorability ratings among those who watched it, but it also exerted an independent, positive effect on support for the Democratic ticket when those favorability ratings were controlled.

Palin Interviews

Not since presidential aspirant Edward Kennedy's inarticulate response to questions by CBS's Roger Mudd in late 1979 have interviews with a prospective president drawn as much attention as did the Gibson and Couric exchanges with Governor Sarah Palin in September 2008. Watching the Gibson-Palin interview had a significantly negative effect on white women's perceptions that the Alaska governor was ready to be president. The importance of the finding is magnified by the fact that initially Palin's nomination had attracted this demographic.

Although the effects of the attacks by conservative critics and the caricature by Tina Fey are difficult to separate from exposure to the Couric interview, our data show that people who reported being more likely to see information about the 2008 presidential campaign on CBS than on other broadcast or cable networks were more inclined to rate Palin negatively on our "ready to be president" question than were those who did not report CBS as their most often seen broadcast or cable source about the campaign. However, since CBS viewers were more likely to be Democrats than Republicans, this finding potentially may be attributable to selective exposure.[1]

Palin Parodies on Saturday Night Live

On *Saturday Night Live,* comedian Tina Fey translated Palin's meandering answers to Couric into laughs at the Alaskan's expense. Those who regularly watched the show were more likely to believe that Palin was not ready to be president. The relationship between *SNL* viewing and views of Palin's readiness was especially pronounced with independents, a group with which McCain had to make inroads in order to obtain enough votes to win the election. Again, since the number of *SNL* viewers in our sample was small, in this case as with the CBS finding, party identification was our only control on selective exposure.

The Debates

Political lore has it that debates tend to advantage a candidate accused of being too unprepared or extreme to serve as president. In the presence of controls, viewing the first presidential debate predicted a significant increase in the perception that Obama would do a better job than McCain in handling the economy. Watching the debate also predicted a significant jump in the perception that electing McCain would in effect produce a third Bush term.

A comparison of debate viewers to nonviewers in the presence of controls suggests that the vice presidential debate upped Biden's favorability ratings without affecting Palin's one way or the other. While viewing the vice presidential debate improved perceptions of Biden, six in 10 (59%) felt that Palin's performance exceeded their expectations. Confirming that expectations affect evaluation, those holding that view gave her higher favorability ratings. Although the postdebate polls called the face-off a win for Biden, our survey registers a short-term post-debate boost in favorability for Palin as well as Biden. Since our comparisons of debate watchers and nonviewers found that viewing did not significantly alter respondents' evaluations of Palin, the changes in her trend lines may have been a result of the media coverage reporting that she had exceeded expectations.

Obama may have gained additional ground in the second debate. Watching it is positively related both to the view that he would handle the economy better and the perception that a McCain election would equal a Bush third term. While these relationships do not reach conventional levels of statistical significance, viewing that debate is significantly associated with higher favorability ratings for Obama but not McCain.

Consistent with our view that the final debate on October 15 helped the Republican nominee, watching it predicted the belief that Obama would raise taxes and McCain would not. That conclusion was significantly related to higher favorability scores for McCain. The strength of this relationship increases directly after the third and final debate. This findings remain in the presence of controls.

The Joe the Plumber Argument in the Two Weeks after the October 15 Presidential Debate

Enwrapped in the saga of Joe the Plumber, the McCain tax charge against Obama gained traction in the final month of the campaign. A majority of middle-income Americans making between $35,000 and $150,000 believed, contrary to his often-stated pledge, that under Obama their taxes would go up not down. An even larger number of households in the $150,000–$249,999 income range (whose taxes would remain unchanged under Obama's plan) foresaw an Obama tax increase. Those making over $250,000, however, got the message that under an Obama administration a tax increase was in their future.

Holding that Obama will raise your taxes and McCain won't, and thinking that Obama proposes a tax cut plan that would provide a government check to millions of people who pay no federal income taxes were positively related to beliefs that: 1) the Obama plan is socialist, 2) black elected officials will favor blacks, and 3) Obama is liberal. Two of these three, the exception being the belief that black officials will favor blacks, predict a belief that McCain will be better at handling the economy than Obama.

The Biden Gaffe: "Tested"

Although Biden made his assertion that Obama would be tested by foreign nations on October 19, declines in public perception of the Delaware senator's readiness to be president did not start in earnest until the McCain camp launched ads tying the gaffe to its theme: Obama as a risky candidate in a time of national crisis. However, even at its low point, ratings of Biden's readiness safely topped the midpoint on a 10-point scale and handily bested Palin's.

Powell Endorsement

Taking several demographic and attitudinal variables into account, our results suggest that the attack on Governor Palin's candidacy that General Colin Powell embedded in his endorsement of the Obama-Biden ticket hurt both her favorability ratings and perceptions of the Alaskan's readiness "to be president." Interestingly, we did not find a direct effect from the endorsement on feelings about Obama. Nor did it affect ratings of McCain.

Obama Half-Hour Program

Where McCain cast his rival as risky, Obama used two-minute ads and a multinetwork half-hour program to reassure. Even after including the candidate favorability measures as controls, a move that takes the effects of selective exposure out of the equation, those who watched the Obama infomercial were significantly more likely to vote for him. During the last few days of the election, those who tuned in to the program also rated the Democratic nominee more highly on the traits of "experience," "judgment," and "shares my values."

At the same time, exposure to the Obama half-hour decreases the perception of Palin's competence, a finding we explain as the byproduct of its emphasis on preparedness and experience. A boost in perceptions that Obama was ready to be president may have caused voters to ask, "What of the other candidate whose experience was at issue?" Palin's perceived lack of preparedness and Obama's rhetoric of reassurance help explain why his lead opened back up in the final days of the campaign.

McCain Is Erratic

Just as they emphasized the notion that McCain was a synonym for Bush, the Democrats repeatedly used the word "erratic" to describe their opponent's behavior. Thinking that the term applied to the Arizonan increased our respondents' reports that he was too old to be president, a finding that holds in the presence of controls. Seeing age as a liability for the Republican nominee undercut voters' perception that McCain shared their values. And belief that a candidate shares one's values predicted vote preference.

News exposure also magnified the notion that McCain's age disqualified him. Attending to television news, newspapers, and Internet news are significantly related to discounting McCain's credentials because of his age.

Obama Is Unpatriotic

As part of their plan to establish that Obama was not ready to lead, Republican groups and the Republican vice presidential nominee impugned the Democratic standard-bearer's patriotism. Throughout their convention, the Democrats inoculated against the charge. The move paid off. At the event's end, the public rated

Obama more highly on that attribute than it had before the event had began. Those who watched some or all of the Illinois senator's acceptance speech gave him a rating of 7.2 on a 10-point patriotic evaluation scale; those who had not viewed the speech situated him at the scale's midpoint with a rating of 5.2.

In the final weeks of the election, the patriotism charge pervaded the ads of the independent Republican groups. An analysis of survey responses in the last three weeks suggests that perceptions of Obama and McCain on this attribute were significantly associated with vote preference, even when sociodemographic and political characteristics, news media exposure, and the presidential and vice presidential favorability ratings were taken into consideration.

This range of communication effects elicited by exposure to communication as dissimilar as that at Saddleback and on *Saturday Night Live* suggests that campaigns are not simply black boxes that telegraph that one candidate is tied to the incumbent and should be credited or castigated for the state of the economy. Campaign messages also change the standards of judgment that voters use in evaluating the candidates and frame the way that the contenders, their stands on issues, and their character and temperament are understood. And those factors can shape attitudes that in turn affect vote preference.

The Relative Impact of Messages

In the instances that we just reprised, we concentrated on the direct effect of isolated messages in the presence of sociodemographic and ideological controls. This process helped us identify not only the communication that affected voters' agendas but also its effects on candidate assessment and selection of interpretive frames. With this menu in place, we now take on the larger task of determining what additional explanatory power, if any, we gain in predicting vote preference by combining the main messages of the campaign into a single source of potential influence.

In chapter 1, we showed that political scientists have predicted electoral outcome with a handful of variables, such as partisanship, ideological placement, incumbent approval rating, and economic indicators. Months before the 2008 Election Day, they accurately forecast the margin by which a Democrat would win in 2008.[2] When we used data from the 2008 NAES phone postelection panel to replicate the standard forecasting models, we found that the "fundamentals" we were able to capture accounted for a bit over 75 percent of variance in respondents reported vote choice—an impressive amount of predicative power for only six variables.

In this chapter we are interested in the impact of messages and rely on the data from the 2008 NAES rolling cross-sectional data collected during the campaign.

In the first chapter, we analyzed the NAES telephone postelection panel because we believe that it more accurately reflects a respondent's actual vote decision. In that chapter, the analyses were limited to the impact of "fundamentals." The telephone postelection panel survey, however, does not contain all of the variables needed for this chapter so we turn to the rolling cross-sectional data. Whereas in the model found in chapter 1, the dependent variable simply asked after the election was over for whom the respondent voted, here we rely on the question that asks for whom the respondent would have voted "if the election were held today?" Since the variables asking which candidates would raise taxes were not added to the NAES until October 8, we ran this model on the answers provided by 3,848 respondents surveyed between October 8 and Election Day. The convergence between the model from chapter 1 and the model we will report in a moment is apparent in the similar amount of variance explained by the "fundamentals," 76.6 percent in chapter 1 and 77.8 percent here.

As in chapter 1, here we will be talking in terms of "explained variance," which is the percentage of variability in a dependent variable that can be statistically attributed to independent variables. Examining explained variance allows us to see the combined impact of campaign messages on vote choice relative to the "fundamental" variables found in the traditional political science forecasting models.

It is important to note that variance of a dependent variable can be "unique" and "shared" among predictor variables. For example, the belief of a devout Democrat that McCain is too old to be president can be attributed to both campaign messages and to the fact that a Democrat is disposed to embrace negative perceptions about a Republican nominee. So in a statistical model, there may be shared variance among the campaign messages and political orientation variables or even shared variance among the campaign messages themselves.

This phenomenon is different from an interaction in which two or more variables have a multiplicative impact. Because campaign messages play on each other and on the political landscape of the campaign, a message may share predictive power with a number of other variables. Parsing out shared variance in the saturated, conservative[3] statistical models is not feasible, because doing so would require hours of hand calculations of what is known as "commonality analysis."[4] Moreover, interpreting such analysis becomes a Herculean task when the model contains more than five variables. Consequently, we focus on the combined unique variance of campaign messages in this chapter. Because it dismisses the variance and predictive power that many of the campaign messages may share with the other variables, this strategy underestimates their collective impact.

To identify the contribution of messages to vote preference above and beyond the fundamentals on which some models rely, we construct a probit regression model in which groups of variables are added incrementally to assess the additional explanatory power that each group of variables contributes to our prediction of an Obama vote preference. Our base model is the one found in chapter 1. The second block of variables contains the sociodemographic factors that have been used as controls in earlier chapters. The third uses the news use variables as controls. Finally, the fourth section of the model captures the main campaign messages. These variables are: (1) the belief that electing John McCain is the same as electing Bush for a third term (chapter 2); (2) McCain is too old to be president (chapter 4); (3) Obama is a liberal (chapter 3); (4) the difference in the rating "has the experience" to be president (McCain minus Obama—chapters 5 and 12); (5) the difference in the rating "has the judgment" to be president (McCain minus Obama—chapters 5 and 12); (6) the difference in rating of "patriotic" (McCain minus Obama—chapter 4); (7) rating of Palin "not ready to be president" (chapter 8); (8) rating of Biden "ready to be president" (chapter 8); (9) believing that Obama can handle the economy better than McCain (chapter 9); (10) believing that Obama will raise taxes and McCain will not (chapter 12); and (11) difference rating in "shares my values" (Obama minus McCain—chapter 4 and throughout whole book).

Notice that the variables for "judgment," "experience," and "patriotic" are constructed by subtracting Obama's ratings from McCain's, while the assessment of "shares my values" is calculated by subtracting McCain's ratings from Obama's. This is done to maintain consistency with the narrative of the book. McCain trumped Obama on judgment, experience, and patriotism, whereas Obama bested McCain on "shares my values." The Palin and Biden variables are not computed together as the presidential candidate variables are. We made this move because of the nondichotomous messages about the two that pervaded the campaign. Specifically, Governor Palin was not as often contrasted with Senator Biden as she was negatively tied to McCain. To capture this difference, the Palin variable is coded as "not ready to be president," while the Biden variable is coded as "ready to be president."

We have discussed the direct effects of these campaign messages in previous chapters and so will not heavily concentrate on individual relationships here. Instead, we will focus on the McKelvey & Zavonia R^2, a statistic that indicates the percentage of variance in the dependent variable explained by the blocks of independent variables. In table 13.1, after each block there is a McKelvey & Zavonia R^2 as well as an entry called "Incremental McKelvey & Zavoina's R^2 change." This R^2 change is the unique variance explained in the dependent variable by each block of independent variables.

Analyzing a probit regression with variables entered in four blocks—(1) fundamentals, (2) sociodemographics, (3) news media use, and (4) campaign messages—we see the amount of incremental variance explained by the addition of each group of variables. As Table 13.1 shows, the amount of variance explained by the fundamental variables used in the political science models is 77.8 percent (as indicated by McKelvey and Zavoina's R^2).[5] This is similar to our findings using the telephone postelection panel data in chapter 1 where we found that fundamentals predicted around three-quarters of the variance in vote preference. As in chapter 1, here we see that economic perceptions are not significantly related to vote preference. Party identification, ideology, and Bush approval are the driving forces.

The next two blocks do not add very much to the explained variance in preference. The sociodemographic variables incrementally added 1.9 percent and the news media variables 0.3 percent. However, the campaign messages account for a substantial portion of the explained variance in vote preference by adding 14.2 percent for a total of 94.2 percent of the variance explained in the vote preference model.

Out of 11 campaign message variables, three were not significant: perceiving that McCain is too old to be president, perceiving Obama as liberal, and the difference in ratings of the candidates' patriotism. This is probably attributable to the fact that these messages were enmeshed with others included in the model. As a result, any unique effect may simply have washed out. For example, advertising tied each of these messages to the notion that a candidate does not share the values of the voter. Consistent with this explanation, in our model (table 13.1) we see that

TABLE 13.1. Probit Regression Predicting Obama Two-Party Vote (Coefficients are from full model)

	Probit Coefficient		Standard Error	Z
Block 1—Fundamentals				
Intercept	−2.473		0.629	−3.93
Party identification	0.180	***	0.038	4.77
Ideology (Conservative high)	0.15	*	0.069	2.18
Vote for Bush in 2004	−0.257	#	0.141	−1.83
Approve Bush	−0.141	#	0.077	−1.83
National economic conditions worse	0.010		0.121	0.09
Personal economic conditions worse	−0.258		0.138	−1.87
McKelvey and Zavoina's R^2:			0.778	
Block 2—Sociodemographics				
Female (1 = yes, 0 = no)	−0.186		0.121	−1.54
Age (in years)	0.003		0.004	0.78

(continued)

TABLE 13.1. (Continued)

	Probit Coefficient		Standard Error	Z
Black (1 = yes, 0 = no)	1.089	**	0.410	2.66
Hispanic (1 = yes, 0 = no)	0.333		0.245	1.36
Education (in years)	0.000		0.029	−0.01
Household income (in thousands)	0.002	#	0.001	1.80
McKelvey and Zavoina's R^2:			0.797	
Incremental McKelvey & Zavoina's R^2 change:			0.019	
Block 3—News Media				
Number of days saw presidential campaign information on TV in past week	0.019		0.030	0.65
Number of day heard about presidential campaign on talk radio in past week	−0.001		0.023	−0.03
Number of days saw presidential campaign information in newspapers in past week	−0.032		0.022	−1.47
Number of days saw presidential campaign information on Internet in past week	0.017		0.021	0.84
McKelvey and Zavoina's R^2:			0.800	
Incremental McKelvey & Zavoina's R^2 change:			0.003	
Block 4—Campaign Messages				
Electing John McCain is the same as electing Bush for third term	0.505	***	0.134	3.78
McCain too old to be president	0.225		0.142	1.59
Rating of Obama's ideology (liberal high)	0.013		0.064	0.20
Difference in the rating of "has the experience to be president" (McCain minus Obama)	−0.088	**	0.029	−3.04
Difference in the rating of "has the judgment to be president" (McCain minus Obama)	−0.097	**	0.031	−3.13
Difference in the rating of "patriotic" (McCain minus Obama)	−0.011		0.027	−0.40
Rating of Palin "not ready to be president"	0.113	***	0.028	4.12
Rating of Biden "ready to be president"	0.084	**	0.032	2.65
Believing that Obama will raise taxes and McCain will not	−0.471	**	0.146	−3.22
Believing that Obama can better handle the economy than McCain	0.974	***	0.126	7.71
Difference in the rating of "shares my values" (Obama minus McCain)	0.177	**	0.02*	6.30
McKelvey and Zavoina's R^2:			0.942	
Incremental McKelvey & Zavoina's R^2 change:			0.142	
N			3,848	

$\# p < .10 * p < .05 ** p < .01 *** p < .001$

Data: NAES08 telephone survey. Dates: 10/08/08 to 11/03/08. Note: Coefficients are from the full model.

the difference in ratings of the candidates on the attribute "shares my values" produced one of the most robust relationships of the campaign messages along with the belief that Obama can better handle the economy than McCain.

The belief that electing John McCain is like electing Bush for a third term was a particularly strong and positive predictor of an Obama vote. Perceptions of the vice presidential candidates' "readiness to be president" produced robust relationships as well. The belief that Obama will raise taxes and McCain won't was negatively related to an Obama vote preference. As shown in earlier chapters, McCain trumped Obama on the traits "has the experience to be president" and "has the judgment to be president." Difference in these traits in McCain's favor predicted a preferring McCain for president.

Connecting Advertising to the Main Campaign Messages

Relying on ad-buy data, we formulated 11 statistical models, each predicting one of the campaign message variables outlined above. In the presence of the controls used in the models outlined in chapter 12 (socio-demographics, political orientation variables, news media, and measures for aggregate competitiveness at the county level), we find evidence that Obama's advertising directly affected the respondents' embrace of some of the central campaign messages. Looking at the per-100 GRP difference between the two campaigns in three media, we found that Obama's advertising advantage was positively related to believing that electing McCain was like electing George W. Bush for a third term. The GRP difference was significantly and negatively related to McCain's ratings on the trait "has the judgment to be president." Thinking that Obama could handle the economy better than McCain was significantly related to Obama GRP advantage, as was the perception that Obama "shares your values" more so than does McCain.*

One finding in this model is puzzling. An Obama advertising advantage was positively related to the belief that Palin was not ready to be president. Because differences in GRP by individual media (spot broadcast, spot cable, and radio) do not produce a significant decrease in the perception of Palin's readiness, and her preparedness was a central theme only in radio, we suspect that our significant finding on that item is spurious. As we argue in the relevant chapter, we attribute the finding in the message model to media priming. The plausibility of our other ad findings is increased by the fact that the Obama message strategy stressed that McCain equals Bush, Obama "shares your values," Obama can better handle the economy, and Obama is ready and has the judgment to be president.

What all of this means is that the fundamentals—specifically, an unpopular incumbent, a faltering economy, and a party-identification advantage for the

Democrats—had impressive predictive power in 2008. After all, they explain over three-fourths of the variance in vote disposition. But with almost 15 percent of the variance in their satchels, messages shifted vote intention as well. And the effects of the advertised messages were in part a function of Obama's capacity to significantly outspend McCain on advertising.

While Obama's prodigious fund-raising may not have changed the outcome of the 2008 election, the campaigns' sophisticated microtargeting and the Democrats' rejection of federal financing forecast a changed election landscape for those seeking the presidency in years to come. So too do the dramatic 2008 increase in early voting and the widespread public use of new media as a source of campaign information and misinformation. In the afterword, we speculate about the impact these changes will have on how and whom we elect.

Afterword

S OME EARTHQUAKES SEND FLUTTERS ONLY THROUGH THE HEARTS
of seismologists. Others shake and roll in ways that rattle even those inca-
pable of finding the San Andreas Fault on a topographical map. When these
occur, water and gas lines crack; bridges crumble; I-beams crash to the earth;
books cascade from their shelves onto the heads of sleeping professors. Put differently, a Richter scale reading of 6.7 captures the brute fact that the ground has
shifted in ways that change our relationship to otherwise taken-for-granted parts
of our world.

Although the McCain campaign might be inclined to analogize its counterpart's destructive force to that of an earthquake, we have adopted the analogy for
a different reason. In its impact on the structures likely to arise in its aftermath,
the 2008 Obama campaign is best analogized to the Northridge California quake
of 1994. So important were the changes that his campaign precipitated that subsequent presidential campaigns will be built to guarantee that no major-party candidate is ever again vulnerable to such an accumulation of forces. If we are correct,
future campaigns will be constructed to replicate the Obama model and forestall
the kind of damage it did to the McCain candidacy.

The changes we see as ground-shifting include the creation of a general election campaign timed to affect early voting, commandeering the capacities of
digital technology to inform and mobilize, pioneering the pathbreaking use of
interpersonal, cable, and radio microtargeting to turn agnostics into true believers and true believers into missionaries, and amassing an unprecedented bankroll
after rejecting federal financing. If this combination of factors can be reassem-
bled in election years that are unburdened (or unblessed) by a toxic incumbent

and tanking economy, then presidential campaigns will have been transformed, perhaps irrevocably. While some of these changes improve the system, others are cause for concern.

Early Voting

In anticipation of high levels of early balloting, the Obama strategists rethought how to run a general election campaign. Early voting "didn't change our strategy," noted Obama's national field coordinator, Jon Carson. "It was our strategy. We sat down and said 'where early vote is no excuse, and convenient...[we engaged in] voter contact as though it was Election Day."[1] The Democratic effort, noted Obama campaign manager David Plouffe, "consisted of radio ads reminding people of early vote [sic] and explaining how it worked; a fusillade of Internet ads to push the concept; repeated e-mail and text messaging to people on our list from these states; and a blizzard of door-knocks and phone calls to remind voters person-to-person about early vote."[2] For the Obama campaign, the fact of early voting altered campaign communication and expenditures. That campaign's spending levels peaked between October 6–12, dates coinciding with the arrival of early ballots in mailboxes. By concentrating on those votes, Obama locked in voters who as a result were not subject to the arguments McCain made in period three about "sharing the wealth." "Even if the race turned against us toward the end," noted Plouffe, "in those states where we had banked a huge number of votes early, the math got awfully hard for McCain."[3]

By contrast, those who balloted for McCain during the weeks in which that argument was resonating did not have the benefit of hearing the final exchanges of the election. It is possible, in other words, that a voter not tightly anchored by party or a high level of information would vote one way if motivated to do so in early October—the opposite way than if that motivation occurred just after October 15—and cast a different ballot if called on to do so in a voting booth on Election Day. In 2008, for approximately one-third of the national electorate Election Day occurred before November 4. The high percentage reflects the fact that two-thirds of the states permitted some type of early voting.[4]

The implications of this topographical change in the campaign landscape are unsettling for a number of reasons. Using microtargeting, the better financed campaign is more likely to not only locate these persuadable voters but also to tell them what they want to hear. The campaign with the resources to find those "soft" voters and lock them in early protects them from information and influence that might have shifted their vote. The party without resources may lack the wherewithal to counter those appeals. Yet it remains possible that were the voter fully informed, he or she would cast a vote different from the one cast early.

If every person casting an early ballot had all of the information available by the traditional Election Day, then changed voting patterns probably would not change election outcomes. Still early voting would have cost those whose Election Day happened in a private moment at an earlier time some of the communal sense one gains by actually joining neighbors at a polling place on a set day.

But for the sake of worrying aloud, impose the patterns of early voting found in 2008 on the election held in 1972 and then add a second hypothetical to the mix. Assume that the Watergate hearings are ongoing in the fall and transcripts of the tapes that ultimately led to Richard Nixon's resignation released in the final week of the campaign. Or ask how the outcome or the winner's capacity to govern might have been affected if John Kennedy's Addison's disease had been documented midway through early voting season in 1960, instead of at his autopsy, or conjure up conclusive confirmation in the closing days of that election that, contrary to Democratic allegations, not only is there no missile gap, but the United States has clear superiority in this domain. In effect what early voting does is create 30 or more election days. On each of them, one electorate with a set range of available information casts its ballots. In effect, the victor on November 4, 2008, was not elected by one electorate but by 30 or more. And once a vote has been cast, there is no legal way to translate buyer's remorse into a new vote, even if circumstances or available knowledge change to the point that one might wish to do so. In 2008, less than 1 percent of those who cast ballots early maintained that their votes would have been cast differently had they waited to vote on Election Day. While this spread would not have made a difference in the 2008 election, such a spread could make a difference in future elections.[5]

Digital Technology and the Internet

Dampening concerns about a paucity of information is the fact that in 2008 there was more readily available campaign-generated political information and misinformation in more places than ever before. "Our e-mail list had reached 13 million people," recalled Plouffe. "We had essentially created our own television network, only better, because we communicated directly with no filter to what would amount to about 20 percent of the total number of votes [sic] we would need to win....And those supporters would share our positive message or response to an attack, whether through orchestrated campaign activity like door knocking or phone calling or just in conversations they had each day with friends, family and colleagues."[6]

Access to the Internet made possible experiences that could not have happened in other media. Individuals spent "more than 14 million hours watching over 1,800 Obama campaign-related videos on YouTube that garnered more than 50 million views."[7] Will.i.am's 'Yes We Can' YouTube video homage to Obama drew more than 20 million views.[8] During the typical week in the general election, 20 percent of our NAES respondents reported getting political information from Internet sources such as You Tube. Those who reported seeing political campaign information on the Internet in the past week were 1.033 more likely to vote for Obama, a positive effect as strong as the negative effect produced by hearing about the campaign on talk radio.

Despite these positive effects for the Democrats, the Web was a two-edged sword that undercut the Obama campaign at key points in the election season. Repeated playing of a YouTube video featuring vignettes from Rev. Jeremiah Wright's sermons helped fuel the spring controversy that slowed Obama's march to the nomination. Moreover, the audio captured by citizen journalist Mayhill Fowler helped drive the revival of Hillary Clinton's candidacy in the Pennsylvania primary. Her recording revealed that in a closed-door San Fransisco fund-raiser, the Democrat had suggested that small-town dwellers in Pennsylvania and the Midwest whose jobs are gone and who did not do well under past administrations "get bitter [and], they cling to guns or religion or antipathy to people who aren't like them or anti-immigrant sentiment or anti-trade sentiment as a way to explain their frustrations."[9]

Microtargeting

Microtargeting in media changed the political playing field in 2008, not because it was new but because the Obama campaign placed large differences in dollars in service of narrowcast messages, some of them deceptive. Because voters are not equally susceptible to persuasion, reaching the susceptible citizen matters. As we noted in the introduction, partisans and those with high levels of knowledge are more resistant[10] than not. But even their minds can be changed if they are subjected to cross-pressuring on issues that they care about.[11] As a result, campaigns have always been preoccupied with reaching susceptible voters with messages designed to sway them.

Addressing one's message to those likely to embrace it has been part of the structure of U.S. campaigns since the partisan newspapers that proliferated in the early days of the republic. Indeed, prior to the advent of national radio, such targeting was the norm, not the exception.[12] With the rise of extensive databases housing information on individuals' purchasing patterns, lifestyle, voting history, and group affiliations, targeting has moved from art to science, a transformation apparent in the uses of these technologies by the Bush campaign in 2004.[13]

Interpersonal Microtargeting

Harnessing the capacities of the new technologies, the Obama campaign delivered traditional messages in nontraditional ways, gathered and managed an impressive army of volunteers, and garnered the funds to ensure that every attack was anticipated, the answer tested, and the resulting message deployed in the channels most likely to swing votes. Better than any campaign before it, the Democratic one located channels of direct communication with its supporters. By the campaign's end, the Democrats had sent more than a billion e-mails.[14] A million people registered as part of the Obama campaign's texting program.[15] An Obama ad targeting the young asked people to text "hope" to 62262 (Obama). Those who responded to that appeal were enlisted as volunteers and as such received regular personalized e-mails on how and where to volunteer, recruit others, phone friends, and help the campaign. The Obama campaign also used direct forms of communication to minimize the need of its supporters to rely on the press for information. So for example, instead of announcing it to the press, the Obama campaign text-messaged its supporters with the name of its vice presidential nominee.

Just as the digital world opened new ways to inform, engage, and mobilize, it expanded the opportunities to inflame and deceive. Those who received e-mail in the final weeks of the campaign were more likely to report that candidate Obama was a Muslim, for example, and palled around with terrorists and was a close friend of former Weather Underground leader William Ayers, charges debunked by impartial organizations. In our postelection deception survey, we found that 19 percent of respondents believed that Obama was a Muslim. Of those who reported that Obama's religion was Muslim, 25 percent voted for him, while 63.9 percent voted for McCain.

Like the messages enthusing about the qualifications of a candidate, these viral messages represent a form of interpersonal microtargeting. An individual generates or relays a message with which he or she agrees to likeminded friends and associates. And in these insular worlds, individuals find shelter from counterarguments and scrutiny of their candidate's problematic claims.[16] For practical purposes, the Obama campaign's regular e-mails to supporters enveloped them in a blanket of reinforcing information that recontextualized events from the campaign's point of view and offered talking points to be used to defend Obama and attack the Republicans. Those circulating viral slurs against him did the same.

Microtargeting in Cable and Radio

Where others have focused on broadcast advertising focused on the battleground states[17] and direct mail as a means of delivering targeting messages,[18] in this book we concentrated on uses of radio and cable to show that differences in spending on these media translated into impact for the Democrats. In particular, narrowcasting of radio messages made it possible for that campaign to affect moderate women's level of information about the candidates' positions on the key wedge issues of abortion and federal funding of stem cell research.

For a campaign, the targeting process works optimally when the narrowcast messages are not overheard by those likely to be alienated by them, when the national media either fails to observe or chooses to ignore the targeted content, and when one side either has the desired audience to itself, offers a better conceived and executed message, or gains the advantage of disproportionate exposure. Consistent with this view, we showed in chapter 12 how narrowcast messages on stem cell research and abortion were tailored to specific radio audiences. This worked for Obama for two reasons. News reports did not alert unsympathetic voters to the whispered content by transforming the narrowcast message into a broadcast one. And Obama drowned out McCain's message with massive targeted buys of ad time.

To the dismay of the McCain campaign, news accounts of paid campaign messages either disappeared entirely or were relegated to parenthetical mentions in a nation transfixed by the economic meltdown. So when the Obama campaign began using evocative radio ads to persuade moderate women that McCain opposed stem cell research, the press did not respond by deploring the deception. Nor did discussion of the Obama strategy top the national news or reverberate through cable talk. The same was true of another problematic Obama statement in radio and TV ads targeting Hispanics with the claim that McCain opposed immigration reform, a charge that flew in the face of the fact that he had bucked many in his own party by co-authoring a major reform bill. Nor did the media pay much attention to the misleading attacks that independent expenditure groups launched against Obama's votes on abortion policy while a state senator.

The Illinois senator's ability to outspend his opponent on ads was only one of a number of advantages he gained by both casting off the constraints that come with federal financing and by successfully raising vast sums.

Forgoing Federal Financing

When the ability to draw large contributions becomes a test of a presidential candidate's viability and has the potential to ensure his success, three worries arise. What, if anything, are large donors given in return for their support? Can money ensure that the less-qualified candidate is elected over the more-qualified one?

And does fund-raising ability translate into a capacity to govern well or does it undercut that possibility? Fueled by the corruption associated with Watergate, federal financing of campaigns was designed to reduce these sorts of concerns.

In their pursuit of their party's nominations, John McCain, Barack Obama, and Hillary Clinton rejected federal financing and the constraints that accompany it. George W. Bush and John Kerry had done the same in 2004. But where from 1976 through the general election of 2004 the major-party nominees had relied on federal funds in the general election, Barack Obama calculated that his campaign was better off without them. Not so John McCain. As a result, the Arizonan based his run on $84.1 million in public funds,[19] while his opponent was able to spend whatever he could raise. This meant that in September alone, Obama raised funds almost double the amount of federal funding McCain had banked to cover his whole fall campaign.

By rejecting federal financing, the Obama campaign reintroduced a world remembered by those who participated in, studied, or were the objects of persuasion by presidential campaigns before 1976. As a result, the Democrat had the capacity to both outspend his opponent in 2008 and to do so on a grand scale. For practical purposes, as Plouffe recalled, the Obama campaign had the "financial capacity to employ just about every tool at [its] disposal." "We even ran ads on evangelical radio," noted Obama's campaign manager, "just to try to hold the McCain margin." It was, he concluded, "like fantasy camp for political operatives."[20]

Scholars of communication have long believed that opposed messages cancel each other out when two sides spend comparable amounts airing them. In chapter 12, we confirmed that the difference between Obama's media spending and McCain's moved votes to the Democrat. Specifically, Obama's paid messages on broadcast, cable, and radio drove home three perceptions important to Obama's candidacy: McCain equaled Bush, Obama could handle the economy better than McCain, and Obama shared voters' values.

Drawing on its substantial bankroll, the Obama campaign created and tested likely attacks against its own candidate while at the same time assessing the likely effectiveness of McCain's messages. Money also made it possible for the Democrats to fashion forms of reassurance carried in two-minute ads and the half-hour national telecast as well. Where McCain was reduced to running a single track of attack ads with only an occasional burst of reassurance, Obama simultaneously aired multiple tracks. In the process, the Democrats could build the case for the Illinois senator while undercutting it for McCain. With less to spend, the Republican campaign turned to hybrid ads, a move that diluted the impact of the ads' message and resulted in confusing presentations.

No Penalty

Increasing the likelihood that candidates will reject the limits that come with federal financing if possible is the fact that in 2008 the public didn't seem to care one way or the other. At the end of October, Gallup reported that most Americans had no idea whether the candidates had taken federal financing or not. Moreover, when told which candidate stayed in the system and which stepped outside it, the overwhelming majority reported that that information didn't affect their opinion of the nominees one way or the other.[21] Although Barack Obama reneged on his pledge to accept federal finance, beyond protests from editorial page writers,[22] that reversal elicited no apparent penalty.

A Campaign with an All but Limitless Bankroll

In a demonstration of the relationship between the digital world and the one in which it is possible to raise large numbers of dollars, online fund-raising bankrolled the most expensive campaign ever mounted for the U.S. presidency. In 21 months, the Obama campaign's online fund-raising operation collected a half billion dollars from three million individuals who made "a total of 6.5 million donations online.... Of those 6.5 million donations, six million were in increments of $100 or less."[23] What this meant was that in broadcast, cable, and radio advertising alone, Barack Obama outspent McCain by almost as much as McCain received in federal financing. The 2008 election broke records for campaign contributions and spending by presidential campaigns. "For the first time ever in U.S. history, the candidates raised more than $1 billion."[24]

Raising Large Sums Required Reliance on Large Donors

Three arguments were front and center in mid-June when the Obama campaign informed its supporters in a Webcast[25] that it would not accept public funding in the general election.[26] First, participating in a broken system made no sense. Second, his millions of small donors were in effect a form of public financing. Finally, his money was not suspect because none of it came from lobbyists. These rationales were disingenuous. The system was as badly broken in summer as it had been when Obama championed public financing a year earlier. Moreover, as the fact checking groups pointed out, his rejection of lobbyist money was only accurate if phrased "no money from currently registered federal lobbyists."[27] And the notion that more than half of the campaign's donations came from those contributing small amounts was artfully framed misdirection.

By featuring single individual donations, not the totals given by those donors, the Democratic campaign fed the false impression that it had created a new political order uncluttered by the baggage that comes with big money donors. However, after the election, a study of Federal Election Commission records by the nonpartisan Campaign Finance Institute revealed that only 24 percent of Obama's donations through October 15 came from those who gave a total of less than $200, a proportion comparable to that of George W. Bush in 2004.[28] "Throughout the election season, this organization and others have been reporting that Obama received about half of his discrete contributions in amounts of $200 or less," said the CFI report. "After a more thorough analysis of data from the Federal Election Commission (FEC), it has become clear that repeaters and large donors were even more important for Obama than we or other analysts had fully appreciated."[29] "The myth is that money from small donors dominated Barack Obama's finances," CFI's executive director Michael Malbin told the *Los Angeles Times*.[30]

How Money Matters

In politics, money provides the media with a measure of momentum and the candidate with a megaphone and a means of bankrolling grassroots activity. And not only can it affect outcome, raising large dollar amounts from contributors may provide them with access and influence that affects governance.

Momentum

"The money was very impactful," David Plouffe told Richard Wolffe about the primary contest between Clinton and Obama, "because for the first time people thought maybe this guy could really give her a run for her money."[31] "With more than $20 million, Obama reports strong quarter" noted a headline in the October 2, 2007, edition of the *Washington Post*.[32] "Clinton and Obama each pull in over $100 million," proclaimed the *Post* on January 1, 2008.[33] "Obama donors pick up pace: A $32 million month," noted the same outlet a month later.[34] "Clinton's fund-raising success is outshined by Obama's," observed the *New York Times* in a front-page article a week later.[35]

Megaphone

In addition to signaling that a candidate is a serious contender, money purchases the media time that carries the campaign's messages into America's cars, living rooms, dens, and handheld devices. Although the rule is not absolute, absence does not make the heart grow fonder in campaigns. In key moments in the 2000 and 2004 contests, the Democrats felt hobbled by their inability to match Republican spending. Had Gore done so in Florida in the final weeks of 2000, he might well have won the electoral college as well as the popular vote.[36] Moreover, because the early date of the Democratic convention in 2004 meant that Kerry had to spread the same number of federal dollars over more weeks than Bush, during the crucial month of August, as independent expenditure groups, such as the Swift Boat Veterans for Truth, hammered his reputation for heroism, the Democrat's campaign conserved its available funds rather than counteradvertising.

Bankrolls Grassroots Activity

The Obama campaign's financial advantage also translated into greater funding for ground operations and a higher level of funding for Internet messages mobilizing its vote. The FEC report issued in summer 2008 revealed that Senator Obama had given more than twice as much money to Democratic committees as McCain had handed over to Republican ones. "President Obama's campaign transferred more than $41 million to Democratic Party committees at both the national and state levels, with $8.5 million going to the Democratic Senatorial Campaign Committee and the Democratic Congressional Campaign Committee," said the document. "The committee ended 2008 with $18.3 million in cash on hand and $1.9 in outstanding debt. Sen. McCain's presidential primary campaign transferred more than $18.6 million to state and local party committees."[37] "The transfers to the state committees not only helped drive turnout in key states (Obama won 13 of the 15 states to which his campaign transferred the most cash), but they also reinforced the effects of his coattails and could boost Democrats in both the 2010 midterms and Obama's own 2012 reelection bid," noted a report on Politico.com:

> Among the top beneficiaries of the Obama campaign's largesse were the Democratic parties in Florida, which received $5.5 million, Virginia ($3.1 million), North Carolina ($2.3 million), Colorado ($1.9 million), Nevada ($1.6 million), Indiana ($1.4 million), Iowa ($700,000) and New Mexico ($450,000)—all states Obama won that had gone Republican in the 2004 presidential election. The only states that Obama lost where the Democratic parties were among the top recipients of Obama's generosity were Missouri, to which he transferred $2 million, and Montana, where the party received $738,000.[38]

Money Can Affect Outcome

As we noted in chapter 12, outspending a presidential rival on a cogent message can increase its impact on voters and potentially swing a close election. "In five cases, their [Republican candidates] popular vote margin was at least four points larger than it would have been, and in two cases—1968 and 2000—Republican candidates won close elections that they very probably would have lost had they been unable to outspend incumbent Democratic vice presidents."[39] Political scientist Larry Bartels estimated, "Since Republican candidates spent at least slightly more money than their Democratic opponents did in each of those elections [1952–2004], it is not surprising," he notes, "to find that they did at least slightly better in every election than they would have if spending had been equal."[40] Although they disagree about the size of the effect, scholars also surmise that spending more on ads than one's presidential rival secures votes.[41]

The Future?

We assume that advertising on the Internet will play an increasing role, driven by the fact that the Obama campaign made extensive use of it to motivate voters to cast their ballots. We also suspect that campaigns able to raise large amounts of money will follow the Obama campaign's lead, and that of Ross Perot before him, by offering longer forms of communication, such as the two-minute ads and half-hour program that made up the Obama campaign communication profile. Capitalizing on the interactive potential of the new media, we expect to see a 2012 equivalent of the call-in telethons that characterized the closing hours of the 1968 campaign. If voters tune in to the resulting programming, as they did in both 1992 and 2008, the return of longer forms could increase voter knowledge. And that would be all to the good.

What is troubling, however, is the possibility that these longer forms of communication will be purchased in a Faustian bargain. Candidates who are willing to barter promises for dollars will raise more cash than those who demur. Big spenders will win against candidates unwilling to please prospective patrons. History suggests that this scenario is not simply pessimism writ large. Had he been able to sideline his conscience long enough to champion a position favorable to big oil, for example, Democratic Party nominee Hubert Humphrey might have stayed on the air during the week of October 13th, 1968 and, since he was closing in the polls when the decision occurred, won rather than lost that close contest.[42] In particular, had he been willing to promise that he would protect the oil depletion allowance, a wealthy Texas oilman was prepared to provide the $700,000 that the campaign required to continue advertising.[43]

Also worrisome is the possibility that a better-financed candidate will microtarget in ways that draw voters to his candidacy based on unrebutted deception. Alternatively, "soft" voters will be more readily persuaded not by the merits of one case over another but by better microtargeted messaging and larger-volume ad buys.

Rather than actually electing the better person with better policies, voters swimming in an ocean of one candidate's ads and micromessages may confuse appearance with reality, promises with plausible solutions, confusion that might not occur if each side had comparable access to their hearts and minds. Moreover, in a country built on confidence in the value of the clash of competing ideas, the notion that one side might be able to dominate any channel of communication is problematic, even if that side is championing this century's Washington, Jefferson, or Lincoln.

To counter this doomsday scenario, the communication media or public dollars could provide candidates with forms of effective, cost-free access that would increase the likelihood that the financially stressed candidate would nonetheless be able to take on the messages of the opponent and get his or her own message through. The fact that candidates have to raise money to pay to reach voters over the publicly owned airwaves is, after all, one of the stranger aspects of our electoral system.

The news media, particularly those emerging on the Web, also could contribute to the solution by vigilantly policing microtargeted messages, including viral e-mail, and by aggressively vetting candidate claims to ensure that the next Watergate is exposed before the election, not after, and that, if elected, a future John F. Kennedy is not surprised to find the country with a missile advantage. In an age in which newsroom staffs are being slashed, bureaus shuttered, papers folding, and network news audiences and revenues declining, we are not optimistic about any of this happening. There are, however, small signs of hope, and it is to one of them that we turn as we close.

Mayhill Fowler was an Obama supporter who had given money to his campaign. As a result, she was in the room when the candidate uttered his dismissive remarks about small-town voters. Although she reports being torn about filing a report on the *Huffington Post*, Fowler recognized the importance of the statement she had captured. In a fashion worthy of a journalist, she wrote up the story and posted the audio online.

If candidates know that citizen journalists are waiting to supplement the work of those who are part of the established profession, and if these newly empowered citizens aggressively monitor the selective forms of communication that arrive in in-boxes, on radios, and in closed-door meetings, some of the accountability needed to keep the candidates honest may survive. Add to this hope a healthy dose of free airtime, confidence that the best of traditional journalism, however delivered, will find a way to survive and prosper, and new models of Web-based journalism—some for profit, some not—and the new world, while different from the old, seems less troubling.

Appendix

W HEN EXAMINING THE IMPACT OF ADVERTISING, SCHOLARS
should consider the lasting effects of exposure that can be expressed in
terms of a "decay parameter." Past work has suggested political advertising decay parameters range from zero (nonpersistence) to .99 (almost complete
persistence). For example, studying the 2000 presidential campaign and marrying
data from the Wisconsin Advertising Project to the 2000 NAES, scholars at UCLA
found a decay parameter or .88 for the whole sample.[1] What this means is that a given
day's advertising is weighted by 0.88 to the power of each lagged day. Therefore, the
day the ad aired is weighted by 0.88^0, which produces a weight of 1. The weight of
an ad aired three days prior is .51, which is produced by the decay coefficient to the
power of 3 or 0.88^3. These scholars continued this decay rate out to 28 days.

Below we provide results using four different decay parameters: (1) the 28-day
0.88 decay rate outlined by the UCLA study, (2) a less steep decay of 0.93, (3) a
steep decay 0.38, and (4) no decay. At the suggestion of Professor John Zaller, one
of the authors on the UCLA study, we ran different decay rates on vote choice and
different decay rates for different media. To do this, we started with 0.88 decay
parameter and then longer and shorter decay rates by increments of 0.05. Our
purpose was locating the decay parameter where the impact on vote would be
strongest. We assumed that the relationship between decay parameter and the
strength of our GRP variable as a predictor of vote would be quadratic and that we
needed to identify the apex of this relationship to find the correct decay parameter
for advertising in the 2008 presidential election for each medium. To our surprise,
we found a linear relationship with the nonpersistent value of zero producing the
largest coefficients in our models across the three media.

This result is counter-intuitive as the effect of an ad is surely to last more than one day, as found by the study of the 2000 presidential campaign by the UCLA team. The reason for these disparate findings lies in the communication environment of these two different campaigns. In 2000 the advertising stream was intermittent leaving room for a decay effect to be found. In 2008 the advertising stream was largely continuous with an Obama spending advantage supplying a consistent stream of messages. As shown below, when we use a decay parameter, we still show

APPENDIX TABLE 1. Logistic Regression Predicting Obama Two-Party Vote "If Election Were Held Today"

	0.93 Decay	0.88 Decay	0.38 Decay	No Decay
Intercept	2.611***	2.610***	2.613***	2.613***
Female (1 = yes, 0 = no)	.061	.061	.061	.061
Age (in years)	−.004#	−.004#	−.003#	−.003#
Black (1 = yes, 0 = no)	2.841***	2.842***	2.845***	2.845***
Hispanic (1 = yes, 0 = no)	.797***	.797***	.795***	.795***
Education (in years)	.039**	.039**	.039**	.039**
Household income (in thousands)	−.002**	−.002**	−.002**	−.002**
Republican (1 = yes, 0 = no)	−1.997***	−1.997***	−1.999***	−2.000***
Democrat (1 = yes, 0 = no)	1.723***	1.723***	1.720***	1.719***
Ideology (1 = very liberal to 5 = very conservative)	−.929***	−.929***	−.927***	−.927***
Average of number of days saw or heard presidential campaign information in past week across television, newspaper, talk radio, and Internet	.028	.028	.029	.029
2004 presidential vote margin by county (FIPS—Kerry percent of total vote minus Bush Percent of total vote)[a]	1.355***	1.352***	1.354***	1.357***
Squared 2004 presidential vote margin by county	−.632#	−.634#	−.654*	−.657*
Difference in total GRP by campaigns (Obama–McCain and RNC) (Per 100 GRPs) (Broadcast, Radio, & Cable)	.011***	.016***	.057***	.079***
N		11,612		
Percent Correct	85.0	85.0	85.0	85.0
Cox and Snell R-Squared	.494	.494	.494	.494
Nagelkerke R-Squared	.656	.656	.659	.659

# $p < .10$ * $p < .05$ ** $p < .01$ *** $p < .001$

[a] Data for the county level election results were compiled by Dave Leip at Atlas of U.S. Presidential Elections, http://www.uselectionatlas.org

Data: Entries are logit coefficents NAES08 telephone survey; dates: 9/1/08 to 11/03/08.

significant effects. When we pinpoint our variable to the day of airing, however, we find stronger effects as these ads are in front of the message stream (see appendix table 1).

It is important to note that there is not an actual exposure measure being analyzed when marrying ad-buy data to individual-level survey data. Our analyses produce results that are in terms of a respondent living in a target zip code not direct exposure. Therefore we need some way to address endogenetity in the targeted zip codes. To do this, we include the 2004 vote margins (percent of Kerry vote minus percent of Bush vote) and this variable squared as measures of aggregate competiveness of the county that each respondent lives in. We are analyzing data from both an aggregate level and at the individual level. This raises the possibility of nonindependence of observations because respondents are nested within their county. At a first glance, multilevel modeling seems like the appropriate technique for analyzing these data. However, more careful examination of the data show that multilevel modeling is inappropriate due to the small n of respondents in each higher level group and the n of higher order groups, in this case, county. To illustrate this point, the calculation of the variance of our dependent variable (an Obama vote if the election we held today) using the intercept-only model by county produced an estimate of the covariance parameter for intercepts of 0.015 and an estimate of the covariance parameter for the residual error term of 0.234 meaning that the intraclass correlation within county is (0.015/0.234) 0.064. The main reason for using multilevel modeling is that observations from the same group are generally similar, at least more so than observations from different groups. In our data, individuals within counties are not more similar than individuals of different counties for the simple reason we have data from some many people in so many counties. Looking only at the 2008 NAES from September 1, 2008 to Election Day we have data from respondents living 2,117 counties.

Notes

INTRODUCTION

1. John Zaller, *The Nature and Origins of Mass Opinion* (Cambridge: University of Cambridge, 1992).

2. D. Sunshine Hillygus and Todd G. Shields, *The Persuadable Voter: Wedge Issues in Presidential Campaigns* (Princeton: Princeton University Press, 2008).

3. Rick Berke, "Aftermath of the Keating Verdicts: Damage Control, Political Glee," *New York Times,* March 1, 1991, http://www.nytimes.com/1991/03/01/us/aftermath-of-the-keating-verdicts-damage-control-political-glee.html; Joanne M. Miller and Jon A. Krosnick, "News Media Impact on the Ingredients of Presidential Evaluations: A Program of Research on the Priming Hypothesis," in *Political Persuasion and Attitude Change,* edited by Dianna C. Mutz, Paul M. Sniderman, and Richard Brody (Ann Arbor: University of Michigan Press, 1996): 79–99; Shanto Iyengar, "The Accessibility Bias in Politics: Television News and Public Opinion," *International Journal of Public Opinion Research* 2 (1990): 1–15; Shanto Iyengar and Donald R. Kinder, *News that Matters* (Chicago: University of Chicago Press, 1987); Shanto Iyengar, Mark D. Peters, and Donald R. Kinder, "Experimental Demonstrations of the 'Not So Minimal' Consequences of Television News Programs," *American Journal of Political Science Review* 76 (1982): 848–58.

4. Vincent Price, David Tewksbury, and E. Powers, "Switching Trains of Thought: The Impact of News Frames on Readers' Cognitive Responses," *Communication Research* 24 (1997): 481–506.

5. Thomas E. Nelson, Rosalee A. Clawson, and Zoe M. Oxley, "Media Framing of a Civil Liberties Conflict and Its Effect on Tolerance," *American Political Science Review* 91 (1997): 567; for perspectives on framing, see Joseph N. Cappella and Kathleen Hall Jamieson, *Spiral of Cynicism: The Press and the Public Good* (New York: Oxford University Press, 1997); Stephen D. Reese, Oscar H. Gandy Jr., and August E. Grant, eds., *Framing Public Life: Perspectives on Media and Our Understanding of the Social World* (Mahwah, N.J.,

Erlbaum, 2001); William A. Gamson and Andre Modigliani, "Media Discourse and Public Opinion on Nuclear Power: A Constructionist Approach," *American Journal of Sociology* 95 (1989): 1–37.

6. Vincent Price and David Tewksbury, "News Values and Public Opinion: A Theoretical Account of Media Priming and Framing," in *Progress in Communication Sciences*, vol. 13, edited by George A. Barnett and Franklin J. Boster (Greenwich, Conn.: Ablex, 1997): 173–212.

7. Thomas E. Nelson, Zoe M. Oxley, and Rosalee A. Clawson, "Toward a Psychology of Framing Effects," *Political Behavior* 19 (1997): 236; William A. Gamson and Kathryn E. Lasch, "The Political Culture of Social Welfare Policy," in *Evaluating the Welfare State*, edited by Shimon E. Spiro and Yuchtman-Yarr (New York: Academic Press, 1983): 398.

CHAPTER 1

1. Peter Brown, "How Much Will Bush Hurt McCain," *Real Clear Politics*, March 27, 2008, http://www.realclearpolitics.com/articles/2008/03/how_much_will_bush_hurt_mccain.html

2. Jeffrey Bell, "The Politics of a Failed Presidency: How John McCain and the Republican Party Should Deal with the Bush Record," *Weekly Standard*, March 17, 2008: 13, 26, http://www.weeklystandard.com/Content/Public/Articles/000/000/014/857bstgi.asp

3. Consistent with these figures, from mid-December 2007 to Election Day, the National Annenberg Election Survey (NAES) found public approval of the President's performance hovering in the 30 percent range. There were exceptions. Using raw daily percentages, the NAES telephone survey showed Bush approval at 40.3 percent on 1/6/08, 41.1 percent on 2/23/08, 41.1 percent on 6/30/08, and 42.6 percent on 8/19/08; those exceptions are potentially attributable to sampling error.

4. "Bush and Public Opinion: Reviewing the Bush Years and the Public's Final Verdict," *The Pew Research Center for the People and the Press*, December 18, 2008, http://people-press.org/report/478/bush-legacy-public-opinion

5. John Maggs, "Despite Crisis, Bush's Legacy Isn't Written Yet: The Financial Meltdown Has Sent Bush's Approval Ratings Near Truman's Record Low," *National Journal Magazine*, October 18, 2008.

6. NAES08 telephone survey. Full dataset (weighted). 12/17/07 to 11/3/08. $N = 57,972$.

7. NAES08 telephone survey. Dataset (weighted). 9/3/08 to 11/3/08. $N = 15,329$.

8. Throughout the 2007–8 election season, veteran pollster Peter Hart conducted focus groups throughout the country for the Annenberg Public Policy Center of the University of Pennsylvania. Many of these sessions were carried by C-SPAN.

9. September 17, 2008.

10. Sarah Palin, interview with Brian Williams, *NBC Nightly News*, October 24, 2008.

11. Peak was reached October 9, 2007.

12. "Fourth-Quarter U.S. GDP Registers Minus-3.8 Percent," *Kansas City Business Journal*, January 30, 2009, http://www.bizjournals.com/kansascity/stories/2009/01/26/daily58.html

13. Peter S. Goodman, "Sharper Downturn Clouds Obama's Spending Plans," *New York Times,* February 28, 2009, 1.

14. Sue Kirchoff, "GDP Down 3.8% in Q4, Biggest Drop Since '82," *USA Today,* http://www.usatoday.com/money/economy/2009-01-30-gdp-q4_N.htm

15. Kelly Evans, "Economy Dives as Goods Pile Up," *Wall Street Journal,* January 31–February 1, 2009: 1.

16. Sue Kirchoff, "GDP Down 3.8%."

17. Ibid.

18. "Fourth-quarter U.S. GDP registers minus-3.8 percent," *Kansas City Business Journal,* January 30, 2009, http://www.bizjournals.com/kansascity/stories/2009/01/26/daily58.html

19. Bill McInturff, "The Role of Polling," in *Electing the President 2008: The Annenberg Election Debriefing,* edited by Kathleen Hall Jamieson (Philadelphia: University of Pennsylvania Press, 2009), 87.

20. Lydia Saad, "Democratic Party Winning on Issues," *Gallup Poll,* December 7, 2007, http://www.gallup.com/poll/103102/democratic-party-winning-issues.aspx

21. Ibid.

22. Ibid.

23. The Pew Research Center for the People and the Press, "Increasing Optimism about Iraq," February 28, 2008, http://people-press.org/report/398/obama-has-the-lead-but-potential-problems-too

24. *Washington Post*/ABC News Poll, November 2, 2008, http://www.washingtonpost.com/wp-srv/politics/documents/postpoll_110208.html

25. Ibid.

26. NAES08 telephone survey. Full dataset (weighted). $N = 57{,}972$.

27. Center for the Study of the American Electorate, "Moderate Registration Increase Propels New Record," November 2, 2008, http://www1.media.american.edu/electionexperts/Voter%20Registration_08.pdf

28. David R. Mayhew, *Parties and Policies: How the American Government Works* (New Haven and London: Yale University Press, 2008), 360.

29. NAES08 telephone survey. Full dataset (weighted). $N = 57{,}972$.

30. Juliana Horowitz, "Winds of Political Change Haven't Shifted Public's Ideology Balance," *Pew Research Center for the People and the Press,* November 25, 2008, http://pewresearch.org/pubs/1042/winds-of-political-change-havent—shifted-publics-ideology-balance

31. In the NAES08 postelection panel study (telephone), the bivariate relationship between self-reported vote and party produced a Lambda coefficient of 0.414 ($p < .001$), while the bivariate relationship between ideology and self-reported vote produced a lambda coefficient of 0.376 ($p < .001$).

32. Examining the NAES08 postelection panel showed party identification to be more stable than self-placement on the ideological spectrum, as the bivariate relationship indicates. Party identification produced a Lambda coefficient of 0.676 ($p < .001$), while ideology produced a coefficient of 0.407 ($p < .001$).

33. Cf. Gerald Kramer, "Short-Term Fluctuations in the U.S. Voting Behavior, 1896–1964," *American Political Science Review* 65 (1971): 131–43; Michael Lewis-Beck and Tom

Rice, *Forecasting Elections* (Washington, D.C.: CQ Press, 1992); Larry Bartels and John Zaller, "Presidential Vote Models: A Recount," *PS: Political Science and Politics* 34 (2001): 9–20; James A. Campbell and James C. Garand, eds., *Before the Vote: Forecasting American Political Science and Politics National Elections* (Thousand Oaks, Calif.: Sage, 2000).

34. We treat the terms *fundamentals* and *structural factors* as synonyms.

35. David Brady, "Reflecting on the Election and Its Consequences," *Bulletin of the American Academy* (Spring 2009): 16.

36. Richard Johnston, Michael Hagen, and Kathleen Hall Jamieson, *The 2000 Presidential Election and the Foundation of Party Politics* (New York: Cambridge University Press, 2004).

37. Andrew Gelman and Gary King, "Why Are American Election Campaign Polls So Variable When Votes Are So Predictable?" *British Journal of Political Science* 23 (1993): 409–51.

38. Party identification and ideology were coded to standardize scales. For party identification, Republican was coded as −1, independents as 0, and Democrat as +1. Concerning ideology, "very" and "somewhat" conservative were coded as −1, moderate as 0, and "very" and "somewhat" liberal were coded as +1.

39. See "Symposium: Forecasting the 2008 National Elections," *PS: Political Science & Politics* 41, no. 4 (2008).

40. Richard D. McKelvey and William Zavoina, "A Statistical Model for the Analysis of Ordinal Level Dependent Variables," *Journal of Mathematical Sociology*, 4 (1975): 103–120; Alfred DeMaris, "Explained Variance in Logistic Regression: A Monte Carlo Study of Proposed Measures," *Sociological Methods & Research* 31, no. 1 (2002): 27–74.

41. Party identification produced a slightly larger coefficient than ideology, and the estimated marginal effects are not that much different, suggesting that the predictive power of party identification is not that much greater than ideology.

42. We used the Consumer Confidence Index (CCI), which is released weekly by ABC, as our aggregate level economic indicator. It is comparable to Michigan's Consumer Sentiment Index, yet the CCI is preferable because of the frequency of data release (i.e., weekly as opposed to monthly), which gives us more data points across the election to analyze. Therefore we aggregated the Obama two-party vote preference variable in the NAES08 telephone survey by week. Aggregate level correlation was moderate ($r = -.348$, $p = .055$, $N = 31$, 4/6/08 to 11/2/08). We then conducted an autoregressive integrated moving average model (ARIMA) and found no causal relationship between shifts in CCI and shifts in Obama vote preference. We also tested to see if aggregate-level Bush favorability was related to the CCI in that perhaps the economy was working through perceptions of the incumbent president. Here we found a stronger relationship, as they both declined as the campaign progressed ($r = .562$, $p < .001$, $N = 44$, 1/13/08 to 11/2/08). Yet an ARIMA did not produce any significant result that would suggest a causal relationship with CCI predicting Bush favorability ratings.

43. John R. Zaller, *The Nature and Origins of Mass Opinion* (Cambridge: Cambridge University Press, 1992).

44. Andrew Gelman and Gary King, "Why Are American Presidential Election Campaign Polls So Variable When Votes Are So Predictable?" *British Journal of Political Science* 23 (1993): 409–451.

45. Thomas M. Holbrook. *Do Campaigns Matter?* (Thousand Oaks, Calif.: Sage, 1996).

46. "Occasionally, campaign events do seem to prime an electoral consideration where one party or the other enjoys a marked advantage in the distribution of opinion in the electorate" (Larry M. Bartels, "Priming and Persuasion in Presidential Campaigns," in *Capturing Campaign Effects*, edited by Henry E. Brady and Richard Johnston (Ann Arbor, MI: University of Michigan Press, 2006): 78–115, 91.

47. Larry M. Bartels, "Priming and Persuasion in Presidential Campaigns," in *Capturing Campaign Effects*, edited by Henry E. Brady and Richard Johnston (Ann Arbor, MI: University of Michigan Press, 2006): 78–115, 97; Andrew Gelman and Gary King, "Why Are American Presidential Election Campaign Polls So Variable When Votes Are So Predictable?": 409–451, 412.

48. "Symposium: Forecasting the 2008 National Elections," *PS: Political Science & Politic* 41, no. 4 (2008).

49. Stephen Ansolabehere, "The Paradox of Minimal Effects," in *Capturing Campaign Effects*, edited by Henry E. Brady and Richard Johnston (Ann Arbor, MI: University of Michigan Press, 2006): 29–44.

50. Center for Responsive Politics, "U.S. Election Will Cost $5.3 Billion, Center for Responsive Politics Predicts," October 22, 2008, http://www.opensecrets.org/news/2008/10/us-election-will-cost-53-billi.html

CHAPTER 2

1. David Axelrod is the founder of AKPD Message and Media, a Chicago-based political consulting firm, and was the chief strategist for President Obama during the 2008 election. He is currently President Obama's top political advisor.

2. David Axelrod, "Campaign Organization and Strategy" in *Electing the President 2008: The Annenberg Election Debriefing*, edited by Kathleen Hall Jamieson (Philadelphia: University of Pennsylvania Press, 2009): 68.

3. "McCain has been hailed by liberals and lionized in the mainstream news media for being a rebel," noted an article in *Time* in early February. "This maverick reputation, so prized for its general-election appeal, makes it difficult for McCain to pass the primary threshold" (James Carney, "The Phoenix," *Time*, February 4, 2008, 35).

4. David D. Kirkpatrick, "As McCain Wins, Critics on Right Look Again," *New York Times*, February 1, 2008, A20.

5. James Carney, "The Phoenix."

6. See Kathleen Hall Jamieson and Joseph N. Cappella, *Echo Chamber: Rush Limbaugh and the Conservative Media Establishment* (New York: Oxford University Press, 2008); Kathleen Hall Jamieson and Bruce W. Hardy, "Media, Endorsements and the 2008 Primaries," in *Reforming the Presidential Nomination Process*, edited by S. S. Smith and M. J. Springer (Washington: Brookings Press, 2009): 64–84.

7. Kathleen Hall Jamieson and Joseph N. Cappella, *Echo Chamber: Rush Limbaugh and the Conservative Media Establishment*.

8. Michael Luo and David D. Kirkpatrick, "As Primary Day Looms in New Hampshire, Republican Rivals Go After One Another," *New York Times*, January 7, 2008, A16.

9. Elisabeth Bumiller and Michael Luo, "Reasons Vary, but McCain and Romney Compete for the Same Prize," *New York Times*, February 2, 2008: A13.

10. "Primary Choices: John McCain," *New York Times,* January 25, 2008, A24.

11. David Brooks, "The Character Factor," *New York Times,* November 13, 2007, A29.

12. John McCain voted for four of George W. Bush's budgets: May 10, 2001, Senate Vote #98, March 12, 2004, Senate Vote #58; April 28, 2005, Senate Vote #114; March 16, 2006, Senate Vote #74. See the U.S. Senate Legislation and Records, http://www.senate.gov/legislative/LIS/roll_call_lists/vote_menu_107_1.htm

13. When Bush took office on January 20, 2001, the national debt was $5.73 trillion. When he left office on January 20, 2009, it was $10.63 trillion. "The Daily History of Debt Results," *Treasury Direct,* http://www.treasurydirect.gov/NP/BPDLogin?application=np

14. Michael Abramowitz, "McCain Lawyers Push back on Obama Keating Five Charges," The Trail, *Washington Post,* October 6, 2008, http://voices.washingtonpost.com/44/2008/10/06/mccain_lawyers_push_back_on_ob.html

15. Rick Berke, "Aftermath of the Keating Verdicts: Damage Control, Political Glee," *New York Times,* March 1, 1991, http://www.nytimes.com/1991/03/01/us/aftermath-of-the-keating-verdicts-damage-control-political-glee.html

16. David Plouffe is a partner at AKPD Message and Media, a Chicago-based political consulting firm, and served as campaign manager for President Obama during the 2008 election.

17. Quoted by Michael Abramowitz. "McCain Lawyers Push back on Obama Keating Five Charges," The Trail, *Washington Post,* http://voices.washingtonpost.com/44/2008/10/06/mccain_lawyers_push_back_on_ob.html

18. David Axelrod, "Campaign Organization and Strategy," in *Electing the President 2008: The Annenberg Election Debriefing,* edited by Kathleen Hall Jamieson (Philadelphia: University of Pennsylvania Press, 2009): 68–9.

19. Ibid.

20. Ron Suskind, "Change: How Political Eras End, and Begin," *New York Times Magazine,* November 16, 2008, 55.

21. David Plouffe, "Campaign Management and Field Operations," in *Electing the President 2008*: 37. Plouffe is the author of *The Audacity to Win* (New York: Penguin, 2009).

22. Second Presidential Debate, Belmont University, Nashville Tenn., October 7, 2008.

23. Change meant turning from failure to embrace success, rejecting pessimism for hope. In his closing statement in the second debate, Obama reiterated the notion that, "We need fundamental change. That's what's at stake in this election. That's the reason I decided to run for president, and I'm hopeful that all of you are prepared to continue this extraordinary journey that we call America. But we're going to have to have the courage and the sacrifice, the nerve to move in a new direction." His concluding statement in the last debate made the same point. "[T]he biggest risk we could take right now is to adopt the same failed policies and the same failed politics that we've seen over the last eight years and somehow expect a different result. We need fundamental change in this country, and that's what I'd like to bring" (Hofstra University, Hempstead, New York, October 15, 2008).

24. Obama for America, "President WA," February 1, 2008.

25. Obama for America, "We Can Revised," February 3, 2008.

26. Obama for America, "Leader Ohio 120," March 3, 2008.

27. Obama for America, "President PA," April 15, 2008.

28. Obama for America, "Reason Rev," April 19, 2008.

29. Obama for America, "Next Door OR," May 9 2008.

30. Obama for America, "Take It Back," August 1, 2007.

31. Obama for America, "Low Road Rev" August 4, 2008.

32. Obama for America, "Embrace," August 13, 2008.

33. Obama for America, "Pocket," August 5, 2008.

34. Obama for America, "Hands," August 9, 2008.

35. Obama for America, "Sold Us Out," September 16, 2008.

36. Joel Benenson is a Founding Partner at and the President of Benenson Strategy Group, a New York–based strategic research and polling firm. He was the lead pollster and a senior strategist for President Barack Obama during the 2008 election.

37. Joel Benenson, "The Role of Polling," in *Electing the President 2008: The Annenberg Election Debriefing*, edited by Kathleen Hall Jamieson (Philadelphia: University of Pennsylvania Press, 2009): 96.

38. McCain-Palin 2008/RNC, "Ambition," October 10, 2008; McCain-Palin 2008/RNC "Unethical," October 14, 2008.

39. McCain-Palin 2008, "Special," October 29, 2008.

40. McCain-Palin 2008, "Jeb Bush," October 31, 2008.

41. McCain-Palin 2008/RNC, "Your Choice," October 31, 2008.

42. John McCain 2008, "Global," June 17, 2008

43. John McCain 2008, "Love 60," July 8, 2008.

44. Ibid.

45. John McCain 2008, "Broken," August 5, 2008.

46. McCain-Palin 2008, "Original Mavericks" (Web ad), September 7, 2008.

47. Bill McInturff is a partner and cofounder of Public Opinion Strategies, a national political and public affairs survey research firm. He served as the lead pollster for John McCain 2008.

48. Bill McInturff, "The Role of Polling," in *Electing the President 2008*: 89. Republican McInturff and Democrat Peter D. Hart codirect the NBC News/*Wall Street Journal* survey.

49. Estimated expenditure figures provided by Campaign Media Analysis Group (CMAG). Throughout the book when we mention the amount spent on a broadcast ad we are relying on CMAG data. In light of the very different process through which ad buys are recorded when made on cable, unless specifically stated otherwise, we are not reporting dollars spent on ads carried in that venue.

50. Barack Obama in Third Presidential Debate, Hostra University, Hempstead, N.Y., October 15, 2008.

51. John McCain in Third Presidential Debate, Hostra University, Hempstead, N.Y., October 15, 2008.

52. Obama for America, "90 Percent" (Web ad), October 16, 2008.

53. Barack Obama in Third Presidential Debate.

54. McCain: "Whether it be bringing climate change to the floor of the Senate for the first time. Whether it be opposition to spending and earmarks, whether it be the issue of torture, whether it be the conduct of the war in Iraq, which I vigorously opposed. Whether it be on fighting the pharmaceutical companies on Medicare prescription drugs, importation.

Whether it be fighting for an HMO patient's bill of rights. Whether it be the establishment of the 9/11 Commission."

55. John McCain, "Fight" (Web ad), October 15, 2008.

56. Joseph Curl and Stephen Dinan. "McCain Lambastes Bush Years," *Washington Times,* October 23, 2008.

57. *Meet the Press,* NBC, October 26, 2008.

58. Joel Benenson, "The Role of Polling," in *Electing the President 2008: The Annenberg Election Debriefing,* edited by Kathleen Hall Jamieson (Philadelphia: University of Pennsylvania Press, 2009): 94.

59. Axelrod, "Campaign Organization and Strategy," in *Electing the President 2008*: 70. On voter knowledge, see M. Alvarez, *Issues and Information in Presidential Elections* (University of Michigan Press, 1997).

60. Obama for America, "Embrace," August 13, 2008.

61. Axelrod, "Campaign Organization and Strategy," in *Electing the President 2008*: 70.

62. John McCain on *Your World with Neil Cavuto,* Fox News Network, May 22, 2003.

63. Obama for America, "Same," August 31, 2008.

64. *Saturday Night Live,* NBC, October 23, 2008.

65. Analyses of the aggregated NAES08 data between 6/9/08 and 11/3/09 show that there is a significant upward linear trend (R-square = .093, p < .001).

66. Steve Schmidt is a partner at Mercury Public Affairs, a strategic communications firm, and served as a senior advisor to Senator John McCain's 2008 presidential campaign.

67. Schmidt, "The Vice Presidential Campaign," in *Electing the President 2008*: 29. On V. P. impact, see Danny M. Adkison, "The Electoral Significance of the Vice Presidency," *Presidential Studies Quarterly* 12 (1982): 330–36.

68. The "heavy" and "light" news users variables were constructed by averaging the number of days respondents said they got campaign information from television and Internet and then selecting those who scored 5 or higher and those who score 3 or less, which corresponded to the top and bottom quartiles of the distribution.

69. Lydia Saad, "Democratic Part Winning on Issues," Gallup Poll, December 7, 2007, http://www.gallup.com/poll/103102/democratic-party-winning-issues.aspx

70. That reputation didn't mean that Republicans were misers, however. While Republicans preferred opening the public coffers for defense (or military) programs, Democrats were more prone to raid them for social programs. The corollary holds as well. Until the administration of Bush 43, one rarely would lose a bar bet by assuming that Democrats would favor cuts or slower growth in defense and the Republicans cuts or reductions in the rate of increase in social spending.

71. *U.S. Department of Treasury,* "The Debt to the Penny and Who Holds It," Treasury Direct, http://www.treasurydirect.gov/NP/BPDLogin?application=np

72. First Presidential Debate, University of Mississippi, Oxford, Miss., September 26, 2008.

73. Second Presidential Debate, Belmont University, Nashville, Tenn., October 7, 2008.

74. Third Presidential Debate.

75. Barack Obama in First Presidential Debate.

76. John McCain 2008, "Family," August 6, 2008.

77. John McCain 2008/RNC, "Expensive Plans," September 1, 2008.

78. McCain-Palin 2008/RNC, "Dome," September 17, 2008.

79. McCain-Palin 2008, "Folks," October 8, 2008.

80. McCain-Palin 2008/RNC, "Tax Cutter" (Web ad), October 3, 2008.

81. John McCain 2008, "Celeb," July 30, 2008.

82. Kathleen Hall Jamieson, *Packaging the Presidency* (New York: Oxford, 1996): 48.

83. In his 2004 autobiography, *Dreams from My Father,* Obama wrote, "But an old, sepia-toned photograph on the bookshelf spoke most eloquently of their roots. It showed Toot's grandparents, of Scottish and English stock, standing in front of a ramshackle homestead, unsmiling and dressed in coarse wool, their eyes squinting at the sun-baked flinty life that stretched out before them. Theirs were the faces of American Gothic, the WASP bloodline's poorer cousins, and in their eyes one could see truths that I would have to learn later as facts: that Kansas had entered the Union free only after a violent precursor to the Civil War, the battle in which John Brown's sword tasted the first blood; that while one of my great-great-grandfathers, Christopher Columbus Clark, had been a decorated Union soldier, his wife's mother was rumored to have been a second cousin of Jefferson Davis, president of the confederacy" (p. 13). Also, during his speech on race, Obama asserts, "I am married to a black American who carries within her the blood of slaves and slave owners, an inheritance we pass on to our two precious daughters." ("A More Perfect Union," Philadelphia, Pa., March 18, 2008). Michelle Obama's great-great grandfather, Jim Robinson, was born into slavery and lived on a plantation in Georgetown, South Carolina.

84. Barack Obama, Selma Voting Rights March Commemoration, March 4, 2007.

85. Lynn Sweet, "Obama's Gaffes Start to Pile Up," *Chicago Sun-Times,* March 28, 2007, 27.

86. "Obama Overstates Kennedys' Role in Helping His Father," *Washington Post,* March 30, 2008, A01.

87. Barack Obama, Candidate Forum on Public Service, Columbia University, N.Y., *NBC,* September 11, 2008.

88. Tim Harper, "The Making of a President," *Boston Globe,* August 16, 2008, AA01.

89. For an insightful exploration of both the narrative of his life and his time in Chicago, see David Remnick, *The Bridge: The Life and Rise of Barack Obama* (Alfred A. Knopf: New York, 2010).

90. For evidence of the effectiveness of the Republican attacks, see Richard Johnston, Michael Hagen and Kathleen Hall Jamieson, *The 2000 Presidential Election and the Foundation of Party Politics* (New York: Cambridge University Press, 2004).

91. For an examination of the role of the press in creating this anti-Gore frame, see Kathleen Hall Jamieson and Paul Waldman, *The Press Effect: Politicians, Journalists and the Stories That Shape the Political World,* 53–4.

92. Those who believe that the press was biased in Obama's favor (a question outside the scope of this book) are likely to see confirming evidence in this pattern of treatment. An alternative explanation might suggest that the press is unlikely to make an issue of a misstatement by a non-front runner. The odds of coverage increase if the front runner uses it to attack or the statement becomes part of a serious challenger's core campaign message.

Neither was the case with these three lapses. As soon as the error was flagged by the national press, it disappeared from Obama's rhetorical repertoire.

93. See Rick Pearson, "McCain Ad Takes on Obama and 'Chicago Machine,'" *Chicago Tribune,* September 22, 2008, http://newsblogs.chicagotribune.com/clout_st/2008/09/mccain-ad-takes.html

94. Obama for America, "The Country I Love 60," June 20, 2008.

95. The exact question wording for the dependent variable is, "Which of the following best describes the views of Barack Obama? 1) Very Conservative, 2) Somewhat Conservative, 3) Moderate, 4) Somewhat Liberal, 5) Very Liberal."

96. "A New Stitch in a Bad Pattern," FactCheck.org, September 2, 2008, http://www.factcheck.org/elections-2008/a_new_stitch_in_a_bad_pattern.html; Politifact, 2 October 2008, http://www.politifact.com/truth-o-meter/statements/2008/oct/02/joe-biden/mccains-tax-plan-doesnt-ignore-middle-class/

97. Obama for America, "Three Times," August 19, 2008.

98. Obama for America, "On Your Side," October 8, 2008.

99. Obama for America, "Work Hard NV," October 9, 2008.

100. Obama for America, "Ayers Response," August 25, 2008.

101. Obama for America, "Bush Economics," September 9, 2008.

102. Obama for America, "Foreign Vehicles MI," September 23, 2008.

CHAPTER 3

1. So for example, when President Obama stumbled verbally during his July 8, 2009, visit to Moscow, the *New York Times* attributed the fumbles to his being "tired." (Peter Baker, "Family Night for Obamas Miffs Some in Moscow," *New York Times,* July 8, 2009, A10). "Mr. Obama has seemed tired here, several times fumbling the pronunciation of Mr. Medvedev's name and Mr. Putin's title. Beginning a speech here, he mistakenly said he first met his wife in school instead of at the law firm where they actually met. And he misstated his young daughter's age."

2. "Tavis Smiley Show," NPR, March 29, 2004.

3. Mark Leibovich, "The Man of the Hour; Barack Obama Is the Party's New Phenom," *Washington Post,* July 27, 2004, C01.

4. Dan Balz, "Obama takes first steps in N.H." *Washington Post,* December 11, 2006, http://www.washingtonpost.com/wp-dyn/content/article/2006/12/10/AR2006121000167.html

5. Obama for America, "Future" (Ohio, La., Miss., N. Mex., R.I., Vt.), February 27, 2008.

6. Obama for America, "Represent," April 15, 2008.

7. Obama for America, "America is Listening TX," February 29, 2008.

8. Barack Obama, Remarks in town hall style fund-raiser in Ball State University, San Francisco, Calif., April 6, 2008.

9. Hillary Clinton for President, "Pennsylvania," April 14, 2008.

10. Obama for America, "Same," August 31, 2008.

11. Obama for America initially aired "Still" on September 12, 2008. Had the ad not aired at a time when news of the faltering economy was crowding out campaign coverage, it

might have produced a backlash for, as the McCain campaign quickly noted, the Senator's infrequent computer use was a byproduct of discomfort created by torture at the hands of his Hanoi captors. At the Annenberg debriefing, the Democrats noted that had they known that McCain's war injuries limited his ability to use a computer, they probably would have forgone the attack on his computer skills.

12. Obama for America, "Still," September 12, 2008.

13. Obama for America, "On Your Side," October 8, 2008; Obama for America/DNC, "Impuestos," October 19, 2008.

14. Obama for America, "Looking Out For," October 17, 2008.

15. Obama for America, "The Subject," October 9, 2008.

16. The Constitution sets 35 as the minimum age: "No person except a natural born Citizen, or a Citizen of the United States, at the time of the Adoption of this Constitution, shall be eligible to the Office of President; neither shall any Person be eligible to that office who shall not have attained to the Age of thirty-five Years, and been fourteen Years a resident within the United States" (Article II, Section I, Clause 5).

17. McCain's age at nomination did not, however, merit inclusion in the *Guinness Book of World Records*. At age 73 the 1996 Republican nominee was older than McCain by a year when he accepted his party's nomination. The moves that incumbent Bill Clinton made against Republican Party standard-bearer Dole presaged Obama's against his Republican rival. It wasn't Dole's age that was the problem, the incumbent Democrat told the audience during one of the 1996 debates, but rather the age of his ideas. "I can only tell you that I don't think Senator Dole is too old to be president. It's the age of his ideas that I question." In Democratic ads, black-and-white footage underscored Dole's age. Pages of a calendar flipped from year to year to tie him to the past.

18. Anna Quindlen, "How Old Is Too Old?" *Newsweek*, February 4, 2008, 84.

19. Second Presidential Debate, Kansas City, Mo., October 21, 1984.

20. For a treatment of Reagan's rebuttal of the age issue in 1984, see Kathleen Hall Jamieson, *Eloquence in an Electronic Age* (New York: Oxford University Press, 1988).

21. For a discussion, see Kathleen Hall Jamieson, *Packaging the Presidency: A History and Criticism of Presidential Campaign Advertising* (New York: Oxford University Press, 1996): 102–10.

22. Joel Benenson, "The Role of Polling," in *Electing the President 2008: The Annenberg Election Debriefing*, edited by Kathleen Hall Jamieson (Philadelphia: University of Pennsylvania Press, 2009): 106.

23. Bill McInturff, "The Role of Polling," in *Electing the President 2008: The Annenberg Election Debriefing*, edited by Kathleen Hall Jamieson (Philadelphia: University of Pennsylvania Press, 2009): 107.

24. This search was conducted by Annenberg researcher Jackie Dunn.

25. Evan Thomas, "What These Eyes Have Seen," *Newsweek*, February 11, 2008, 27.

26. James Carney, "The Phoenix," *Time*, February 4, 2008, 37.

27. The Cultural Communication Index (CCI) is a map of the media environment using data collected by Dr. Steven Skiena and his associates at Stony Brook University for the Annenberg Public Policy Center. The data that they provided us are based on their Lydia system that identifies the occurrences of predefined "entities" in online newspaper texts, blogs, and television news show transcripts and analyzes these occurrences temporally,

specially, and linguistically. The Lydia system uses "Web spiders" that identify the pre-defined entities and then archives the article, page, blog, or transcript. Once archived they are "then run through a pipeline that performs part-of-speech tagging, named entity iden-tification and categorization, geographic normalization, intra-document co-reference reso-lution, extraction of entity descriptions and relations between entities, and per-occurrence sentiment score calculation" (Mikhail Bautin, Akshay Patil, and Steven Skiena, News/Media Analysis for National Annenberg Election Survey, p. 1). For the Annenberg Public Policy Center, Dr. Skiena and his team collected data from October 2007 to January 2009 based on a custom list of entities specific to the 2008 election that the NAES team provided the Stony Brook team. For data, they relied on 1000–2000 daily U.S. online newspapers, around 45 political blogs, and 13 political television shows that were crawled daily. The Stony Brook team took our list of 626 entities and manually grouped our entities with "synonym sets"— for example, the synonym set for "Barack Obama" includes synonyms such as "Obama," "Barack," "Barack Hussein Obama," "Senator Obama," "Senator Barack Obama," and all similar entities and all entities with various capitalizations.

In the analyses, we look at co-occurrences between different entities and/or "synonym sets" by date. A co-occurrence or concurrence occurs when that two entities (or a single member from a synonym set) appear within a sentence in the overall sample of online newspapers, blogs, and TV transcripts. For example, in chapter 3 we show the co-occur-rences between the synonym set "Barack Obama" and the synonym set "William Ayers" and how daily co-occurrences shift.

Although the Lydia system is not designed to give a complete count on the number of times that two entities appear in the same sentence in the universe of news media—mainly because it is based on "crawling" the Internet and even within that domain it has a limited and nonrandom sample—it does provide us with a barometer measuring the agenda-set-ting function of news because we can track these co-occurrences by date allowing us to see relative shifts. The actual numbers reported in our graphs are, in reality, quite meaningless but are still useful as we can tie relative shifts to actual events in time during the 2008 cam-paign. The Lydia system is extremely complex technically and we invite the readers to go to www.annenbergpublicpolicycenter.org/obamavictory for a complete discussion of the data collection process.

28. The Television News Frequency Index (TNFI) is constructed by conducting a Lexis Nexis searches of the frequency of a co-occurrence of our search terms in transcripts from NBC, CBS, ABC, FOX News, CNN, and MSNBC.

29. Anna Quindlen, "How Old Is Too Old?" 64.

30. James Fallows, "Rhetorical Questions," *The Atlantic,* September 2008, 50.

31. Joseph Carroll, "Which Characteristics Are Most Desirable in the Next President?" Gallup Poll, September 17, 2007, http://www.gallup.com/poll/28693/which-characteristics-most-desirable-next-president.aspx

32. *Special Report with Brit Hume,* Fox News Network, January 21, 2008.

33. John McCain, Remarks at the Citadel, Amman, Jordan, March 18, 2008.

34. *CNN Newsroom,* CNN, July 19 2008.

35. Lawrence K. Altman, "Many Holes in Disclosure of the Nominees' Health," *New York Times,* October 20, 2008, A20.

36. "The other thing that was a 4:15 in the morning wake-up-in-a-cold-sweat moment was the question, every time that you use John McCain footage of Vietnam, does it make him an old guy? Among my other losing presidential campaigns was Bob Dole's in '96. One of the things I know from that was every time you'd set Bob Dole in World War II, everyone would say, "Is he old?" So I was worried about that." Chris Mottola, "Advertising," in *Electing the President 2008: The Annenberg Election Debriefing*, edited by Kathleen Hall Jamieson (Philadelphia: University of Pennsylvania Press, 2009): 113.

37. *The Daily Show with Jon Stewart,* Comedy Central, October 8, 2008.

38. *The Tonight Show with Jay Leno,* NBC, April 10, 2008.

39. *The Tonight Show with Jay Leno,* NBC, October 17, 2008.

40. *Jimmy Kimmel Live,* ABC, October 23, 2008.

41. *Late Show with David Letterman,* CBS, September 24, 2008.

42. *Late Late Show with Craig Ferguson,* CBS, October 21, 2008. Other jokes pivoted on exaggerating McCain's actual age. "The former chairman of the Fed, Alan Greenspan, was in Washington today," said Craig Ferguson. "And he said that the current financial crisis is a 'one in a century' occurrence. And John McCain was like: 'He's right. I've been through three of 'em.'" (October 23, 2008); "In a speech earlier this week, John McCain said, 'I've been fighting for the United States since I was 17,'" noted Conan O'Brien. "Then he said, 'Of course, back then, it was called Pangaea.'" (October 20, 2008).

43. "The Comedy Campaign: The Role of Late-Night TV Shows on the Campaign," *Media Monitors,* XXII, 3, (Winter 2008): 4, http://www.cmpa.com/pdf/08winter.pdf

44. Brave New PAC & Democracy for America, "McCain Medical Records" September 25, 2008.

45. *New York Times,* October 3, 2008, A07.

46. Lawrence K. Altman, "Many Holes in Disclosure of Nominees' Health."

47. Obama for America, "Old Politics General," July 28, 2008.

48. Obama for America, "New Energy Rev," July 30, 2008.

49. Obama for America, "Low Road Rev," August 4, 2008.

50. Obama for America, "Embrace," August 13, 2008.

51. Obama for America, "Never," August 20, 2008.

52. Obama for America, "Seven," August 22, 2008.

53. Obama for America, "Out of Touch," August 25, 2008.

54. Obama for America, "Burden," September 15, 2008.

55. Obama for America, "Floridians Hurting," October 7, 2008.

56. Obama for America, "Erratic," October 20 2008.

57. Obama for America, "Audio Tapes," October 27, 2008.

58. Bush then stealthily repudiated his own public embrace of McCain's position with an exception-taking signing statement that functioned for practical matters as a de facto line item veto. For a discussion, see Karlyn Kohrs Campbell and Kathleen Hall Jamieson, *Presidents Creating the Presidency: Deeds Done in Words* (Chicago: University of Chicago Press, 2008): 209–10.

59. Obama for America, "Social Security," September 16, 2008; Obama for America, "Out of Touch"; Obama for America, "Risk," September 30, 2008.

60. Obama for America, "Out of Touch."

61. Audio replayed on *CNN Election Center,* CNN, August 21, 2008.

62. Robert Gibbs, *Morning Joe,* MSNBC, September 30, 2008. In *Huffington Post,* "Obama Spokesman on McCain, We 'Know Who Is Erratic In a Crisis,'" http://www.huffingtonpost.com/2008/09/30/obama-spokesman-on-mccain_n_130514.html

63. Robert Gibbs and Chris Wallace, *Fox News Sunday,* Fox News Network, August 24, 2008.

64. Barack Obama, *The Situation Room,* CNN, May 8, 2008.

65. John McCain and Mark Saltar, *Worth Fighting For: A Memoir* (New York: Random House, 2002).

66. "McCain's Temper Is Legitimate Issue: Hull's Account of Outbursts Not Unusual," *Arizona Republic,* October 31, 1999, 6B.

67. Nancy Gibbs, October 15, 2008, http://www.time.com/time/politics/article/0,8599,1850921,00.html

68. David Lightman and Matt Stearns, September 7, 2008, http://www.mcclatchydc.com/227/story/51660.html

69. David Kirkpatrick, October 25, 2008, http://www.nytimes.com/2008/10/26/weekinreview/26kirkpatrick.html

70. Michael Leahy, April 20, 2008, http://www.washingtonpost.com/wp-dyn/content/article/2008/04/19/AR2008041902224.html

71. Ralph Vartabedian and Michael Finnegan, May 22, 2007, http://articles.latimes.com/2007/may/22/nation/na-outburst22

72. Mark Benjamin, "It's 3 A.M. Who Do You Want Answering the Phone?" *Salon,* March 6, 2008, http://www.salon.com/news/feature/2008/03/06/commander_in_chief/

73. "Mr. McCain's snap choice of Ms. Palin reflects his impulsive streak," editorialized the *New York Times* ("Candidate McCain's Big Decision," September 3, 2008, A24). "The best evidence is that she was a somewhat impulsive choice," noted *Times'* columnist Bob Herbert (Bob Herbert, "Running from Reality," September 6, 2008, A17). "The desire to win, and the impulsiveness, converged in his decision to pick Palin—a bold move that has allowed McCain to regain his maverick identity," argued David Ignatius in the *Washington Post* ("Stopping at Nothing to Win," September 14, 2008, B07). "[T]he choice of Sarah Palin, as controversial as it`s turning out to be, was a bold stroke on John McCain`s part to try and reclaim the change side of this debate in 2008, to show himself to be decisive, perhaps impulsive, but decisive, and to be somebody who really stood for change. And that change is from George W. Bush," observed commentator Mark Shields on PBS's *NewsHour* ("Hurricane-Shortened Republican National Convention Begins in Earnest Tonight," September 2, 2008). "McCain's problem is not only one of substance but perhaps more crucially of temperament," claimed Fareed Zakaria in *Newsweek* near the end of the campaign. "Throughout the campaign, he has been volatile and impulsive.… He apparently wanted to name as his vice presidential candidate Joe Lieberman, a pro-choice semi-Democrat with decades of experience, but then instead picked someone close to the opposite—Sarah Palin, a rabble-rousing ultraconservative with limited experience and knowledge of the issues" ("The Case for Barack Obama," October 27, 2008, 43). Conservative columnist George Will makes the same point in different language when he wrote on September 23, 2008, "McCain's selection of her is applied McCainism—a visceral judgment by one who is confidently righteous.

But the viscera are not the seat of wisdom" ("Impulse, Meet Experience," *Washington Post*, September 3, 2008).

74. David Plouffe, *The Audacity to Win: The Inside Story and Lessons of Barack Obama's Historic Victory* (New York: Penguin Group, 2009): 311.

75. $R^2 = .190, p < .001$

76. Question wording: "I am going to read you some phrases. For each one, please tell me how well that phrase applies to the following candidates. Please use a scale from 0 to 10, where 'zero' means it does not apply at all and 10 means it applies extremely well. Of course you can use any number in between. 'Shares my values.'"

77. James Carney, "The Phoenix." McCain repeated the "Frankenstein" line in the January 5, 2008 Republican primary debate in Manchester, N.H.

78. Michael Luo and David Kirkpatrick, "As Primary Day Looms in New Hampshire, Republican Rivals Go After One Another," *New York Times*, January 7, 2008, http://query. nytimes.com/gst/fullpage.html?res=9B0CE0D91331F934A35752C0A96E9C8B63

79. Robert Kurzban, John Tooby, and Leda Cosmides, "Can race be erased? Coalitional Computation and Social Categorization," *Proceedings of the National Academy of Sciences* 98, 26 (December 18, 2001): 15387–15392; Leda Cosmides, John Tooby, and Robert Kurzban, "Perceptions of race," *Trends in Cognitive Science* 7, 4 (April 2003): 173–179.

80. By contrast, with a white mother from Kansas and black father from Kenya, Barack Obama was ancestrally as white as he was black and reminded viewers regularly of that fact with ads that prominently featured his mother and her parents.

81. For example, the National Institute on Aging's Web site reports, "The rate and progression of this process can vary greatly from person to person, but generally over time every major organ of the body is affected. As we age, for instance, lung tissue loses much of its elasticity, and the muscles of the rib cage shrink. As a result, maximum vital breathing capacity progressively diminishes in each decade of life, beginning at about age 20. With age, blood vessels accumulate fatty deposits and lose much of their flexibility, resulting in arteriosclerosis or "hardening of the arteries." In the gastrointestinal system, production of digestive enzymes diminishes, and as a result, tissues lose much of their ability to break down and absorb foods properly." http://www.nia.nih.gov/HealthInformation/Publications/AgingUndertheMicroscope/chapter01.htm

Scholars report that there is no genetic basis for distinguishing one supposed race from another. Richard Lewontin, "The Apportionment of Human Diversity," *Evolutionary Biology* 6 (1972): 381–98; Masatoshi Nei and Arun K. Roychoudhury, "Evolutionary Relationships of Human Populations on a Global Scale," *Molecular Biology and Evolution* 10 (1993): 927–43.

CHAPTER 4

· 1. Dan Balz and Keith B. Richburg, "Historic Decision Renews Old Debate," *Washington Post*, June 27, 2008, http://www.washingtonpost.com/wp-dyn/content/article/2008/06/26/AR2008062604247.html

2. Jonathan Weisman, "Obama Signals Support for Wider Offshore Drilling," *Washington Post*, August 2, 2008, http://www.washingtonpost.com/wp-dyn/content/article/2008/08/01/AR2008080103199.html

3. United States Senate Roll Call, H.R. 6304, http://www.senate.gov/legislative/LIS/roll_call_lists/roll_call_vote_cfm.cfm?congress=110&session=2&vote=00168

4. Michael D. Shear, "GOP Sharpens Attacks on Obama," *Washington Post,* June 30, 2008, A4.

5. John McCain 2008, "Troop Funding," July 19, 2008.

6. Let Freedom Ring, "Both Ways Barack," July 22, 2008.

7. John McCain 2008, "Joe Biden on Barack Obama," August 25, 2008.

8. Republican National Committee, "Chair," October 16, 2008.

9. Republican National Committee, "Listen to Biden," October 25, 2008.

10. *The Daily Show with Jon Stewart,* Comedy Central, July 22, 2008.

11. "Iraq Leader Maliki Supports Obama's Withdrawal Plans," *Spiegel,* July 19, 2008, http://www.spiegel.de/international/world/0,1518,566841,00.html

12. "Iraqi PM Backs Obama Troop Exit Plan: Report," *Reuters,* July 19, 2008, http://www.reuters.com/article/vcCandidateFeed2/idUSL198009020080719

13. Steve Schmidt, "Campaign Organization and Strategy," in *Electing the President 2008: The Annenberg Election Debriefing,* edited by Kathleen Hall Jamieson (Philadelphia: University of Pennsylvania Press, 2009): 59.

14. *CNN Newsroom,* CNN, February 24, 2008.

15. John McCain 2008, "The One" (Web ad), August 1, 2008, http://www.youtube.com/watch?v=mopkn01PzM8

16. In Oprah's speech endorsing Obama, the talk show host observed:

But I do remember when Jane Pittman would encounter young people throughout that film. And she would ask, "Are you the one? Are you the one?" I remember her standing in the doorway, her body bowed, frail, old, and holding the baby in her arms and saying, "Are you the one, Jimmy? Are you the one?" Well I believe in '08, I have found the answer to Miss Pittman's question. I have found the answer. It is the same question that our nation is asking. "Are you the one? Are you the one?" I'm here to tell you, Iowa, he is the one. He is the one! Barack Obama. (Remarks from Campaign Rally in Des Moines, Iowa, C-SPAN Video Library, December 8, 2007, http://www.c-spanvideo.org/videoLibrary/)

17. *This Week,* ABC, August 3, 2008.

18. E-mail correspondence among Chris Mottola, Fred Davis and Kathleen Hall Jamieson, 13 August 2009.

19. Sarah Wheaton, "Your Tube," *New York Times,* November 4, 2008, A24.

20. Barack Obama, Remarks to Gridiron Club, Washington, D.C., December 2005.

21. John McCain 2008, "Higher," August 22, 2008.

22. John McCain 2008, "Painful," August 8, 2008.

23. Ibid.

24. John McCain 2008/RNC, "Expensive Plans," September 1, 2008.

25. Barack Obama, Remarks at Al Smith Dinner, New York City, New York, October 16, 2008.

26. John McCain 2008, "Maybe," August 18, 2008.

27. Michael Powell, "Barack Obama: Calm in the Swirl of History," *New York Times*, June 4, 2008, A1.

28. Barack Obama, *The Audacity of Hope* (New York: Crown Publishers, 2006).

29. *CNN Newsroom*, Interview with McCain Economic Adviser Nancy Pfotenhauer, CNN, October 6, 2008.

30. Susan T. Fiske, Monica H. Lin, and Stephen L. Neuberg, "The Continuum Model: Ten Years Later," in Shelly Chaiken and Yaacov Trope, *Dual-Process Theories in Social Psychology* (New York: Guilford, 1999): 231ff.

31. Blascovich, James et al., "Perceiver Threat in Social Interactions with Stigmatized Others," *Journal of Personality and Social Psychology*, 80, 2 (2001): 253–267.

32. See "Two Canadian Diplomats, One Evasion by Obama," *Washington Post*, March 3, 2008. "I do not have to clarify it," Obama told an Ohio TV station on February 29. "The Canadian embassy already clarified it by saying that the story was not true. Our office has said that the story was not true. I think it is important for viewers to understand that it was not true... It did not happen." "This is a case where the technical parsing of the truth by the Obama campaign falls well short of the whole truth," said Michael Dobbs of the *Washington Post* while awarding the Obama campaign two Pinocchios for its maneuveurs (Michael Dobbs, "Obama Parses his Words," *Washington Post*, March 3, 2008, http://blog.washingtonpost.com/fact-checker/2008/03/obama_parses_his_words.html).

33. Both YouTube and Nexis records of this event indicate that Obama instead said "Come on now. I mean I just answered like eight questions" (*Anderson Cooper 360 Degrees*, CNN, March 3, 2008; "Obama Avoids Answering about Rezko," YouTube, March 3, 2008, http://www.youtube.com/watch?v=rbkhzsTwz_g&feature=player_embedded).

34. Aswini Anburajan, "Obama Tangles with the Press," MSNBC'S First Read, March 3, 2008, http://firstread.msnbc.msn.com/archive/2008/03/03/726268.aspx

35. Dan Balz and Haynes Johnson, *The Battle for America 2008* (New York: Penguin Group, 2009): 164.

36. Democratic Presidential Candidates Debate, ABC, Manchester, New Hampshire, January 5, 2008.

37. Susan T. Fiske, Amy J. C. Cuddy, Peter Glick, and Jun Xu, "A Model of (Often Mixed) Stereotype Content: Competence and Warmth Respectively Follow from Perceived Status and Competition," *Journal of Personality and Social Psychology*, 82, 6 (2002): 878–902.

38. David Axelrod, "Campaign Organization and Strategy," in *Electing the President 2008: The Annenberg Election Debriefing*, edited by Kathleen Hall Jamieson (Philadelphia: University of Pennsylvania Press, 2009): 72.

39. "Michelle Obama: 'Proud' vs. 'Really Proud,'" YouTube, http://www.youtube.com/watch?v=EGjR81pFJI4

40. Ibid.

41. Jake Tapper, "Michelle Obama: 'For the First Time in My Adult Lifetime, I'm Really Proud of My Country,'" Political Punch, ABC, http://blogs.abcnews.com/politicalpunch/2008/02/michelle-obam-1.html

42. Cf. Evan Thomas, "Alienated in the USA," *Newsweek,* March 13, 2008, http://www.newsweek.com/id/123024

43. ABC News first aired the footage including the statement "god damn America" during *Good Morning America* on March 13, 2008. The day before, a number of shows on Fox played tape of Wright saying, "Barack knows what it means to be a black man living in a country and a culture that is controlled by rich white people. Hillary can never know that. Hillary ain't never been called a nigger!" The Fox segments included a second clip in which the minister said, "Bill did us just like he did Monica Lewinsky. He was riding dirty!" (*Special Report with Brit Hume,* March 12, 2008).

44. "Obama Weathers the Wright Storm, Clinton Faces Credibility Problem," The Pew Research Center for the People and the Press, March 27, 2008, http://people-press.org/report/407/

45. Sarah Wheaton, "Your Tube."

46. Bill McInturff, "The Role of Polling," in *Electing the President 2008: The Annenberg Election Debriefing,* edited by Kathleen Hall Jamieson (Philadelphia: University of Pennsylvania Press, 2009): 31.

47. Our Country Deserves Better, "Different Values," October 13, 2008.

48. Pennsylvania Republican Party, "Obama Consider This," November 1, 2008.

49. Judicial Confirmation Network, "Choose 60," October 2, 2008.

50. See Martin Gilens, *Why Americans Hate Welfare: Race, Media, and the Politics of Antipoverty* (Chicago: University of Chicago Press, 1999); David O. Sears, Jim Sidanius and Lawrence Bobo, *Racialized Politics: The Debate about Racism in America* (Chicago: University of Chicago Press, 2000); Lawrence Bobo, "Race and Beliefs about Affirmative Action: Assessing the Effects of Interests, Group Threat, Ideology and Racism," in *Racialized Politics: The Debate about Racism in America,* edited by David O. Sears, Jim Sidanius, and Lawrence Bobo (Chicago: University of Chicago Press, 2000): 137–64.

51. Tali Mendelberg, *The Race Card: Campaign Strategy, Implicit Messages, and the Norm of Equality* (Princeton, N.J., Princeton University Press, 2001). This finding is called into question by two randomized experiments conducted by Gregory A. Huber and John S. Lapinski (see "The 'Race Card' Revisited: Assessing Racial Priming in Policy Contests," *American Journal of Political Science* 50, 2 [April 2006]: 421–40). That study found that "individuals do tend to reject explicit appeals outright" but also finds that "implicit appeals are no more effective than explicit ones in priming racial resentment in opinion formation." It concludes as well that "education moderates both the accessibility of racial predispositions and message acceptance" (p. 421).

52. Tali Mendelberg, *The Race Card;* Nicholas A. Valentino, Vincent L. Hutchings, and Ismail K. White, "Cues that Matter: How Political Ads Prime Racial Attitudes during Campaigns," *American Political Science Review* 96 (2002): 75–90.

53. Jon Hurwitz and Mark Peffley, "Playing the Race Card in the Post-Willie Horton Era," *Public Opinion Quarterly* 69, 1 (2005): 99–112.

54. Anita Huslin, "On the Outside Now, Watching Fannie Falter," *Washington Post,* July 16, 2008, D01.

55. McCain-Palin 2008, "Advice," September 20, 2008.

56. Rightchange, "Fighting," October 3, 2008.

57. Rightchange, "Fought Reform," October 3, 2008.

58. Our Country Deserves Better, "Ayers Wright Kilpatrick 60," October 23, 2008.

59. National Rifle Association, "Intruder SP," October 31, 2008.

60. For a study of "welfare" as a race-coded concept see Martin Gilens, "'Race Coding' and White Opposition to Welfare," *American Political Science Review* 90 (1996): 593–604. See also Mark Peffley, Jon Hurwitz and Paul Sniderman, "Racial Stereotypes and Whites' Political Views of Blacks in the Context of Welfare and Crime," *American Journal of Political Science* 41 (1997): 30–60.

61. Obama for America, "Dignity," June 30, 2008.

62. Obama for America, "Education," November 16, 2007.

63. Our Country Deserves Better, "Different Values," October 13, 2008.

64. Our Country Deserves Better, "Patriotism Problem 60," October 22, 2008.

65. Our Country Deserves Better, "Shameful 60," October 14, 2008.

66. Julie Bosman, "Palin Plays to Conservative Base in Florida Rallies," *New York Times,* October 8, 2008, A20.

67. *Anderson Cooper 360°,* CNN, October 24, 2008.

68. Michael Cooper, "Palin, On Offensive, Attacks Obama," *New York Times,* October 5, 2008, A31.

69. The advertisement "624787" first aired March 31, 2008:

JOHN MCCAIN: "Keep that faith. Keep your courage. Stick together. Stay strong. Do not yield. Stand up. We're Americans. And we'll never surrender.

ANNOUNCER: What must a president believe about us? About America? That she is worth protecting? That liberty is priceless? Our people, honorable? Our future, prosperous, remarkable and free? And, what must we believe about that president? What does he think? Where has he been? Has he walked the walk?

INTERVIEWER: "What is your rank?"

JOHN MCCAIN: "Lieutenant Commander in the Navy."

INTERVIEWER: "And your official number?"

JOHN MCCAIN: "624787"

ANNOUNCER: John McCain. The American president Americans have been waiting for.

JOHN MCCAIN: "I'm John McCain and I approve this message."

GRAPHIC: Paid for by John McCain 2008. Approved by John McCain.

(*Electing the President 2008: The Annenberg Election Debriefing,* edited by Kathleen Hall Jamieson [Philadelphia: University of Pennsylvania Press, 2009]: 110–11).

70. "In the blogosphere, there was this whole thing about our tag line that said 'the American President America's been waiting for.' Bloggers said, 'Oh, they're saying he's a Muslim and he's born in a foreign country.' Where that came from was, frankly, totally me. I'm showing my cards here. 'We are the ones we've been waiting for?' Instead I said, 'The president we've been waiting for.' But when Powers Boothe, who was the voiceover, was in the booth, the rhythm was wrong on it. And so I added the 'American' president America's been waiting for. That was really the basis for it'" (Chris Mottola, "Advertising," in *Electing the President 2008: The Annenberg Election Debriefing,* edited by Kathleen Hall Jamieson [Philadelphia: University of Pennsylvania Press, 2009]: 111).

71. Julie Bosman, "Palin Plays to Conservative Base in Florida Rallies."

72. "Dishonorable," FactCheck.org, October 6, 2008, http://www.factcheck.org/elections-2008/dishonorable.html

73. NAES08 telephone survey, 10/15/08 to 11/3/08. $N = 3,681$

74. John McCain 2008, "Housing Problem," August 22, 2008.

75. The Claims/Deception Survey, sponsored by the Annenberg Public Policy Center, obtained telephone interviews with a nationally representative sample of 3,008 adults living in continental United States telephone households. The survey was conducted by Princeton Survey Research International. The interviews were conducted in English by Princeton Data Source, LLC from November 5 to November 18, 2008. The interview averaged 31 minutes in length. Statistical results are weighted to correct known demographic discrepancies. The margin of sampling error for the complete set of weighted data is ±2.3%.

76. There, Clinton said that she was fighting bad Republican ideas "when you were practicing law and representing your contributor, Rezko, in his slum landlord business in inner-city Chicago." Democratic Presidential Candidates Debate, Myrtle Beach, S.C., January 21, 2008.

77. Republican National Committee, "Chicago Way," October 10, 2008.

78. National Republican Trust PAC, "Licenses," October 17, 2008.

79. Let Freedom Ring, "Puzzle 60," October 29, 2008.

80. Let Freedom Ring, "Trust 60," October 29, 2008.

81. Annenberg Claims/Deception Survey, weighted data. The Annenberg Public Policy Center Claims/Deception Survey was first conducted in 2004. For reports based on this data set, see Bruce W. Hardy and Kathleen H. Jamieson, "Unmasking Deception: The Capacity, Disposition, and Challenges Facing the Press," in *The Politics of News: The News of Politics* (2nd ed.), edited by Doris A. Graber, Denis McQuail, and Pippa Norris (Washington, D.C.: CQ Press, 2007): 117–38; Kathleen Hall Jamieson and Joseph N. Cappella, *Echo Chamber: Rush Limbaugh and the Conservative Media Establishment* (New York: Oxford University Press): 212, 229–36.

82. *Lou Dobbs Tonight,* CNN, October 10, 2008.

83. Colin Powell, *Meet the Press*, NBC, October 19, 2008.

84. Colin Powell, *CNN Newsroom*, CNN, October 19, 2008.

85. Exact question wording of the dependent variables in the regression: (1) Could you tell me what you think Barack Obama's religion is? (2) Senator Barack Obama is nearly half Arab. How truthful do you think that statement is? Would you say it is very truthful, somewhat truthful, not too truthful, or not truthful at all?) (3) Barack Obama pals around with terrorists. How truthful do you think that statement is? Would you say it is very truthful, somewhat truthful, not too truthful, or not truthful at all? (4) How close do you think the relationship between Senator Obama and William Ayers was? Do you think they were very close, somewhat close, or not close at all? (5) Senator Obama was able to buy his house because a man named Tony Rezko purchased the lot next door at full price. How truthful do you think that statement is? Would you say it is very truthful, somewhat truthful, not too truthful, or not truthful at all?

86. When explicitly asked about his racial identity, Obama told Steve Kroft of *60 Minutes* on February 6, 2007, "I think if you look African-American in this society, you're treated as an African-American. And when you're a child in particular, that is how you begin to identify yourself. At least that's what I felt comfortable identifying myself as."

87. Obama for America, "The Country I Love 60," June 20, 2008.

88. Michelle Obama in speech at Democratic National Convention, Denver, Colorado, August 26, 2008.

89. Obama for America, "Strickland," October 18, 2008.

90. Obama for America, "Mother General," September 9, 2008.

91. Obama for America, "Choices RI," February 17, 2008; Obama for America, "Choices OH," February 19, 2008.

92. Obama for America, "Inspiring 60," February 19, 2008.

93. Obama for America, "Caroline," January 30, 2008.

94. Susan T. Fiske, Hilary B. Bergsieker, Ann Marie Russell and Lyle Williams, "Images of Black Americans," *Du Bois Review: Social Science Research on Race* 6 (2009): 83–101, http://journals.cambridge.org/action/displayFulltext?type=6&fid=5884268&jid=DBR&v olumeId=6&issueId=01&aid=5884264&fulltextType=RA&fileId=S1742058X0909002X# ref025

95. These questions were developed by Annenberg School for Communication graduate student Seth Goldman. Exact question wording: "I'm going to read you some statements. For each one, please tell me to what extent you agree or disagree with it. Do you think black elected officials are more likely to 1) Favor blacks for government jobs over white applicants 2) Support government spending that favors blacks 3) Give special favors to the black community." (Alpha = .877).

96. For 2004: "Election Results," CNN, http://www.cnn.com/ELECTION/2004/pages/results/

For 2008: "Election Center 2008," CNN, http://www.cnn.com/ELECTION/2008/

97. "Election Results 2008," *New York Times,* http://elections.nytimes.com/2008/results/president/national-exit-polls.html

98. Chuck Todd and Sheldon Gawiser, *How Barack Obama Won* (New York: Random House, 2009): 42.

CHAPTER 5

1. Dan Harris, "Record Price; Through the Roof," *Evening News*, ABC, May 19, 2008.

2. Brian Williams, "Gas, Food Prices Rise; Home Prices Fall," *NBC Nightly News,* NBC, February 27, 2008.

3. Dan Harris, *World News with Charles Gibson*, ABC, April 28, 2008.

4. *This Week with George Stephanopoulos,* ABC News, May 4, 2008.

5. "Candidates Clash on Gas Tax Holiday," CNN, April 29, 2008, http://www.cnn.com/2008/POLITICS/04/29/campaign.wrap/index.html

6. NPR News Blog, "Clinton Support Gas Tax Holiday Because of 'Leadership,'" May 1, 2008, http://www.npr.org/blogs/news/2008/05/clinton_support_gas_tax_holida.html

7. Joseph Doyle Jr., and Krislert Samphantharak, "$2.00 Gas! Studying the Effects of a Gas Tax Moratorium," *National Bureau of Economic Research,* May 2006, http://www.nber.org/papers/w12266.pdf?new_window=1

8. "A Holiday from Gas Prices?" *Washington Post,* April 29, 2008, http://voices.washingtonpost.com/fact-checker/2008/04/a_holiday_from_gas_prices.html

9. "Candidates Clash on Gas Tax Holiday," CNN, April 29, 2008, http://www.cnn.com/2008/POLITICS/04/29/campaign.wrap/index.html

10. Remarks, "Obama on Gas Tax Holiday: A Gimmick Instead of a Real Solution," Winston-Salem, N.C., April 29, 2008.

11. Hillary Clinton for President, "What's Happened," May 5, 2008.

12. Brian Faler, "Economists Criticize Clinton-McCain Gas Tax Plans," Bloomberg.com, May 5, 2008, http://www.bloomberg.com/apps/news?pid=20601110&sid=aza2XQB.kk0k

13. Ibid.

14. Existing studies also suggest that: when elites are divided along party lines, the public becomes polarized; the influence of expert opinion on public opinion is reduced if there is disagreement between expert opinion and political elite opinion with the public following the lead of those whose ideology it shares; and citizens' level of disagreement with experts opinion is in part a function of such personal attributes as education, issue knowledge, and personal experience with the issue.

15. In our analysis of the gas tax, we focused on whites only.

16. Matthew Hay Brown, "Reid: No Holiday for the Gas Tax," The Swamp, *Chicago Tribune,* May 6, 2008, http://www.swamppolitics.com/news/politics/blog/2008/05/reid_no_holiday_for_the_gas_ta.html

17. Jonathan Weisman, "Pelosi Comes Out Against Proposed Gas Tax Holiday," The Trail, *Washington Post,* May 1, 2008, http://voices.washingtonpost.com/44/2008/05/01/pelosi_comes_out_against_propo.html

18. "Over a Barrel; Drop in the Bucket," *World News with Charles Gibson,* ABC, May 16, 2008.

19. Christopher Joyce, "Candidates Clash on Impact of Offshore Drilling," NPR, July 16, 2008, http://www.npr.org/templates/story/story.php?storyId=92570077

20. Sheryl Gay Stolberg, "Bush Will Seek to End Offshore Oil Drilling Ban," *New York Times,* June 18, 2008.

21. Jad Mouawad, "Oil Prices Take a Nerve-Rattling Jump Past $138," *New York Times,* June 7, 2008, http://www.nytimes.com/2008/06/07/business/070il.html

22. "Year-End Review of Markets and Finance: June 10," *Wall Street Journal,* January 2, 2009, R10

23. Brian Williams, *NBC Nightly News,* NBC, June 6, 2008.

24. Michael D. Shear and Juliet Eilperin, "McCain seeks to End Offshore Drilling Ban," *Washington Post,* June 17, 2008, www.washingtonpost.com/wp-dyn/content/article/2008/06/16/AR2008061602731.html

25. Ed Hornick and Alexander Marquardt, "Obama Says Offshore Drilling Stance Nothing New," CNN, August 3, 2008, http://www.cnn.com/2008/POLITICS/08/02/campaign.wrap/index.html

26. McCain for President, "Purpose," June 26, 2008.

27. Ibid.

28. John McCain 2008, "Celeb," July 30, 2008.

29. Obama for America, "New Energy," July 8, 2008.

30. Obama for America, "New Energy Rev," July 30, 2008.

31. *Anderson Cooper 360°*, CNN, July 30, 2008.

32. Michael C. Bender, "Obama Would Consider Off-Shore Drilling as Part of Comprehensive Energy Plan," *Palm Beach Post*, August 1, 2008, http://www.palmbeachpost.com/state/content/state/epaper/2008/08/01/08010bama1.html

33. Ibid.

34. Mike Glover, "Obama Shifts on Offshore Oil Drilling," *Associated Press*, August 1, 2008.

35. Ed Hornick and Alexander Marquardt, "Obama Says Offshore Drilling Stance Nothing New."

36. Andrea Mitchell, "McCain, Obama Spar on Energy Policies; Iraqi Money in American Banks Due to Oil," *NBC Nightly News with Brian Williams*, NBC, August 5, 2008.

37. Kent Garber, "Obama Shows New Openness to Offshore Drilling," *U.S. News and World Report*, August 4, 2008, http://www.usnews.com/articles/news/campaign-2008/2008/08/04/obama-shows-new-openness-to-offshore-oil-drilling.html

38. "Inflation up 5.6 percent in July," *NBC Nightly News with Brian Williams*, NBC, August 14, 2008.

39. David Axelrod, "Campaign Organization and Strategy," in *Electing the President 2008: The Annenberg Election Debriefing*, edited by Kathleen Hall Jamieson (Philadelphia: University of Pennsylvania Press, 2009): 71.

40. Third Presidential Debate, Hofstra University, Hempstead, N.Y., October 15, 2008.

41. Ibid.

42. NAES08 telephone survey (weighted), 8/18/08 to 8/22/08. $N = 1,194$.

43. "Year–End Review of Markets and Finance, July 3, July 10," *Wall Street Journal*, January 2, 2009, R11.

44. Ibid., R12.

45. Nicolle Wallace served as a senior advisor for John McCain during the 2008 election. Prior to joining the campaign, she worked as a political analyst at CBS News and served as director of communications for the White House from January 2005 to June 2006.

46. Nicolle Wallace, "The Vice Presidential Campaign," in *Electing the President 2008: The Annenberg Election Debriefing*, edited by Kathleen Hall Jamieson (Philadelphia: University of Pennsylvania Press, 2009): 13–44.

47. "Inside Obama's Sweeping Victory," Pew Research Center for People and the Press, November 5, 2008, http://pewresearch.org/pubs/1023/exit-poll-analysis-2008

CHAPTER 6

1. Statement from McCain Campaign on Sen. Obama's Selection of Sen. Biden as Running Mate from "John McCain 2008—Press Office," August 23, 2008.

2. McCain for President, "Joe Biden on Barack Obama," August 25, 2008.

3. Michael Cooper, "At 70, McCain Takes on Talk of His Age," *New York Times*, August 25, 2007, http://www.nytimes.com/2007/08/25/us/politics/25mccain.html?_r=2&oref=slogin

4. *The Daily Show with Jon Stewart*, Comedy Central, August 2, 2005.

5. Adam Nagourney and Jeff Zeleny, "Obama Chooses Biden as Running Mate," *New York Times,* August 23, 2008.

6. Margaret Talev and David Lightman, "Obama Names Sen. Joe Biden as His Vice-Presidential Pick," *McClatchy Newspapers,* August 23, 2008.

7. *Good Morning America,* ABC, August 23, 2008.

8. Ron Fournier, "Analysis: Biden Pick Shows Lack of Confidence," *Associated Press,* August 23, 2008.

9. Kyle Trygstad, "Obama Goes with Biden," Real Clear Politics, *Time,* August 23, 2008, http://realclearpolitics.blogs.time.com/2008/08/23/obamabiden_08/

10. A comparison of NAES08 data (weighted) from before the Republican convention (8/28 to 8/31) to after the convention (9/5 to 9/10) shows that the public increased its perceptions of McCain's experience from 6.6 to 6.9 on a 10-point scale ($t = -3.23$, df $= 2,566$, $p < .01$) and judgment from 5.9 to 6.2 on a 10-point scale ($t = -2.57$, df $= 2,534$, $p < .05$). The data also show that McCain had higher ratings than Obama on "experience" before and after the Republican convention ($t = 11.47$, df $= 1,991$, $p < .001$ and $t = 19.19$, df $= 3,142$, $p < .001$, respectively). Before the Republican convention, McCain and Obama received statistically comparable ratings on "judgment." After the convention, McCain received statistically higher ratings than Obama on "judgment" ($t = 4.31$, df $= 3,103$, $p < .001$).

11. Barack Obama, CNN/YouTube Presidential Debate, CNN, Charleston, S.C., July 23, 2007.

12. Barack Obama, *Meet the Press,* NBC, November 11, 2007; Barack Obama, *Situation Room,* CNN, February 4, 2008.

13. David Axelrod, "Campaign Organization and Strategy," in *Electing the President 2008: The Annenberg Election Debriefing,* edited by Kathleen Hall Jamieson (Philadelphia: University of Pennsylvania Press, 2009): 73.

14. *The Tonight Show with Jay Leno,* NBC, August 26, 2008.

15. Writing on WashingtonPost.com, Eugene Robinson noted, "I'll leave it to Joe Biden to explain (or figure out) why he used 'clean' as one of a logorrheic string of adjectives describing his Senate colleague Barack Obama. I'm not sure his initial revision and extension of his remarks—that he meant 'clean as a whistle'—get him off the hook. Just a suggestion, but Biden might fall back to 'clean as the Board of Health,' meaning sharply dressed; the last time I saw Obama he was, indeed, wearing an impeccable navy suit" ("An Inarticulate Kick-Off," February 2, 2007, http://www.washingtonpost.com/wp-dyn/content/article/2007/02/01/AR2007020101495.html).

16. Jason Horowitz, "Biden Unbound: Lays into Clinton, Obama, Edwards," *New York Observer,* January 31, 2007, updated February 4, 2007, http://www.observer.com/2007/politics/biden-unbound-lays-clinton-obama-edwards

17. In response, the Obama campaign issued a statement from the Illinois senator saying, "I didn't take Senator Biden's comments personally, but obviously they were historically inaccurate. African-American presidential candidates like Jesse Jackson, Shirley Chisholm, Carol Moseley Braun and Al Sharpton gave a voice to many important issues through their campaigns, and no one would call them inarticulate." (Statement released January 31, 2007).

18. Rush Limbaugh, on *World News with Charles Gibson,* ABC, January 31, 2008.

19. Biden remarks, C-SPAN, June 17, 2006, http://www.c-spanarchives.org/library/index.php?main_page=product_video_info&products_id=193258–1

20. Biden remarks, *Fox News Sunday*, Fox News Network, August 27, 2006.

21. Massimo Calabresi, "Behind Obama's Bet on Biden," *Time*, August 23, 2008, http://www.time.com/time/politics/article/0,8599,1835478,00.html

22. Michael Saul, "Foreign Policy? Joe Biden's No Schmo," *New York Daily News*, August 23, 2008, 4.

23. Howard Fineman, "No Ordinary Joe: The Politics of the Veep Pick—and What He Brings to the Party," *Newsweek*, August 23, 2008.

24. Mark Halperin, "Halperin on Biden: Pros And the Cons," *Time*, August 23, 2008, http://www.time.com/time/world/article/0,8599,1835480,00.html

25. *The Tonight Show with Jay Leno*, NBC, January 15, 2006.

26. Democratic Primary Presidential Debate, MSNBC, Orangeburg, South Carolina, April 26, 2007.

27. McCain for President, "Passed Over," August 25, 2008.

28. Joe Biden, remarks at rally in Nashua, N.H., September 10, 2008, http://www.youtube.com/watch?v=9qzyLc30JC4

29. Jill Serjeant, "John McCain Speech Draws Record TV Ratings," *Reuters*, September 5, 2008, http://www.reuters.com/article/politicsNews/idUSN0439266820080905; Leigh Holmwood, "Sarah Palin Republican Convention Speech Watched by 37 Million in US," *Guardian*, September 5, 2008, http://www.guardian.co.uk/media/2008/sep/05/ustelevision.tvratings

30. Steve Gorman, "Obama Acceptance Speech Believed to Set TV Record," *Reuters*, August 29, 2008, http://www.reuters.com/article/vcCandidateFeed1/idUSN2948169620080829

31. David Axelrod, "Campaign Organization and Strategy," in *Electing the President 2008: The Annenberg Election Debriefing*, edited by Kathleen Hall Jamieson (Philadelphia: University of Pennsylvania Press, 2009): 73.

32. Ibid.

33. Bill Clinton, remarks at the Democratic National Convention, Denver, Colo., August 27, 2008.

34. Joe Biden, remarks at the Democratic National Convention, Denver, Colo., August 27, 2008.

35. Ibid.

36. Ibid.

37. JibJab, "Time for Some Campaignin,'" http://www.youtube.com/watch?v=adc3MSS5Ydc

38. Joe Biden, remarks at Democratic National Convention.

39. Ibid.

40. Peter S. Canellos, "In Bid to Capture Lapsed Democrats, Biden Casts Self as 'Just Your Average' Joe," *Boston Globe*, August 28, 2008.

41. "Rove at RNC: Biden a 'Big Blowhard Doofus,'" *Huffington Post*, September 1, 2008, http://www.huffingtonpost.com/2008/09/01/rove-at-rnc-biden-a-big-b_n_122998.html

42. Not only do we control for sociopolitical demographic variables and overall news media use, we also include Obama and McCain favorability ratings. This means that the relationship outlined here is not a function of selective exposure with Biden fans and Obama supporters more likely to watch the Biden speech.

43. Barack Obama, remarks at the Democratic National Convention, Denver, Colo., August 28, 2008.

44. Comparing data collected five days before the Democratic convention to the five days after the convention reveals that the increase in perceptions of Obama being "patriotic" was statistically significant ($p < .001$). Despite the significant increase, the Democratic aspirant's patriotism ratings were significantly lower than his Republican opponent's ($p < .001$).

45. NAES08 telephone survey. 9/5/08 to 9/10/08. $N = 1,250$. The difference between the groups was significant ($p < .001$). The difference between Obama speech viewers and nonreviews was robust and detected when several demographic characteristics, party identification, ideology, and media variables were taken into consideration.

46. McCain for President, "Convention Night," August 28, 2008.

47. The statement read: "Governor Palin is a tough executive who has demonstrated during her time in office that she is ready to be president. She has brought Republicans and Democrats together within her Administration and has a record of delivering on the change and reform that we need in Washington. Governor Palin has challenged the influence of the big oil companies while fighting for the development of new energy resources. She leads a state that matters to every one of us—Alaska has significant energy resources and she has been a leader in the fight to make America energy independent. In Alaska, Governor Palin challenged a corrupt system and passed a landmark ethics reform bill. She has actually used her veto and cut budgetary spending. She put a stop to the 'bridge to nowhere' that would have cost taxpayers $400 million dollars. As the head of Alaska's National Guard and as the mother of a soldier herself, Governor Palin understands what it takes to lead our nation and she understands the importance of supporting our troops. Governor Palin has the record of reform and bipartisanship that others can only speak of. Her experience in shaking up the status quo is exactly what is needed in Washington today."

48. "Obama Campaign Highlights Palin's 'Zero' Experience," Breitbart, August 29, 2008, http://www.breitbart.com/article.php?id=080829171140.5123i228&show_article=1

49. Sarah Palin, remarks at Republican National Convention, St. Paul, Minn., September 3, 2008.

50. John Heilemann, "The Sixty Day War," *New York Magazine,* September 15, 2008.

51. "Sliming Palin," FactCheck.org, September 8, 2008, http://www.factcheck.org/elections-2008/sliming_palin.html

52. Steve Schmidt, remarks to Katie Couric, "Campaign 08: Republican National Convention," September 2, 2008, docs.cbsconventionpress.com/0902.doc

53. Sarah Palin, remarks at Republican National Convention.

54. "As a Candidate, Yes; As Governor, No," *PolitiFact,* August 30, 2008, http://www.politifact.com/truth-o-meter/statements/680/

55. Stephen Branchflower Report to the Legislative Council, October 10, 2008, http://msnbcmedia.msn.com/i/msnbc/Components/Interactives/Politics/Election2008/branch-flower_report_to_the_legislative_council.pdf

56. "Report of Findings and Recommendations," *State of Alaska Personnel Board,* November 3, 2008, http://media.adn.com/smedia/2008/11/03/12/report-sept12008-complaint.source.prod_affiliate.7.pdf

57. *Anderson Cooper 360°*, CNN, September 1, 2008.

58. Sam Harris, "Palin: Average Isn't Good Enough," *Los Angeles Times*, September 3, 2008, http://www.latimes.com/news/opinion/commentary/la-oe-harris3–2008sep03,0,3801278.story

59. Todd S. Purdum, "It Came From Wasilla," *Vanity Fair*, August 2009, 97.

60. Sarah Palin, remarks at Republican National Convention.

61. Ibid.

62. Ibid.

63. Ibid.

64. Ibid.

65. Ibid.

66. "Republican National Convention Coverage," NBC, September 3, 2008.

67. Ibid.

68. *Nightline*, ABC, September 3, 2008.

69. *Morning Joe*, MSNBC, September 4, 2008.

70. "Ms. Palin's Introduction," *Washington Post*, September 4, 2008, A14.

71. "CNN Election Center," CNN, September 3, 2008.

72. "MSNBC Special," MSNBC, September 3, 2008.

73. Tom Raum and Liz Sidoti, "Palin Delivers Star-Turning Performance for GOP," *Associated Press*, September 4, 2008.

74. John Dickerson, "A Pit Bull with Lipstick," *Slate*, September 4, 2008, http://www.slate.com/id/2199250/

75. "CNN Election Center," CNN, September 3, 2008.

76. "Ms. Palin's Introduction," *Washington Post*.

77. Michael D. Shear, "Palin Comes Out Fighting," *Washington Post*, September 4, 2008, A01.

78. Jeanne Cummings and Beth Frerking, "Palin Wows GOP, Puts Dems on Notice," Politico, September 4, 2008, http://www.politico.com/news/stories/0908/13147.html

79. "Palin Assails Critics And Electrifies Party," *New York Times*, September 4, 2008.

80. A significant downward linear trend was detected in perceptions of Palin's readiness to be president from August 31 to November 3 (R-square = .385, $p <.001$).

81. Susan Milligan, "A Pledge of Bipartisanship," *Boston Globe*, September 5, 2008.

82. "CNN Election Center," CNN, September 4, 2008.

83. Robert Barnes, "'Change Is Coming,' McCain Says," *Washington Post*, September 5, 2008.

84. Gerald F. Seib, "McCain Vows End to 'Rancor,' Betting on Maverick Appeal," *Wall Street Journal*, September 5, 2008, A1.

85. David Brooks, "A Glimpse of the New," *New York Times*, September 5, 2008.

86. "CNN Election Center," CNN, September 4, 2008.

87. Steve Schmidt, "Campaign Organization and Strategy," in *Electing the President 2008: The Annenberg Election Debriefing*, edited by Kathleen Hall Jamieson (Philadelphia: University of Pennsylvania Press, 2009): 60.

CHAPTER 7

1. Cf: Danny M. Adkison, "The Electoral Significance of the Vice Presidency," *Presidential Studies Quarterly* 12 (1982): 330–336.

2. For a discussion of the strategic importance of balance in selection of a vice presidential nominee see: Marie D. Natoli, *American Prince, American Pauper: The Contemporary Vice Presidency in Perspective* (Westport, Conn.: Greenwood Press, 1985); Michael Nelson, *A Heartbeat Away: Twentieth Century Fund's Taskforce on the Vice Presidency* (New York: Priority Press, 1988).

3. See Danny M. Adkison, "The Electoral Significance of the Vice Presidency."

4. Michael Nelson, "Choosing the Vice President," *PS: Political Science & Politics* 21 (1988): 858–868.

5. Nelson Polsby and Aaron Wildavsky, *Presidential Elections: Contemporary Strategies of American Electoral Politics,* 8th ed. (New York: Free Press, 1991): 168.

6. Nicolle Wallace, "The Vice Presidential Campaign," in *Electing the President 2008: The Annenberg Election Debriefing,* edited by Kathleen Hall Jamieson (Philadelphia: University of Pennsylvania Press, 2009): 27.

7. The impact on the home state of the vice presidential nominee however may be smaller than many assume, where the presidential candidate may gain a home state advantage of 4 percent (Michael Lewis-Beck and Tom W. Rice, "Localism in Presidential Elections: The Home State Advantage," *American Journal of Political Science* 27 [1983]: 548–556). Dudley and Rapoport conclude that from 1884–1984, "On average the vice-presidential candidate gains only about. 3 percent more in his home state than expected" (Robert L. Dudley and Ronald B. Rapoport, "Vice-Presidential Candidates and the Home State Advantage: Playing Second Banana at Home and on the Road," *American Journal of Political Science* 33 [1989]: 537–540 at 537). Examining the period from 1948 to 1972, Rosenstone found that voters in the home state of the vice presidential nominee were 2.5 percent more disposed than they otherwise would have been to give their votes to the ticket (Stephen Rosenstone, *Forecasting Presidential Elections,* New Haven, Conn.: Yale University Press, 1983: 87ff.)

8. Martin P. Wattenberg, "The Role of Vice Presidential Candidate Ratings in Presidential Voting Behavior," *American Politics Research* 23 (1995): 504–514 at 507.

9. Martin P. Wattenberg, "The Role of Vice Presidential Candidate Ratings in Presidential Voting Behavior," 504–514 at 508.

10. Sarah Palin's second televised interview was on Fox's *Hannity & Colmes* program. The segments aired September 17–18, 2008.

11. "Sarah the Unready," September 13, 2008, http://rossdouthat.theatlantic.com/archives/2008/09/sarah_the_unready.php

12. Joseph Morton, "Hagel Doubts Palin Is Ready," *Omaha World-Herald (Nebraska),* September 8, 2008.

13. Jacques Steinberg, "Palin Reviews Are In, And Gibson Got An…" *New York Times,* September 13, 2008.

14. *World News with Charles Gibson,* ABC, September 11, 2008.

15. Palin would have been correct to say that Alaska produces just over 14 percent of all the *oil produced* in the U.S., leaving out imports and leaving out other forms of power. According to the federal government's Energy Information Administration, Alaskan wells

produced 263.6 million barrels of oil in 2007, or 14.3 percent of the total U.S. production of 1.8 billion barrels. ("Energetically Wrong," FactCheck.org, September 12, 2008, http://www.factcheck.org/elections-2008/energetically_wrong.html).

16. September 17, 2007. See also Michael Abramowitz, "Many Versions of 'Bush Doctrine': Palin's Confusion in Interview Understandable, Experts Say" *Washington Post*, September 13, 2008, http://www.washingtonpost.com/wp-dyn/content/article/2008/09/12/AR2008091203324.html

17. Interview with Katie Couric, *CBS Evening News*, CBS, September 30, 2008.

18. *Late Night with Conan O'Brien*, NBC, September 29, 2008.

19. *Late Show with David Letterman*, CBS, October 1, 2008.

20. *The Jay Leno Show*, NBC, October 1, 2008.

21. Our ability to include a robust set of controls was constrained by the small number of CBS viewers in our sample during the time frame under investigation. Consequently, it is possible that the finding is the result of selective exposure to the content by those who had unfavorable dispositions toward Palin at the outset.

22. "That's why I say I, like every American I'm speaking with, we're ill about this position that we have been put in where it is the taxpayers looking to bail out. But ultimately what the bailout does is help those who are concerned about the health care reform that is needed to help shore up our economy, helping the—it's got to be all about job creation, too, shoring up our economy and putting it back on the right track." (Sarah Palin, *CBS Evening News*, September 24, 2008).

23. Keith Olbermann, *Countdown*, MSNBC, September 29, 2008.

24. Ibid.

25. Interview with Katie Couric, *CBS Evening News*, CBS, September 25, 2008, http://www.cbsnews.com/stories/2008/09/25/eveningnews/main4479062.shtml

26. Chris Weigant, "My 2008 McLaughlin Awards Part 2," December 26, 2008, http://www.huffingtonpost.com/chris-weigant/my-2008-mclaughlin-awards_b_153636.html, Retrieved January 16, 2009.

27. Mike Snider, "Late-Night Laughs Capture the Online Vote," *USA Today*, October 28, 2008, D1.

28. Will Carter, "No Need for a Recount Here. Political Comedy Is Winning, Big Time," *New York Times*, October 9, 2008.

29. Mike Snider, "Late-Night Laughs Capture the Online Vote."

30. Kathleen Parker, "The Palin Problem," *Washington Post*, September 28, 2008, http://www.washingtonpost.com/wp-dyn/content/article/2008/09/26/AR2008092603268.html

31. George Will, "Palin Is Not Qualified," *Huffington Post*, September 30, 2008, http://www.huffingtonpost.com/2008/09/30/george-will-palin-is-not_n_130647.html?view=print

32. *Good Morning America*, ABC, October 2, 2008.

33. *Exxon Shipping Co. et al. v. Baker et al.*

34. Christopher Maag, "Supreme Court Decision on Exxon Valdez Damages a Blow to Alaskans," *New York Times*, June 26, 2008, http://www.nytimes.com/2008/06/26/world/americas/26iht-alaska.4.14027236.html

35. Interview with Katie Couric, *CBS Evening News*, CBS, October 1, 2008.

36. McCain-Palin 2008, "Embarrass," (Web ad), October 2, 2008, http://www.you-tube.com/watch?v=p7RJAnefJKA&feature=channel_page

37. Vice Presidential Debate, Washington University, St. Louis, Mo., October 2, 2008.

38. U.S. Senate Roll Call Votes 106th Congress—1st Session, S.900, http://www.senate.gov/legislative/LIS/roll_call_lists/roll_call_vote_cfm.cfm?congress=106&session=1&vote=00354

39. Ibid.

40. Ibid.

41. Ibid.

42. NAES08 telephone survey, 10/3/08 to 10/6/08. $N = 980$.

43. "CBS Special Coverage," CBS, October 2, 2008.

44. "MSNBC Special Coverage," MSNBC, October 2, 2008.

45. In response to an exchange on energy, she also uttered her most famous line in the October 2 vice presidential debate:

> The chant is "drill, baby, drill." And that's what we hear all across this country in our rallies because people are so hungry for those domestic sources of energy to be tapped into. They know that even in my own energy-producing state we have billions of barrels of oil and hundreds of trillions of cubic feet of clean, green natural gas. And we're building a nearly $40 billion natural gas pipeline which is North America's largest and most expensive infrastructure project ever to flow those sources of energy into hungry markets.
>
> Barack Obama and Senator Biden, you've said no to everything in trying to find a domestic solution to the energy crisis that we're in. You even called drilling—safe, environmentally friendly drilling offshore as raping the outer continental shelf.
>
> There—with new technology, with tiny footprints even on land, it is safe to drill and we need to do more of that. But also in that "all of the above" approach that Senator McCain supports, the alternative fuels will be tapped into: the nuclear, the clean coal.

46. Opinion, "Palin's Failin': What Is It She Stands For? After Seven Weeks We Don't Know," *Wall Street Journal*, October 17, 2008, http://online.wsj.com/article/SB122419210832542317.html

47. See figure 6.2 in previous chapter.

48. Republican Primary Debate, Columbia, S.C., CNN, February 15, 2000, http://transcripts.cnn.com/TRANSCRIPTS/0002/15/lk1.00.html

49. *Meet the Press*, NBC, October 19, 2008.

50. Jeff Zeleney, "Donation Record as Colin Powell Endorses Obama," *New York Times*, October 20, 2008, A1.

51. "Eight Out of 10 Voters Aware of Powell Endorsement," Gallup Poll, October 22, 2008, http://www.gallup.com/poll/111319/Eight-Voters-Aware-Powell-Endorsement.aspx. Retrieved January 12, 2009.

52. *Washington Post*, October 22, 2008, http://voices.washingtonpost.com/behind-the-numbers/2008/10/this_race_goes_to_11.html

53. Data were weighted for the population estimate of knowing who Powell endorsed, as all respondents were asked this question.

54. Maumee, Ohio, September 16, 2008, http://www.youtube.com/watch?v=7rXyTRT-NZg&eurl=http%3A%2F%2Fwww%2Eclean%2Dcoal%2Einfo%2Fdrupal%2Fcomment%2Freply%2F991&feature=player_embedded

55. Obama for America, "American Stories and American Solutions," October 29, 2008.

56. Vice Presidential Debate.

57. "Check Point: The Vice-Presidential Debate," The Caucus, *New York Times,* October 2, 2008, http://thecaucus.blogs.nytimes.com/2008/10/02/check-point-the-vice-presidential-debate/

58. Matthew Jaffe, "Biden to Supporters: 'Gird Your Loins,' for the Next President 'It's Like Cleaning Augean Stables," Political Radar, ABC News, October 20, 2008, http://blogs.abcnews.com/politicalradar/2008/10/biden-to-suppor.html

59. *World News Tonight with Charles Gibson,* ABC News, October 21, 2008.

60. Expenditure estimates from CMAG/TNS Media Intelligence.

61. McCain-Palin 2008, "Listen to Biden," October 25, 2008.

62. "Let Freedom Ring: Frank Gaffney & Joe Biden," *National Journal,* October 24, 2008.

63. Obama for America, "Audio Tapes," October 27, 2008.

64. NAES08 telephone survey. Data unweighted. 10/15/08 to 11/3/08. $N = 3{,}785$.

65. NAES08 telephone survey. Data weighted. 12/17/08 to 6/09/08. $N = 2{,}380$

66. Curve estimation analyses confirm that there was a significant linear decline in Palin's favorability ratings across the general election period ($R^2 = .493$, $p < .001$). A linear trend in Biden's favorability ratings was not found.

67. As shown in table 7.2, Palin's favorability ratings fell by 0.33 points on the 10-point favorability scale, while Biden's ratings increased by 0.12 points when the time periods of 9/5/08–10/14/08 and 10/15/08–11/3/08 were compared.

68. Johnston and Thorson (2009) maintain that "each major Palin rating drop precedes a critical drop in McCain vote intentions by one or two days only." We did not find evidence of a two-day lagged effect of Palin favorability on vote preference for McCain noted by Johnston and Thorson. After taking out the cubic trends in the variables, we did find, however, a significant cross-correlation between a one-day lag of Palin favorability and McCain vote preference. In addition, Kenski (forthcoming) found that Palin favorability ratings were significantly associated with McCain vote preference at the individual level when a robust set of controls were taken into consideration. See: Richard Johnston and Emily Thorson, "The Economy, the Candidates, and the 2008 Campaign," paper presented at the Annual Meeting of the American Political Science Association, September 2009; Kate Kenski (forthcoming), "The Palin Effect and Vote Preference in the 2008 Presidential Election," *American Behavioral Scientist.*

69. *Washington Post*/ABC News Poll, November 3, 2008, http://www.washingtonpost.com/wp-srv/politics/documents/postpoll_110308.html

CHAPTER 8

1. In the coming chapters we will suggest that in period four McCain loosened himself somewhat from both of those perceptions; in period five Obama retied the knot

to produce the outcome the political science models had predicted. On Election Day, 63 percent of those leaving voting booths said that economy was the most important issue facing the country. All other issues drew less than 10 percent. Three quarters of the country thought that it was on the wrong track. Two in three disapproved of George W. Bush's performance as president. Those who thought John McCain would continue George W. Bush's policies voted overwhelmingly (90 percent) for Barack Obama ("Inside Obama's Sweeping Victory," Pew Research Center for the People and the Press, November 5, 2008, http://pewresearch.org/pubs/1023/exit-poll-analysis-2008).

2. Bill McInturff, "The Role of Polling," in *Electing the President 2008: The Annenberg Election Debriefing*, edited by Kathleen Hall Jamieson (Philadelphia: University of Pennsylvania Press, 2009): 89.

3. Mark Jurkowitz, "PEJ Campaign Coverage Index: September 8–14, 2008," Project for Excellence in Journalism: Understanding News in the Information Age, http://www.journalism.org/node/12800

4. "2008 Trends," Project for Excellence in Journalism, http://www.stateofthemedia.org/2009/narrative_yearinthenews_intro.php

5. *World News with Charlie Gibson,* ABC, September 15, 2008.

6. *CBS Evening News,* CBS, September 15, 2008.

7. For example, "The Bush/McCain [Social Security] privatization plan. Can you really afford more of the same?" (Obama for America, "Social Security" September 16, 2008); "Three years ago John McCain campaigned for George Bush's plan to risk your Social Security in the stock market…So imagine if McCain and Bush had gotten their way and invested your future retirement benefits at Lehman Brothers. Bankrupt. AIG. Bailed out. Merrill Lynch. Sold. The risk is too great trying four more years of the same" (Obama for America, "Risk," September 30, 2008).

8. Mr. Milhaven: "Does Sarah Palin—John McCain obviously thinks she has the experience to become president of the United States. Do you think she has the experience to run a major company like Hewlett Packard?" Fiorina: "No, I don't. But you know what, that's not what she's running for." (*McGraw Milhaven Show,* KTRS Radio, St. Louis, Missouri, September 16, 2008); "Well, I don't think John McCain could run a major corporation. I don't think Barack Obama could run a major corporation. I don't think Joe Biden could run a major corporation. But on the other hand, a major corporation is not the same as being the president or the vice president of the United States. It is a fallacy to suggest that the country is like a company" (*Andrea Mitchell Reports,* MSNBC, September 16, 2008).

9. FactCheck.org, "Distorting McCain's Remarks," August 19 2008, http://www.factcheck.org/elections-2008/distorting_mccains_remarks.html

10. Obama for America, "Fix the Economy," August 13, 2008.

11. Obama for America, "Out of Touch," August 25, 2008.

12. *Larry King Live,* CNN, September 15, 2008.

13. Peter Baker, "Obama Voices Optimism on the Economy," *New York Times,* March 14, 2009, A10.

14. Ibid.

15. Dan Balz, "McCain's Fundamentals Problem," *Washington Post,* September 17, 2008.

16. Barack Obama, remarks at campaign rally, Grand Junction, Colo., September 15, 2008.

17. Alone among the networks, NBC played an extended segment of the sentence in which the fundamentals statement was cast but attached the word "tried" to his explanation of what he meant, a word choice suggesting the reporter's view that McCain's effort had failed:

JOHN YANG: At John McCain's first postconvention rally without running mate Sarah Palin and without the huge crowds she attracted today, he argued that America's economic glass is half full.

SENATOR JOHN MCCAIN: Our economy, I think, still—the fundamentals of our economy are strong, but these are very, very difficult times.

YANG: Later, in a town hall meeting, McCain tried to explain.

MCCAIN: The American worker, in their innovation, their entrepreneurship, the small business, those are the fundamentals of America, and I think they're strong. (*NBC Nightly News*, NBC, September 15, 2008).

18. John McCain, remarks at campaign rally, Orlando, Fla., September 15, 2008.

19. In one CBS segment aired September 15, 2008, the context was favorable to McCain:

NANCY CORDES (CBS): Stumping in Florida, McCain explained why he considers the economy fundamentally sound.

SENATOR MCCAIN: Our workers have been the strength of our economy and they remain the strength of our economy today. (*CBS Evening News*).

But in a second CBS piece on the same day, Katie Couric translated McCain's qualified statement into an affirmation of the country's fundamental economic strength and paired it with the Obama attack theme "out of touch." "Despite Wall Street woes, John McCain said that the fundamentals of the economy are strong. And that prompted Barack Obama to mock him as out of touch" (*CBS Evening News*, CBS, September 15, 2008).

20. This search was conducted by Annenberg researcher Jackie Dunn.

21. Beginning September 24, Spanish language TV ads in Colorado and New Mexico evoked the numbers of unemployed and children without health insurance before asking, "How is it possible for John McCain to say 'The fundamentals of our economy are strong'?" As the announcer repeated McCain's statement, it was visually reinforced by text reading, "Que los fundamentos de nuestra economia son solidos?" In both radio and TV ads in the battleground states, the Obama campaign cited the unemployment and foreclosure rates, quoted McCain's "fundamentals" statement, and drew the link between Bush and McCain. A Florida TV spot that began airing October 7, for example, concluded, "And McCain promises more of the same failed Bush economic policies that got our economy into this mess in the first place."

22. John McCain, remarks at a campaign rally, Cedar Rapids, Iowa, September 18, 2008.

23. "The president appoints the SEC chairman but cannot fire him" (Stephen Braun and Noam N. Levey, "Seizing on Wall Street's Woes," *Los Angeles Times,* September 19, 2008, A18); "But while the president nominates and the Senate confirms the SEC chair, a commissioner of an independent regulatory commission cannot be removed by the president" (ABC News, "McCain Flub? Republican Says He'd Fire SEC Chair as President," September 18, 2008); Kelly O'Donnell: "That's tricky. While a president can remove the SEC chair for cause, legal authorities say the president cannot simply fire a member of the commission over policy disagreements" (*NBC Nightly News,* September 18, 2008).

24. "If we keep talking about the economic crisis, we're going to lose" (Thomas M. Defrank, "Insults Fly as Barack Obama & John McCain Prepare for Second Debate," *New York Daily News,* October 5, 2008).

25. Jake Tapper and Sunlen Miller, "Obama Attacks McCain's Response to Crisis on Wall Street," Political Punch, ABC, September 16, 2008, http://blogs.abcnews.com/politicalpunch/2008/09/obama-attacks-1.html

26. David Axelrod, "Campaign Organization and Strategy," in *Electing the President 2008: The Annenberg Election Debriefing,* edited by Kathleen Hall Jamieson (Philadelphia: University of Pennsylvania Press, 2009): 75.

27. Barack Obama, *Lou Dobbs Tonight,* CNN, September 15, 2008.

28. Obama for America, "Plan for Change," September 17, 2008.

29. Obama for America, "Mother General," September 30, 2008.

30. Obama for America, "Same Path," September 30, 2008.

31. Nick Timiraos, "Obama Continue Attack on McCain's Economic Credentials," *Wall Street Journal,* September 16, 2008, http://blogs.wsj.com/washwire/2008/09/16/obama-continues-attack-on-mccains-economic-credentials/

32. Maria Gavrilovic, "Obama: McCain Backs Failed Economic Policy," CBS News blog, September 16, 2008, http://www.cbsnews.com/blogs/2008/09/16/politics/fromtheroad/entry4453126.shtml

The same message got through on network broadcast news. On the September 15 broadcast of *CBS Nightly News,* Dean Reynolds reported:

REYNOLDS: In new, more confrontational remarks. Obama tried to yoke John McCain to an economic philosophy that he says has brought America to the brink.

SENATOR OBAMA: Now instead of prosperity trickling down, the pain has trickled up.

REYNOLDS: And he followed that up by questioning McCain's grasp of the nation's number one issue.

SENATOR OBAMA: This morning he said that the fundamentals of the economy are still strong. Senator McCain, what economy are you talking about?

REYNOLDS: The speech featured a long indictment of past McCain positions, including opposition to increases in Social Security and the minimum wage, and it accused him of being a captive of special interests and whose claims to be a change agent are laughable.

SENATOR OBAMA: And if you think those lobbyists are working day and night for John McCain just to put themselves out of business, well, I've got a bridge to sell you up in Alaska.

33. McCain-Palin 2008/RNC, "Dome," September 17, 2008.

34. McCain-Palin 2008/RNC, "Expensive Plans," September 1, 2008.

35. McCain-Palin 2008/RNC, "Ambition," October 10, 2008.

36. Chris Mottola, "Advertising," in *Electing the President 2008: The Annenberg Election Debriefing*, edited by Kathleen Hall Jamieson (Philadelphia: University of Pennsylvania Press, 2009): 114.

37. Ibid., 57.

38. McCain-Palin 2008, "Advice," September 20, 2008.

39. McCain-Palin 2008, "Jim Johnson," September 21, 2008.

40. FactCheck.org found the attack to be inaccurate. (FactCheck.org, "Obama Trade Trickery" September 26, 2008, http://www.factcheck.org/elections-2008/obamas_trade_trickery.html).

41. McCain-Palin 2008/RNC, "Overseas," September 19, 2008.

42. Adam Nagourney, "McCain Pulls Out of Michigan," *New York Times*, October 2, 2008, http://thecaucus.blogs.nytimes.com/2008/10/02/mccain-pulls-out-of-michigan/

43. Bill McInturff, "The Role of Polling," in Electi*ng the President 2008: The Annenberg Election Debriefing*, edited by Kathleen Hall Jamieson (Philadelphia: University of Pennsylvania Press, 2009): 92.

44. "Many laid-off workers are seeking new skills and new career paths under the assumption that, as Mr. Obama said Tuesday, 'the hard truth is that some of the jobs that have been lost in the auto industry and elsewhere won't be coming back'" (Jim Rutenberg, "Obama Attacks Over Economy and Offers Community College Aid," *New York Times*, July 15, 2009, A14).

45. McCain-Palin 2008, "Ambition," October 10, 2008.

46. McCain-Palin 2008, "Dome," September 17, 2008.

47. The tax indictment was reiterated in an ad titled "Foundation" that tied the two McCain attack lines into one argument: "My opponent's only solutions are talk and taxes" (McCain-Palin 2008, September 18, 2008). It appeared as well in a hybrid ad that defended past Republican behavior by saying that "McCain and his congressional allies led. Tough rules on Wall Street, stop CEO rip-offs, protect your savings and pensions" (McCain-Palin 2008/RNC, "Mum," September 24, 2008). The ad then asked, "Obama and his liberal allies?" and answered with a claim undercut by the specific policy details Obama was offering in his ads. "Mum on the market crisis because no one knows what to do." The ad then returns to the staple of the Republican ads: "More taxes. No leadership. A risk your family can't afford."

In mid-October a McCain hybrid ad tried to ally the tax attack to wasteful spending, the liberal Congress, and Tony Rezco. "Obama rewards his friends with your tax dollars," said the announcer. "Tony Rezko, $14 million. Allison Davis, $20 million. Kenny Smith. $100,000. That's unethical. Congressional liberals promise to raise your taxes to reward their friends with wasteful pork. Taxes for you. Pork for them" (McCain-Palin 2008/RNC, "Unethical," October 14, 2008).

48. Bill McInturff, "The Role of Polling," in *Electing the President 2008: The Annenberg Election Debriefing*, edited by Kathleen Hall Jamieson (Philadelphia: University of Pennsylvania Press, 2009): 89.

49. McCain-Palin 2008/RNC, "Dangerous," October 6, 2008.

50. McCain-Palin 2008, "Hypo," October 7, 2008.

51. McCain-Palin 2008, "Folks," October 8, 2008.

52. McCain-Palin 2008, "Enough Is Enough," September 17, 2008.

53. McCain-Palin 2008, "Foundation," September 18, 2008.

54. Obama for America, "Real Change 120," September 18, 2008.

55. McCain-Palin 2008, "Foundation."

56. Alexandra Twin, "Another Huge Dow Loss," CNN, October 15, 2008, http://money.cnn.com/2008/10/15/markets/markets_newyork/index.htm

57. Gerald F. Seib, "Stocks Should Matter to Obama," *Wall Street Journal*, March 6, 2009, A2.

58. Ibid.

59. Erin Burnett, "Economic Bailout Plan Thought To Be on Its Way, But Hits Snag Thursday," *Today*, NBC News, September 26, 2008.

60. Brit Hume, "Preparing for the Debate," *Special Report with Brit Hume*, Fox News Network, September 26, 2008.

61. Barack Obama, First Presidential Debate, University of Mississippi, Oxford, Miss., September 26, 2008.

62. Ibid.

63. David Axelrod, "Campaign Organization and Strategy," in *Electing the President 2008: The Annenberg Election Debriefing*, 74.

64. At that press conference, House Republican leader John Boehner said, "The speaker [Nancy Pelosi] had to give a partisan voice [*sic*] that poisoned our conference, caused a number of members who we thought we could get to go south" (CQ Transcripts, Washington D.C., September 29, 2008). Not to be outdone, deputy Republican whip Eric Cantor added, "Right here is the reason, I believe, why this vote failed. And this is Speaker Pelosi's speech that, frankly, struck the tone of partisanship that, frankly, was inappropriate in this discussion" (CQ Transcripts, Washington D.C., September 29, 2008).

65. Steve Schmidt, "Campaign Organization and Strategy," in *Electing the President 2008: The Annenberg Election Debriefing*, 62.

66. The House rejected the stimulus bill on September 29, 2008. The Senate passed a version of the bill on October 1, and the House followed suit on October 3, 2008, and the bill was sent to President Bush to sign ("The Crisis: A Timeline," CNN, http://money.cnn.com/galleries/2008/news/0809/gallery.week_that_broke_wall_street/20.html).

67. David Gregory, "Race for the White House with David Gregory," MSNBC, October 2, 2008.

68. *World News Tonight with Charles Gibson*, ABC, October 2, 2008.

69. *The Early Show*, CBS, October 7, 2008.

70. *Hardball*, MSNBC, October 7, 2008.

71. 2000 National Annenberg Election Survey. Exact question wording: "If you voted today in the general election for president and the candidates were George W. Bush the Republican and Al Gore the Democrat (names rotated) who would you vote for?" Included in the analyses are 3,750 white men with a four-year college degree surveyed from June 1, 2000, to Election Day. Weighted data. 2004 National Annenberg Election Survey. Exact

question wording, "If the 2004 presidential election were being held today, would you vote for George W. Bush, the Republican, John Kerry, the Democrat, or Ralph Nader (names rotated)?" Included in the analyses are 5,710 white men with a four-year college degree surveyed from June 1, 2004, to Election Day. Weighted data.

CHAPTER 9

1. John Kerry, remarks during Q&A in Huntington, W. Va., March 16, 2004, http://www.cnn.com/2004/ALLPOLITICS/09/30/kerry.comment/

2. *Anderson Cooper 360°*, CNN, March 24, 2008.

3. "You go into these small towns in Pennsylvania and, like a lot of small towns in the Midwest, the jobs have been gone now for 25 years and nothing's replaced them. And they fell through the Clinton administration, and the Bush administration, and each successive administration has said that somehow these communities are gonna regenerate, and they have not. And it's not surprising then they get bitter, they cling to guns or religion or antipathy to people who aren't like them or anti-immigrant sentiment or anti-trade sentiment as a way to explain their frustrations" (San Francisco fund-raiser, April 6, 2008).

4. *Hannity & Colmes*, Fox News Network, October 28, 2008.

5. Steve Schmidt, "Campaign Organization and Strategy," in *Electing the President 2008: The Annenberg Election Debriefing*, edited by Kathleen Hall Jamieson (Philadelphia: University of Pennsylvania Press, 2009): 63.

6. Bill McInturff, "The Role of Polling," in *Electing the President 2008: The Annenberg Election Debriefing*, edited by Kathleen Hall Jamieson (Philadelphia: University of Pennsylvania Press, 2009): 90.

7. One major fracture line in Obama's pledge to cut taxes for 95 percent, however, was his campaign's inconsistency about whether the figure's denominator included all Americans, working individuals, or working families. In the first debate he stated, "here's what I can tell the American people: 95 percent of you will get a tax cut." In the second, on October 7, he offered both formulations, insisting in one place that "I want to provide a tax cut for 95 percent of Americans, 95 percent," and in another that "what I want to do is provide a middle-class tax cut to 95 percent of working Americans" ("2008 Debates," Commission on Presidential Debates, http://www.debates.org/pages/his_2008.html).

The distinction mattered. "Obama's policies do not provide a tax cut for 95 percent of Americans—it's actually about 81 percent of all tax filers," noted the *St. Petersburg Times'* PolitiFact. "But if you consider only people who work, that number goes up, because part of Obama's plan is a tax credit to offset payroll taxes. If you look only at workers, or 'working families,' as Obama likes to put it, it turns out that 95 percent of workers receive a tax cut under Obama's plans." PolitiFact's finding was consistent with that of the Tax Policy Center, which concluded that Obama proposed tax cuts for 94.3 percent of workers. The extent to which the Obama tax case was built on the 95 percent claim is evident in his reliance on it in the general election debates where it appeared ten times ("Impact of Senator Obama's Tax Proposals as Described by Economic Advisors on Workers," Tax Policy Center, October 14, 2008, http://www.taxpolicycenter.org/numbers/displayatab.cfm?Docid=2007&DocTypeID=2; Angie Drobnic Holan, "A Credit for Workers Cuts Taxes for Middle Class," PolitiFact, September 17, 2008, http://www.politifact.com/truth-o-meter/statements/724/).

8. Under the Obama plan, his campaign contended, families making over $250,000 would once again be subject to the marginal income tax rates of the 1990s—39.6 and 36 percent. Since Obama planned to raise taxes on the upper 2% of income earners and reduce them for 95% of the population, then it stood to reason that 3% (those making $150,000–200,000 according to the campaign) should anticipate no changes in their federal taxes under his plans.

9. Bill McInturff, "The Role of Polling," in *Electing the President 2008: The Annenberg Election Debriefing,* edited by Kathleen Hall Jamieson (Philadelphia: University of Pennsylvania Press, 2009): 90.

10. "The Race for President: Before the Final Debate," *New York Times*/CBS News Poll, October 10–13, 2008, http://www.cbsnews.com/htdocs/pdf/oct08b-politics.pdf

11. Michael Cooper and Dalia Sussman, "Growing Doubts About Palin Take a Toll, Poll Finds," *New York Times,* October 31, 2008, A18.

12. "And I'm not going to raise taxes the way Senator Obama wants to raise taxes in a tough economy" (John McCain, The Third Presidential Debate, Hofstra University, Hempstead, New York, October 15, 2008).

13. Jim Margolis is a senior partner at GMMB, a political consulting and advertising firm, and served as a senior advisor and led advertising efforts for President Obama during the 2008 election.

14. Steve Schmidt, "Campaign Organization and Strategy," in *Electing the President 2008: The Annenberg Election Debriefing*: 63.

15. "The $32,000 Question," FactCheck.org, July 8, 2008, http://www.factcheck.org/elections-2008/the_32000_question.html

16. "A Detailed Timeline of the Healthcare Debate Portrayed in 'The System,'" *NewsHour,* PBS, http://www.pbs.org/newshour/forum/may96/background/health_debate_page1.html

17. "Health Care Spin," FactCheck.org, October 14, 2008, http://www.factcheck.org/elections-2008/health_care_spin.html; "Sorting Out of the Truth on Health Care," PolitiFact.com, October 14, 2008, http://www.politifact.com/truth-o-meter/article/2008/oct/14/sorting-out-truth-health-care/

18. "I'm on record as saying that taxing Cadillac plans that don't make people healthier, but just take more money out of their pockets because they're paying more for insurance than they need to, that's actually a good idea and that helps bend the cost curve. That helps to reduce the cost of health insurance over the long term. I think that's a smart thing to do" (Barack Obama, remarks on National Public Radio interview, December 23, 2009).

19. "McCain wants to eliminate business tax deductions for health spending in favor of individual tax credits and health savings accounts that encourage people to save for medical expenses" (Elaine S. Povich, "Your World: John McCain," *AARP Bulletin,* October 2008, 20).

20. In the first debate, Obama's explanation of the McCain plan was even more confusing than was McCain's. "Just one last point I want to make, since Senator McCain talked about providing a $5,000 health credit," noted Obama in the opening debate on September 26. "Now, what he doesn't tell you is that he intends to, for the first time in

history, tax health benefits. So you may end up getting a $5,000 tax credit. Here's the only problem: Your employer now has to pay taxes on the health care that you're getting from your employer." Obama's rendition of the McCain plan was clearer in the second debate, where he said, "Now, Senator McCain has a different kind of approach. He says that he's going to give you a $5,000 tax credit. What he doesn't tell you is that he is going to tax your employer-based health care benefits for the first time ever. So what one hand giveth, the other hand taketh away" (Obama for America, "Taketh," October 11, 2008).

21. Obama for America, "Tax Healthcare," October 1, 2008.

22. Kevin Sack, "Business Cool toward McCain's Health Coverage Plan," *New York Times,* October 7, 2008, http://www.nytimes.com/2008/10/07/us/politics/07health.html?_r=1&pagewanted=print

23. The Second Presidential Debate, Belmont University, Nashville, Tenn., October 7, 2008.

24. Kevin Sack, "Businesses Wary of Details in Obama Health Plan," *New York Times,* October 26, 2008, http://www.nytimes.com/2008/10/27/us/politics/27healthcare.html

25. The Second Presidential Debate.

26. Video shown on *The McLaughlin Group,* "Joe Rising (the Plumber)," http://www.mclaughlin.com/bb/bb.htm?topicid=2434&pagenumber=9

27. Barack Obama, remarks at campaign stop, Toledo, Ohio, October 12, 2008, http://www.npr.org/templates/story/story.php?storyId=95799684

28. "Joe Wurzelbacher," *New York Times,* http://topics.nytimes.com/topics/reference/timestopics/people/w/joe_wurzelbacher/index.html

29. *Your World with Neil Cavuto,* Fox News Network, October 14, 2008.

30. Third Presidential Debate, Hofstra University, Hempstead, N.Y., October 15, 2008.

31. *Good Morning America,* ABC, October 16, 2008.

32. Rich Lowry, "O's Magic Number," *New York Post,* October 17, 2008.

33. "Vote '08: The Final Debate," ABC, October 15, 2008.

34. McCain Puts Obama on the Defensive," Associated Press, October 15, 2008.

35. "McCain Presses Obama in Last and Pointed Debate," *New York Times,* October 16, 2008, A1.

36. Third Presidential Debate.

37. Ibid.

38. Ibid.

39. Ibid.

40. "Buffett Boosts Goldman Sachs with $5-Billion Investment," *Los Angeles Times* blog, September 23, 2008, http://latimesblogs.latimes.com/money_co/2008/09/warren-buffett.html

41. Third Presidential Debate.

42. Ibid.

43. "Obama Fuzzy on 'Small Business' Exemption," Political Radar, ABC, August 5, 2008, http://blogs.abcnews.com/politicalradar/2008/08/obama-fuzzy-on.html

44. "Overhauling Health Care: Two Divergent Visions," MSNBC News, September 22, 2008.

45. "McCain Presses Obama on Health-Plan Penalties," *Wall Street Journal,* October 16, 2008.

46. *Good Morning America,* ABC, October 17, 2008.

47. *Special Report with Brit Hume,* Fox News Network, October 17, 2008.

48. "Uncertain Times Require McCain's Tested Vigilance," *Tampa Tribune,* October 17, 2008.

49. "Obama's Tax Cut: New Welfare Deal," *Pittsburgh Tribune-Review,* October 14, 2008.

50. "McCain for President," *San Diego Union-Tribune,* October 19, 2008.

51. *The Union Leader* (Manchester, N.H.), October 22, 2008, 8.

52. *World News with Charles Gibson,* ABC, October 21, 2008.

53. *CBS Evening News,* CBS, October 21, 2008.

54. Quoted by Steven Greenhouse, "For Incomes Below $100,000, a Better Tax Break in Obama's Plan," *New York Times,* October 31, 2008, A14.

55. The tax cut debate was formally joined on national television for the first time in mid-August at Saddleback before either candidate had formally secured his party's nomination. "What I can say is under the approach I'm taking," Obama told Rick Warren, "if you make $150,000 or less, you will see a tax cut. If you're making $250,000 a year or more, you're going to see a modest increase. What I'm trying to do is create a sense of balance, and fairness, in our tax code" (Saddleback Civil Forum, "Special Event," CNN, August 16, 2008).

But that isn't what the Democrat had said in the last debate before the Pennsylvania primary. There those making less than $250,000 might reasonably have surmised that they would see a tax cut from him:

QUESTION: Senator Obama, would you take the same pledge? No tax increases on people under $250,000?

OBAMA: I not only have pledged not to raise their taxes, I've been the first candidate in this race to specifically say I would cut their taxes.

Having taken that position in Philadelphia the Democrat then appeared to backtrack to set the tax cut set point not at $150,000 but between $200,000 and $250,000.

OBAMA: Well, it depends on how you calculate it. But it would be between $200,000 and $250,000.

There were other discrepancies in the Obama statements as well. The Democratic nominee's response to Wurzelbacher hinted that those making less than $250,000 would see a tax cut: "[W]e've cut taxes a lot for folks like me who make a lot more than $250,000. We haven't given a break to folks who make less."

In the second presidential debate Obama planted the tax cut threshold $50,000 above Saddleback's $150,000. There Obama said, "If you make less than a quarter of a million dollars a year, you will not see a single dime of your taxes go up. If you make $200,000 a year or less, your taxes will go down." Obama reiterated that position in the third and final debate as well: "let's help families right away by providing them a tax cut—a middle-class tax cut for people making less than $200,000...."

56. Barack Obama, remarks, Powder Springs, Ga., July 8, 2008.

57. Obama for America, "Defining Moment 120," October 26, 2008.

58. Joseph Biden, interview with WNEP-Scranton, October 27, 2008.

59. *Hannity & Colmes*, Fox News Network, October 28 2008.

60. McCain Campaign Press Release, "Just Words: Obama's Ever-Changing Definition of Rich," October 28, 2008.

61. "100 Economists Warn that With Current Weak Financial Conditions Barack Obama's Proposals Run A High Risk of Throwing the US Economy into a Deep Recession," John McCain 2008 press release, October 7, 2008.

62. "McCain Can't Find 100 Economists to Endorse His Plan," *Yglesias*, October 11, 2008, http://yglesias.thinkprogress.org/archives/2008/10/mccain_cant_find_100_economists_to_endorse_his_pla.php

63. John McCain, "What We're Fighting For," *Wall Street Journal*, November 3, 2008.

64. http://www.swamppolitics.com/news/politics/blog/2008/06/obama_willing_to_defer_some_ne.html

65. Barack Obama, *This Week*, ABC, September 7, 2008.

66. Second Presidential Debate.

67. Obama for America, "Defining Moment 120."

68. "The McCain Campaign Experiments with Dishonesty," PolitiFact, October 27, 2008, http://www.politifact.com/truth-o-meter/statements/2008/dec/03/sarah-palin/the-mccain-campaign-experiments-with-dishonesty/

69. The transcript of the McCain radio address was distributed to reporters and available from FactCheck.org files. When asked by Fox's Sean Hannity whether the Obama plan constituted socialism, McCain seemed reluctant to use the term. "But the fact is that it's a far left liberal view that you need to take money from one group of Americans and give it to another, to take people who have built up through their labor and their hard work and their dedication to the free enterprise system and take it away from them," he said instead (*Hannity and Colmes*, October 28, 2008, http://www.foxnews.com/story/0,2933,444671,00.html).

70. Jeff Zeleny, "Donation Record as Colin Powell Endorses Obama," *New York Times*, October 20, 2008, A01.

71. Matthew Mosk, *Washington Post*, October 19, 2008, http://www.washingtonpost.com/wp-dyn/content/article/2008/10/18/AR2008101802212_pf.html

72. John McCain's Weekly Radio Address, October 18, 2008, http://www.johnmccain.com/Downloads/wra1017.mp3

73. Ruth Marcus, "The Socialist Scare," *Washington Post*, October 22, 2008, A19.

74. *Good Morning America*, ABC, October 20, 2008.

75. Mark Z. Barabak and Bob Drogin, "Campaign 08: Race for the White House," *Los Angeles Times*, October 24, 2008.

76. Editorial, "Obama's 95% Illusion," *Wall Street Journal*, October 13, 2008; Editorial, "Obama's Tax Cut: New Welfare Deal," *Pittsburgh Tribune-Review*, October 14, 2008; Editorial, "Ready, Set...Spend!" *New York Post*, October 14, 2008.

77. Janet Hook, "Campaign 2008: The Presidential Race," *Los Angeles Times*, October 24, 2008.

CHAPTER 10

1. The Pew Research Center for the People & the Press, "Increasing Optimism About Iraq," February 28, 2008, http://people-press.org/report/398/obama-has-the-lead-but-potential-problems-too

2. Barack Obama, acceptance speech remarks at Democratic National Convention, "The American Promise," Denver, Colo., August 28, 2008.

3. First Presidential Debate, University of Mississippi, Oxford, Miss., September 26, 2008.

4. Ibid.

5. The Pew Research Center for People & the Press, "Obama Has the Lead, But Potential Problems Too."

6. The Pew Research Center for the People & the Press, "Increasing Optimism about Iraq."

7. RNC, "Chair," October 16, 2008.

8. Obama for America, "Audio Tapes," October 27, 2008.

9. McCain-Palin 2008, "Special," October 29, 2008.

10. Len Burman, Surachai Khitatrakun, Greg Leiserson, Jeff Rohaly, Eric Toder, and Bob Williams, "An Updated Analysis of the 2008 Presidential Candidates' Tax Plans," Urban Institute and Brookings Institute Tax Policy Center, updated September 12, 2008, http://www.taxpolicycenter.org/UploadedPDF/411749_updated_candidates.pdf

11. Like the other statements in the ad, the final one attributed to the Republican nominee is not read by an announcer or played from tape. Instead each is printed to be read. What the viewer sees on the screen is:

"I might have to rely on a vice president that I select" for expertise on economic issues.

The fact that the final five words are not in quotation marks gives the campaign the ability to argue that that part of the statement is a paraphrase. But the sense a reader gets from it bears scant resemblance to what McCain actually said in the cited debate:

ANDERSON COOPER: Senator McCain, has this president given too much authority to the vice president?

SENATOR MCCAIN: Look, I am going to give you some straight talk. This president came to office in a time of peace, and then we found ourselves in 2001. And he did not have as much national security experience as I do, so he had to rely more on the vice president of the United States and that's obvious. I wouldn't have to do that. I might have to rely on a vice president that I select on some other issues. He may have more expertise in telecommunications, on information technology, which is the future of this nation's economy. He may have more expertise in a lot of areas, but I would rely on a vice president of the United States, but, as Fred said, the primary responsibility is to select one who will immediately take your place if necessary.

Presumably the Democrats did not quote McCain's last line instead, because the thrust of the ad was an indictment of his supposedly poor understanding of the economy.

12. Quoted by Michael D. Shear, "McCain Gives Economy Speech in Ohio, Warning Against 'Dangerous Threesome' of Democratic Leaders," *Washington Post,* October 27, 2008.

13. Exit poll table data are drawn from Chuck Todd and Sheldon Gawiser's *How Barack Obama Won* (New York: Random House, 2009): 40–43.

14. "Pennsylvania Hurting," October 27, 2008; "Change We Need SP," October 28, 2008.

15. Obama for America, "Something Happening," October 31, 2008.

16. Obama for America, "Something Happening."

17. Obama for America, "Defining Moment," October 26, 2008.

18. A second two-minute ad titled "Same Path 120" was aired in Florida from October 28 to November 1 and in Montana from October 28 to October 30.

19. Obama for America, "American Stories, American Solutions," October 29, 2008.

20. Mark Kukis, "How the Economy Could Crush Iraq's Hopes," *Time,* May 23, 2009, http://www.time.com/time/world/article/0,8599,1899880,00.html

21. Bill Carter, "Infomercial for Obama Is Big Success in Ratings," *New York Times,* October 31, 2008, A19.

22. We checked to see if those who hadn't decided for whom to vote and those who voted early were significantly different in regard to viewing but did not find any effects.

23. Exit poll tables are reported in Chuck Todd and Sheldon Gawiser's *How Barack Obama Won.*

24. *Washington Post*/ABC News Poll, November 2, 2008, http://www.washingtonpost.com/wp-srv/politics/documents/postpoll_110208.html

CHAPTER 11

1. Adam Nagourney and Jim Rutenberg with Michael Cooper and Jeff Zeleny contributing to the article, "Polls Cause Campaigns to Change Their Itineraries," *New York Times,* October 17, 2008, A20.

2. Paul Gronke and James Hicks, "The Secretary of State's Guidebook to the Early Voting Obstacle Course." Handout prepared for the Voter Participation Committee of the National Association of Secretaries of State, February 7, 2009, http://www.earlyvoting.net/blog/uploads/NASS%20Handout%20FINAL.pdf

3. RealClearPolitics, "October 12: RCP Electoral Count," Prediction of electoral counts by day based on state poll averages, http://www.realclearpolitics.com/epolls/election_2008/presidential_elections_electoral_count-10–12–2008.html

4. The president and vice president of the United States are formally elected by the electoral college. The number of electors granted to each state to send to the electoral college is determined by a state's number of congressional representatives. Washington, D.C., is also allocated three electors. All but two states use a winner-take-all method for allocating their electoral votes. Maine and Nebraska use a congressional district method for assigning their electoral representation. The winner-take-all method means that a candidate merely needs to win a plurality of the vote. This approach was quite different from the voting method used to win delegates in the Democratic primaries and caucuses, but it was more akin to the approach used in Republican primaries and caucuses. To win the presidency, a ticket must obtain 270 of the 538 electoral votes.

5. Henry C. Kenski and Kate M. Kenski, "Explaining the Vote in the Election of 2008: The Democratic Revival," in Robert E. Denton, Jr. (ed.), *The 2008 Presidential Campaign: A Communication Perspective* (Boulder, Colo.: Rowman & Littlefield, 2008).

6. Adam Nagourney with Elisabeth Bumiller and Jeff Zeleny, "In McCain's Uphill Battle, Winning Is an Option," *New York Times,* October 24, 2008, A1.

7. NAES08 telephone survey. Dataset (weighted). 8/8/08 to 8/24/08. $N = 3,663$.

8. NAES08 telephone survey. Dataset (weighted). 10/19/08 to 10/23/08. $N = 1,197$. Rounding error prevents these percentages from adding to 100 percent.

9. Kate M. Kenski, "Gender and Time of Voting Decision: Decision Certainty During the 2000 Presidential Election," *Journal of Political Marketing,* 6, 1 (2007): 1–22.

10. NAES08 telephone survey. Postelection panel. $N = 3,448$.

11. Kate Kenski, "Early Voting Reaches Record Levels in 2004, National Annenberg Election Survey Shows," Annenberg Public Policy Center press release, March 24, 2005, http://annenbergpublicpolicycenter.org/NewsDetails.aspx?myId=67

12. United States Department of Justice, Civil Rights Division, "The Uniformed and Overseas Citizens Absentee Voting Act," http://www.usdoj.gov/crt/voting/misc/activ_uoc.php

13. Center for the Study of the American Electorate, "Two Pro-Participation Reforms Actually Harm Voter Turnout; Other Reforms Suggested," Press release, January 9, 2001.

14. The Early Voting Information Center at Reed College, "States: Absentee and Early Voting Laws," http://earlyvoting.net/states/abslaws.php

15. Paul Gronke and James Hicks, "The Secretary of State's Guidebook to the Early Voting Obstacle Course." Handout prepared for the Voter Participation Committee of the National Association of Secretaries of State, February 7, 2009, http://www.earlyvoting.net/blog/uploads/NASS%20Handout%20FINAL.pdf

16. NAES08 telephone survey. Estimates from 5-day prior moving averages.

17. NAES08 telephone survey. Sample from no-fault absentee and early voting states. Estimates from 5-day prior moving averages.

18. NAES08 telephone survey. Subsample of respondents in competitive states. 10/8/08 to 10/15/08.

19. David Plouffe, "Campaign Management and Field Operations," in *Electing the President 2008: The Annenberg Election Debriefing,* edited by Kathleen Hall Jamieson (Philadelphia: University of Pennsylvania Press, 2009): 47.

20. David Plouffe. *The Audacity to Win: The Inside Story and Lessons of Barack Obama's Historic Victory* (New York: Viking, 2009): 362–363.

21. NAES08 telephone survey. Dataset (weighted). 10/19/08 to 10/23/08. $N = 1,286$.

22. NAES08 telephone survey. Subsample of those who had already cast ballots. 10/19/08 to 10/23/08. $N = 174$. The small sample size yields a large margin of error of +/−7.4 percent.

23. Kate Kenski, "No Excuse Absentee and Early Voting During the 2000 and 2004 Elections: Results from the National Annenberg Election Survey." Paper presented at the 2005 Annual Meeting of the American Political Science Association.

24. The spread between Obama and McCain vote preference is slightly larger in the NAES08 postelection panel than that found in the polls. CNN.com reported that Obama

won 53 percent of the vote to McCain's 46 percent. See CNN's "Election Center 2008, President" http://www.cnn.com/ELECTION/2008/results/president/

25. CNN, "Exit Polls: President," http://www.cnn.com/ELECTION/2008/results/polls/#val=USP00p2. We acknowledge that there is a difference between self-assessments of past vote intentions and actual behavior. The patterns nevertheless suggest that Obama did better than McCain among those who voted and/or decided early.

26. Table 11.4 presents information on the two-party vote. One could, however, look at all vote preference response options. After including all response options on vote preference, the results change very little from the two-party vote results when looking solely at those respondents who reported voting two weeks or more before Election Day. Of respondents in this category, 36.2 percent reported voting for McCain, 60.1 percent for Obama, 0.2 percent said that they did not know for whom they voted, and 3.4 percent refused to answer the question.

27. Richard Wolf, "Dems Get Big Boost in Early Voting; Trend Is a Reversal of Pattern Favoring GOP," *USA Today,* October 22, 2008, A1.

28. Jon Carson, "Campaign Management and Field Operations," in *Electing the President 2008: The Annenberg Election Debriefing,* 45–46.

29. NAES08 telephone survey. Postelection panel. $N = 1,755$ of Obama voters and $N = 1,434$ of McCain voters.

30. Ibid., $N = 3,448$.

31. Ibid., $N = 3,737$.

32. Thomas Fitzgerald, "Clinton Wins Pa., Keeps Drive Alive," *Philadelphia Inquirer* (Web edition), April 23, 2008.

33. "McCain's Last Stand; Swing States: Pennsylvania," *Economist,* October 25, 2008.

CHAPTER 12

1. Larry M. Bartels. *Unequal Democracy: The Political Economy of the New Gilded Age* (New York: Russell Sage Foundation: Princeton and Oxford: Princeton University Press, 2008): 122–3.

2. Larry M. Bartels. *Unequal Democracy*: 120–3. Determining total campaign spending is difficult, a problem complicated by the fact that some campaigns secure more impact per dollar spent than others.

3. Daron R.Shaw, "The Effect of TV Ads and Candidate Appearances on Statewide Presidential Votes, 1988–96" *American Political Science Review* 93, 2 (1999): 345–61; Richard Johnston, Michael G. Hagen and Kathleen Hall Jamieson, *The 2000 Presidential Election and the Foundations of Party Politics* (New York: Cambridge University Press, 2004); Gregory Huber and Kevin Arceneaux, "Identifying the Persuasive Effects of Presidential Advertising," *American Journal of Political Science* 51, 4, (2007): 957–977.

4. Karen Finney in "Political Party Panel," in *Electing the President 2008: The Annenberg Election Debriefing,* edited by Kathleen Hall Jamieson (Philadelphia: University of Pennsylvania Press, 2009): 158.

5. For broadcast, we were able to access commercial records of the GRPs purchased by each campaign in each market during each day of the general election, and we cross-checked these for correlation with independent records of campaign expenditure. For cable and radio, we had access only to spending records, and estimated GRPs by multiplying

spending by the spending-GRP ratios observed in broadcast for each market and week. While the actual spending-GRP ratios for cable and radio are likely to have been different than those for broadcast, we assume that the relative differences between markets and weeks are likely to fluctuate in the same directions (i.e., variation in the price of advertising between markets and weeks will be relatively medium-independent).

6. Because of the degree of estimation involved in computing GRPs for cable and radio, we also analyzed the data with unadjusted spending figures. These analyses did not yield substantively different results, and we report our findings here only in terms of GRP. Converting dollars to GRPs does bring in error that underestimates the impact of Obama's advertising. As the McCain campaign focused solely on 30-second spots, the Democrats, ran 60-second and 120-second spots in addition to their 30-second spots. While more time cost more money, longer spots do not necessarily mean greater reach and higher GRPs. For example, a 30-second spot that reaches an estimated 1 percent of the population receives the same GRP score as a 120-second spot that reaches 1 percent of the population. One would assume that longer spots would have a greater impact and as a result we are using a conservative estimation of the Obama advertising advantage in analyses below.

7. Chris Mottola in "The Roll of Polling," in *Annenberg Election Debriefing*, edited by Kathleen Hall Jamieson (Philadelphia: University of Pennsylvania *Electing the President 2008: The* Press, 2009): 118.

8. Bill McInturff in "The Roll of Polling," in *Electing the President 2008: The Annenberg Election Debriefing*, edited by Kathleen Hall Jamieson (Philadelphia: University of Pennsylvania Press, 2009): 90.

9. The formula for turning logodds to probability is $1/(1+\exp(-\text{logodds}))$.

10. This estimation is calculated by $\exp(b)^x$ where x is number of increments in the base unit of the independent variable (i.e–GRP). The natural log of this number is then used in the calculation of a new logit coefficient that is used to estimate the greater impact. For example the impact of a 300 GRP Obama advantage on a individual with a baseline probability of 50 percent equals $1/(1+\exp(-(LN(\exp(.079)^3)))) = 1/(1+\exp(-(LN(1.082)))) = 1/(1+\exp(-(LN(1.2677)))) = 1/(1+\exp(-(0.236))) = 0.559$ which is the new probability.

11. Radio and broadcast: $r = .167$, $p < .001$; radio and cable: $r = .235$, $p < .001$; and broadcast and cable: $r = .194$, $p < .001$.

12. The logit coefficient for advertising in the model was 0.108, $p < .10$.

13. Nicolle Wallace in "The Campaign and the Press," in *Electing the President 2008: The Annenberg Election Debriefing*, edited by Kathleen Hall Jamieson (Philadelphia: University of Pennsylvania Press, 2009): 144.

14. Kathleen Hall Jamieson and Jeffrey Gottfried. "Are There Lessons for the Future of News in the 2008 Presidential Campaign?" *Daedalus* (Forthcoming).

15. Daniel Frankel, "Cablers Shine, Broadcast Struggles," *Variety*, October 28, 2009, http://www.variety.com/article/VR1117997882.html?categoryid=14&cs=1&nid=2565

16. E-mail communication with Kyle Roberts, November 8, 2009.

17. PEW Project for Excellence in Journalism, "Audience," The State of the News Media, http://www.stateofthemedia.org/2009/narrative_networktv_audience.php?cat=2&media=6

18. Ibid.

19. Figures provided by National Cable Communications.

20. From 5:00 P.M. to 7:00 A.M., 12:00 P.M. to 1:00 P.M., 4:00 P.M. to 6:00 P.M. and 11:00 P.M. to 11:30 P.M., stations typically offer viewers locally produced news. Because the stations originate the content, they control the ad space. (We thank Tim Kay for confirming these figures).

21. Nielsen, http://en-us.nielsen.com/tab/industries/media

22. Mediamark Research & Intelligence (MRI), http://www.mediamark.com/

23. Scarborough Research, http://www.scarborough.com/

24. E-mail communication with Tim Kay, September 10, 2009.

25. We are grateful to Kyle Roberts, President of Smart Media Group, for providing the illustrations in this paragraph.

26. Tim Kay, "The Shift Occurring in Paid Media," NCC Political, March 28, 2009, http://www.spotcable.com/spot_downloads/ShiftOccurringinPaidMediaAAPC.pdf

27. E-mail correspondence between Sarah Simmons and Kathleen Hall Jamieson, August 17, 2009.

28. E-mail correspondence between Jim Margolis and Kathleen Hall Jamieson, September 10, 2009.

29. Exact question wording: "Which candidate or candidates running for president supports federal funding for embryonic stem cell research? Barack Obama, John McCain, both, or neither?

30. These percentages reflect the percentage difference in popular vote (in favor of Obama).

CHAPTER 13

1. The small number of CBS viewers in our sample during the time frame under investigation limited our ability to include a robust set of controls.

2. See PS: Political Science & Politics, 41, 4 (2008).

3. "Saturated and conservative" models refers to the fact that our statistical model in this chapter (table 14.1) includes 27 independent variables, which comparatively is a large number of predictor variables in social science statistics. Additionally, the more relevant variables one includes in a model the more conservative the results.

4. David R. Seibold and Robert D. McPhee, "Commonality analysis: A method for decomposing explained variance in multiple regression analyses," Human Communication Research, 5, 4 (1979): 355–365.

5. Richard D. McKelvey and William Zavoina, "A Statistical Model for the Analysis of Ordinal Level Dependent Variables," Journal of Mathematical Sociology 4 (1975): 103–120; Alfred DeMaris, "Explained Variance in Logistic Regression: A Monte Carlo Study of Proposed Measures," Sociological Methods & Research 31, 1 (2002): 27–74.

AFTERWORD

1. Jon Carson in "Campaign Management and Field Operations," in Electing the President 2008: The Annenberg Election Debriefing, edited by Kathleen Hall Jamieson (Philadelphia: University of Pennsylvania Press, 2009): 44.)

2. David Plouffe, *The Audacity to Win: The Inside Story and Lessons of Barack Obama's Historic Victory* (New York: Penguin Group, 2009): 350.

3. Ibid.

4. http://www.ncsl.org/Default.aspx?TabId=16604

5. NAES08 telephone survey. Postelection panel. $N = 1,811$.

6. David Plouffe, *The Audacity to Win*, 364.

7. http://www.bluestatedigital.com/casestudies/client/obama_for_america_2008/

8. http://newsblaze.com/story/20090128105841zzzz.nb/topstory.html

9. http://www.huffingtonpost.com/mayhill-fowler/obama-no-surprise-that-ha_b_96188.html

10. John Zaller, *The Nature and Origins of Mass Media* (Cambridge University Press: New York: 1992).

11. See D. Sunshine Hillygus and Todd G. Shields, *The Persuadable Voter: Wedge Issues in Presidential Campaigns* (Princeton New Jersey: Princeton University Press, 2008).

12. Kathleen Hall Jamieson, *Packaging the Presidency: A History and Criticism of Presidential Campaign Advertising* (New York: Oxford University Press, 1996).

13. Douglas B. Sosnik, Matthew J. Dowd, and Ron Fournier, *Applebee's America: How Successful Political, Business, and Religious Leaders Connect with the New American Community* (New York: Simon and Schuster, 2006).

14. Jose Antonio Vargas, "Obama Raised Half a Billion Online," *Washington Post*, http://voices.washingtonpost.com/44/2008/11/20/obama_raised_half_a_billion_on.html

15. Ibid.

16. For an analysis of these insular tendencies, see Jamieson and Cappella, *Echo Chamber: Rush Limbaugh and the Conservative Media Establishment* (New York: Oxford University Press, 2008).

17. Richard Johnston, Michael Hagen, and Kathleen Hall Jamieson. *The 2000 Presidential Election and the Foundation of Party Politics* (New York: Cambridge University Press, 2004).

18. D. Sunshine Hillygus and Todd G. Shields, *The Persuadable Voter* (Princeton New Jersey: Princeton University Press 2008): 145–182.

19. Additionally he raised "$46.4 million for legal and accounting expenses" ("Federal Election Commission, 2008 Presidential Campaign Financial Activity Summarized: Receipts Nearly Double 2004 Total," June 8, 2009, http://www.fec.gov/press/press2009/20090608PresStat.shtml).

20. Plouffe, *The Audacity to Win*, 327–28.

21. Jeffrey M. Jones, "Campaign Financing Appears to Be Non-Issue for Voters," Gallup, October 30, 2008, http://www.gallup.com/poll/111652/campaign-financing-appears-nonissue-voters.aspx

22. The *Washington Post* editorialized, "Mr. Obama didn't mention his previous proposal to take public financing if the Republican nominee agreed to do the same—the one for which he received heaps of praise from campaign finance reform advocates such as Mr. Wertheimer,

president of Democracy 21, and others, including us. He didn't mention, as he told the Federal Election Commission last year in seeking to preserve the option, that "Congress concluded some thirty years ago that the public funding alternative…would serve core purposes in the public interest: limiting the escalation of campaign spending and the associated pressures on candidates to raise, at the expense of time devoted to public dialogue, ever vaster sums of money" ("The Politics of Spare Change," June 20, 2008, A18, http://www.washingtonpost.com/wp-dyn/content/article/2008/06/19/AR2008061903026.html).

On the same day the *New York Times* argued that "The excitement underpinning Senator Barack Obama's campaign rests considerably on his evocative vows to depart from self-interested politics. Unfortunately, Mr. Obama has come up short of that standard with his decision to reject public spending limitations and opt instead for unlimited private financing in the general election" ("Public Funding on the Ropes," June 20, 2008, http://www.nytimes.com/2008/06/20/opinion/20fri1.html).

23. Jose Antonio Vargas, "Obama Raised Half a Billion Online."

24. http://www.opensecrets.org/pres08/index.php

25. Obama for America, Webcast, June 19, 2008.

26. A mid-February headline in the *Washington Post* revealed, "Mr. Obama's waffle; his commitment to pursue public financing for the fall campaign suddenly looks soft." By mid-June the die had been cast. "Obama to reject public funds for election," noted the *Post* on June 20 (Shailagh Murray and Perry Bacon Jr., "Obama to Reject Public Funds for Election," *Washington Post*, June 20, 2008, A1). At the Annenberg debriefing, David Plouffe explained, "A junior researcher filled out a questionnaire from some campaign finance institute, and said, 'Yes-period.' That really boxed us in. That was not a position of the campaign, to be that declarative" (David Plouffe in "Campaign Management and Field Operations," in *Electing the President 2008: The Annenberg Election Debriefing*, edited by Kathleen Hall Jamieson [Philadelphia: University of Pennsylvania Press, 2009]: 37).

27. "That distinction is important for Obama. As we've written before, Obama is doing a bit of a tightrope act here. He does not accept funds from registered federal lobbyists, but he does accept money from spouses of lobbyists, non-lobbying partners who work for lobbying firms or for law firms that do lobbying, ex-lobbyists, and state lobbyists." (FactCheck.org, "PAC-ing Heat," April 21, 2008, http://www.factcheck.org/elections-2008/pac-ing_heat.html).

28. Campaign Finance Institute, "Reality Check: Obama Received about the Same Percentage from Small Donors in 2008 as Bush in 2004," November 24, 2008, http://www.cfinst.org/pr/prRelease.aspx?ReleaseID=216

29. Ibid.

30. "Obama's Small Donor Base Image Is a Myth, New Study Reveals," *Los Angeles Times*, November 28, 2008, http://latimesblogs.latimes.com/washington/2008/11/obama-money.html

31. Richard Wolffe, *Renegade: The Making of a President* (New York: Crown Publishers, 2009): 75.

32. Matthew Mosk, "With More than $20 Million, Obama Reports Strong Quarter," *Washington Post*, October 2, 2007, A4.

33. Matthew Mosk and John Solomon, "Clinton and Obama Each Pull in Over $100 Million," *Washington Post,* January 1, 2008, A4.

34. Matthew Mosk and Shailagh Murray, "Obama Donors Pick Up Pace: A $32 Million Month," *Washington Post,* February 1, 2008, A9.

35. Patrick Healy and Jeff Zeleny, "Clinton's Fund-Raising Success Is Outshined by Obama's," *New York Times,* February 8, 2008.

36. See Richard Johnston, Michael Hagen and Kathleen Hall Jamieson, *The 2000 Election and the Foundation of Party Politics* (New York: Cambridge University Press, 2004).

37. Federal Election Commission, "2008 Presidential Campaign Financial Activity Summarized: Receipts Nearly Double 2004 Total," June 8, 2009, http://www.fec.gov/press/press2009/20090608PresStat.shtml

38. Kenneth P. Vogel, "FEC: President Obama Funneled Money to Swing States," Politico, June 9, 2009, http://www.politico.com/news/stories/0609/23543.html

39. Larry M. Bartels, *Unequal Democracy: The Political Economy of the New Gilded Age* (New York: Russell Sage Foundation: Princeton and Oxford: Princeton University Press, 2008), 122–3.

40. Ibid.

41. Daron R. Shaw, "The Effect Of TV Ads and Candidate Appearances on Statewide Presidential Votes, 1988–96," *American Political Science Review* 93, 2 (1999): 345–61; Richard Johnston, Michael G. Hagen, and Kathleen Hall Jamieson, *The 2000 Presidential Election and the Foundations of Party Politics* (New York: Cambridge University Press, 2004); Gregory Huber and Kevin Arceneaux, "Identifying the Persuasive Effects of Presidential Advertising." *American Journal of Political Science* 51, 4 (2007): 957–977.

42. Jamieson, *Packaging the Presidency.*

43. Ibid., 234.

APPENDIX

1. Seth Hill, James Lo, Lynn Vavreck and John Zaller, "The Duration of Advertising Effects in the 2000 Presidential Campaigns," Paper presented to the 2008 Midwest Political Science Association.

Index

Note: Page numbers followed by *f*, *t*, and *n* denote figures, tables, and endnotes.

Abramoff, Jack, 30
absentee voting, 173, 255–59, 256–58*f*,
   260*t*, 261, 264 (*see also* voting)
Adair, Bill, 206
Adams, John, 245
Adkison, Danny M., 346*n*1, 346*n*3
advertisement campaign
  "Celeb," 79, 115–16
  "Dangerous," 37, 93
  "Dome," 45, 187, 192, 206
  five-minute straight-to-camera
    advertisement, 240
  "Foundation," 194, 353*n*47
  "Fundamentals," 184
  "Grandfather," 101
  half-hour program, 242–47, 295
  "The One," 77, 78
  "Real Change," 193
  spending for
    differences in ad spending shifted
     votes, 267–68
    national ad buys, impact of, 266–67,
     267*f*
  "Tax Healthcare," 209
  two-minute ads, 186, 193–94, 223–24,
    241–42, 295
age, 69
  impact in presidential election, 55–57
  -related threads in ads, 62–65

Agnew, Spiro, 150
Ahmadinejad, Mahmoud, 125, 238
Alito, Sam, 129
American Economic Association, 224
American National Election Study, 151
Andrews, Wyatt, 221
Annenberg Claims/Deception Survey, 96,
  97–98, 338*nn*75,81
Annenberg Public Policy Center, 185,
  330*n*27, 338*n*75
Annenberg School for Communication,
  339*n*95
Ansolabehere, Stephen, 323*n*49
Arceneaux, Kevin, 363*n*3, 368*n*41
Arctic National Wildlife Refuge, 113
Arizona Republic, The, 65
Associated Press, 37, 117, 125, 144
Atlantic, The, 58
Audacity to Win, The, 259
"Audio Tapes," 167
Axelrod, David, 27, 32, 39, 119, 127, 131,
  197, 206, 323*n*1
Ayers, William, 5, 90, 92, 95*f*, 97–99, 102,
  188, 307

Balz, Dan, 82, 183
Bartels, Larry, 25, 265, 313, 322*n*33,
  323*n*46, 323*n*47, 363*n*1–2, 368*n*39
Bautin, Mikhail, 330*n*27

Bell, Jeffrey, 14
Benenson, Joel, 35, 39, 57, 325*n*36
Bennett, Robert, 31
Bentsen, Lloyd, 140, 151
Bergsieker, Hilary B., 339*n*94
Bernanke, Ben, 185
Biden, Joseph, 9, 73, 149, 237–38, 245, 298
    acceptance speech, 133–35
    chair of Senate Foreign Relations
        Committee, 125, 166
    against clean coal, 164–65
    competence, 9
    convention speeches, 291–92
    favorability ratings of, 141*f*, 142, 161,
        162*f*, 168–74, 168*t*, 170*t*, 171*f*, 173*f*
    knowledge, 9
    as "ready to be president," 9, 146*f*,
        163–64, 167–68, 167*f*, 294
    as vice presidential candidate, 123–30
    vice presidential debate, 157–61
    vote for Gramm-Leach-Bliley Act, 159
Bipartisan Campaign Reform Act, 32
Blagojevich, Rod, 47
Blascovich, James, 335*n*31
Bobo, Lawrence, 336*n*50
Boston Globe, The, 46, 134, 146
Brady, David, 322*n*35
Brave New Films, 61
Broadcast (see also cable television; media;
        radio; television)
    availabilities in local news, impact of, 278
    high spending on, 276–78
Brokaw, Tom, 144, 162
Brooks, David, 30, 147
Brown, Peter, 14
Buffet, Warren, 217, 227, 241
Burnett, Erin, 195
Bush, George H.W., 17, 59, 112, 113
Bush, George W., 2, 13, 33, 43–44, 72, 131,
        134, 138, 235
    federal financing, rejecting, 309
    ideology of, 21*f*
    Iraq war and, 14
    and John McCain, similarity between,
        118–19, 119*f*, 132*f*, 309
    "my way or the highway" foreign policy,
        76
    as president
        public opinion of, 14–16
Bush, Jeb, 35

Bush Doctrine, 9
Byrd, April, 229

cable television, 277–78
    microtargeting in, 307–8
    spending differences in gross ratings
        points, 268–70, 269*f*
        impact on vote, 270–275, 271*t*,
            272–74*f*, 275*t*
Campaign Finance Institute (CFI), 311
Campaign Media Analysis Group (CMAG),
        229, 268, 278, 325*n*49
Campbell, Karlyn Kohrs, 331*n*58
Cappella, Joseph N., 319*n*5, 323*n*6–7,
        366*n*16
Carroll, Joseph, 330*n*31
Carson, Jon, 261, 304
Carter, Jimmy, 16*f*, 17, 56, 72, 240
Cavuto, Neil, 213, 229
Clawson, Rosalee A., 319*n*5, 320*n*7
CBS Evening News, 154, 187
CCI. See Cultural Communication Index
        (CCI)
"Celeb," 79, 115, 116
Center for Media and Public Affairs, 61
CFI. See Campaign Finance Institute (CFI)
"Chair," 237, 238
Charleston Daily Mail, The, 60
"Chicago machine," 47, 48–50
Chicago Sun-Times, 46
Chisholm, Shirley, 128
clean coal, 143, 151, 164–66, 167*f*, 243
Clinton, Bill, 56, 72, 82, 129, 131, 133, 144,
        150, 222
    Gramm-Leach-Bliley Act and, 159
    windfall profits tax on oil companies,
        110
Clinton, Hillary Rodham, 44, 54, 77, 82, 92,
        110, 125, 127, 130, 131, 133, 141,
        144, 204, 306
    federal financing, rejecting, 309
    support for gas tax holiday, 110–11
CMAG. See Campaign Media Analysis
        Group (CMAG)
Comedy Central, 60, 124, 279
Consumer Confidence Index, 322*n*42,
        329–30*n*27
Consumer Sentiment Index, 16–17, 16*f*, 18*f*
Cooper, Anderson, 147
Cosmides, Leda, 333*n*79

Cordes, Nancy, 180
Couric, Katie, 9, 137, 152, 157, 164
    interview with Sarah Palin, 151, 152,
        154–55
Cox, Christopher, 185
Cultural Communication Index (CCI), 10,
    57, 58f, 64f, 88f, 90f, 91f, 95f, 96f,
    97f, 329n27
Cuddy, Amy J.C., 335n37

Daily News, 34
Daily Show with Jon Stewart, 60, 76, 124
"Dangerous," 93
Davis, Fred, 79
Davis, Teddy, 218
"Defining Moment," 241–42
DeMaris, Alfred, 322n40, 365n5
Democratic advantage
    on argument for change, 33–35
    in early voting, 259–63, 260t
    on handling economy, 17–18, 19f
    in party identification, 19–22
Democratic Congressional Campaign
    Committee, 312
Democratic National Committee, 266, 276
Democratic Senatorial Campaign
    Committee, 312
Department of Energy, 113
Department of the Interior, 113
Der Spiegel, 77
digital technology, 305–6
Discovery, 279
Dobbs, Michael, 206
Dole, Bob, 60
"Dome," 45, 187, 192, 206
Douthat, Ross, 153
Dow Closing Average, 194–95, 194t, 195f,
    197–98
Dowd, Matthew J., 366n13
Doyle, Jr., Joseph, 339n7
Dreams from My Father, 100
Dreher, Rod, 153
Dudley, Robert L., 346n7
Dukakis, Michael, 129, 140, 235
Durbin, Dick, 245

early voting, 251, 255–59, 256–58f, 261–64,
    260t, 302–5 (see also voting)
economic crisis, 5, 35, 62, 176, 177f, 179,
    187, 191, 224, 238, 244

Economist, 264
economy, 13, 18f, 176–78, 177f
    Democratic advantage on handling,
        17–18, 19f
    faltering, 16–17
    impact in 2008 general election, 23t,
        22–25
Edwards, John, 44
Eisenhower, Dwight D., 28, 56
    as "The Man from Abilene," 46
enlightened preferences, 24
European Union (EU), 239

FactCheck.org, 115, 137, 153
Faler, Brian, 111
Fallows, Jim, 58
Falwell, Jerry, 33
Fannie Mae. See Federal National Mortgage
    Association
Federal Election Commission (FEC), 311,
    312
federal financing, 308–9
Federal Home Mortgage Corporation
    (Freddie Mac), 38, 179
Federal National Mortgage Association
    (Fannie Mae), 38, 89, 179
Feingold, Russ, 38
Ferguson, Craig, 60
Ferrell, Will, 41
Fey, Tina, 1, 9, 152, 154–57, 156f, 242, 292,
    293
Fineman, Howard, 128
Finney, Karen, 363n4
Fiorina, Carly, 181, 350n8
first presidential debate, 194–97, 194t, 195f,
    253f, 357n20
Fiske, Susan, 83, 102, 335n30, 335n37,
    339n94
five-minute straight-to-camera
    advertisement (Ronald Reagan),
    240 (see also advertisement
    campaigns)
"Foundation," 194, 353n47
Fournier, Ron, 125, 342n8, 366n13
Fowler, Mayhill, 306, 314
Fox News, 29, 83, 195, 223–24, 229, 243,
    277, 279
Freddie Mac. See Federal Home Mortgage
    Corporation
Freeland, Chrystia, 144

funding, public
    Obama declination, 310–311
fund-raising, 302, 310, 311
Furman, Jason, 218

Gaffney, Frank, 167
Gallup, 18, 43, 59, 123, 163, 207, 310
Gamson, William A., 320n5, 320n7
gas tax holiday, 110, 111, 112–13
Gawiser, Sheldon, 103, 339n98, 361n13,
    361n23
Gelman, Andrew, 24, 322n37, 322n44,
    323n47
general election 2008
    vote, predicting, 22–25, 23t
        party identification, 24
        ideology of candidates, 24
        economy, 24–25
Gergen, David, 78, 147
Giamei, Rosaria, 109
Gibbs, Robert, 63, 64
Gibson, Charles, 9, 157, 198
    interview with Sarah Palin, 146f, 151,
        152–54, 156f, 157, 161, 162f, 173f,
        291, 292
Gilens, Martin, 336n50, 337n60
Gingrich, Newt, 220
Glenn, John, 31
Glick, Peter, 335n37
Goldman, Seth, 339n95
Good Morning America, 220, 222, 226
Gore, Al, 22, 48, 150, 235, 251, 255, 259,
    312
    ideology of, 21f
    truthfulness in ads, 47–48
Gottfried, Jeffrey, 276, 364n14
Gramm-Leach-Bliley Act, 159
"Grandfather," 101
Gregory, David, 144, 198
Gronke, Paul, 361n2, 362n15
gross ratings points (GRPs), 267

Hagen, Michael G., 322n36, 327n90, 363n3,
    366n17, 368n36, 368n41
half-hour program, 242–47, 291, 295,
    309, 313 (see also advertisement
    campaigns)
Halperin, Mark, 129
Hammond, Darrell, 40
Hannity, Sean, 157
    interview with John McCain, 223–24

Hanoi Hilton, 30, 45, 147
Hardy, Bruce W., 323n6
Harris, Dan, 109
Harris, Sam, 140
Hart, Peter, 14, 320n8
Heflin, Howell, 31
Heston, Charlton, 78
Hicks, James, 362n2, 362n15
Hill, Seth, 368n1
Hillygus, D. Sunshine, 319n2, 366n11, 366n18
Hilton, Paris, 79, 115, 116
Holbrook, Thomas M., 25, 322n45
Hoover, Herbert, 224
Horowitz, Juliana, 321n30
Huffington Post, 314
Huber, Geogory A., 336n51, 364n3, 368n41
Humphrey, Hubert, 14, 255, 313
Hurwitz, Jon, 336n53, 337n60
Hutchings, Vincent L., 336n52

ideology of candidates, 21, 21f, 23t, 24, 190f
IncomeTaxFacts.org, 229
in-person absentee voting, 257 (see also
    voting)
Internet, 6, 47, 57, 88, 156, 180, 229, 262,
    305–6
interpersonal microtargeting, 307–8 (see
    also microtargeting)
Iraq war, 14, 17, 177f, 234–35, 234f
    Obama's opposition against, 76–77
Iyengar, Shanto, 319n3

Jackson, Brooks, 206
Jackson, Jesse, 128
Jamieson, Kathleen Hall, 276, 319n5,
    322n36, 323n6, 323n7, 327n82,
    327n89–91, 329n20–1, 331n58,
    363n3, 364n14, 366n12, 367n16–7,
    368n36, 368n41, 369n42–3
Jester, Danny, 274
"Joe the Plumber," 5, 45, 203, 205, 212–19,
    213f, 219f, 222, 226, 228, 229, 231,
    294
Johns, Deborah, 92
Johnson, Haynes, 82
Johnson, James, 89, 188–89
Johnson, Lyndon, 150
Johnston, Richard, 322n36, 327n90,
    349n68, 363n3, 366n17, 368n36,
    368n41
Jones, Jeffrey M., 366n21

Kagan, Robert, 235
Kaine, Tim, 125
Kay, Tim, 279, 280
Keating, Charles, 31, 32
   savings and loan scandal, 31–33
Kellman, Jerry, 102
Kennedy, Carolyn, 102
Kennedy, Edward, 38, 46, 292
Kennedy, John F., 56, 72, 150, 166, 197, 305,
   314
Kenski, Henry C., 362n5
Kenski, Kate M., 349n68, 362n5, 362n9,
   362n11, 363n23
Kerry, John, 22, 91, 131, 150, 181, 197, 204,
   235, 312
   federal financing, rejecting, 309
   ideology of, 21f
   white voters for, 103–6, 104–6f
Keyes, Alan, 128
Kilpatrick, Kwame and Barack Obama,
   90–91, 91f
Kimmel, Jimmy, 60
Kinder, Donald R., 319n3
Kindler, David, 102
King, Gary, 24, 322n37, 322n44, 323n47
Kinnock, Neil, 125
Kramer, Gerald H., 24, 321n33
Krosnick, Jon A., 319n3
Kurzban, Robert, 333n79

Lapinski, John S., 336n51
Lasch, Kathryn E., 320n7
Leno, Jay, 60, 61, 128, 129, 154
Letterman, David, 60, 61, 154
Lewis-Beck, Michael, 321n33, 346n7
Lewontin, Richard, 333n81
Lieberman, Joe, 59
Limbaugh, Rush, 29, 128
Lin, Monica H., 335n30
Lincoln, Abraham, 72, 314
Lincoln Savings and Loan Association, 31,
   32
Lo, James, 368n1
Los Angels Times, 129, 140, 229, 311
Lowry, Rich, 153, 214
Lydia system, 329–30n27

Malbin, Michael, 311
Margolis, Jim, 206, 281, 356n13
Matthews, Chris, 198
Mayhew, David, 20, 321n28

McCain, John, 1, 14, 15, 53, 130
   acceptance speech, 146–47
   advertisement spending versus
      favorability rating, 266–67, 267f
   age in news, priming, 57–59, 58f, 329n17
   media, role of, 69
   allegations about temper and
      temperament, 65–66
   and Bush, similarity between, 118–19,
      119f
   campaign finance reform, 32, 36–37
   celebrity attack into tax-and-spend
      allegation, 238–39
   "Chicago machine," 47, 48–50
   convention speeches, 291–92
   debate over abortion, 281–84, 284f
   debate over embryonic stem cell
      research, 281–83, 283f
   Democratic argument on taxes against,
      207–11, 210f
   as "experience needed to be president,"
      73, 73f, 126f, 199f
      by party identification, 74f
   favorability ratings of, 132f, 171f, 202f,
      204f, 282f
   and George W. Bush, similarity between,
      132f
   economy, handling, 18, 19f, 178f, 225f,
      289–91
   as erratic, 63–64, 64f, 183–84, 185, 192,
      295
   fear-based attacks against Obama,
      234–35, 234f
   first presidential debate, 194–97, 194t,
      195f
   on fundamentals of country's economy,
      181–85
   healthcare reform, handling, 34, 208f
   ideology of, 21f
   inaccurate tax claims, 211–12
   Internet use in campaign, 77–79
   interviewed by Sean Hannity, 223–24
   as "Joe the Plumber," 212–14
   as "judgment needed to be president,"
      126f, 200f
   Keating Five savings and loan scandal
      and, 31–33
   as maverick, 30, 36–43, 288–89
   as McSame, 27, 39–43, 41f, 42f, 180–181,
      192, 289, 295
   on Obama's argument for change, 35–36

McCain, John (*continued*)
    one-party rule, raising, 240
    opposition to stem cell research, 308
    "Original Mavericks," 37
    "our dependence on foreign oil,"
        eliminating, 114–15
    as out of touch, 54–55, 181
        and old, link between, 58–61
    party identification of, 20
    as patriotic, 92–95, 93f, 94f
    as "ready to be Commander-in-Chief,"
        73, 75f, 127f, 234
        by party identification, 75f
    as reassuring leader, 192–93
    role in Vietnam War, 30–31
    at Saddleback forum, 291
    second presidential debate, 198–202
    "shares my values," 200f
    spending on cable, 277
    spending on local broadcast, 276–77
    spending reform, 38
    support for gas tax holiday, 110, 111,
        112–13
    tax-and-spend argument against, 50–51
    as tax cutter, 212, 213f, 219f
    tax on employer-provided health
        benefits, 207–11, 237
    as tax raiser, 205–7
    as "too old to be president," 66–69,
        67–68f
        by party identification, 68f
        on shares my values, 69–70
    as trustworthy, 79f
        by party identification, 80f
    vote preference for, 148f, 202f, 230f
    weak on defense, 235–38
    Worth Fighting For, 65
McCain-Feingold, 29, 32
"McCain's Own Words," 239–40
"McCain Your Choice," 229–30
McCaskill, Claire, 102, 245
McInturff, Bill, 17, 37, 57, 87, 167, 178, 179,
    191, 205, 270, 325n47
McKelvey, Richard D., 322n40, 365n5
McPhee, Robert D., 365n4
Meckler, Laura, 219
media (*see also* broadcast; cable television;
        radio; television)
    microtargeting in, 306, 307–8
    role in priming McCain's age, 69

spending differences in gross ratings
        points, 268–70, 269f
    impact on vote, 270–275, 271t,
        272–74f, 275t
Mediamark Research & Intelligence (MRI),
        279
Meet the Press, 38, 140, 162
Mendelberg, Tali, 89, 336n51–52
messages, 287–302
    campaign, 299, 300t
        advertising, role of, 301–2
        contribution to vote preference, 296–300
        campaign messages, 299, 300t
        fundamentals, 299, 299t
        news media use, 299, 300t
        sociodemographics, 299, 299–300t
    half-hour program, 295
    two-minute ads, 295
    microtargeting, 304, 306–8
        in cable and radio, 278–81, 307–8
    interpersonal, 307
Miller, Joanne M., 319n3
Mitchell, Andrea, 161
Modigliani, Andre, 320n5
Mondale, Walter, 56, 58
money, 310–313
Mottola, Chris, 79, 188, 268
MRI. *See* Mediamark Research &
        Intelligence (MRI)
Mudd, Roger, 292
Muskie, Edmund, 151, 204

NAES. *See* National Annenberg Election
        Survey (NAES)
Nagourney, Adam, 253
narrowcast messages, 308
    on stem cell research, 308
National Annenberg Election Survey
        (NAES), 10
National Cable Communications (NCC),
        279, 280
National Institute on Aging, 333n81
National Journal, 14, 45
National Press Club, 87
National Republican Trust, 98
National Rifle Association Victory Fund, 91
National Security Political Action
        Committee, 90–91
NATO, 239
Natoli, Marie D., 346n2

NBC News, 16, 243
NBC Nightly News with Brian Williams, 278
NCC. *See* National Cable Communications (NCC)
Nei, Masatoshi, 333n81
Nelson, Michael, 346n2, 346n4
Nelson, Thomas E., 319n5, 320n7
Neuberg, Stephen L. 335n30
"New Energy," 116
"New Energy-Revised," 116
Newsweek, 57, 58, 65
New York Observer, 128
New York Post, 229
New York Times, 30, 31, 60, 61, 82, 86, 125, 163, 165, 206, 210, 214, 229, 311
Nixon, Richard, 14, 150, 197, 235, 255, 305
no-fault absentee voting, 255–58, 256–58f
   (*see also* voting)
Noonan, Peggy, 161
Norris, Chuck, 59
Nuri-al-Maliki, 77

Obama, Barack, 1 (*see also individual entries*)
   acceptance speech, 135–36
   advertisement spending versus
      favorability rating, 266–67, 267f
   age-related threads in ads, 62–65
   as angry black male, 82–83
   to angry black rhetoric, 87–88
   argument on taxes against McCain, 207–11f
   attack on McCain's defense priorities, 235–38
   call for withdrawal of U.S. troops from Iraq, 76–77
   campaign's texting program, 307
   "Celeb," 115, 116
   changes to campaign strategy, 263–64
   convention speeches, 292
   credibility by charging inconsistency, 72
   as criminal, 91–92
   deal with domestic crises, 238–39
   debate over abortion, 281–84, 282f, 283f, 284f
   debate over embryonic stem cell research, 281–83, 282f, 283f
   declines public funding, 310–311
   Dreams from My Father, 100, 327n83
   economy, handling, 18, 19f, 178f, 289–91, 225f

as "experience needed to be president," 73, 73f, 126f, 199f
   by party identification, 74f
favorability ratings of, 86f, 132f, 171f, 202f, 204f
federal financing, rejecting, 309
first presidential debate, 194–97, 194t, 195f, 357n20
and Franklin Raines, 89–90, 90f
general election GRP advantage, 268–70, 269f
half-hour program, 242–47, 295
healthcare reform, handling, 208f
ideological placement of
   by news consumption, 48–50, 49f
   by party identification, 48, 49f
ideology of, 21f
inaccurate tax claims, 211–12
Internet use in campaign, 86, 262, 313
and Jeremiah Wright, 88f
as "judgment needed to be president," 84f, 126f, 200f
on Keating Five savings and loan scandal, 32–33
and Kwame Kilpatrick, 90–91, 91f
as lightweight, unprepared celebrity, 76–81
linking to crime, corruption, and terror, 95–98
locking up early votes, 259–63, 260t
on McCain's health care plan, 34
on McCain's reputation as maverick, 43
as member of Senate Foreign Relations Committee, 239
microtargeting in cable and radio, 307–8
"New Energy," 116
"New Energy-Revised," 116
as "not ready to lead," 191–92
on offshore oil drilling, 115–18
one-party rule, raising, 240
online fund-raising operation, 310
opposition to gas tax holiday, 110–111
as out-of-touch, 111
party identification of, 20
as patriotic, 92–95, 93f, 94f
Powell's endorsement on feelings about, 294–95
pre-convention speech in Berlin, 2
radio ads, 43
radio, cable and TV GRPs advantage, 268–70, 269f

Obama, Barack (*continued*)
  readiness to deal with crisis
    fear-based attacks on, 234–35, 234*f*
  as "ready to be Commander-in-Chief,"
    73, 75*f*, 76*f*, 84*f*, 127*f*
  by party identification, 76*f*
  as reassuring leader, 192–93
  rebuttal, 100–2
  rhetoric of reassurance, 240–241
  Reverend Wright revelations on, 83–87
  second presidential debate, 198–202
  spending on cable, 277
  spending on local broadcast, 276–77
  "shares my values," 200*f*
  shared voters' values, 319
  socialist view of, 226–30
  strategy of change, 33–35
  and Tony Rezko, 96, 96*f*
  as tax-and-spend liberal, 27, 43–48
  as tax cutter, 205–7
  as tax raiser, 212–14, 213*f*, 219*f*
  as "too young to be president," 66–69,
    67–68*f*
  by party identification, 68*f*
  tour to Europe, 76
  tour to Middle East, 76
  as trustworthy, 79*f*, 84*f*
  by party identification, 80*f*
  two-minute ads, 193–94, 295, 224,
    241–42
  two-party vote, predicting, 22–25,
    23*t*, 270–271, 271*t*, 274, 275*t*,
    296–300, 299–300*t*, 315–17,
    316*f*
  as "unpatriotic," 295–96
  as "unprepared to be president," 73
  viral arguments against, 98–100
  vote preference for, 148*f*, 202*f*, 230*f*
  white voters for, 103–6, 104–6*f*
  and William Ayers, 95*f*
Obama, Michelle, 83, 101
O'Brien, Conan, 154
Office of President, eligibility for,
  329*n*16
Offshore oil drilling, 113–14
Olbermann, Keith, 155
"One, The" 77, 78
one-party rule, raising, 240
Oxley, Zoe M., 319*n*5, 320*n*7
Our Country Deserves Better, 87, 90

Palin, Sarah, 5, 9, 15, 35, 60, 66, 281, 149,
  295, 298
  acceptance speech, 142–46
  attack on, 157
  Colin Powell's attack on qualifications,
    162–63
  competence, 9
  Couric interviews with, 292–93
  Democrats low-cost attack on, 239–40
  favorability ratings of, 141*f*, 142, 161,
    162*f*, 168–74, 168*t*, 170*t*, 171*f*, 173*f*
  interviewed by Charles Gibson, 146*f*,
    151, 152–54, 156*f*, 157, 161, 162*f*,
    173*f*, 292
  interviewed by Katie Couric, 146*f*, 151,
    152, 154–55, 156*f*, 157, 161, 242, 292
  parodies on *Saturday Night Live*, 151,
    152, 155–57, 293, 296
  as "ready to be president," 9, 146*f*, 156*f*,
    157, 252
  as vice presidential candidate, 136–42
  vice presidential debate, 157–61
Parker, Kathleen, 157
party identification, 19–22, 23*t*, 24, 41–43,
  74–76*f*, 94*f*
"Passed Over," 130
Patil, Akshay, 330*n*27
Patriot-News, 34
Peffley, Mark, 336*n*53, 337*n*60
Pelosi, Nancy, 112, 240
Perot, Ross, 242, 313
persuadable voters, characteristics of,
  251–55, 252*t*, 253*f*
  versus not persuadable voters, 254*t*
Peters, Mark D., 319*n*3
Pew Research Center for the People & the
  Press, 14, 19, 277
Pittsburgh Times Review, 220
Plouffe, David, 32, 33, 66, 259, 304, 305,
  309, 311, 324*n*16
PolitiFact, 138, 206, 226
Polsby, Nelson, 149
Powell, Colin, 60, 99, 152, 227, 241, 294–95
  attacks on Palin's qualifications, 162–63
  endorsement on feelings about Obama,
    294–95
Powers, Elizabeth, 319*n*4
Price, Vincent, 319*n*4, 320*n*6
priming, 8, 25, 57, 69, 89, 90, 290, 301
"Purpose," 115

Quayle, Dan, 59, 150
Quindlen, Anna, 56, 65

race, 103–6, 104–6*f*
    impact in presidential election, 56–57
racial identity, 33, 100
radio
    microtargeting in, 278–81, 307–8
    role in abortion and embryonic stem cell
        research debate, 281–83, 282*f*, 283*f*
    spending differences in gross ratings
        points, 268–70, 269*f*
        impact on vote, 270–275, 271*t*,
        272–74*f*, 275*t*
Raines, Franklin and Barack Obama,
    89–90, 90*f*
Rapoport, Ronald B., 346*n*7
Reagan, Ronald, 56, 58, 129
    five-minute straight-to-camera ads, 240
"Real Change," 193
RealClearPolitics.com, 123, 251, 252*t*, 259,
    263*t*
Reid, Harry, 112, 240
Republican Federal Committee of
    Pennsylvania, 88
Republican National Committee, 71, 266
Republican Party
    advantage in party identification, 19–20
    "crisis management" argument, 247
    "fear of the unknown" scenario, 238
Rezco, Tony, 5, 47, 82, 96, 96*f*
Rice, Tom W., 322*n*33, 346*n*7
Richardson, Bill, 92
RightChange.com, 89
Roberts, Kyle, 276, 277
Robinson, Eugene, 342*n*15
Rodriguez, Maggie, 198
Roe v. Wade, 158, 281, 283, 284*f*
Roosevelt, Teddy, 56
Rosenstone, Stephen, 346*n*7
Rove, Karl, 235
Roychoudhury, Arun K., 333*n*81
Russell, Ann Marie, 339*n*94

Saad, Lydia, 321*n*20, 326*n*69
Sachs, Goldman, 217
Saddleback Forum, 118, 119*f*, 120, 132*f*,
    291, 296
Samphantharak, Krislert, 339*n*7
San Diego Union-Tribune, 220

Saturday Night Live, 9, 40, 141, 296
    parodies of Sarah Palin on, 151, 155–57,
        293
Sawyer, Diane, 214, 222, 226
Schieffer, Bob, 161, 229
Schmidt, Steve, 42, 77, 120, 121, 131, 137,
    197, 205, 326*n*66
second presidential debate, 198–202
Seibold, David R., 365*n*4
selective exposure, 9
Senate Ethics Committee, 31, 32
Senate Judiciary Committee, 129
"Share the wealth," 203, 205, 210, 214–19, 222
Sharpton, Al, 128
Shaw, Daron R., 364*n*3, 368*n*41
Shields, Todd G., 319*n*2, 366*n*11, 366*n*18
Simmons, Sarah, 281
Skiena, Steven, 329*n*27
Sniderman, Paul M., 337*n*60
socialism, 226–30
Sosnik, Douglas B., 366*n*13
"Spread the wealth," 219–21
Spears, Britney, 78, 79, 115, 116
spending
    broadcast availabilities in local news,
        impact of, 278
    on cable, 277
    differences, 265
        in ad spending shifted votes, 267–68
        in cable GRPs, 268–70, 269*f*
        dollar differences, 266
        national ad buys, impact of, 266–67,
            267*f*
        in radio GRPs, 268–70, 269*f*
        in spot TV GRPs, 268–70, 269*f*
    on local broadcast, 276–77
Stephanopoulos, George, 124, 144, 157,
    214, 224
Stevens, Ted, 136
Stevenson, Adlai, 28, 56
Stewart, Jon, 60, 76, 124
Stockdale, James Bond, 58
"Storm," 238
Strategic Petroleum Reserve, 113
Strickland, Ted, 102
"Sweat Equity," 229
Swift Boat Veterans for Truth, 91

Tampa Tribune, 220
Tapper, Jake, 83, 125, 180, 183–84, 221, 228

tax-and-spend liberalism, 43–48
"Tax Healthcare," 209
television, 276–77
    "Audio Tapes," 167
    microtargeting in, 278–81
    "New Energy," 116
    "Passed Over," 130
    spending differences in gross ratings
        points, 268–70, 269*f*
        impact on vote, 270–275, 271*t*,
        272–74*f*, 275*t*
Television News Frequency Index (TNFI),
    57, 58*f*, 64*f*, 90*f*, 330*n*28
Ten Commandments, The, 78
terrorism, *18f*, *90*, 177*f*, 234, 235, 237
Tewksbury, David, 319*n*4, 320*n*6
text messaging, 304, 307
Thorson, Emily, 349*n*68
Time, 57
TNFI. *See* Television News Frequency
    Index (TNFI)
Todd, Chuck, 103, 339*n*98, 361*n*13,
    361*n*23
Tonight Show, 60
Toobin, Jeffrey, 144
Tooby, John, 333*n*79
Tribe, Laurence, 102
Truman, Harry, 14, 28
Trygstad, Kyle, 125
TV News Frequency Index, 10
TV One, 243
two-minute ad, 193–94, 224, 241–42
two-party vote, predicting, 260–261, 260*t*,
    270–271, 271*t*, 274, 275*t*, 296–300,
    299–300*t* (*see also* voting)

Uniformed and Overseas Citizens Absentee
    Voting Act of 1986, 255
University of Michigan
    Consumer Sentiment Index, 16–17, 16*f*,
    18*f*
Univision, 243, 279
Unpopular President, 14–16, 28–30
USA Today, 261

Valdez, Exxon, 158
Valentino, Nicolas A., 336*n*52

Variety, 277
Vavreck, Lynn, 368*n*1
vice presidential debate, 197–98
Violence Against Women Act, 158
vote-only-by-mail, 256 (*see also* voting)
voting
    early, 255–58, 256–58*f*, 304–5
        locking up, 259–63, 260*t*
    in-person absentee, 257
    no-fault absentee, 255–58, 256–58*f*
    two-party, 260–261, 260*t*, 270–71, 271*t*,
        274, 275*t*, 296–300, 299–300*t*
    vote-only-by-mail, 256

Waldman, Paul, 327*n*89, 327*n*91
Wallace, Gregory, 218
Wallace, Nicolle, 121, 341*n*45
Wall Street Journal, 16, 224, 229
war on terror, 235
Warren, Rick, 118, 120, 291
Washington Post, 31, 46, 89, 112, 144, 153,
    163, 227, 235, 311
Washington Times, 38
Wattenberg, Martin P., 151, 346*n*8–9
Weekly Standard, 14
Weigant, Chris, 155–56
welfare, 92, 220, 221, 228, 229
White, Ismail K., 336*n*52
"Who is Barack Obama?," 81–82, 192
Wildavsky, Aaron, 149
Will, George, 157
Williams, Brian, 15, 109, 129
Williams, Lyle, 339*n*94
winner-take-all method, 362*n*4
Wolffe, Richard, 311, 368*n*31
Worth Fighting For (John McCain), 65
Wright, Jeremiah, 1, 306, 88*f*
Wurzelbacher, Joe, 226

Xu, Jun, 335*n*37

Yglesias, Matthew, 224
YouTube, 77, 79, 83, 86, 239, 306

Zaller, John, 315, 319*n*1, 322*n*33, 366*n*10,
    368*n*1
Zavoina, William, 322*n*40, 365*n*5